WHY
BOSNIA?

WHY BOSNIA?

Writings on

the Balkan War

Edited by Rabia Ali & Lawrence Lifschultz

THE PAMPHLETEER'S PRESS, INC.
STONY CREEK, CONNECTICUT

ACKNOWLEDGMENTS

Serbia's Blood War by T. D. Allman is the extended version of the article originally published by *Vanity Fair* in March 1993.

Bosnia Tune by Joseph Brodsky. First appeared in *The New York Times,* 18 November 1992. Copyright © 1992 by Joseph Brodsky. Reprinted by permission of Farrar, Strauss & Giroux, Inc.

The poems of Mak Dizdar are reprinted courtesy of the Croatian Writers' Association and PEN, Sarajevo, Bosnia-Hercegovina

Women Hide Behind a Wall of Silence by Slavenka Draculić was originally published by *The Nation,* 1 March 1993.

On Nationalism by Danilo Kiš. English translation copyright © Farrar, Strauss & Giroux, Inc. Reprinted by permission of Farrar, Strauss & Giroux, Inc.

Appointment in Sarajevo: Why Bosnia Matters by Christopher Hitchens was originally published by *The Nation,* 14 September 1992.

The Final Solution of Bosnia-Hercegovina by Mark Thompson is adapted from *A Paper House: The Ending of Yugoslavia* by Mark Thompson. Copyright © 1992 Mark Thompson. It is reprinted by permission of Pantheon Books, a division of Random House, Inc.

Caught in Another's Dream in Bosnia by Slavoj Žižek was originally published by *Alphabet City,* December 1992.

The cover shows a detail from *Guernica* by Pablo Picasso. Giraudon/Art Resource, NY.
© 1993 ARS, New York / SPADEM, Paris.

COVER AND BOOK DESIGN BY BARBARA MARKS

10 9 8 7 6 5 4 3 2 1

Library of Congress Catalog Card Number 93-84170

ISBN 0-9630587-9-7 (Paperback)   0-9630587-8-9 (Hardcover)

THE PAMPHLETEER'S PRESS
P.O. Box 3374, Stony Creek, Connecticut 06405
Fax (203)483-1429

A Note of Thanks

The editors wish to thank the authors and the many friends and fellow workers who generously gave of their time, labor, and talents to make this book possible. Salko Kriještorac's commitment, advice, and help was invaluable at every stage of the journey. Dorothea Hanson, Marko Prelec, Paul Jukić, and Andrea Feldman not only helped with the translation of Serbo-Croatian into English, but also provided many hours of lively discussion on the history and politics of former Yugoslavia. Francis Jones gracefully responded to every insistent call on his time to write about, translate, and interpret a Bosnia the world does not know. Ivo Banac's many masterly discourses on Balkan history were always welcome and his part in the selection of verse for this volume is gratefully acknowledged. Alan Fogelquist's detailed research on the history and politics of the Balkans was a valuable source of reference. Smail Balić, Jasna Samić, Mark Thompson, Joanne Landy, Thomas Harrison, Jennifer Scarlott, Christopher Hitchens, Branka Magaš, Jamie Harrison, Eqbal Ahmad, Cemal Kafadar, David Weiman, Dušan Zavišić—all, in different ways, helped to bring this project to fruition. Thanks also to James Morris for his insights into the arcane world of publishing; to Karen Suchenski and Joshua Lane not only for meticulous copy editing but for friendship and solidarity; to Andrew Greenawalt for his assistance with technology; and to Dinah McCleod at the MacNeil/Lehrer Newshour for cheerfully meeting peremptory requests for transcripts. Finally, the editors wish to express their appreciation to Barbara Marks for her skills, her advice, and her patience invested in the design and production of this book.

*This book is dedicated to the citizens of
Bosnia-Hercegovina—Muslims, Serbs, Croats—
who have fought and died for the right
to live in a secular, multinational, undivided land.*

Contents

Introduction

In Plain View

Rabia Ali & Lawrence Lifschultz

HE DESTRUCTION OF Bosnia-Hercegovina is proof, if proof were needed, that the actions of states wielding great power in the international system are not determined by ethical or humanitarian considerations. The war of conquest launched by Serbia, and joined by Croatia, was allowed to take its genocidal course because the defense of Bosnia and its citizens was not an imperative dictated by the "national" or "security interests" of any state. There is nothing new here; nothing new to lament. This is the way we have ordered our world.

It needs only to be recalled that the war against Nazi Germany was fought not to defend Czechoslovakia or Poland against aggression, or to save the Jews and Gypsies of Europe from extermination. By sacrificing Czech interests, the British and the French believed their Munich bargain with Hitler would preserve their security and position in Europe. Denied by the British the guarantee of an "anti-fascist" military alliance, the Soviet Union under Stalin proceeded to sign its own "non-aggression pact" with Germany. The United States, for its part, stood aloof from Europe's distant wars. Only when it became amply apparent that the Nazis posed a far greater threat to their own world and way of life did the Allied powers go to war. This, however, did not prevent either Britain or the United States, on the eve of the war, from turning away thousands of Jewish refugees fleeing Germany and clamoring for refuge at their borders.

A half century later the citizens of Bosnia could still reflect on other examples of modern European history to illuminate their dilemma. On the eve of the Second World War neither Britain nor the United States had come to the aid of the Republican government in Spain as it confronted a fascist military rebellion. While Franco received the full military backing of Hitler and Mussolini, the Republicans essentially fought alone. The defense of Republican Spain was not in the Western powers' national interests. Those like George Orwell who went to fight in the international brigades were Europe's "premature anti-fascists." In the forty years that followed the defeat of democratic forces, Franco imposed a fascist dictatorship, hunted down and executed those who had fought for a democratic Spain, but invited no sanctions from the "Free World."

Beyond Europe, the onset of the Cold War led to Western support for an array of hideous dictatorships that were often established through the destabilization of governments attempting to build democracy and more just societies for their citizens. Guatemala in 1953 and Iran in 1954 were two salient examples among many. Relatively independent nationalist policies were perceived as a threat to the interest of Western powers and invited coups, sanctions, embargoes, and war. Within the Soviet bloc, attempts by any country or internal force to exercise autonomy in the pursuit of forms and structures of socialist society other than the Soviet variant were opposed or crushed by similarly harsh military and political measures.

The reality of how powerful states conduct their affairs and shape the world, however, has never prevented their representatives from defining and refining the ideals by which the world should live. Since the Second World War, an elaborate architecture of international institutions has been developed to reflect the new standards of international law which emerged from the trials of Nazi war criminals and the formal adoption of numerous accords regarding standards of human rights and the conduct of war. The Nuremberg principles, the United Nations Charter, the Universal Declaration on Human Rights, the Convention on the Prevention of Genocide, the Geneva Conventions, and the Helsinki Declaration made up this new canon. But noble principles or ideals have rarely, if ever, been permitted to complicate the ordering of world affairs in accordance with the cold principles of great-power politics.

Bosnia showed once again how the canon of international law was in reality not a universal standard but only an instrument to be utilized in their own interests by those with the power to do so. What has made the tragedy of Bosnia unique is the breadth and premeditation of the destruction directed against an entire people because of who they were and where they lived. And these acts occurred not in obscurity but in plain view of the world.

IN DANILO KIŠ'S words, Bosnia was "that exotic country in the heart of Europe"— a land with a six-hundred-year heritage made rich with the intermingling of many cultures and civilizations. Multinational, multicultural, multireligious, its many communities—Muslims, Serbs, Croats, Hungarians, Jews—had lived together for generations. It was in Bosnia under the Ottomans that large numbers of Jews fleeing the Inquisition in Spain found welcome refuge, and there they had stayed, weaving another strand into the country's variegated tapestry. It was this Bosnia, recognized as a historically distinct entity, that was accorded constitutional status as a separate and multinational republic of three equal constituent nations—Muslim, Serb, and Croat—as part of the new Yugoslav federal state established under Tito at the end of the Second World War.

This ancient land, the new republic of a modern state, had long been a center of a distinctly cosmopolitan way of life. The intermingling of peoples and cultures had continued apace in the twentieth century with more than one-fourth of the marriages in modern Bosnia cutting across ethnic divides. Ethnicity had ceased to be the defining criterion of identity for Bosnia's new generation of "Yugoslavs." Remembering his days as a university student in Sarajevo in the late seventies, Francis Jones recalls in this volume the way life once was.

> For the students I knew in Sarajevo all of whom spoke the Bosnian dialect (about halfway between Serbian and Croatian, but generously spiced with Turkish loan-words), fine ethnic distinctions had little meaning . . . If asked my friends would have regarded themselves as Yugoslavs. Perhaps also as Bosnians, though all I recall is normal home-town pride: you must come with me back to Tuzla, to Banja Luka. Ironically, what I missed among many of these thoroughly modern Yugoslavs was a sense of deeper heritage, of faithfulness to traditional roots—little suspecting that history would return not as wisdom, but as vengeance.[1]

History returned as vengeance in the 1990s as Yugoslavia disintegrated and the revivified blood-and-soil nationalisms of its more powerful neighboring republics of Serbia and Croatia brought war to Bosnia. For the new nationalist ideologues a "hybrid" state and civilization such as the one Bosnia represented belonged, with Yugoslavia, in the graveyard of history. Bosnia as it had existed for six centuries had to be destroyed; the fabric which wove the lives of its many peoples together torn beyond repair; the loyalty of its indigenous Serb and Croat communities to a multi-ethnic Bosnian nation subverted; its native Muslim population terrorized. The objective was to "cleanse" Bosnia not only of the Muslims but also of the unique and dangerous cosmopolitanism of its cities which clearly had no place in the new "pure" nation-states emerging from the ruins of Yugoslavia. A "cleansed" Bosnia could then be carved up and annexed to the national states of "Greater Serbia" and "Greater Croatia."

At stake in Bosnia were two visions of society and democracy. Those who came under assault in the newly formed Bosnian state made clear that they stood for a society of equal citizens where the rights of all constituent nations (Muslims, Croats, and Serbs) would be secured and protected under law as a matter of constitutional right. This was a vision of a multi-ethnic society in the tradition of the European Enlightenment. The embodiment of "rights" inherent in the status of citizenship was one of the more significant advances which the French Revolution had spread and integrated into the constitutional orders of European states over a period of two centuries. Yet, in the final decade of the twentieth century, it was to be a standard which Europe, led in this instance by France and Britain, would cynically abandon.

The opposing vision was the one promoted by the nationalist leaders of

Serbia and Croatia. Insular, parochial, ethnocentric, this was a vision of a puri-
fied nation-state in which there was no room for the "Other." The in-gathering
of a people into the bosom of the "mother country" meant in this instance the
acquisition of the territory on which they lived. Serbia's nationalist ideology
was unequivocal on this issue: the destiny of all Serbs was to live in one state,
and since all land on which Serbs lived was by definition Serb land, it rightfully
belonged to "Greater Serbia." They, alone, would unilaterally define its boundaries and remove any community which by their account did not "belong."

For their part, Croatian nationalists—depending on the fervor of their
nationalism and, accordingly, the degree of irredentist manipulation of history—claimed large swaths of Bosnian territory as their own. According to
this view, Bosnia-Hercegovina had no legitimacy as a separate nation, civilization, or state. Those who had lived in the land for generations and were not
Serb (or Croat) were foreigners who had to be removed from it by all means
necessary.

T. D. Allman describes in his essay an encounter with a Serbian official
which splendidly captures the mentality of tyrannical bigotry prevailing
among modern Serb nationalists. During a visit to a Serbian-run concentration camp where he was able to see "how grown men starve differently from
the way children do," Allman encountered among the prisoners a small group
of Ukrainians known as Ruthenians. They had been a tiny minority living in
Yugoslavia and Allman was mystified to find them prisoners in the Serbian
camp. It was bad enough that the Muslim and Croat civilians who made up
the majority of the starving detainees were being held in complete violation of
the Geneva Convention. But, Ruthenians! Why Ruthenians? "The Serb officer answered benignly," writes Allman, "as though explaining the obvious to a
child: 'They are not Serbs.'"[2]

The shock troops in Bosnia for this brand of nationalism promoted by
Serbia were Radovan Karadžić, General Ratko Mladić and their confreres in
the Serbian Democratic Party (SDS). Tihomir Loža, a journalist at *Oslobodjenje,* explains the logic underlying the strategy and the tactics adopted by the
Serbian nationalists in Bosnia.

> What actually is the crime in Bosnia, the practice known in the
> West as "ethnic cleansing"? Undoubtedly it has been anything but a
> coincidence: the key component of a grand greater state project,
> and conducted through all political, psychological, and military
> means. The aim is not only to expel the ethnically "unclean" popu-
> lation from the desired territory but also to destroy all possibilities
> for their return—completely to dismantle the spiritual and material
> structure of the civilization of the unwanted population . . . the
> expelled populations will stay away because they have no homes,
> mosques, schools, etc.—literally nothing to go back to. The prob-
> lem is that since no one can destroy everything perfectly, not even
> [the] Serb armed forces, there is always the danger of the expelled

population returning to the burnt remains of their existence. So the real guarantee is fear: the knowledge that their neighbors remain in wait, should they try to go back. According to numerous testimonies, special military expeditions from Serbia and Montenegro have sought not only to slaughter and expel but also to inspire or force the indigenous Serbs to do the same. The formula for territorial occupation that the expelled are compelled to accept is "either them or us". At the present score, the reality of course is "them".[3]

It had been a long time since Europe had heard anything like the phrase, *Judenfrei.* It returned again to Europe but it had a fresh ring: "ethnic cleansing." Entire villages were wiped out. Specific forms of assault were developed to inspire terror. Concentration camps were set up again on European soil reviving an earlier continental innovation. It was all part of the war that the Serbian nationalists waged against the unwanted inhabitants of Bosnia to remove them from the landscape.

The other intrinsic dimension of the war, of course, was the destruction or "disappearance" of all that represented the unique history and character of Bosnia and the intermingling of its diverse cultures. The country's architecture, its buildings, bridges, monuments built by the Ottomans were the most visible, most immediately tangible signs of Bosnia's "otherness." These became targets of relentless artillery bombardment or straightforward demolition. As if the intent was to destroy all recorded history, libraries housing rare books and priceless manuscripts were deliberately destroyed. Hundreds of delicately designed mosques, large and small, that had stood for centuries unharmed, untouched, disappeared overnight. Smail Balić in this volume has chronicled the assault on Bosnia's architectural heritage which took place in the course of one year.[4]

It needs to be remembered that there were Serbs who never endorsed such acts. In March 1993, the inhabitants of Bijeljina, both Muslim and Serb, watched in silent terror as Serbian forces from outside the region demolished in one evening a cluster of exquisite mosques which had graced the center of the town. The mayor of Bijeljina, a Serb, who condemned the destruction was powerless to stop the marauding military forces which prowled through his city.[5] Although such practices brought shame and sorrow to non-nationalists among Bijeljina's Serbian community, they were cause for praise and promotion in Belgrade. In August of 1993, Serbia's President, Slobodan Milošević appointed General Momčilo Perišić as Chief of Staff of the Yugoslav Army. In Bosnia a year earlier, Perišić had distinguished himself by ordering the destruction of the old city of Mostar, the Venice of the Balkans, once ranked among the greatest architectural jewels of the region.[6]

Catholic churches, symbols of Croat existence in Bosnia's mixed communities did not escape the "purifying" zeal. Unmarked, untouched among the jumble of architecture in Bosnia's cities, among the rubble, the burnt mosques and Catholic churches, stood the Serb Orthodox church. And on walls of buildings still standing—THIS IS SERBIA—was the unmistakable mes-

sage written for those who thought that another Bosnia was possible.[7] In tear-
ing the complex fabric that held Bosnia's many communities together, and in
destroying its heritage, Serbian nationalists were erasing history, preparing a
tabula rasa for the remaking of Bosnia according to their own design, their
own vision. It is thus important, as Jones reminds us, to remember that Bosnia
was not always a wasteland.

> [I]t is important to keep faith with memory . . . for the sake of a
> land where memory may soon be all we have to cling to. Invaders
> down the ages have been drawn to conquest by Bosnia's rich upland
> pastures and the orchards of her valleys. Other enemies have burnt
> her fields, have put her villages to the knife or sword . . . And yet,
> fields can be sown again, the blackened plum tree puts forth new
> shoots, the massacre's cowed survivors come down from their caves
> and build shacks from the rubble.
>
> But the new overlords are not content with conquest, with
> subjugation. They mean to obliterate a people; and they know full
> well that the most effective obliteration comes from within, by set-
> ting neighbor against neighbor. But to wipe out a people, it is not
> enough to harry, to burn and kill. Memory itself must be
> cleansed—memory that there ever was such a land, a land where the
> living was good, a land that all its people knew as home.[8]

An entire way of life, a whole civilization in the heart of Europe was being
wiped out. The world watched the events as if it were a Roman spectacle, taking no action to bring the massacre to a halt. Perhaps, the most egregious
aspect of the war was not merely that the international community failed to
intervene against Serbia's campaign of "ethnic cleansing," but that it intervened in a manner which denied the Bosnians the means to defend themselves
militarily.

A UN-imposed arms embargo guaranteed that a well-armed Serbia
could annex territory and expel over a million civilians while facing only limited resistance. While heavily armed Serbian and Croatian nationalist forces
consolidated their territorial claims, Western powers in the European Community and the Security Council, through their appointed mediators, worked
at the drafting board to translate these military conquests into blueprints for
the dismemberment of Bosnia. These blueprints for "peace," appropriately
termed the West's modern version of classical "apartheid" by Kemal
Kurspahić, went through several metamorphoses to keep up with the pace of
Serbian and Croatian gains.[9] Thus "cantonization" led to "ethnic provinces"
and, finally, to "partition." The Bosnians, at each step of their defeat, were
asked to accept "reality."

The reality, as the Bosnians saw it, was that the West was complicit in
engineering their defeat and the destruction of their society. Their emphatic
denials to the contrary notwithstanding, the Western powers had made their

position unmistakably transparent: they would not intervene in the war to defend Bosnia; they would not permit Bosnians to defend their country themselves or allow others to join in their defense; and they would compel them to surrender, accept defeat, and accede to the internationally legitimized carve-up of their country. As Loža points out, the "reality" that the West finally demanded that Bosnia accept was a reality that the West had itself helped to create.

> The authentic reality of Bosnia before the war and the supposedly inevitable reality after ethnic cleansing are completely different. From the pre-war perspective, any idea of division was nonsense, because the regions, towns, streets, flats, and beds were so mixed . . . Opposing division meant, in the first point, simply recognizing that reality. With the Bosnia of today, however, it is possible to think of the idea of division. After ethnic cleansing, Bosnia is like a blank piece of paper. The existing structure has been all but erased, and theoretically could be replaced by any other. "Realities" are created, and the present one would never have happened peacefully. The version [of reality] now plumped for by Lord Owen looks like this: A typical eastern Bosnia town may have had 70 percent Muslims and 30 percent Serbs and today has no Muslims. No one is willing to change that new reality, and there is no hope otherwise that they would return. So under the present logic, the town will be given to the Serbs.[10]

WHAT MADE BOSNIA such a singular moment in international relations was that in the end the European Community, the United States, and the United Nations actively collaborated in the advancement of a final solution for Bosnia-Hercegovina. To achieve this stage significant sections of the Western intelligentsia and their counterparts in various national governments had to walk quite a distance. It ultimately developed into a veritable long march back from the principles of the Enlightenment. Rousseau, Locke, Voltaire, Paine, and Jefferson were summarily abandoned. The process took the form of a remarkable "policy debate," a discourse in search of rationales, while, in Diego Arria's apt phrase, "slow-motion genocide" was systematically carried out in Bosnia.[11]

The intellectual features of this discussion took unusual forms. Many false representations were necessary to establish the full repertoire of rationalizations which would then preclude effective action. It was necessary, for instance, to advance a new interpretation of history, undercutting the legitimacy of Bosnia as a political entity and a civilization, and to present the conflict as a civil war in which all sides were, more or less, guilty; a war in which there were no principles or ideals worth defending, or identifying with.

The debate began with the thesis of "ancient hatreds." The Balkans were presumably very unlike other, more "western," societies in this respect. Thus, the war was characterized as the product of centuries-old enmities between the Serbs, Croats, and Muslims—a tribal blood-feud, a "typical" Balkan convulsion which could not be understood much less mediated by any intervention by the civilized world. "A problem from hell," was US Secretary of State Warren Christopher's repeated refrain as he tried to explain, with appropriately furrowed brow, why the world stood by as the Serb nationalist forces steadily "cleansed" and occupied Bosnia. These people, he would state over and over and again, have hated each other for hundreds of years.

Patronizing, superior pronouncements from statesmen and commentators, of course, relied heavily on willful amnesia regarding the "ancient hatreds" which "provoked" centuries of bloodletting in Europe, the Americas, and across the globe between, among and by the now civilized states—Britain, France, Germany, Russia, and the United States. In the Balkans "ancient hatreds" became the central motif of every cliché. "Their" wars were irrational, insensate, primeval bloodletting; "our" wars were fought for principles—democracy, freedom, God and Free Trade.

Such views were expressed at the highest levels of the American foreign policy establishment. In early February 1993, the former editor of *Foreign Affairs*, William Hyland described the war in Bosnia as "a fight among gangsters."[12] No distinction was made between an aggressor state and a state under attack—they were simply all "gangsters." This crude and uneducated statement went unchallenged on the premier newscast of the Public Broadcasting System. The concept of equivalence was part of a broader notion that the war in Bosnia was a "civil war" in which the international community ought not to become involved militarily lest it enter the ubiquitous "quagmire." For those who preferred to stand aloof and observe the consummation of the "Greater Serbia" project, it became crucial to designate the conflict as "civil" in form.

This view was propagated despite the fact that Bosnia had received international recognition as an independent and sovereign state. Unlike the other new states in the Balkans it had followed very precise procedures laid down by the European Community in order to secure recognition. The United States supported this process and accorded recognition following an internationally monitored plebiscite in March 1991 where 68 percent of the electorate voted in support of a multi-ethnic independent state. Despite demands and threats by extreme Serbian nationalists, including Radovan Karadžić, in Sarajevo "substantial numbers of Serbs voted in favor of independence and against the recommendations of Karadžić's extremists."[13]

On April 6, 1992, the day Bosnia-Hercegovina's independence was recognized by the European Community, tens of thousands of citizens drawn from all of Bosnia's nationalities, gathered before Bosnia's Parliament on the embankment of the Miljačka River. They demanded that "the ethnic nationalists who began dominating Bosnia and Hercegovina's politics . . . [after the December 1990 elections] form a government of national unity." True to Sarajevo's long tradition of tolerance, the crowd held signs declaring: "We Can Live Together."

However, Radovan Karadžić, the Serbian nationalist leader, had declared that Sarajevo's streets would "run with blood," if Bosnia's declaration of independence were confirmed by the European Community. As the crowd stood before the Bosnian Parliament calling for "peace" and "reconciliation" among all national groups, one of Karadžić's bodyguards opened fire from the Holiday Inn. Karadžić made his way out of Sarajevo and that evening Serbian heavy artillery opened fire from the hills overlooking the city. It was the beginning of the siege of Sarajevo.[14]

With direct collaboration and instigation from Belgrade "Serbian paramilitary forces invaded Bosnia en masse and, with assistance from federal army units, unleashed a wholesale military assault on the newly recognized nation."[15] International borders were crossed and supply convoys from Serbia became a permanent feature of the war's military logistics. General Momčilo Perišić of the Yugoslav Army would later openly acknowledge the commanding role played by his forces in conquering southeastern Bosnia which was then handed over to local Serbian paramilitary units.[16]

Nevertheless, James Hogue, editor of *Foreign Affairs,* repeatedly emphasized in public appearances that "this is a civil war," and like William Hyland, assured the American public that "there [were] no good guys in this battle."[17] This insistence on the existence of perfect symmetry led eventually to US Secretary of State, Warren Christopher, declaring before the Congress that all three sides shared responsibility for atrocities in Bosnia. However, as *The New York Times* soon revealed, Christopher's testimony "ran counter to State Department reports to the United Nations on human rights abuses." In fact, the State Department had for more than a year been reporting Serbian responsibility for an "overwhelming majority" of the atrocities and the "complicity by the Milošević regime and the Government of Croatia in atrocities of both regular and paramilitary forces." The State Department's own internal reports showed "an absence of support by the Bosnian Government" for any excesses.[18] Despite the Hyland-Hogue-Christopher thesis no such symmetry existed. Nevertheless, it became a crucial pretext for policy.

Throughout the war there were those who called it by its real name. On the fiftieth anniversary of the Warsaw Ghetto uprising, Marek Edelman, the last surviving commander of that heroic resistance to the Nazis, said that "in Bosnia, we are witnessing mass slaughter, and Europe is behaving the way it did toward the resistance in the Ghetto."[19] In Sarajevo, Mustafa Spahić, a Muslim cleric, said: "Bosnia's Muslims are the new Jews of Europe. But we have no America to lean on. We have no one to lean on . . . This is the first genocide to be committed under the protection of the United Nations. This is the first world-class crime to be carried out like a football game before the eyes of the entire world on television."[20] Bozidar Milicević, a Croat fighting in the Bosnian Army, said: "In Sarajevo, we're fighting so all nations of this country can live together. Europe has sold out its own values."[21]

What the soldier Milicević, a Croat and a Bosnian, had expressed represented that other vision which insisted that human beings, were not like "cats

and dogs," as Radovan Karadžić had once described the nature of coexistence
between Serbs and non-Serbs. There were hundreds of thousands in Bosnia
who did not believe in apartheid or consider themselves to be like animals in
the manner which the Serb nationalist leader had managed, inadvertently, to
characterize himself and stigmatize his own followers. Close to eighty thousand Serbs shared the siege of Sarajevo with their Croat and Muslim neighbors. Indeed, throughout the war thousands fought and died for the idea of a
multinational, cosmopolitan, pluralist society—an idea Bosnia had embodied
for centuries.

It was this tradition which was defended in Bosnia and placed in great
peril. It was defended by those who held the principle of ethnic or national
solidarity to be precious. Colonel Jovan Divjak, the Deputy Commander of
the Bosnian Army is a Serb. His colleague, Colonel Stjepan Siber, also a
Deputy Commander is a Croat. Nearly one third of the Bosnian Army is Serbian. At Sarajevo's main daily newspaper, *Oslobodjenje,* the Deputy Editor is
Serbian, as are a third of the active staff of the paper.[22] Vladimir Stanka, a
young Serbian reporter at *Oslobodjenje* explained, "My job is to try and capture something of the truth. My Serbian roots are irrelevant in this. What does
matter is what is happening here, and that is plain. The city I live in, the city
where I was born, is being terrorized by militarists."[23] But it was as if the
Bosnians were speaking into a void; the world seemed not to hear them.

The characterization of the conflict in Bosnia advanced by the United
States and its European partners was entirely self-serving and, of course, misleading. According to Ivo Banac, Professor of History at Yale University, the
constant talk about "civil war" and "ancient hatreds" represented merely a useful caricature by which to rationalize a policy designed "to abandon Bosnia
and do nothing." The war in Banac's view was "essentially a war of aggression
conducted by Serbia against an internationally recognized independent state
with a democratic constitution that guaranteed rights to all citizens, including
Serbs . . . If one wishes to think in terms of historical analogies, the Serbian
war policy in Bosnia-Hercegovina resembles to a very large extent the
approach adopted by the German administration against Czechoslovakia in
the late 1930s. Therefore, one could view Radovan Karadžić as being Konrad
Henlein and the Serbian Democratic Party as the Sudetendeutsche Partei."[24]

John Burns of *The New York Times* discovered in Sarajevo just how burning a comparison the Czechoslovak events of 1938 had become for many
Bosnians. In an interview with the Bosnian President, Alija Izetbegović, Burns
explored various similarities between the events of 1938 and the negotiations
conducted with Slobodan Milošević by UN and EC mediators, Cyrus Vance
and David Owen. Izetbegović told him, reports Burns, that "the negotiators
had spoken frequently of their horror at the excesses, including mass executions
of Muslims and brutality against Muslims in detention camps, but that they
had told him, 'We have no army, we have only the power to negotiate.' What
this has led to, Mr. Izetbegović said, was appeasement similar to that shown in
Munich in 1938, when Britain and France let Hitler dismember Czechoslo-

vakia, forcing the President, Eduard Benes, into exile in London. 'I have often thought of this,' he said. 'Instead of Munich, it is Geneva. Instead of little Czechoslovakia, it is little Bosnia. Instead of negotiating for a real peace, they are negotiating for an imaginary one. And instead of Benes, it is me.'"[25]

The decision to abandon "little Bosnia," to permit the destruction of the actual "reality" it represented, and to assist in the carve-up of the territory it inhabited was readily acceptable if one believed that as an independent political entity Bosnia was, at best, an entirely artificial construct and, at worst, illegitimate. This view, based on untruths and half-truths, was promoted by several influential commentators. Typical among these were the columns in *The New York Times* by former editor A. M. Rosenthal who was forever warning against any ill-considered move to rescue the Bosnians. "As for the Muslim leaders," he wrote attacking those who suggested that Bosnia's defense was imperative, "they had declared the independence of a Bosnia which had not existed as a nation and in which they did not have a majority. There are no 'Bosnians'—just Slavs who call themselves Serbs, Croatians or Muslims."[26] The arrogance of such ostensibly authoritative pronouncements was only matched by the underlying ignorance of historical and political facts.

THERE HAD BEEN a Bosnia since the Middle Ages—the last of the major South Slav states to emerge in the fourteenth and fifteenth centuries. According to Ivo Banac, the Kingdom of Bosnia was "a major regional power which, at moments, included sections of present-day Croatia and Serbia." The land's continuity as a distinct political and geographic entity was maintained through the Ottoman and the Austro-Hungarian period, and at the end of the Second World War it became part of Tito's Yugoslavia as one of the constituent republics of the federation—the only republic which was multinational by definition. "Thus from the medieval period to Tito's federalism there has been a Bosnia . . . a land which has its own distinctive cultural flavor." While the presence of a large Muslim community has been an important influence in shaping the character of Bosnia, the national cultures of the Bosnian Serbs and Croats also have their distinct Bosnian character which distinguishes them from the national cultures of Serbia and Croatia. Now, of course, if the world wants to abandon Bosnia and do nothing, says Banac, let it be frank about it and not distort the historical record to rationalize its position. "The rich history of coexistence between [Bosnia's] communities is also part of the record."[27]

The refusal to take account of the country's history, of the fact that it was a pre-existing entity which preceded and was not a consequence or creation of Yugoslavia, has led many to conclude that Bosnia invited its own destruction by seeking independence from Yugoslavia. The Serbs of Bosnia, the argument runs, did not wish to secede from Yugoslavia and made their wishes clear by boycotting the referendum which put the question of independence to vote in Bosnia in March 1991. This is the sort of argument made, for instance, by Misha Glenny who takes the view that the declaration of independence—the majority vote in favor notwithstanding—was a violation of the established political norms of Bosnia-Hercegovina which had required the consent of all three of its ethnic communities to any constitutional change in the Republic. Since the Bosnian Serbs would not consent to an independent Bosnia, the decision to secede was illegitimate and self-destructive because it invited the Serbs' wrath.[28]

It is, on the face of it, a compelling argument but it is only half right. Given the war that has engulfed Bosnia, it is clear that the country's declaration of independence proved to be a catastrophe for many of its citizens. The Bosnian parliament had declared independence without adequate preparations to either secure or defend it. The country's political leadership had, instead, succumbed to a certain political naiveté and placed its faith in European and American commitments. As Slavoj Žižek points out,

> Slovenia and Croatia moved fast and aggressively against the will of the West. They proclaimed independence, and attained their goal, including being recognized by the West, whereas Alija Izetbegović, the Bosnian president, behaved like a model pupil of the West: he followed closely Western suggestions and proceeded with extreme caution, always ready to give another chance to any formula of a "new Yugoslavia," abstained from "provoking the Serbs" even when the Yugoslav army was already fortifying artillery sites on the mountains around Sarajevo—all in exchange for Western assurances that they would keep in check the Serbs and prevent the Yugoslav army from attacking non-Serbs in Bosnia. He was paid for trusting the West and for playing its "civilized" game by the total destruction of his country. When Western promises proved void and the army did attack, the West quickly threw up its hands and assumed the convenient posture of a distant observer, appalled at the outburst of "primitive Balkan passions."[29]

Events and outside actors had propelled Bosnia into a declaration of independence—an independence it could not defend. Abandoned by Slovenia and Croatia, threatened by Serbia, and, desperately in search of allies, lulled into assurances that Europe and the United States would stand behind the newly independent state, the Bosnian government had acted—only to discover, the morning after, that it would have to fight alone. "It is true that the Bosnian government could have done the same thing the Croat [and the Slovene] government[s] did—that is, to start arming in advance with the expectation of the worst," Miloš Vasić observed. "But the possibility of a war in Bosnia-Hercegovina was so appalling to everyone that it bordered on the unthinkable—like a global thermonuclear war, from the Yugoslav standpoint."[30]

The fact that the Bosnian leadership had been caught unprepared to defend the independence of Bosnia-Hercegovina did not, however, negate the republic's right to self-determination—a right recognized by the Yugoslav constitution. By the time Bosnia declared independence, Yugoslavia had effectively ceased to exist with the failure of its constituent republics to negotiate a new confederal structure and with the subsequent secession, or "disassociation," of Slovenia and Croatia from the federation. What remained was the Great Serb bloc—Serbia and Montenegro—masquerading as "Yugoslavia." In declaring independence, therefore, Bosnia (together with Macedonia) was not seceding from Yugoslavia; it was attempting to secure its territorial, political, and cultural autonomy by separating itself from Serbia. Bosnia was *not* part of Serbia. The demand of the Bosnian Serbs—by no means entirely the product of a home-grown movement—to keep Bosnia within "Yugoslavia" was, in effect, a demand for the absorption of Bosnia into Serbia. It was the project for "Greater Serbia", surfacing with renewed force in the twilight years of the Yugoslav state and given its "modern" ideological expression in the 1986 Memorandum of Serbia's Academy of Sciences and Arts, which presented a direct and powerful threat to an independent—and disarmed—Bosnia.

Backed by the military might of the Yugoslav People's Army (JNA), the Milošević regime had moved aggressively to extend the frontiers of Serbia. In 1989 it had revoked the autonomous status of the provinces of Vojvodina and Kosovo, placing the latter's Albanian majority under virtual military occupation, and in the autumn of 1991, following Croatia's declaration of independence, it had launched a war against the new state, occupying its Krajina region inhabited by the Croatian Serbs and constituting one-fourth of Croatia's territory.[31] The assault on Bosnia, when it came in April 1992, was only the most brutal phase of the campaign to conquer and eventually to annex "Serb" territory to "Greater Serbia." However, while the severing of the putatively Serb lands from Croatia was a relatively swift and easy operation, the conquest of Bosnia—a small country which embarked on independent statehood with no organized military force and hardly any weaponry—turned into a protracted, seemingly endless war.

An important factor in this comparative "failure" of Serbian arms in Bosnia was the difficulty, of course, of "redeeming" Serbs and "Serb" land in a patchwork quilt of a country where the terrain had been made inhospitable to expansionary nationalist projects by the intermingling of populations and communities. To secure slabs of "pure" Serb territory required "cleansing" it of non-Serbs, village by village, house by house. This process itself was bound to make Serbia's Bosnian campaign a protracted affair. What compounded the task, however, was the long and complex process of securing the support of the Bosnian Serb community in the drive for "Greater Serbia." To do so, as Banac puts it, the nationalists in Serbia "had to turn a relatively peaceful population . . . into a group that would become auxiliary to the aims of the aggressors." This was one of the reasons the instigators of the process had to proceed very slowly, gradually implicating the Bosnian Serb community in their project of aggression and expansion. This could not be done overnight; it had to be done in stages. First, they had to isolate those who were opposed to their plans and had struggled against them. Then they had to implicate all the others in what initially were small acts of repression against the other communities and, ultimately, in very large and horrid crimes."[32]

Myths disguised as history were designed to breed fear and insecurity among Serbs, wherever they lived. The cultivation of group paranoia became an important task for Serb nationalists. The Muslims of Bosnia suddenly became the enemy within. By conflating the demons of yesteryear with the stereotypes of today, neighbors were converted into the conquering Turks of the Middle Ages who had occupied "Serb" lands and oppressed the Serb nation. This vision of the Ottoman Turk was fused with a caricature of Islamic "Mujahideen" descending on the Balkans intent on establishing a terrorist state in Bosnia. The safety and the future of the Bosnian Serbs, therefore, lay not with an Islamic enemy that might destroy them but with brother Serbs in a powerful "Greater Serbia." This was the essential or, rather, crude argument against cohabiting with Muslims in Bosnia—and, therefore, an argument for the elimination of Muslims *from* Bosnia. As Serbia's war of "self-defense" took its murderous course, the argument was further refined. The war became Christianity's last stand against Islamic hegemony over Europe. The Serbs were fighting the last Crusade.

The propaganda underlying the ethnic stereotype became an essential part of a prolonged process in which the Bosnian Serb community was gradually subverted. It had begun prior to the first multiparty elections of 1990 in the republic. Led by Karadžić, a psychiatrist turned nationalist redeemer, the campaign of the Serbian Democratic Party in Bosnia was shaped by the agenda set by the Milošević regime in Serbia. From the start, therefore, Karadžić's party was entirely uninterested in any political future for the Bosnian Serbs within an undivided, multinational Bosnia. Accordingly, Karadžić had initially threatened to boycott the 1990 elections on the grounds that the elections would be "against Serbian interests."[33] In other words, free elections, freely held, would further strengthen Bosnia's autonomy while the Milošević regime was intent on drastically reducing the autonomy ceded to the republics by Tito in the 1974 Constitution and on recentralizing the Yugoslav state as a means of asserting Serbia's domination over the federation.

When threats did not prevent the election in Bosnia as they had also failed to do in Slovenia or Croatia, Karadžić and his mentors in Belgrade— canny as always—clearly realized that to boycott the election would be to marginalize the SDS and leave the field open to other claimants to Serb votes. In the meantime, however, Karadžić had proceeded to establish a national council to run Serbian affairs in Bosnia—a signal that the SDS considered itself the sole representative of the Bosnian Serbs.

The elections of December 1990, held to inaugurate a new democratic order in the Republic, placed the fate of Bosnia-Hercegovina in the hands of its nationalists: the Party for Democratic Action (SDA), the Serb Democratic Party (SDS), and the Croat Democratic Union (HDZ). These parties, having won the largest number of seats, dominated the parliament and the multinational presidency led by SDA's Alija Izetbegović. Despite the emergence of the nationalist parties, the reality of a Bosnia that was not and could not be an exclusive nation-state of the Muslims, or the Serbs, or the Croats, and therefore could only be governed as a multinational state of all its citizens seemed to swiftly reassert itself. The multinational character and evenly balanced structure of the new government appeared in themselves proof of the fact that in a country such as Bosnia-Hercegovina there was no place or rationale for exclusionary nationalist politics. This, of course, was illusion. The logic of the nationalists' divisive, millenarian political agendas would rend Bosnia from end to end.

While the SDA, the largest party in parliament and drawn from the largest community—the Muslims—in Bosnia, appeared to recognize from the outset that the survival of Bosnia as the homeland for the region's Muslims was inseparably linked to its survival as a pluralist, multinational state secured against neighboring Serbia and Croatia's expansionist ambitions, the SDS had very different objectives. Elections for the Serb nationalists were only going to be a stepping stone to the "Serbianization" of Bosnia. And if an independent Bosnia was going to be imperiled by the votaries of "Greater Serbia," the Croat nationalists in the Bosnian HDZ—an offshoot of, and drawing inspiration and support from, Franjo Tudjman's party of the same name in Croatia—were more than willing to jettison their very tenuous commitment to an undivided Bosnia in order to secure their own territorial fiefs.

The SDS had made its position very plain: not only was it strongly opposed to Bosnia leaving Yugoslavia but, supported by a chorus of political parties in Serbia demanding the "cantonization" of Bosnia, it also sought the division of the republic into "a confederation of three national communities" within Yugoslavia. The idea of cantonization found great favor with the HDZ, since "the idea of a Bosnian nationality in our time", declared the party's spokesman to the BBC, "is unacceptable."[34]

Of course "cantonization"—subsequently adopted with great enthusiasm by a parade of international mediators—was only a code word for the dismemberment of Bosnia. In March 1991, Slobodan Milošević of Serbia and Franjo Tudjman of Croatia met in Karadjordjevo on the Croat-Serb border to define the meaning of "cantonization" by agreeing on the carve-up of Bosnia-Hercegovina between the two larger states.[35] "The division of Bosnia-Hercegovina," writes Jelena Lovrić, "was the subject of their deepest mutual understanding."[36] This understanding on their common goal was reached between the two foes a full year before Bosnia-Hercegovina declared its independence—a point worth remembering for those who blindly argue that the Serbian assault on Bosnia was a consequence of the Bosnian declaration of independence. As far as Milošević and Tudjman were concerned, Bosnia's fate was settled regardless of whether or not it declared its independence from Yugoslavia.

The March meeting between the paramount leaders of Serbia and Croatia was followed by a meeting between their Serb and Croat surrogates in Bosnia. On May 6, 1991, Radovan Karadžić of the SDS and Mate Boban of the HDZ met at Gratz, Austria, to define their separate territorial shares of Bosnia-Hercegovina.[37] The same year, in November 1991, the SDS proceeded "to stage a 'plebiscite' in which more than one hundred percent of the Serbian population of Bosnia was said to have voted in favor of an 'Independent Serbian Republic of Bosnia' encompassing more than two-thirds of Bosnian territory including the capital city of Sarajevo. Such a demand was patently absurd," writes Alan Fogelquist, "if one considers the fact that Serbs comprised only 31 percent of the population while Muslims represent 44 percent, Croatians 18 percent, and others 7 percent. In staging such a 'plebiscite' Karadžić was following the precedent set earlier by extremist Serb leaders of the Krajina Republic in Croatia."[38] In July 1992, months after the "proclamation" of the Serbian Republic, the Croats of the HDZ had followed suit, establishing the "Republic of Herceg-Bosna" in the Croat-majority areas of Bosnia-Hercegovina.

The Milošević-Tudjman scheme for the two-way partition and annexation of Bosnia was reviving old ghosts. In 1939, a similar agreement on the carve-up of Bosnia had been reached between then Yugoslav president Dragiša Cvetcović and the Croat national leader Vlatko Maček with the blessings of the regent Pavle of the Kingdom of Yugoslavia. The only determinant of the division was to be the relative majority of Serbs or Croats in a given area, with no consideration given to the existence of the Muslims. When questioned about the apparent oversight, the response of Cvetoković and Maček was starkly simple: "Let's pretend they do not exist."[39]

Such collusion over Bosnia between Serbia and Croatia had been thwarted in the past by the Ottoman and Austro-Hungarian empires and then by the Yugoslavia built by Tito. With Tito dead and Yugoslavia dying, Bosnia did not have the resources to withstand the predatory moves of its neighbors. It was precisely for this reason that in 1991 Alija Izetbegović desperately tried to forestall the collapse of Yugoslavia. As John Newhouse noted in *The New Yorker*, "Bosnia's leaders pleaded with Western capitals to withhold recognition of Slovenia and Croatia, fearing that if granted Serbs and Croats would instantly fall upon Bosnia. Macedonia, frightened of the Serbs made the same plea."[40]

Together with Kiro Gligorov, the president of Macedonia, Izetbegović attempted to secure the agreement of Slovenia, Croatia, and Serbia to a decentralized and reorganized federal structure of sovereign Yugoslav states which would persuade the Slovenes and the Croats to stay within the union rather than opt for independence. If Slovenia and Croatia left Yugoslavia, the Bosnian and Macedonian leaders announced, they would have no option but to seek independence as well. But the nationalist governments that had come to power in all the three major republics had very different and conflicting perspectives on a future Yugoslavia and the fears and insecurities of the smaller republics were not their primary concerns. While the Slovenes and the Croats wanted the fullest autonomy, a step short of independence, the Serbian leadership was steadily dismantling the existing federal structures to construct a state dominated by Serbia, and was in no mood for compromise. Milošević and the military leadership of the JNA rejected both the joint Slovenian and Croatian proposals for a confederation as well as the compromise plan proposed by Bosnia and Macedonia for a looser federation.[41]

The predicament of the government of Bosnia-Hercegovina was dire. If Slovenia and Croatia were to abandon the federation, Bosnia would be left to the tender mercies of the Milošević regime which had embarked upon its journey to replace Yugoslavia with "Greater Serbia." The Serbian leadership's intentions were clear; the supporting statements and actions of the SDS in Bosnia left no space for illusions. Even so the Bosnian government continued to seek means of avoiding a confrontation with Serbia. In the autumn of 1991, after Slovenia and Croatia had declared independence and Serbia had declared war on Croatia, and while Serbian paramilitary groups began appearing in the Serbian villages of Bosnia, Izetbegović acceded to the diktat of the JNA to disarm the Republic's territorial defense units and allowed the "federal" army to confiscate their weapons. At this time JNA forces were withdrawing from Slovenia and Croatia, Bosnia was virtually under military occupation, and weaponry was being distributed openly to Serbian militias.

It was in December 1991 that the Bosnian parliament finally voted in favor of a declaration of sovereignty and asked for diplomatic recognition from the European Community and United States. This declaration had followed the declaration of the "Independent Serbian Republic of Bosnia" by the SDS in November. The Bosnian parliament's move towards independence was immediately denounced by Radovan Karadžić who threatened war if Bosnia withdrew from Yugoslavia. "It takes two to fight," Izetbegović had responded. "There will be no war."

WHILE BOSNIA'S TOWNS and villages were set ablaze, governments in Paris, London, New York, and Washington, unencumbered by any great sense of urgency, engaged in a protracted, contentious and, in the end, sterile debate over the options available to them to stop the war. A remarkable turn to this debate came early on in the United States when, in September 1992, the Chairman of the Joint Chiefs of Staff, General Colin Powell declared his opposition to the use of American ground forces in Bosnia. Powell's remarks became a key moment in a fateful miscasting of the debate which would have tragic consequences for the Bosnians. Powell noted that tens or hundreds of thousands of American troops might be required to staunch the war. Powell's reluctance about committing forces on such a scale were countered by General William Odom's open advocacy of deploying hundreds of thousands of NATO forces in former Yugoslavia. The bogey of massive intervention had been unleashed on a fearful and confused public.

For months Americans engaged in earnest and intense argument over whether to deploy or not to deploy hundreds of thousands of soldiers at a cost of tens of billions of dollars. Arthur Schlesinger, scorched like Colin Powell by the Vietnam war, warned the new American President, Bill Clinton, that

Bosnia could "destroy his domestic hopes as surely as Vietnam destroyed Lyn-
don Johnson's Great Society." Schlesinger intoned that America "must accept
the sad necessity of living with tragedies" when "vital US interests" were not
"directly threatened."[42]

The debate was remarkable for its narcissism. From afar Bosnians listened in exasperated disbelief. Much of the American intelligentsia, its press,
its military, and its politicians were living in a peculiar world all their own.
They argued, wrung their hands, and expressed great angst over the question
of massive intervention and what it might cost the United States. The last
superpower could only conceive of itself being involved on some extraordi-
narily grand scale or not at all. No one took note of the fact that the Bosnians
had not asked for massive intervention. Sefer Halilović, at the time the Commander of the Bosnian Army, repeatedly stated that Bosnia did not want the
United States or any other power to deploy its ground forces in the Balkans.
The Bosnian request was straightforward. If the United States or Europe
would not assist Bosnia in defending its integrity as an integral state or
believed they were under no obligation to forcefully deter acts of genocide,
then at the very least these Great Powers should cease to deliberately obstruct
the ability of Bosnia to act in its own self-defense. The simple, yet fundamental, maxim of the Bosnians was: If you cannot or will not help, then have the
moral decency to cause us no harm.

In September 1991, at the request of the Belgrade authorities, the UN
Security Council adopted Resolution 713 which imposed an arms embargo
on a still extant Yugoslavia. As Albert Wohlstetter observed, "Milošević
wanted UN 713 because a continuing monopoly of heavy guns and armor
made it easier for his 'federal' army to complete his program of ethnic cleansing."[43] It was this embargo which the Great Powers through their domination
of the Security Council continued to relentlessly apply to Bosnia following the
break-up of Yugoslavia.

The Serbs had a virtual monopoly of heavy weapons having acquired
nearly the entire military assets of the Yugoslav Army, including production
facilities. On December 18, 1992, the UN General Assembly woke up to the
perversity of an embargo which denied a member state the right to self-
defense under Article 51 of the UN Charter. It therefore voted by an overwhelming majority to lift the arms embargo against Bosnia and asked the
Security Council to immediately revoke resolution 713 and authorize "all
means possible" to preserve Bosnia's territorial integrity. The General Assembly's request to the Security Council was ignored.

The enormous dichotomy between the standpoint of the General
Assembly and that of the Security Council went largely unnoticed in much of
the press. Ian Williams, a journalist with *The New York Observer*, was one of
the few writers to note the disparity.

> The sordid maneuverings in the Security Council in April [1993]
> raise the question of whether the carnage in the Balkans could

actually have continued for the past year *without* the UN. The most notable example of the UN's contribution to the mayhem in the region has been the lopsided arms embargo against Bosnia-Hercegovina, which in principle favors the Serbs . . . The Balkan crisis has shown that, far from being the keystone of the new world order, the United Nations has no independent volition apart from the Security Council, which can and does ignore the will of the General Assembly . . . A series of creeping procedural changes since the end of the Cold War have virtually made the Council a tight cabal of the five [permanent members'] foreign ministries.[44]

Despite intense diplomatic pressures against them, three non-permanent members of the Security Council, New Zealand, Pakistan, and Venezuela, consistently opposed the position of Britain and France on the arms embargo. Following a visit to the besieged town of Srebrenica in April 1993, Diego Arria, Venezuela's Ambassador to the United Nations, appealed once again to the Security Council to lift the one-sided arms embargo against Bosnia. Arria's speech was "reported to have brought tears to the eyes of listening UN staff members."[45] The Venezuelan request was rejected at the behest of Britain, France, and Russia. Articulating diametrically opposite positions from week to week, the United States continued to intermittently call for a lifting of the embargo while in practice sanctioning its continuance.

In late June 1993, Venezuela and Pakistan again appealed to the Security Council to lift the embargo against Bosnia. Addressing the Council, Diego Arria, responded to the British and French objections:

We are told that lifting the arms embargo would increase violence. Already nearly two hundred thousand people have died. More than two million people have been displaced from their homes. Twenty thousand women have been raped. The International Court of Justice and the World Conference on Human Rights have indicated that Bosnia-Hercegovina is a victim of genocide and "ethnic cleansing," among other unspeakable crimes. For this Council, then, what precisely does it mean to say that violence would increase and spread?

If an armed people possess a greater ability to defend themselves, this does not mean that violence would necessarily increase. Until now the Serbs have been able to easily trample and vandalize the Bosnian Muslims. When the Bosnians are in a position to defend themselves, circumstances may deter the Serbs and, above all, place limits on their capacity to act with impunity.

More war? Rather, it is the international community's inconsistent attitude in the adoption of measures to stop aggression that has given free reign to the escalation of the conflict. It has essentially meant a massacre of mainly the Bosnian Muslim com-

munity. This is the reality . . . To do all that one can possibly do
to prevent a people from exercising its right to defend itself in
order to survive means to shoulder moral and political responsibilities of extraordinary significance.[46]

Despite Arria's repeated appeals the Security Council did not revoke the arms
embargo against Bosnia. In an attempt to parry the issue, the British and
French governments instead advocated the establishment of "safe havens" in
six Bosnians towns. The Americans endorsed the idea with some equivocation, acknowledging in the words of one American intelligence official that a
"polka dot solution" would result in "six little West Banks in Western Europe
with enormous problems." The American official explained whimsically, "You
can't create a viable economy inside a polka dot."[47]

   The Bosnian government denounced the proposal as one in which a formal UN vote was providing international sanction for the formation of "ghettos" on its territory. Alija Izetbegović, the Bosnian President, declared on
Radio Sarajevo, "If the international community is not ready to defend the
principles that it itself has proclaimed and which it proclaims to be a reflection
of its fundamental values . . . [and instead] prefers to close its eyes before the
most ruthless violations of human rights and international law, even more to
reward both aggression and genocide, let it then say this openly both to our
public and its own . . . Let it proclaim that the UN Charter and all the carefully and patiently built rules of international law are no longer valid."[48]

   The Bosnians reminded the United Nations that earlier Security Council resolutions had already authorized UN forces to use all available means to
protect the delivery of relief supplies and that the UN had the authority under
international law to break a military siege directed exclusively at the slaughter
of non-combatants. Arria told the Security Council on June 4, 1993, "We
should call them what they are: ghettos, refugee camps, open jails, areas under
threat; but we should never be so brazen as to call them 'safe areas.'"[49] Nevertheless, on June 4 a resolution declaring that six designated "safe areas" be
placed under UN protection was voted in the Security Council.

   As the Council passed yet another toothless resolution the Serbs
attacked Goražde with impunity. Sixty thousand civilian refugees in the town
came under a relentless artillery barrage, electricity and water were cut, and
food convoys blockaded in yet another violation of the Geneva Convention.
Hadžo Efendić, a Deputy Prime Minister in the Bosnian government and a
former Mayor of Goražde told the press, "We have thousands of people in
Goražde who are just like sacrificial lambs. Europe is responsible for this. It
has tied our hands, and all that the rest of the world has done is watch."[50]

AS THE WORLD watched, a shadow play of negotiations moved between London, Lisbon, New York, Athens, and Geneva. The talks began in earnest during August 1992 in London, four months after Bosnia's independence had

been recognized by the international community, and quickly took on the pattern of a farce.

In London the Serbs had agreed to cease all hostilities, to place all their heavy weapons in Bosnia under UN supervision, to end Serbia's involvement in the conflict, and to permit humanitarian relief to flow unimpeded to civilian population centers. Yet, after the London Conference not a single element in the agreement was implemented. At this stage the EC and the UN mediators made a fateful choice. Rather than insist firmly that the first principles had to be enacted before further negotiations could proceed, the mediators allowed the breach of key understandings to become an operating premise.

The London Conference had recognized the territorial integrity of Bosnia-Hercegovina and implicitly identified the aggressor by imposing specific sanctions against Serbia. However, a month later in September 1992 as negotiations resumed in Geneva, the arrival of David Owen, the new EC interlocutor, heralded a radical alteration in the terms of reference for the conference. The mandate of the Geneva conference was clear: to implement the London principles. Kasim Trnka, former Chief Justice of Bosnia's Constitutional Court, argues in his contribution to this volume that "the Geneva Conference deviated from its mandate and in so doing significantly degraded the entire peace process." Vance and Owen began to take steps which led ultimately to the evisceration of the principles upon which the negotiations for a settlement had been based. In August 1992 the London Conference had recognized Bosnia's territorial integrity as indivisible. Ten months later, in June 1993, David Owen would reveal his willingness to accept the Milošević-Tudjman plan to "partition" Bosnia by declaring, "I am a realist."[51]

In Trnka's view, Vance and Owen introduced two fundamentally flawed assumptions into the negotiation process which were "responsible for all the subsequent weaknesses of the peace negotiations sponsored by the EC and the UN." In London, it had been determined "without ambiguity that Bosnia was a sovereign state which had the legal right to defend itself against the aggression of another state," but Trnka insists that the negotiators abandoned "the starting position of the London Conference . . . and thus abandoned their mandate." When they reached Geneva, Vance and Owen fundamentally altered the underlying formulation which had focused on Bosnia as a target of externally backed aggression. Instead, argues Trnka they "imposed the formulation of 'three warring factions' upon the negotiations."

> They brought delegations into the negotiation process which they, as mediators, chose to identify as representatives of the three largest nationalities in Bosnia-Hercegovina. The implications of this change were to prove tragic. The new formulation ignored the fact of aggression which the London principles had recognized. By ignoring the element of aggression the EC and UN mediators gave preeminence to the view that the war was essentially a civil, interethnic, and religious war. Although the Bosnian government

reflected a multi-ethnic, cosmopolitan, and pluralistic constituency, it was now designated a 'faction.' This formulation
placed the legitimate and legally elected organs of state power on
a par with illegitimate self-proclaimed structures which were
engaged in acts of aggression backed by external forces.

Thus, the Geneva Conference accepted, as legitimate representatives of the three nationalities, the leaders of three particular
national political parties. None of these individuals had ever been
given any mandate in an election to negotiate away the existence
of Bosnia-Hercegovina as an integral, undivided state. They represented parties which had been elected to the parliament of the
country, but they could not even pretend to represent the entire
community to which they belonged; there existed several other
parties representing other political tendencies and drawing support from varied national and multinational constituencies. In
addition, in the last elections, more than one-fourth of the electorate did not support any of the three political parties which
Vance and Owen elevated to the status of the national representatives of the 'warring factions.'[52]

The framework imposed upon the peace talks by the West's mediators effectively disenfranchised a large segment of the Bosnian population. Analysis of
the 1990 election shows that one-half of the voting population of Bosnia was
not represented at the peace negotiations.[53] In the election, one-third of the
eligible voters had abstained, while one-third of those who voted did not vote
for any of the nationalist parties, casting their votes instead across ethnic lines
for non-national liberal or social democratic parties. The election rules had
also provided for a "Fourth List" for elections to the Bosnian Presidency which
allowed Bosnians to vote for independent candidates who refused to define
themselves by ethnicity. The Bosnian Vice-President, Ejup Ganić, a "Muslim"
was elected to the Presidency from the fourth list. Thus fifty percent of the
republic's citizens had—by voting or by abstaining—clearly demonstrated
that the nationalist current was not strong enough to overwhelm all of Bosnia.
The so-called "warring factions" at the UN-EC negotiating tables had among
them the votes of only half the electorate of Bosnia—and even these votes
were not necessarily votes for the partitioning of Bosnia. The exclusion of a
significant group of Bosnian society from the peace talks revealed the ideological assumptions of the negotiators who had set their minds at arriving at some
form of ethnic division of Bosnia as the only permissible basis for a solution.

According to Tihomir Loža, the men and women who had voted against
the various nationalist currents were "those who were born in or now live in
mixed marriages, and who by definition can have no place in the national
states. The group [would] also include those Serbs, Muslims, and Croats
whose political beliefs reject any chauvinistic, clerical formula" for the ordering of state and society.[54] There was, thus, a "fourth estate" which could not

and would not be defined by ethnicity. Their presence at the negotiating table—objectively sharing the same vision of society that the Bosnian government was seeking to defend—would have made it virtually impossible to premise the debate and the solutions on the notion—zealously advanced by the Serb and Croat nationalists—of an ancient and irreconcilable conflict which could only be resolved through partition. For when the electoral strength of the SDA and the non-nationalist parties was combined it represented a clear majority in favor of maintaining Bosnia-Hercegovina as a unitary multinational state. By consciously excluding the "fourth estate" of non-nationalists from the peace negotiations Vance and Owen narrowly confined their mediation effort inside the prison of ethnic politics.

When the political representatives of the non-nationalist parties arrived in Geneva in August 1993 to protest, along with the SDA, the Owen-Stoltenberg partition plan, they were treated with contempt by mediators apparently incapable of assimilating the phenomenon of Bosnians who failed to fit neatly into the Owenite category of a faction driven by ethnic nationalism. Thus, although the "fourth estate" had received more votes than Mate Boban's HDZ, they were excluded from the EC-UN peace negotiations.

"According to Lord Owen, we are nothing at all. We thought the negotiators should come up with a fourth republic where all the normal and mixed-marriage people could live," a young woman doctor of Croat and Serb parents told a *New York Times* reporter in Sarajevo. Sitting with her best friend, a Muslim woman, whose fiancé is a Croat soldier fighting in the Bosnian Army, the doctor explained, "We're neither Muslim, nor Croat, nor Serb. A normal person in this situation is one who has an identity that goes beyond his or her nationality. Imagine asking people who they are and the only thing they can come up with is 'I'm a Croat' or 'I'm a Serb' or whatever. Imagine, these people were born that way and they haven't made any progress since."[55] The "normal people" were not permitted representation.

Although he would later claim regretfully that he had never intended the peace talks to end in the partition of Bosnia, Cyrus Vance nonetheless went along with David Owen for most of the ride. Three days after Owen publicly embraced Milošević's partition plan in June 1993, Vance discreetly distanced himself from the scheme, when he told *The New York Times,* "Right from the beginning, we always said there can be no partition. It's wrong. It's the equivalent of endorsing ethnic cleansing."[56] Vance's disavowal came too late to make any difference. Moreover, it represented dissembling after the fact. Vance and Owen early on had changed course together and taken the road which would lead to partition. For this reason George Kenney, the American diplomat who resigned in 1992 as State Department desk officer for Yugoslavia, declared that Owen and Vance "bear a heavy responsibility for collaborating with Serbian aggression."[57]

Had the mediators stayed faithful to their original mandate of preserving Bosnia's territorial integrity, they would have had to confront the dilemma which they avoided at every turn. In Kasim Trnka's words it would have required them to advance "a plausible military option to deter the ongoing aggression."[58] After the Serbs failed to implement the key provisions of the London meeting which called upon them immediately to cease the practice of "ethnic cleansing" and to place their heavy artillery under UN control, the original mandate would have logically compelled Owen and Vance to return to the European Community and the United Nations in order to propose that specific actions be adopted to defend the territorial integrity of a UN member state and enforce the provisions of the London conference.

Vance and Owen not only failed to proceed in this direction, but they also failed to establish a key negotiating principle. At no point did they firmly insist on a cease-fire in place as a pre-condition for negotiations to proceed. Nor, did they declare that the failure to observe such a cease-fire would bring into force clear military countermeasures on the part of the EC and UN. Furthermore, at no stage did the negotiators categorically demand as a pre-condition for all further negotiations that existing concentrations camps for Croat and Muslim civilians be closed and their dismantlement be monitored strictly. Press and intelligence reports had confirmed the enormously high mortality rates prevailing in Manjača, Omarska, and other camps where non-combatants were being held in violation of the Geneva Convention.[59]

Instead, Vance and Owen proceeded to negotiate while an escalating atmosphere of mass terror engulfed the Bosnian population. Regardless of innumerable outrages, broken agreements, and violations of UN resolutions the negotiations proceeded in a manner in which they soon became little more than a procedural ruse from the Serbian side. Milošević's assessment of Vance's and Owen's inclinations and weaknesses proved to be remarkably astute. Whatever the world's press might say, Milošević understood that Serbia in the end would set the terms and David Owen would be his "realistic" accomplice.[60] According to Marko Prelec,

> Milošević chose his tactics astutely . . . master of manipulating the peace process to serve his own ends, he cultivated the Serbs' image of dangerous unpredictability, violating countless agreements and committing spectacular outrages. The result of this was that the United Nations mediators ceased being surprised or angered by the Serbs' failures to live up to their promises and came to see keeping them at the peace table as a valued goal in itself. Milošević could therefore negotiate at no cost, dragging out the peace talks and buying valuable time to complete the work of ethnic cleansing . . . While Milošević steadfastly refused to buckle under any threat short of force, he gave the impression of being on the brink of compromise, thus dragging out the peace process and winning concessions from the mediators."[61]

The concessions to Milošević were many and they began almost immediately after the London Conference. No action was taken to impede the steady advance of ethnic cleansing; no steps were taken to control the attacks on civilian centers by Serbian artillery; and firm measures were not implemented to guarantee the delivery of relief supplies to refugees marooned in isolated ghettos. While more than a million persons were driven in terror from their homes, Vance and Owen crafted a proposal which would divide Bosnia into ten ethnic provinces.

In their critique of the Vance-Owen proposals, Stjepko Golubic, Susan Campbell, and Thomas Golubic have argued persuasively that solutions "defined by the principle of a carve-up on the basis of ethnicity are inherently unworkable attempts to divide the indivisible." In a detailed review of demographic statistics they show the high level of integration of Bosnian society. In order to achieve the scale of ethnic segregation which David Owen on behalf of the European Community proposed as the basis for a solution, the permanent—*not temporary*—rending of Bosnian society was required. The dislocation from homes and villages where families had traditional links extending back five centuries or more would for the first time in history be given international sanction. Such a solution in the end represented "a clear case of *realpolitik* that sacrifices the interests of the very people it purports to protect."[62]

If the Milošević-Tudjman partition plan—adopted by David Owen in June 1993 on the heels of the Serbs' rejection of the earlier Vance-Owen plan—actually became a reality, a classified State Department report concluded that an additional two million persons would be forced to leave their homes.[63] The prospect of such a plan actually becoming a reality disturbed even normally staid voices. *The New Yorker* warned in July 1993 that the United States had one "last chance" not to become implicated in an EC-UN scheme of apartheid.

> There are many unhappy precedents for this kind of scheme. In South Africa, the mad dreamers of apartheid forcibly resettled three and a half million people in a cynical hopeless quest to create a chain of ethnically 'pure' states. What they created instead was untold suffering, chaos, and a ferocious new breed of petty tyrant: the Bantustan leader . . . What South Africa and the former Yugoslavia really have in common is simply their pain and their manipulation by politicians who exploit the idea that only ethnically homogeneous societies can be successful. What is in some ways most frightening at this point in the Yugoslav tragedy is the willingness of Western governments to accept this patently false and racist idea—to agree, in effect, to the creation of Bantustans in Europe.[64]

Alternative measures could have been adopted at almost any stage. The most critical would have been the lifting of the arms embargo. The timing was ideal in 1993. In the United States a new administration was taking power in Washington and appeared at first willing to confront the question of Serbian aggression head on. But in early February 1993 David Owen and Cyrus Vance shifted the Geneva peace negotiations to UN headquarters in New York. In a series of well-publicized appearances before the world press the two mediators condemned the new Clinton Administration for suggesting there was any alternative to their plan. Vance attacked his critics within the Administration declaring his effort to be "the best settlement you can get" and asserting that it was a "bitter irony to see the Clinton people block it."[65] Meanwhile, Owen with characteristic arrogance declared the proposals to be "not just the best act in town, [but] the only act in town." He publicly denounced the US government declaring it to be "largely the fault of the Americans" that he could not "get the Muslims on board." Frequently referring to the multi-ethnic government in Bosnia as "the Muslims," Owen demanded that the American President "make it clear to Izetbegović [the Bosnian President] that he's got no real alternative."[66]

Owen and Vance had persuaded the Croat "factional leader" Mate Boban to sign on to their proposals. Boban, a former officer in Yugoslav military intelligence and a protégé of the Croatian President, General Franjo Tudjman, had gained prominence through an internal *putsch* within the Bosnian wing of the HDZ following the December 1990 elections in Bosnia. It had been engineered by Tudjman and Boban in order to oust Stjepan Kljuić from the leadership of the party. An elected member of the Bosnian presidency, Kljuić was a representative of the Croats of central Bosnia who constituted the majority of the country's Croat population. Uncompromising in his commitment to the integrity and independence of Bosnia as a multinational state, he had refused to yield to the Croatian regime's pressure to endorse the cantonization of Bosnia. Backed, financed, and armed by the Tudjman regime, Boban became the unelected representative of Croat interests as defined by the proponents of "Greater Croatia." Thus, Owen and Vance secured the first signature to their plan from an unelected intelligence officer whom they chose to accept as the "representative" of the Bosnian Croat population.

The next step was to secure Izetbegović's signature. Owen continued to condemn Washington saying the Bosnian President would not sign "as long as the Muslims think that military help may be on the way." As always, the cardinal sin for the EC's representative was the horrifying prospect of Bosnia securing the means to fight for its own defense. Owen demanded that Clinton "stop all this loose talk about using force" and promised that the Vance-Owen plan "could be the big prize for Clinton."[67] Of course, in three months time when the Serbs cavalierly rejected Owen's plan ("Bosnia never existed, and it will never exist," Karadžić had exulted) and demanded that Owen instead agree to *their* proposal for partition, no word was heard from Lord Owen that Clinton should make it "clear to Milošević and Karadžić that they've got no real alternative." It appeared, as Branka Magaš noted early on, that Owen and Vance "were more interested in saving their conference than in saving Bosnia-Hercegovina."[68]

In February 1993 a timid and uncertain Clinton Administration finally yielded to Vance and Owen by publicly endorsing a settlement based on ten ethnic provinces and accepting for the first time that territory seized by Serbian forces in their campaign of "ethnic cleansing" would be recognized as a fait accompli. Categorical American statements regarding the impossibility of accepting any settlement that endorsed the forcible seizure of territory which had been ethnically cleansed were now replaced by meager utterances by senior US officials. Madeleine Albright, the American representative to the United Nations, awkwardly announced that the United States *"will try* to make a peace settlement which does not punish the victims and does not award the aggressors."[69]

The transparent contradictions of such a policy were self-evident. Magaš observed in the *Manchester Guardian Weekly:*

> The map proposed by Vance and Owen openly ratifies the results of ethnic cleansing, which international public opinion has condemned. In reducing the country's multi-national government and army to its Muslim component alone, the plan betrays all Serbs and Croats who, by remaining faithful to the ideal of a single Bosnian state, have given the lie to the claims of Karadžić and Boban to represent all Serbs and Croats in Bosnia-Hercegovina. Besides being unprincipled, the plan is also unworkable because it contains no provisions for disarming the aggressor, while denying to the central state authority that "monopoly of legal violence" (i.e. exclusive control of the army and police) without which no normal state can function, and in the absence of which Bosnia-Hercegovina cannot return to normal life, rebuild its shattered economy or ensure the return of its expelled population. It is obvious that a Bosnia-Hercegovina constructed in accordance with the Vance-Owen plan could not pretend to sovereignty, integrity or independence . . . Far from being a step towards peace, the plan will only stimulate further war for territory . . . The "peace plan" becomes an instrument for punishing the victim rather than the aggressor.[70]

Enormous pressures were brought to bear upon the Bosnian government to sign the Vance-Owen plan and formally accept the ethnic division of their country. With a Bosnian signature in hand the two negotiators confidently predicted that Milošević would see to it that the Bosnian Serbs signed. Owen told the *Financial Times* that Milošević was a man who could be counted on. "Cy's [Vance] relationship with [Milošević] is a very important one," said Owen. "There is trust there, at a level of man for man."[71]

With the Bosnian government's last slender hope of finding support in Washington dashed by the mediator's diplomatic maneuvers, a bitter Bosnian delegation under obvious duress signed the Vance-Owen proposals at the end of March 1993. They declared, without much conviction, that the Clinton Administration had promised that if the Bosnians signed the accord and the

Serbs continued their assaults, then Washington would genuinely do "every-thing in its power" to lift the arms embargo.[72]

The cheery optimism of Vance and Owen quickly proved to be a chimera. As predicted, their plan provided a perverse rationale for one of the most violent phases of land grabbing and "ethnic cleansing" yet seen in the Balkan war "by tempting the 'owners' of the national provinces to full posses-sion of their mini-states."[73] Kemal Kurspahić had warned of the terrible dan-gers inherent in the mediators casually advancing "solutions" based on ever changing proposals designed to establish arbitrary boundaries where none had ever existed.

> People in Bosnia still live in very ethnically mixed towns. It is impossible to draw even the tiniest line between them without leaving vast numbers in some else's ethnic "state." To pursue such a "solution" would turn entire sections of the population into sec-ond class citizens. What is even worse, the so-called "solution" along these lines is likely to generate even more victims of violence by encouraging new waves of "ethnic cleansing" designed to create ethnically exclusive Muslim, Serbian, or Croatian mini-states . . . The evidence, already, is staring the peace makers and the cartog-raphers in the face. The maps of a divided Bosnia-Hercegovina passed around at international conferences have become more a continuing *cause* for the tragedy that has befallen us than a *solu-tion.* When those maps were first introduced into the negotiation process in March 1992, in Lisbon, Serbian forces started an inten-sive campaign to "cleanse" the territory designated on the maps as "theirs." They embarked upon yet another campaign of killing, raping, imprisoning, and expelling all non-Serbs. When these maps were again re-introduced in January 1993, during the Vance-Owen negotiations in Geneva, incidents of the same type occurred in areas classified as supposedly Croatian—Gornji Vakuf, Busovaca, Vitez.[74]

In early February 1993, as Vance and Owen insisted in New York upon ten ethnic provinces being the "best game in town," intensive new assaults by Ser-bian forces in eastern Bosnia rapidly turned tens of thousands of terrified civil-ians into refugees in the depth of winter. *The New York Times* reported "a renewed Serbian campaign to expel Muslims from towns and villages in Bosnia-Hercegovina [that] appears to have been set off by the United Nations [Vance-Owen] proposal to divide the country into semi-autonomous provinces."[75] By April it had reached a crescendo as an estimated sixty thou-sand refugees poured into a tiny besieged enclave in eastern Bosnia known as Srebrenica. Under a constant barrage of Serbian artillery fire, starved of basic supplies, and death tolls mounting each day, Srebrenica became, for a period, a modern-day Guernica.

As the Serbian offensive gathered speed in eastern Bosnia, the Croatian government abruptly broke off its tactical military alliance with the Bosnian Army. In spite of vociferous dissent within the Croatian community, the Tudjman government in Zagreb reverted to its old arrangement agreed with Milošević in 1991—the partition of Bosnia between Croatia and Serbia.[76] The Vance-Owen plan provided the perfect entrée. By defining the basis of a solution to be ten ethnically defined provinces, extreme nationalist elements in both Serbia and Croatia acted unilaterally to ensure that Vance's and Owen's theoretical framework would reflect a territorial minimum for the final carve-up of Bosnia. The diplomatic niceties imagined by the mediators of a step-by-step agreement were bluntly shunted aside as the "theory of ten provinces" became *facts* defined by military occupation.

Whether the mediators used the phrase "cantonization," "ethnic provinces," or "partition," they all amounted to a code word for the dismemberment of Bosnia. In early April 1993, Gojko Sušak, the Croatian Minister of Defense, crossed the border of Bosnia-Hercegovina and in the town of Travnik (granted to the Croats under the Vance-Owen plan) demanded that the Croatian national flag be flown over a city within the borders of Bosnia. At the prodding of the Zagreb government, Croatian paramilitary units began a violent assault on the civilian Muslim populations in Travnik, Vitez, Zenica, and Mostar. The Croatian military offensive in Bosnia was carried out relentlessly throughout the spring and summer of 1993. In late August the UN High Commission for Refugees (UNHCR) accused the Croat forces under Mate Boban's command of carrying out atrocities against Bosnian Muslims "as brutal as any so far witnessed."

The UNHCR stated that Bosnian Croat forces had waged a campaign of "brutal ethnic cleansing, murder, looting, rape and other abuses" against Muslims in south-western Bosnia. The UN also revealed that fifteen thousand draft-age Muslim men were being illegally held in concentration camps in western Bosnia following their detention by Croat forces in the summer of 1993. In September 1993 UN officials described civilians who had been released from Croatian detention centers as looking "like concentration camp victims from the Second World War."[77]

In a replay of the Vance-Owen tactics in February 1993, the Bosnians in August were given an ultimatum by David Owen and Thorvald Stoltenberg to accept a new partition plan which left the country "virtually landlocked and geographically disjointed . . . sandwiched between the new Greater Serbia and Greater Croatia." *The Financial Times* reported that Bosnia's President, Alija Izetbegović, had been given a "chance to choose peace—at the risk of losing his country." Observing that "Serb enthusiasm of the [Owen-Stoltenberg] plan" reflected this fact, the newspaper quoted a member of the Bosnian Serb delegation who "gleefully boasted" that Owen's ultimatum to the Bosnians meant that "the Turks [a derogatory term for Bosnia's Muslims] are going to be like walnuts in a Serbo-Croat nutcracker."[78]

The United Nations' and the European Community's entanglement in the center of an ugly paradox was evident. The UNHCR and other international organizations had clearly identified paramilitary formations and specific individuals responsible for a preponderance of the war's worst atrocities. Nevertheless, UN and EC negotiators in Geneva continued to engage with such elements as "acceptable" interlocutors. And in the end they went one astonishing step further. They accepted the proposals of men who had been publicly identified with war crimes as a valid diplomatic basis upon which Bosnia-Hercegovina would be partitioned and thus cease to exist.

THE ROLE OF THE United States in ultimately sanctioning the ruin of Bosnia requires special mention. In early February 1993, three weeks after the Clinton administration assumed power, the new Secretary of State Warren Christopher issued an idealistic statement on Bosnia: "Bold tyrants and fearful minorities are watching to see whether ethnic cleansing is a policy the world will tolerate . . . [O]ur answer must be a resounding no."[79] Within six months a "resounding no" became a "perhaps," then a "maybe," and finally an inaudible "yes."

The new American administration was a spectacle rich in irony and contradiction. In early February the US expressed grave reservations about the Vance-Owen proposals. Yet, by the end of that same month Clinton and Christopher had endorsed the Vance-Owen framework which accepted Serbian territorial conquests in Bosnia and the forced removal of non-Serb populations from those territories. By July 1993, Warren Christopher was able to declare that Bosnia was not of "vital interest" to American foreign policy and bemoan the fact that Washington had become a "one-issue city." *The New York Times* noted that Christopher "made no secret of his desire to move attention away from Bosnia."[80]

Lee Hamilton, the Democratic Chairman of the House Committee on Foreign Affairs, argued against lifting the arms embargo on Bosnia and chuckled on public television when he noted that it was unfortunate for the Bosnians that unlike Kuwait there was no oil in their country which might have made Bosnia's resources, if not its population, a strategic interest to the US.[81] At the Pentagon, the first African-American Chief-of-Staff, General Colin Powell, continued to wargame the problem of massive deployment involving hundreds of thousands of troops, but appeared conceptually incapable of assessing what the simple option of lifting the arms embargo might have meant for an unarmed population resisting the imposition of ethnic apartheid upon its society.

In April 1993, as Srebrenica was about to be overrun, twelve State Department officials specializing in the Balkans condemned American policy in a letter to the Secretary of State. By August, three officials—Marshall Harris, Jon Western, and Stephen Walker—had resigned from the Department. Harris, the desk officer for Bosnia, left on the eve of a crucial turn in American policy. In early August, Warren Christopher was preparing an important

American démarche on Bosnia which went largely unnoticed in the press. A letter was drafted to the Bosnian president, Alija Izetbegović, formally insisting that the Bosnians accept the final partition of their state along lines originally proposed by Slobodan Milošević and Franjo Tudjman and approved by David Owen and Thorvald Stoltenberg. Harris and other State Department officials fought to dissuade their seniors from making the ethnic partition of Bosnia official US policy. They failed and Christopher's letter to Izetbegović went out on August 19th.

Whatever the disclaimers, American pressure on the Bosnian government to accept the ethnic partition of their state had placed the imprimatur of the United States on the irreversibility of Serbia's "ethnic cleansing." In his letter of resignation Harris said he could not be a party to the ongoing "pressure on the Bosnian government to agree to partition . . . I can no longer serve in a Department of State that accepts the forceful dismemberment of a European state and that will not act against genocide."[82] Explaining the depth of disaffection in the State Department, George Kenney, the desk officer for Yugoslavia who resigned during the Bush Administration, stated that "virtually all the staff working on these issues agree that our Balkan policy is a total failure" and "that American policy borders on complicity in genocide."[83]

In April 1993, Bill Clinton declared without equivocation that "[e]thnic cleansing is the kind of inhumanity that the Holocaust took to the nth degree. The idea of moving people around and abusing them and often killing them, solely because of their ethnicity, is an abhorrent thing and it is especially troublesome in that area where people of different ethnic groups lived side by side for so long together. I think you have to stand up against it. I think its wrong." Yet, the following September in his first public meeting with the Bosnian President, Clinton told Izetbegović he had to accept ethnic partition. According to *The New York Times,* Clinton explained that "Washington and its allies were not going to commit the military resources to fundamentally change the balance of power."[84] The Bosnians bitterly understood the policy of cynical realism which had long prevailed against them. As Miloš Vasić observed, they had learned their diplomacy the "hard way" and disposed of "their illusions about 'justice,' 'the sovereignty of an internationally recognized state,' and being victims who should be protected."[85]

On September 7th, a day before the Washington encounter, Izetbegović appeared before the UN Security Council and made clear how little he expected from an organization which had repeatedly failed to implement any of the nearly fifty resolutions it had passed on Bosnia. Yet, in one final and utterly unavailing appeal, the Bosnian president insisted that if the Security Council would not stand behind its own resolutions, it still had a moral responsibility to lift the arms embargo and allow Bosnia to defend itself. "Defend us or let us defend ourselves. You have no right to deprive us of both," he told the Council.[86] The stone-faced men who sat listening to him may not have had the right, but they had the power. "The French ambassador Jean Bernard Merimée," Ian Williams reported, "dismissively referred to the

President as sounding like a beggar, which came badly from someone who had played such a large part in reducing Bosnia to penury."[87]

Shortly after his meeting with Izetbegović, Clinton was pressed by journalists to explain the seeming incoherence of his Bosnia policy. His answer was perhaps more revealing then he intended. "When [Britain and France] refused to lift the arms embargo," said Clinton, "it was the biggest single disappointment I've had as President, because I thought then and I think today that it delayed getting a decent peace agreement for Bosnia."[88] It was clear that if Britain and France were not inclined toward a "decent peace" for Bosnia, the US would agree to the imposition of an indecent one. It would do so because its "vital interests" lay in not placing an excessive strain on the Atlantic Alliance over unpleasant developments in the Balkans. Thus in May 1993, when Christopher had toured European capitals to persuade the British and the French to lift the arms embargo and to strike at Serbian forces besieging civilian centers, so tentative were his representations that he had, by all accounts, underwhelmed his counterparts and "practically asked to be dissuaded."[89] Where Eisenhower had sharply broken with Britain, France, and Israel over the invasion of Suez, Clinton yielded to London and Paris on Bosnia and then publicly wrung his hands.

Clinton was also frank in telling journalists that they had "to see this Bosnia thing in the context of everything else that's going on in the world including Russia."[90] A key American consideration had always been not to act in any manner in the Balkans which might provide the slightest provocation to pan-Slavic nationalists in Russia who opposed American led efforts to structure a transition to capitalism in the former Soviet Union. Writing in *The New York Times,* Dimitri Simes, senior associate at the Carnegie Endowment for International Peace, argued that Boris Yeltsin, and not Bosnia, was and ought to be America's prime concern: "In contrast to Kuwait, Bosnia has never been an American ally. And there is no oil there either . . . Also, disciplining Serbia may damage our ability to address a more important issue: aid to Russia . . . Yet, support is badly needed for Boris Yeltsin's democratic government. No peripheral causes should be allowed to divert US attention from that fundamental issue."[91] Thus, as Dr. Eqbal Ahmed observed, any American "action against genocide had to be indefinitely postponed for the sake of Boris Yeltsin's political viability."[92]

In the Great Game of Great-Power politics, Bosnia like many small nations in history had merely become a sideshow to ostensibly greater imperatives. During their meeting with the American President, the hard-bitten Bosnian delegation was stunned to hear Clinton explain that John Major, the British Prime Minister, had told him that the Conservative government in England would fall if the arms embargo on Bosnia were lifted.[93] This was offered as a rationale for the continuance of the embargo. The British government apparently stood on a perilously thin reed if its fate rested upon its Bosnia policy. Nevertheless, Major, and not the Bosnians, had found a sympathetic ear in Washington. Therefore, Ian Williams writes, "Bosnia, a small country, far away, is to be left to its own devices, so that small grey men around

Major can maintain the dubious perks of office in the face of disdain at home and abroad."[94]

For the Bosnian delegation it was obvious that Clinton was more concerned with sustaining the most unpopular government in Britain since the Second World War than he was about the survival of their country. For men who had come from the maelstrom of war it was a set of priorities which were difficult to comprehend. It was a surreal encounter. In one year ten percent of their country's population had been killed. They were returning to a devastated country of besieged and starving cities, wounded children, and raped women, empty-handed, with the recommendation that they surrender. The United States had more important matters on its agenda.

BY FAILING TO support the defense of Bosnia-Hercegovina against Serbian aggression, the West, in effect, was coming to terms with a war of conquest which had been fueled by the emergence of an essentially fascist political movement in Serbia. The sense of injured nationalism which can be mobilized into an enormously destructive force had appeared once again in Europe. Since it did not arise in a powerful industrialized European state which could threaten the order of the entire continent, it was tolerated by the liberal democratic order in much the same way as Third World regimes of similar character have been readily accommodated for decades.

In the half century since the defeat of fascism in Europe a new generation of leaders and intellectuals had come of age who had had no direct experience of the regimes that rose in Italy, Germany, and Spain in the early decades of the twentieth century. Four decades of the Cold War had intervened to obscure from view the dangerous consequences of the aggressive nationalist projects embodied in Europe's fascist movements. In light of events in southeastern Europe today, however, it would not be inappropriate to reflect anew on the question of fascism.

Thomas Mann had spoken of the need for vigilance when he described fascism as "a disease of the times which is at home everywhere and from which no country is free."[95] Although the term has been often used loosely and inappropriately in modern political discourse, political parties and movements with fascist characteristics have continued to endure in many societies. Hugh Trevor-Roper pointed out long ago that fascism as a philosophy had "no . . . intellectual rigor, no agreed prophets . . . Its origins are plural, divergent, imprecise."[96] Paul Sweezy also observed, "So far as internal economic or social problems are concerned the program of fascism is a mass of ill digested and often mutually contradictory proposals which are notable chiefly for their unmistakably demagogic character. Hardly any of these proposals is novel or original; almost without exception they have appeared and reappeared in earlier periods of social distress. What gives to fascism coherence and vitality is its stress on nationalism, its demand for the restoration of a strong state power, and its call for a war of revenge and foreign conquest."[97]

European fascism, despite similarities and borrowings, had many variants revealing significant differences between each national experience. Mussolini defined fascism as an "organized, concentrated, authoritarian democracy on a national basis." But unlike their German counterparts the Italian *fascisti* were not possessed by a fanatical, and, in the end, murderous, hostility toward their ethnic minorities. The German and Italian movements were similar in the contempt in which they held the Church even though innumerable accommodations of mutual interest were made between the robe and the party. In Spain, however, the Church and Franco had fought under the same banner in their campaign to cleanse Spain of the contagion of democracy and radical social ideas that threatened the established hierarchy.

Whether or not the Milošević regime in Belgrade and its associates in Pale can be considered an integral part of Europe's fascist legacy requires careful consideration which is impossible within the setting of an introduction. It needs to be recognized, however, that the revival of Serbian nationalism—which the Serb poet Mirko Kovač has called "that sick phenomenon . . . the aim of which was the annihilation of everything that did not belong to the Serbs,"—represents a blending of many antecedents.[98]

Unquestionably, it is possessed by a fanatical hostility towards the "Other", those who are not part of the Serb nation. Furthermore, Serb nationalism is deeply imbued with the sense of a religious crusade and draws its inspiration and its sanctification from a zealous Orthodox Church. Like Franco who had once portrayed himself as a soldier of the cross, Mladić and Karadžić have sought and gained the endorsement of the Church patriarchs for the expansionist drive to set new borders for a "Greater Serbia." And the intoxicated frenzy and the war fever which Milošević's demagoguery infused into the movement to bring all Serbs into one state has created like "all European fascisms the impression that the movement was open-ended, a continuous Nietzchean ecstasy."[99]

There is, of course, a particularly backward element to the modern Serb revival which distinguishes it from other somewhat comparable experiences in twentieth-century Europe in that it lacks a coherent economic rationale. In the context of the Great Depression, the Nazi program of German rearmament and extensive public works directly addressed, for better or for worse, the crisis of effective demand and acute industrial depression. In Italy, Mussolini had earlier advanced a "corporatist" program of national planning and investment which, unlike Germany, met with rather limited success. It was principally his promise of imposing order in an unstable environment of social unrest which had won the support of a wide coalition of conservative and middle class parties fearful of socialist agitations among workers in Milan and other industrial centers.[100]

Fascism's promise of stability and order appealed to conservative elements worried by the emergence of mass parties on the left. "Fascism, as an effective movement, was born of fear," writes Trevor-Roper. "Faced by the terrible threat of bolshevism, the European middle classes, recently so confident, took fright. And in their fright they found themselves crouching in the same postures and adapting some of the ideas which they had once ridiculed."[101] A half-century later the Serb nationalist revival emerged as a leading alternative to the "bolshevism" of the Yugoslav communists. What is confusing, as Banac notes, is that the Milošević regime emerged from the shell of the League of Communists of Serbia. "But it is entirely misleading to say, as is frequently said, that Milošević is some sort of unreconstructed Bolshevik. He is certainly not that," argues Banac. "There is no connection with his origins . . . the basic defining element is fascism."[102] The European Community and the United States came to terms with this variant of Serb nationalism, the segregationist ideas and cold-blooded practices of which they had so volubly condemned. While not an ideal option, it was certainly to be preferred to any variant of socialist *perestroika,* in Yugoslavia or anywhere else in Europe.

The earlier naive presumption parlayed about by the European and American political establishments in the aftermath of the Cold War was that the new epoch, then dawning, would deliver to the populace of the "other camp" the capitalist cornucopia. Indeed, this had been the alluring promise. However, the great celebration over the demise of "actually existing socialism" obscured the emergence of darker realities. Long suppressed traditions which the West might have preferred to deny as part of the legacy of Western civilization surfaced from the locked caverns of its history, and any illusions that the transition from "socialism" would evolve naturally toward stable and liberal democratic structures fell victim to a recrudescence of domestic bigotry and revanchist violence. As Žižek, citing Hegel, reminds us, the moment of victory of a political force is the very moment of its splitting apart.[103] The illusion that old structures would be replaced by firm constitutional guarantees of civil liberties and new forms of economic prosperity soon disintegrated as post-socialist elites in several states succumbed to an unseemly scramble of primitive accumulation or nationalist wars of conquest.

But the pragmatic men of the West came to terms with fascism in the manner of their fathers. "These men could feel emotion for Czechoslovakia," observed the *Manchester Guardian* regarding 1938, "but their rational judgment told them that what they desired was not possible in practical terms."[104] Milošević, Karadžić, and Šešelj were only nasty little fascists on the periphery of Europe; unlike Hitler, they represented no significant threat to the Great Powers other than the setting of an awkward precedent. In the end, the Serbs were offered exactly what they had killed for.

THE DECISION TO keep the Bosnians unarmed and defenseless was essentially made by the governments of Britain and France. Their adamant opposition in the Security Council to the lifting of the arms embargo against Bosnia-Hercegovina was based on the persistent argument by these states that arming the Bosnians would prolong the war. In effect this meant that arming the victims of aggression would give them the means to resist, fight back, and possibly regain lost territory. Such a development might preclude a swift Serbian (and Croatian) victory, and, therefore, a tidy conclusion to the war. A "peace" settlement at any price, was the paramount objective.

The British and French positions had, in light of the history of this century, an ignoble and paradoxical aspect. Just over fifty years ago both countries—one threatened with invasion and the other under occupation—had fought a long war for survival against German fascism. At the time neither Britain nor the French resistance had to struggle against a crippling arms embargo. In fact, Britain had been massively armed by Franklin Roosevelt's adroit use of the Lend-Lease program. Without liberal American financing for the purchase of weapons and munitions on the eve of the Second World War, the "Battle of Britain" might well have had a different outcome.

In a rare dissenting article in the *Wall Street Journal*—a paper that took the sanguine view that there was no profit or vital interest for the United States to engage in an area where the battle was neither for oil nor against communists— Albert Wohlstetter argued critically against the European position on Bosnia:

> It is hard to separate realpolitik from moralpolitik . . . [when] the grim farce of a mediation only encourages the continuation of ethnic cleansing. It seems that these 'realists' are out to test Milošević's sincerity until the destruction of the last Bosnian child. The Dane who held the rotating EC presidency last month argues that lifting the embargo to let the Bosnians defend themselves will only 'lead to more fighting.' Mr. Major and his ministers have been making that argument for more than a year. They should think about how the US prolonged World War II all the way to 1945 by transferring ships to Britain early in 1941 and persisted in sending convoys to keep England fighting. Hitler might have ended the war handily in 1941 or '42.[105]

In June 1993, when the foreign ministers of the twelve members of the European Community gathered in Copenhagen to consider the partition of Bosnia rather than its defense, the political and moral contradictions of the European position did not go unrecognized. Hans van den Broek, the European Community's External Affairs Commissioner and a former Dutch Foreign Minister asked his colleagues at the Copenhagen meeting, "If you do not see any possibility of helping these people out, how can you morally deny them the right of letting them arm themselves?"[106]

The British and French determination to keep the Bosnians defenseless was not a profound enigma requiring complex tools of investigation to unravel. In a discussion with the British Defense Secretary, Malcolm Rifkind, Christopher Hitchens promptly reached the heart of the matter. In May 1993, in a macabre parody on the plight of the Bosnians, Rifkind had "come to Washington to strike an attitude at the unveiling of the Holocaust Museum." When Hitchens asked Rifkind why Britain fervently supported the embargo,

Rifkind "said he thought that lifting the arms embargo would be the worst of all possible 'options'. And why was that? Because 'it would mean we lost control.' A revealing slip." Noting that Britain and other NATO states regularly "deny that they *have* control, meekly asking Serbian and Croatian permission for every bandage shipment," Hitchens concluded that Rifkind's unwittingly truthful yet utterly cynical position had made "the case, in both logic and morality, for ceasing the actual surreptitious intervention that is represented by the arms embargo, and for freeing (and helping) the people of Bosnia to fight for their own survival."[107]

The cynical truth was crisply expressed by Mark Helprin, the American novelist who long ago had discovered a fertile terrain for his imagination in the decade of the First World War. As the war intensified, Helprin argued that "the first requirement of morality is that the war [in Bosnia] be contained." To this end, it was necessary to construct an arrangement which placed tight boundaries around the violence regardless of what depravities occurred within the contained area. Helprin's implicit hope was that the hungry devotees of a "Greater Serbia" would be sated by Bosnia. Writing in the *Wall Street Journal* Helprin observed, "On the one hand, given what is happening to these people, this may seem to be *Realpolitik* at its cruelest, but on the other hand the imperative of this exercise has never been territorial justice for Bosnian Muslims at the expense of their lives."

The "exercise" Helprin referred to had little to do with the Bosnians' struggle to sustain a democratic and multi-ethnic society and the consequent resistance to any settlement that would force them into indefensible ghettos. Rather, the "exercise" concerned the dilemma of European and American diplomacy faced with a recalcitrant people unwilling to surrender their notion of "territorial justice" despite every diplomatic tactic designed to force them into a permanent oblivion. Having painlessly grasped this thorn Helprin was ideally equipped to understand the cynical realism of the European powers. "The British and French cannot say so publicly," he wrote, "but they know that the Serbian conquest is drawing to a close, and they do not want to arm the Bosnian Muslims for fear that it would prolong the war indefinitely should the Muslims attempt to regain what they have lost."[108] The policy was clear: to permit the Bosnians to arm themselves as Malcolm Rifkind, the British Defense Secretary, had said, would mean that the Europeans would lose control and the Bosnians might be tempted to commit the most cardinal of sins: "to regain what they have lost."

John Newhouse in *The New Yorker* described how a leading French diplomat had put the point quite bluntly. He explained that the Europeans "want to prevent a wider war or the emergence of a rump Muslim state in southeastern Europe—one that might become rich, militant, and an inspiration for ethnic or communal strife elsewhere. Europeans also want to discourage a Bosnian diaspora of the kind that was generated by the war in Palestine half a century ago. *'Our interests are closer to the Serbs than you think,'* a senior French diplomat says. *'We worry more about the Muslims than about the Serbs.'*"[109]

In many European foreign ministries important functionaries appeared to have adopted Radovan Karadžić's argument regarding the emergence of a "Muslim state" on European soil. In an interview with John Burns, "Karadžić said Serbian war aims had to take account of what he described as the risk to Europe of allowing any Muslim state in Bosnia. 'The biggest concern for us is that any Muslim state can be a stronghold for Muslim terrorism in Europe,' he said. This threat would be greatest, he added, if Bosnia became a state with a central government that Muslims would be in a position to control."[110]

The French fears—echoing Karadžić's warnings—of a "Muslim" state in Europe were shared equally by the Russians who also saw a greater commonalty of interests with their historic Slav allies, the Serbs. In June 1993, at a polite Master's Tea at a Yale college, Boris Yeltsin's adviser on the Balkans and Director of Russia's Institute of Balkan Affairs, Dr. Vladimir Volkov, had warned incredulous students and faculty of the dangers of Islamic expansionism. In the scenario he painted, Bosnia could become a bridgehead for Turkish and Albanian imperialist ambitions in Europe. In his view therefore, while certain Serb actions in the Balkans were regrettable, it was the perfidious "Muslims" the world—and, certainly, Europe—had to watch out for.

On the eve of the twenty-first century it was hard to believe that a small country such as Bosnia, which in both economic or political terms could represent no credible threat to the European powers, would nevertheless revive phantoms from a medieval era when Christian Europe had fought its holy crusades against the world of Islam. The Muslim presence and power in Europe had been effectively ended in Spain in the fifteenth century with the destruction of Moorish Andalusia, and formally extinguished at the turn of the twentieth by the defeat and dismemberment of Ottoman Turkey. Bosnia-Hercegovina was not and could not be the Trojan horse for an Islamic "reconquest" of Europe—a fact that would surely be obvious to the ostensibly sophisticated, secular, modern men and women who staffed Western governments and constituted the West's intelligentsia. And yet here were a French diplomat and a Russian intellectual expressing fears that a Bosnia which had not been militarily defeated might represent an "Islamic" threat to Europe.

The question of Bosnia, for Europe and for the world, needed to be viewed from an entirely different perspective. The survival and, therefore, the defense of Bosnia ought to have been a clear, uncompromising imperative precisely because the country was a rare and unique phenomenon—a secular, richly heterogeneous, multi-ethnic, tolerant society—in a continent where race, tribe, and religion had once again begun to threaten the forces of reason. Bosnia should have mattered to Europe, writes Hitchens in this volume, because it was defending not only its own self-determination but "the values of multicultural, long-evolved and mutually fruitful cohabitation. Not since Andalusia has Europe owed so much to a synthesis, which also stands as a perfect rebuke to the cynical collusion between the apparently "warring" fanatics. If Sarajevo goes under, then all who care for such things will have lost something precious, and will curse themselves because they never knew its value while they still had it."[111]

By keeping Bosnia disarmed, legitimizing Serbia's and Croatia's wars of "ethnic cleansing," and accepting the dismemberment of Bosnia into ethnic ghetto-states, Western powers had intervened not on the side of reason but on the side of fanaticism and bigotry. The message was that all means were permitted to destroy the Bosnias of the world, to kill the "Other," to secure *lebensraum* for a pure nation-state. Having colluded in the destruction of Bosnia and what it had represented over the centuries, Europeans in high places were now raising the specter of Bosnia as a "militant" or "terrorist" Muslim state from which Europe had to be made secure. Having extinguished Bosnia, the imperative now was to prevent a Bosnian diaspora. Memories of a half-century of Palestinian exile were beginning to trouble the sleep of the Europeans. Hence the determination to herd the Bosnians (or the "Muslims," as the world insisted on calling them) into Gaza-like reservations surrounded by the great impenetrable slabs of Greater Serbia and Greater Croatia.

The injustice and injury done to the Bosnians were to be compounded by insults. The suspicions and fears underlying the stance of the Western powers toward the prosecution of war crimes revealed once again that accountability and universal principles would have selective application. Thus the suspicion that the "Muslims" of the world might seek to right some wrongs through the moribund institutions of international law led to the opposition by Britain, France, and Russia to the appointment of Professor Cherif Bassiouni, an Egyptian, as chief prosecutor for the Yugoslav War Crimes Tribunal. According to *The New York Times*, "[n]ations opposed to Mr. Bassiouni maintain that he lacks prosecutorial experience and that his Muslim background makes him an unsuitable choice for prosecuting crimes committed in a war between Christians and Muslims."[112] At the Nuremberg trials, Jews had not been excluded from the prosecution staff, yet an Egyptian Muslim was ruled out of court by the Security Council when it came to the question of Bosnia.

Lack of prosecutorial experience, as Ian Williams pointed out, was the official reason. "In fact, diplomats candidly admit that his [Bassiouni's] real problem is an excess of efficiency," wrote Williams in the *New Statesman*. "He is a year ahead of any other potential candidate in assembling war crimes evidence and among the chief suspects are the 'leaders' to whom David Owen and the West are urging the Bosnians to surrender most of their country."[113] The determination to keep Muslims away from Bosnia was also apparent in the selection of the eleven judges for the War Crimes Tribunal. "Although Muslims have been the victims of many of the atrocities," reported *The New York Times*, "none of the members of the tribunal are Muslim." In fact, it seemed important to ensure that the judges selected even from countries with large Muslim majorities—Pakistan, Egypt, Malaysia—should not be Muslim.[114]

This judgment emerging from the heart of secular, liberal Europe on the inherent "unsuitability" or unreliability of any and all "Muslims"—prosecutors, judges, or peacekeeping forces (troops from Turkey, a NATO member, were deemed unacceptable for the same reason)—exposed the deeply ingrained prejudices that were influencing the decisions of the Western pow-

ers. In "a war between Christians and Muslims," "Christian" judges and soldiers—British, French, American, even Russian (Russia's support for Serbia
notwithstanding)—could be trusted to be fair and just, but "Muslims" could
not. Serbia's "holy war," it seemed, had won converts in the unlikeliest of
places: religion and ethnicity are now be the determinant of all things.

It has taken a long period for the Muslims of Bosnia to learn to think of
themselves in other than secular terms. They thought they were citizens of
Europe and clung to the illusion that their fellow Europeans and the Americans would rally to their cause. When it did not happen, disbelief, disillusionment, and, finally, anger led many to the conclusion that the only reason they
had been abandoned was because they were "Muslim." The West had forced
them to see the world in categories which in the Bosnia that had once shaped
their lives and their history had little relevance.

Needless to say—Samuel P. Huntington's grand new theory on the clash
of civilizations notwithstanding—not all Europeans or Americans view Islam
and Muslims as a threat to Europe or Western civilization.[115] There still are
rational people who reject stereotypes and propaganda, who see and appreci-
ate both complexity and diversity, and who understand the multilayered economic and political realities that shape this world. But their voices are not
loud enough; and they have not made themselves heard. Should Bosnia fall, its
dismemberment on Europe's "peace" tables will further divide the world,
widening the chasm between the West and the Islamic world, watering the soil
in which nationalist hatreds and religious myths grow and which are steadily
strangling all reason. Not only Europe but the world of Islam itself owed a
tremendous debt to the synthesis that was Andalusia. The spirit of Andalusia
had survived in Bosnia-Hercegovina until modern Inquisitors came to
expunge heresy from the land. With the death of Bosnia, that spirit may be
lost forever and the world will have surrendered to the Holy Warriors of modern barbarism. This is why Bosnia matters.

NOTES

1. Francis Jones, "Return" in *Why Bosnia? Writings on the Balkan War,* edited by Rabia Ali and Lawrence Lifschultz (Stony Creek, CT: The Pamphleteer's Press, 1993), p. 29.

2. T. D. Allman, "Serbia's Blood War" in *Why Bosnia?,* pp. 42–44.

3. Tihomir Loža, "A Civilization Destroyed," *Balkan War Report: Bulletin of the Institute for War and Peace Reporting* (London: July 1993), p. 1.

4. Smail Balić, "Culture Under Fire" in *Why Bosnia?,* pp. 75–83.

5. "Report from Bijeljina" by Niki Rado, ITN News, March 1993.

6. Laura Silber, "Bosnian Peace Plan Awaits Final Moslem Verdict," *Financial Times,* August 27, 1993.

7. That the irreverent, indomitable spirit of Bosnia still lived was evident in the answering graffiti Mark Thompson came upon in Sarajevo: "Wrong, dimwit, it's a post office," said the rejoinder. See Mark Thompson, *A Paper House: The Ending of Yugoslavia* (New York: Pantheon, 1992), p. 196.

8. Jones, pp. 31–32.

9. Interview with Kemal Kurspahić, May 6, 1993, New Haven, Connecticut. See also Kemal Kurspahić, "Serbian Sincerity, and Ours," *The New York Times,* May 7, 1993.

10. Loža, "A Civilization Destroyed," p. 15.

11. Paul Lewis, "UN Visitors Say Srebrenica is 'An Open Jail,'" *The New York Times,* April 26, 1993.

12. *McNeil-Lehrer Newshour,* PBS, February 10, 1993. William Hyland, a Professor at Georgetown University, also served as Deputy National Security Adviser in the Ford White House.

13. Alan F. Fogelquist, *The Break Up of Yugoslavia, International Policy and the War in Bosnia-Hercegovina* (Whitmore Lake, MI: AEIOU Publishing, 1993), p. 26.

14. John Burns, "Bosnians in Besieged Sarajevo Look Back on Year of Horror," *The New York Times,* April 6, 1993.

15. Fogelquist, p. 28.

16. "In Bosnian City, UN Finds Terror with Misery" (AP), *The New York Times,* August 27, 1993. The AP report refers to an interview General Perišić gave to the Belgrade newspaper, *Duga,* shortly before his appointment to the position of Chief of Army Staff in August 1993.

17. Interview with James Hogue, *The Charlie Rose Show,* PBS, February 12, 1993, Program Transcript, p. 6.

18. "US Memo Reveals Dispute On Bosnia: Christopher's View That All Share Guilt for Atrocities Is Attacked By Official", *The New York Times,* June 25, 1993.

19. Edelman is quoted in Peter Schneider, "Serbian Barbarism—And Ours," *The New York Times,* May 30, 1993.

20. Chuck Sudetic, "In Sarajevo, Silence Turns To Despair," *The New York Times,* June 25, 1993.

21. Chuck Sudetic, "UN Team Enters A Muslim Enclave," *The New York Times,* June 18, 1993.

22. Talk by Kemal Kurspahić, Editor-in-Chief, *Oslobodjenje,* at Pierson College, Yale University on May 6, 1993. See also John Burns, "Sarajevo Paper Defies War by Stay-ing in Print," *The New York Times,* October 7, 1992. Describing to Burns how *Oslobodjenje* had become a priority target for Serbian artillery, Kurspahić said, "I think they are attempt-ing to destroy us with a special intensity because of what we stand for. We have a staff that reflects the national composition of our society almost exactly—one-third of our reporters and editors are Serbs, about the same as the population of Bosnia as a whole. And we write

about Sarajevo and Bosnia in a way that reflects something that Serbian forces deny—that Serbs and Muslims and Croats can work and live together in harmony."

23. John Burns, "Sarajevo Paper Defies War."

24. Ivo Banac, "Separating History from Myth" in *Why Bosnia?*, p. 135.

25. John Burns, "A Plea to Clinton: Keep Bosnia United," *The New York Times,* February 3, 1993.

26. A.M. Rosenthal, "Muslims Broke the Truce," *The New York Times,* April 16, 1993.

27. Banac, pp. 137–138

28. See Misha Glenny, "What Is To Be Done?", *New York Review of Books,* May 27, 1993 and *The Fall of Yugoslavia: The Third Balkan War* (London: Pengin, 1992).

29. Slavoj Zižek, "Caught in Another's Dream in Bosnia" in *Why Bosnia?*, p. 237.

30. Miloš Vasić, "The Pattern of Aggression: Two Against One in Bosnia," *Balkan War Report,* January 1993, p. 8. Vasić is an editor at *Vreme,* Belgrade.

31. Shkelzen Maliqi, "The Albanians of Kosovo: Self-determination through Non-Violence," in *Why Bosnia?*, pp. 331–338, and Fogelquist, pp. 2–4.

32. Banac, p. 134.

33. Thompson, *The Paper House,* p. 96.

34. Thompson, p. 97.

35. Thompson, p. 282, and Glenny, "Yugoslavia: the Revenger's Tragedy", *New York Review of Books,* August 13, 1992.

36. Jelena Lovrić, "Things Fall Apart" in *Why Bosnia?*, p. 285.

37. Fogelquist, pp. 45–46.

38. Fogelquist, p. 24.

39. Loža, "Croatia's Territorial Options," *Balkan War Report,* June/July 1993, p. 8.

40. John Newhouse, "The Diplomatic Round: Dodging the Problem," *The New Yorker,* p. 63.

41. Fogelquist, p. 6.

42. Arthur Schlesinger, Jr.,"How To Think About Bosnia", *The Wall Street Journal,* May 3, 1993.

43. Albert Wohlstetter, "Why We're In It—Still", *The Wall Street Journal,* July 1, 1993.

44. Ian Williams, "Will Bosnia Break the UN?," *Balkan War Report,* April/May 1993, p. 28. See also Williams, "A Shameful Deadlock on Bosnia—And What Else Is New?," *The New York Observer,* April 26, 1993.

45. Williams, "A Shameful Deadlock On Bosnia."

46. "Statement By Venezuelan Ambassador Diego Arria to the UN Security Council," June 29, 1993. Transcript provided by Republic of Venezuela, Mission to the United Nations, New York.

47. Michael Gordon, "U.S. Experts Say 'Safe Havens' Won't Help Much," *The New York Times,* June 10, 1993.

48. "Statement by Alija Izetbegović," Radio Sarajevo, May 23, 1993.

49. "Statement of Diego Arria, Venezuelan Ambassador to the United Nations Security Council, June 4, 1993." Transcript provided by Republic of Venezuela, Mission to the United Nations, New York.

50. Chuck Sudetic,"Shelling By Serbs Is Said To Kill 50 In First-Aid Center: 'Safe Area' Under Attack," *The New York Times,* June 13, 1993.

51. The day David Owen accepted Slobodan Milošević's proposal for the partition of Bosnia he stated, "I am a realist and we have to make the best of what has happened on the ground." Paul Lewis, "Balkan Negotiator, In Shift, Backs Plan Dividing Bosnia," *The New York Times,* June 18, 1993.

52. Kasim Trnka, "The Degradation of the Bosnian Peace Negotiations," in *Why Bosnia?*, p. 204.

53. Loža, "A Civilization Destroyed," p. 15.

54. Loža, p. 15.

55. Chuck Sudetic, "Two Sarajevo Women Build a House in Air," *The New York Times*, September 8, 1993.

56. Anthony Lewis, "The Price of Weakness," *The New York Times*, June 21, 1993.

57. George Kenney, "From Bosnian Crisis To All Out War," *The New York Times*, June 20, 1993.

58. Trnka, p. 206.

59. For a detailed description of the Serbian-run concentration camps see Roy Gutman, *A Witness To Genocide* (New York: Macmillan, 1993). See also Orhan Bosnević, "The Road to Manjača" in *Why Bosnia?*, pp. 103–113.

60. Paul Lewis, "Balkan Negotiator, In Shift, Backs Plan Dividing Bosnia," *The New York Times*, June 18, 1993.

61. Marko Prelec, "A House Built On Sand: The Western Response to the War in Bosnia" in *Why Bosnia?*, p. 192–194.

62. Stjepko Golubic, Susan Campbell, and Thomas Golubic, "How Not To Divide The Indivisible" in *Why Bosnia?*, pp. 209–232.

63. "The Last Chance," *The New Yorker*, July 25, 1993.

64. "The Last Chance," *The New Yorker*.

65. Thomas Friedman, "Clinton Neutral On Geneva Plan For Bosnia Peace," *The New York Times*, February 4, 1993.

66. R.W. Apple, "Mediator Is Upset at US Reluctance Over Bosnia Talks," *The New York Times*, February 2, 1993.

67. "Mediator Is Upset At US Reluctance Over Bosnia Talks", *The New York Times*.

68. Branka Magaš, "Unfair to the people of Bosnia-Hercegovina," Letter to the Editor, *Manchester Guardian Weekly*, February 14, 1993.

69. Elaine Scialino, "US Faces a Delicate Task in Intervening in Negotiations on Bosnia," *The New York Times*, February 12, 1993.

70. Magaš, "Unfair to the people of Bosnia-Hercegovina".

71. "Bosnia Negotiators Count Considerable Achievements: Robert Mauthner Talks To Lord Owen About The Peace Process," the *Financial Times*, February 1, 1993.

72. Paul Lewis, "Bosnian Muslims Join Croats in Accepting Peace Pact", *The New York Times*, March 26, 1993.

73. Banac, p. 153

74. Kemal Kurspahić, "Letter From Sarajevo: Is There A Future?," *Why Bosnia?*, p. 16

75. "Bosnia Peace Plan Said to Spur New Attacks by Serbs," *The New York Times*, February 6, 1993.

76. An example of opposition by Croats to the Tudjman government's collusion with the Milošević regime over the partitioning of Bosnia can be found in "The Bosnian Catastrophe" by Ivo Banac, Bojan Bujič, Vesna Domany Hardy, and Branka Magaš in the *New York Review of Books*, August 12, 1993.

77. Laura Silber, "Bosnian peace deal proposed," *Financial Times*, August 21/22, 1993. See also "Bosnian Sees ⌐ e Talks Resuming Soon," (Reuters), *The New York Times*, September 5, 1993.

78. Laura Silber, "Map Poses Dilemma for Izetbegović," *Financial Times*, August 23, 1993.

79. Cited in Roy Gutman, *A Witness To Genocide*, p. xli.

80. Elaine Scialino, "Bosnia's Plight Divides the State Department," *The New York Times*, July 18, 1993.

81. Lee Hamilton, "Air Strikes? Not Yet," *The New York Times,* April 24, 1993. Hamilton was asked on April 28, 1993 by Robin MacNeil what vital US interests, if any, existed in Bosnia. Hamilton responded, "I find it very hard to spell out a vital interest of the United States. You can certainly argue in the Persian Gulf that we had a vital interest because of the oil resources there, and we're all very addicted to oil and gasoline in this country. I don't see a vital interest there." *MacNeil/Lehrer Newhour,* Show #4616, PBS, April 28, 1993, Transcript, p.5.

82. Michael Gordon, "State Department Aide on Bosnia Resigns on Partition Issue," *The New York Times,* August 5, 1993.

83. George Kenney, "American Policy 'Borders on Complicity in Genocide,'" the *Manchester Guardian Weekly,* August 22, 1993.

84. Thomas Friedman, "Clinton Rebuffs Bosnian Leader In Plea For Help," *The New York Times,* September 9, 1993.

85. Vasić, "A Bridge Too Close, A Peace Too Far," *Balkan War Report,* August/September 1993, p.1.

86. Paul Lewis, "At UN Bosnian Presses His Plea For More Land," *The New York Times,* September 8, 1993.

87. Williams, "Bosnia Let Down At UN," *New Statesman,* September 17, 1993.

88. William Safire, "Fuzzy, Was He?," *The New York Times,* September 16, 1993.

89. George Soros, "Bosnia and Beyond," *New York Review of Books,* October 7, 1993, p. 16. See also Newhouse, "The Diplomatic Round: No Exit, No Entrance," *The New Yorker,* June 28, 1993, p. 49.

90. Safire, "Fuzzy, Was He?"

91. Dimitri Simes, "There's No Oil in Bosnia," *The New York Times,* March 10, 1993.

92. "Is A Democratic World Order Possible?," Talk by Dr. Eqbal Ahmed at a conference sponsored by the Campaign for Peace and Democracy, April 17, 1993, New York.

93. Williams, "Bosnia Let Down At UN." See also Safire, "Fuzzy, Was He?"

94. Williams, "Bosnia Let Down At UN."

95. Thomas Mann, "Dieser Friede" in *Gesammelte Werke,* 12 vols. (Frankfurt: A.M.,1960), XII, p. 930. Cited in Ernst Nolte, *Three Faces of Facism* (New York: Holt, Reinehart and Winston, 1963), p. 7.

96. H.R. Trevor-Roper, "The Phenomenon of Fascism" in *European Fascism* edited by S.J. Woolf (London: Weidenfeld and Nicolson, 1968), p. 19.

97. Paul Sweezy, *The Theory of Capitalist Development* (New York: Monthly Review Press, 1968), pp. 333-334.

98. "The Origins of Serbian Jingoism Lie Within Serb Culture: An Interview with Mirko Kovač," *Ljiljan,* Zagreb-Sarajevo, December 7, 1992.

99. George L Mosse, "The Genesis of Fascism" in *Fascism: An Anthology* edited by Nathanael Greene (Arlington Heights: Harlan Davidson, 1968), p. 5.

100. Marco Revelli, "Italy" in *The Social Basis of European Fascist Movements* edited by Detlef Muhlberger (London: Croom Helm, 1987), p. 10.

101. Trevor-Roper, p. 23.

102. Banac, p. 157.

103. Žižek, p. 235.

104. *The Guardian Book of Munich* edited by R. H. Haigh, D. S. Morris, and A. R. Peters (London: Wildwood House, 1988), p. xiv.

105. Wohlstetter, "Why We're In It—Still."

106. John Darnton, "Europeans Turn To Partition Of Bosnia", *The New York Times,* June 19, 1993.

107. Christopher Hitchens, "Minority Report," *The Nation,* May 24, 1993.

108. Mark Helprin, "Military Reality In Yugoslavia," *The Wall Street Journal,* May 6, 1993.

109. Newhouse, "The Diplomatic Round: No Exit, No Entrance." Emphasis added.

110. John Burns, "Serbian Plan Would Deny The Muslims Any State," *The New York Times,* July 18, 1993.

111. Hitchens, "Appointment in Sarajevo: Why Bosnia Matters," in *Why Bosnia?,* p. 11.

112. Paul Lewis, "Disputes Hamper UN Drive For a War Crimes Tribunal," *The New York Times,* September 9, 1993.

113. Williams, "Bosnia Let Down At UN."

114. "War Crimes Panel Chosen," *The New York Times,* September 19, 1993.

115. See Samuel P. Huntington, "The Clash of Civilizations?," *Foreign Affairs,* Summer 1993, pp. 22-49.

A Text About The Land

Mak Dizdar

"There was a part of Illyricum that is now known as Bosnia.
A wild land, but rich in silver ore.
No long-furrowed fields could be found there,
Nor the fields that bore rich harvests,
But only rude mountains, grey mountains, rocks,
And tall turrets at the tops of cliffs."
Janus Pannonius, Sixth Elegy (1463)

One day a certain worthy questioner asked:
Who is she what is she, pray tell,
Where is she whence is
Wither is she
Bosnia
Tell

And the questioned gave him a quick reply:
Bosnia, you see, is a country
Both fasting and bare-footed, you see,
And cold and hungry
And in addition,
you see,
Defiant
After sleep.

WHY BOSNIA?

PART I

The sorrow of parting with Sarajevo acted on my soul.
Farewells with my Sarajevo friends wounded me.
In Sarajevo one is convinced that life is long.
Fountains, the waters of life, flow by thousands.
In winter days cold tightens the city.
All the same, sages and youths meet in large rooms for conversation.
But when the time of spring and blossoms is at hand,
the rose gardens of Sarajevo are like paradise.
[. . .]
I am a narcissus of world meadow, as well as a nightingale of beautiful
    Sarajevan melodies.
Thou may sometimes cry, or laugh like a rose, o sad Nerkesi,
this is the way things are in Sarajevo.

—From a poem of praise for the city of Sarajevo by Nerkesi Muhammed
    (Early Seventeenth Century)

Appointment in Sarajevo

Why Bosnia Matters

Christopher Hitchens

T HE DAILY ROUND in Sarajevo is one of dodging snipers, scrounging for food and water, collecting rumors, visiting morgues and blood banks and joking heavily about near misses. The shared experience of being, along with the city's inhabitants, a sort of dead man on leave, makes for a leveling of the more joyous and democratic sort, even if foreign writers are marked off from the rest by our flak jackets and our ability to leave, through the murderous corridor of the airport road, more or less at will. The friendship and solidarity of Sarajevo's people will stay with all of us for the rest of our lives and indeed, at the present rate of attrition, it may be something that survives only in memory. The combined effect of incessant bombardment and the onset of a Balkan winter may snuff out everything I saw.

On a paved street in the center of town, near the Eternal Flame (already snuffed out by lack of fuel) which consecrates the Partisan resistance in World War II, is a bakery shop. Eighteen people were killed by a shell that hit a bread line a few weeks ago, and mounds of flowers mark the spot. Shortly after I paid my own visit, another shell fell in exactly the same place, randomly distributing five amputations among a dozen or so children. One of the children had just been released from hospital after suffering injuries in the first "incident." A few hundred yards farther on, as I was gingerly approaching the imposing building that houses the National Library of Bosnia, a mortar exploded against its side and persuaded me to put off my researches. All of this became more shocking to me when I went with some Bosnian militiamen to the top of Hum, the only high ground still in the defenders' keep. It was amazing, having spent so much time confined in the saucer of land below, to see the city splayed beneath like a rape victim. This sensation was soon supplanted by outrage. From this perspective, it was blindingly clear that the Serbian gunners can see exactly what they are doing.

Entering the handsome old Austro-Hungarian edifice that houses the presidency of Bosnia and Hercegovina, and that absorbed several hits that day, I saw in the vestibule a striking poster. Executed in yellow and black, it was a combined logo featuring the Star of David, the Islamic star and crescent, the

Roman Catholic cross, and the more elaborate cruciform of the Orthodox Church. *Gens Una Summus* read the superscription. "We are one people." Here, even if rendered in iconographic terms, was the defiant remnant of "the Yugoslav idea." (Pictures of Tito, incidentally, are still common in Sarajevo, in both public and private settings.) And here also was all that was left of internationalism. The display was affecting, and not only because it rebuked the primitive mayhem in the immediate vicinity. All across former Yugoslavia, a kind of mass surrender to unreason is taking place, hoisting emblems very different from the Sarajevan.

Across the street from the Zagreb café where I am writing, there is a display of adoring memorabilia, all of it brashly recalling the rule of Ante Pavelić and his bestial Ustaše in Croatia, which was constituted as a Nazi and Vatican protectorate between 1941 and 1945. Young men in black shirts and warped older men nostalgic for fascism need no longer repress the urge to fling the right arm skyward. Their "militia," long used for harassing Croatian Serbs, is now heavily engaged in the "cleansing" of western Hercegovina, in obvious collusion with the Serbian Chetniks to the east and south. Miraculous Virgins make their scheduled appearance. Lurid posters show shafts of light touching the pommels of mysterious swords, or blazoning the talons of absurd but vicious two-headed eagles. More than a million Serbs attend a frenzied rally on the battle site of Kosovo, where their forebears were humiliated *in 1389,* and hear former Communists rave in accents of wounded tribalism. Ancient insignias, totems, feudal coats of arms, talismans, oaths, rituals, icons, and regalia jostle to take the field. A society long sunk in political stagnation, but one nevertheless well across the threshold of modernity, is convulsed: puking up great rancid chunks of undigested barbarism. In this 1930s atmosphere of colored shirts, weird salutes, and licensed sadism, one is driven back to Auden, that period's clearest voice, who spoke of:

> *The enlightenment driven away,*
> *The habit-forming pain,*
> *Mismanagement and grief:*
> *We must suffer them all again.*

WE MUST SUFFER them all again. But Bosnia, and especially Sarajevo, is not so much the most intense version of the wider conflict as it is the heroic exception to it. During respites from fighting, I was able to speak with detachments of Bosnian volunteers. At every stop they would point with pride and cheerfulness to their own chests and to those of others, saying, "I am Muslim, he is Serb, he is Croat." It was the form their propaganda took, but it was also the truth. I met one local commander, Alija Smet, defending a shattered old peoples' home seventy meters from the Serbian front line, who as well as being a defector from the Yugoslav National Army (JNA) is also an Albanian from the province of Kosovo. There was a Jew among the entrenchment-diggers on

Hum hill. Col. Jovan Divjak, deputy commander of the Bosnian Army, is a Serb. I shook his hand as he walked, with a Serbo-Croat aide-de-camp name Srdjan Obradović ("Obradović is a multinational name"), among the nervous pedestrians on the edge of the Old City, under intermittent fire at noonday. He was unarmed, and popular.

In the Old City itself, you can find a mosque, a synagogue, a Catholic, and an Orthodox church within yards of one another. Almost all have been hit savagely from the surrounding hills, though the gunner is usually accurate enough to spare the Orthodox. ("Burn it all," said Gen. Ratko Mladić, the JNA commander whose radio traffic was intercepted, recorded, and authenticated recently. "It is better to bombard Pofilići . . . there are not many Serbs there," replied his more "moderate" deputy, Col. Tomislav Sipčić. The Jewish Museum is badly knocked about and closed, and perhaps one third of the city's Jews have fled. An ancient community, swelled by refugees from Spain in 1492 and resilient enough to have outlived the Ustaše version of the Final Solution, is now threatened with dispersal. Even so, an Israeli Army Radio reporter, who had come to cover the evacuation of Jews, told me that he was impressed by how many of them wanted to stay on and fight.

The exquisite Gazi Husref Beg mosque, set in the lovely but vulnerable Muslim quarter of wooden houses and shops, has a crude shell-hole in its minaret, and its courtyard garden is growing unkempt. The mosques, very important in the siege for their access to antique stone cisterns or *sadrivan,* normally used for ablution before prayer, have found even those old wells drying up. And thirst is a fiercer enemy even than hunger.

To speak of "quarters" is not to speak of ghettos, or at least not yet. A good estimate puts the proportion of mixed marriages here at one in three, a figure confirmed by anecdote and observation. So to try to make Bosnia "uniform" in point of confession or "ethnicity" is not to put it together but to tear it apart. To call this dirty scheme "cleansing" is to do grotesque violence to both language and society. To turn, for a moment, from the period's greatest poet to its greatest essayist, we find that in 1933, Leon Trotsky wrote in *Harper's:*

> The idea proclaimed by Hitler of the necessity of re-adapting the *state* frontiers of Europe to the frontiers of its *races* is one of those reactionary utopias with which the National Socialist program is stuffed . . . A shifting of the internal frontiers by a few dozens or hundreds of miles in one direction or another would, without changing much of anything, involve a number of human victims exceeding the population of the disputed zone. [Emphasis added.]

The 2.4 million refugees and the numberless dead *already* outweigh the populations of the various "corridors" by which Serbian and Croatian nationalists seek to purify their own states and to dismember Bosnia. As before, their "nationalism" has its counterpart in the axiomatic resort to partition by certain "noninterventionist statesmen." When Lord Carrington, the European Community's mediator and a man obviously bored with the whole business, rec-ommends "cantonization," the Serbian puppet in Bosnia, Radovan Karadžić, and Croatian client there, Mate Boban, both make a little holiday in their hearts. The British Foreign Office's favorite fetish has triumphed again. After Ireland, India, Palestine, the Sudetenland, and Cyprus, partition—or ghet-toization—ceases to look like coincidence. Cantons by all means! say the fas-cists of all stripes. They won't take long for us to cleanse!

Near the town of Novska, on the Croatia-Bosnia border, I came upon a scene that illustrated the process in microcosm. An immaculate contingent of Jordanian UN soldiers was politely concealing its shock at the tribal and atavis-tic brutality of this war between the whites. It had done its task of separating and disarming the combatants in its immediate area. But here came six bus-loads of Bosnian Muslim refugees, many of them injured, who had taken the worst that Christian Europe could throw at them and who were bewildered to find themselves under the care of a scrupulous Hashemite chivalry. They had come perforce to Croatia, but Croatia wants no part of these victim of "Serbian terror," a terror that it denounced only when it was directed at Catholics.

A digression here, on the etymology of "ethnic cleansing." Few journal-ists who employ the expression know where it originated, and its easy one-sided usage has maddened the already paranoid Serbs. Jose-Maria Mendiluce, the exemplary Basque who came to Zagreb from Kurdistan as the special envoy of the United Nations High Commission for Refugees, told me he thought he had coined the term himself (though he blushed to recall he had used the term "cleaning"). But of course there is no "ethnic" difference among the Slavs, any more than there was between Swift's Big-Endians and Little-Endians. Nor is there a linguistic difference. And religion has not yet suc-ceeded (though it has often failed) in defining a nationality. So "cultural cleansing" might cover the facts of the case, if it did not sound more ludicrous than homicidal. At all events, a reporter for Belgrade TV described the gutted, conquered Bosnian city of Zvornik with the single word *"cist"* (clean), after it fell in April. And the unhygienic Serbian militia that did the job, the self-described Chetniks* of the warlord Vojislav Sešelj, also freely used the happy expression. The "camps," which were the inescapable minor counterpart of this process, have at least served to concentrate a flickering European and American mind upon a fading but potent memory, though comparisons to Belsen and Auschwitz show not that people learn from history but that they resolutely decline to do so, and instead plunder it for facile images.

WHO IF, ANYONE, does play the part of the Reich in this nightmare? *Smrt Fašizmu! Sloboda Narodu!* (Death to Fascism! Freedom to the People!) say the wall posters of the Sarajevo Commune. In most of the Western media the role

---

*The name "Chetnik" was first used by Serbian royalist irregulars who, during the Second World War, could not decide whether they detested Tito more, or less, than Hitler.

of fascist is assigned to the Serbs without hesitation. In order to try to comprehend the Serbian political psyche, I had to visit, and indirectly to loot, two highly significant museums.

The first one of these was the Gavrilo Princip Museum in Sarajevo, which stands by the bridge of the same name on the Miljacka River and is normally enfiladed by Serbian gunfire. Its wrecked appearance is deceptive, nonetheless, because although it has taken a round or two of Serbian mortaring, its actual destruction was wrought by enraged Sarajevan citizens. Gavrilo Princip, who stood quivering on this corner on June 28, 1914, waiting to fire the shot heard round the world at the fat target of the Austrian Archduke Franz Ferdinand, was a member of the Young Bosnia organization, which yearned and burned for the fusion of Bosnia with Serbia. No cause could be less fashionable in Sarajevo today, and the crowd had even dug up the famous two "footprints" sunk in the pavement to memorialize Princip's supposed stance. Until recently, this was the museum of the national hero, and it bore witness that Serbia, in alliance with Russia, was the historic guarantor of all Slavs. Princip appears to have chosen the date for the assassination to coincide with the exact anniversary of the Serbian defeat by the Muslim Turks at Kosovo in 1389, which testifies to the power of aggrieved memory and to the Serbians' conviction that *they* are the victims of regional history, underappreciated by those for whom they have sacrificed.

The second museum I visited was the site of the Jasenovac concentration camp, a real one this time, where during the Nazi period some hundreds of thousands of Serbs and Jews, as well as Gypsies and Croatian Communists, were foully slaughtered by the Croatian Ustaše regime of Ante Pavelić. No Germans even supervised this "cleansing," which was an enthusiastic all-volunteer effort to rival the butchery in Latvia or the Ukraine. Here is the Serbian Babi Yar, a piercing wound in the heart. It sits on a broad, handsome field where the rivers Sava and Una converge. During the appalling Serb-Croat combat last year, it was occupied for a while by Croatian forces. They methodically trashed the museum and the exhibits, and left only the huge, ominous mounds that mark the mass graves. As in Sarajevo, I was able to salvage a few gruesome souvenirs from the debris. My Serbian guide, a friendly metal worker named Mile Trkulja, told me, "The world blames the Serbs for everything, but nobody writes about Jasenovac."

In other words, it was not so very difficult for the Serbs to become that most toxic and volatile of all things—a self-pitying majority. (The man who commanded the now-notorious POW camp at Omarska, unearthed last month, had been born in Jasenovac. "Those to whom evil is done . . .") Faced with the mass expulsion of Serbs from the "new" Croatia and laden with historical resentment, many of them fell for the crudest option, exemplified by the four C's on the Serbian emblem, which translate approximately to mean "Only Unity Can Save the Serbs." Here was a Versailles mentality, replete with defeat and fear on the part of the stronger side.

In March 1992, in an astounding speech given at the last Congress of

Serbian Intellectuals to be held in Sarajevo, the Serbian academic Milorad Ekmečić was so daring as to phrase this consciousness directly:

> The Serbian people do not want a state determined by the interests of the great powers and of European Catholic clericalism, but one which emerges from the ethnic and historical right possessed by every people in the world. In the history of the world, only the Jews have paid a higher price for their freedom than the Serbs. Because of their losses in war, and because of massacres, the most numerous people in Yugoslavia, the Serbs, have in Bosnia-Hercegovina fallen to second place, and today our policy and our general behavior carry within themselves *the invisible stamp of a struggle for biological survival.* Fear governs us . . . . Therefore the internal division of Bosnia-Hercegovina into three national parts is the minimal guarantee of the maintenance by Serbian *and Croatian* peoples of a partial unity with their homes. [Emphasis added.]

Under the dispensation of Serbian leader Slobodan Milošević, notional heir to a vestigial Socialist Party, this combined pathology of superiority/inferiority has become the equivalent of state dogma. With dismaying speed, and by a macabre metamorphosis, the World War II Partisan slogan of "One Yugoslavia" has mutated into yells for a "Greater Serbia," and the army devised by Tito for defence against foreign intervention has been turned loose, along with various militias, against civilians and open cities. You could, without stretching things too much, describe this hybrid as "national socialism."

Yet it is also true that Croatia has a fascist ideology and a contempt for Serbian rights. President Franjo Tudjman does not quite affirm the Ustaše tradition, and can usually contrive to keep his right arm by his side, but he did adopt a near-replica of the Pavelić symbol for his national flag, and he did write a stupid revisionist book that said, one, that the Jasenovac camp had really killed very few Serbs and, two, that in any case it was run largely by Jews! He coupled this crassness with a campaign against Serbs living in Croatia, 200,000 of whom "relocated" as a result. Finally, he solicited support for his egotistical unilateralism from Germany, Austria, and Italy, thus materializing the very geopolitical alliance that every Serb is taught by history to fear.

Yet Serbs had never been persecuted in Bosnia. Nor had Croats. But now the Serbian and Croatian irredentists are allied in a sort of Molotov-Ribbentrop pact against a defenseless neighbor. (Ekmečić was wrong. There will be *two* Bosnias, not three, and he knows it.) Each camp exploits its Sudeten minorities to establish "pure" ministates that will in time demand fusion with the mother- and fatherlands. The Serbs have proclaimed "republics" in Croatian Krajina and in Bosnia. The turn of Kosovo and Macedonia is probably not far behind. Meanwhile, the Croats have begun the annexation of western Hercegovina, on Bosnian soil. There is no guarantee at all that this narcissistic subdivision will not replicate itself across international frontiers (involving Greece and Bulgaria in the case of Macedonia, and Albania in the case of Kosovo) and attract the "protective" interest of outside powers like Turkey, armed with NATO weapons. But then, that's what Balkanization is supposed to mean.

There is no need to romanticize the Muslim majority in Bosnia. But they have evolved a culture that expresses the plural and tolerant side of the Ottoman tradition—some of this subtle and diverse character can be found in the stories of Ivo Andrić, Yugoslavia's Nobel laureate—and they have no designs on the territory or identity of others. The Bosnian President, Alija Izetbegović, is a practicing Muslim, which makes him an exception among his countrymen. I have read his book, *Islam Between East and West,* a vaguely eccentric work that shows an almost pedantic fidelity to ideas of symbiosis between "the three monotheisms" and the humanist tradition of social reform. In the rather surreal atmosphere of a press conference under shellfire, I asked Izetbegović, who is accused by both Serbs and Croats of wanting to proclaim a fundamentalist republic, what he thought of the *fatwa* condemning Salman Rushdie. He gave the defining reply of the "moderate" Muslim, saying that he did not like the book but could not agree to violence against the author.

It is possible to meet the occasional Bosnian Muslim fanatic, and it is true that some of them made an attempt to sequester some Sarajevo Serbs in a football stadium. But that action was swiftly stopped, and roundly denounced in the newspaper *Oslobodjenje* (Liberation). None of the Bosnian Serbs I met complained of cruelty or discrimination, and where they had heard of isolated cases they reminded me that it was the Serbian forces who had stormed the River Drina, thus breaching a centuries-old recognition of the integrity of the Bosnian patchwork. If, however, that patchwork is ripped to shreds and replaced with an apartheid of confessional Bantustans, those who like to talk ominously of Bosnian Muslim fundamentalism may get their wish, or their pretext.

During the Tito and post-Tito years, one used to read *Praxis,* a journal of secular intellectuals, in order to find out what impended in Yugoslavia. Suppressed by the party state in 1975, the magazine continued to publish as *Praxis International* under the aegis of Jurgen Habermas and other European and American sympathizers. Since the push for Greater Serbia began to ignite every other micronationalism in the region, I had not heard the voice of *Praxis* above the snarlings and detonations. But in Zagreb I did find the oldest and the youngest member of this apparently irrelevant collective.

Professor Rudi Supek is a veteran by any definition. For his work in organizing resistance among Yugoslav workers in Nazi-occupied France, he was sent to Buchenwald and is now the last survivor of that camp's successful "Liberation Committee." He left the Communist Party when Tito broke with Stalin in 1948 and now tries to keep alive the ideas of secularism and internationalism in a Croatia that has grown hostile again. "My family is an old Croat family, but I have no choice but to say I am still Yugoslav. In Buchenwald I was the chosen representative of Serbs, Bosnians, and Croats, and they were Yugoslav in a way that I cannot betray."

Supek spoke with regret of the defection of some distinguished Serbian *Praxis* members. Professor Mihailo Marković, on whose behalf I remember signing a petition or two in days gone by, is now a vice president of Slobodan Milošević's Serbian Socialist Party and an ideologue of the diminished Serbian ideal. Svetozar Stojanović, likewise, has become the personal secretary of "Yugoslavia's" exiguous President Dobrica Cosić, whose stories about Partisan martyrdom have now taken on a distinctly Chetnik tone.

Zarko Puhovski, the younger *Praxis* adherent, teaches political philosophy at Zagreb University and bears with stoicism the anti-Semitic cracks that come his way as the son of a Jewish mother and a Croatian Communist father who did hard time in Jasenovac. "If you say you are a Croatian atheist, given that there are no ethnic or linguistic differences," he told me, "the next question is: How do you know you are not a Serb?" For both Puhovski and Supek, the contest with their "own" chauvinism was the deciding one. And for both of them, the defense of multinational Bosnia was the crux.

"Both the Chetniks and the Ustaše should be told to keep out of Bosnia," said Supek. "The fascists on both sides must be defeated and disarmed. If this needs an international protectorate, it should be provided."

"The embargo on 'both sides' is pure hypocrisy," said Puhovsky. "The Bosnians need arms to defend themselves, and the JNA has appropriated to itself the weapons that used to belong to everybody." This, by the way, echoed the street opinion in Sarajevo, which roundly opposed the idea of foreign troops fighting their battles, but bitterly recalled that the lavishly accoutered People's Army had been paid for out of the historic levies of Croats, Bosnians, and Macedonians, and witheringly criticized the moral equivalence that the great powers were using as a hand-washing alibi.

Both Supek and Puhovski do their best to keep in touch with their Serbian counterparts despite reciprocal jeers about "treason" and despite wrenching breakdowns in ordinary means of communication. Supek gave me a printed statement from committed Serbian democrats, who denounced the ruin brought on their country by Milošević's realm of delusion. Puhovski told me of the courageous Mirjana Miocinović, widow of the great novelist Danilo Kiš who wrote to Milošević renouncing her academic privileges and refusing the patronage of conquerors and occupiers.

For now, all these are no more than efforts to "show an affirming flame." But they may not be merely quixotic. Post-Communist Europe is hesitating on the brink of its own version of Balkanization, and Yugoslavia gives an inkling of what could lie ahead for more than one region, to say nothing of more than one culture. Bosnia matters, because it has chosen to defend not just its own self-determination but the values of multicultural, long-evolved, and mutually fruitful cohabitation. Not since Andalusia has Europe owed so much to a synthesis, which also stands as a perfect rebuke to the cynical collusion between the apparently "warring" fanatics. If Sarajevo goes under, then all who care for such things will have lost something precious, and will curse themselves because they never knew its value while they still had it.

LETTER FROM SARAJEVO

Is There a Future?

KEMAL KURSPAHIĆ

"SARAJEVO WILL ALWAYS BE, everything else will pass . . . ," says a song, one of the many composed in this capital city of war-ravaged Bosnia during the first year of its siege. But I often ask myself if the Sarajevo I have loved will ever be the same. Can this most cosmopolitan of cities, not only in former Yugoslavia but in the whole of the Balkans, a unique meeting point between East and West, an exciting mixture of religions, cultures, and splendid architecture survive this terrible war?

Since the beginning of the Serbian aggression in April 1992, so much of Sarajevo's beauty has been destroyed. The hundred-year-old Austro-Hungarian city hall with its thousands of precious books and manuscripts; the main post office, also Austro-Hungarian; the picturesque Ottoman shops and the bazaars of Baščaršija; one of the most beautiful railway stations in Europe; the Winter Olympics sports halls, Zetra and Skenderija—all have been devastated by artillery fire. The same fate has been visited upon government and parliamentary offices and elegant commercial buildings, including the offices of my paper *Oslobodjenje.* The city's communication and transportation facilities are in ruins, as are its hospitals (targets of regular, systematic shelling), and more than half of its apartments have been destroyed. It is hard for a city to be the same as it was after such devastation.

But, above all, can Sarajevo survive the destruction of so many lives? More than ten thousand have been killed and a hundred thousand severely wounded. So many, too many, with arm or leg amputated, have been maimed and crippled for life. Tens of thousands have been separated from their families, not knowing what happened to their loved ones—captured, killed, driven out, made refugees—or whether they will ever see them again.

While the war goes on—shells, grenades, snipers hitting my neighborhood, day after day, around the clock—I try to imagine the first day of peace in Sarajevo. What will it look like then, with all its young men gone, killed defending their city? To whom will the girls of Sarajevo give their first love? And how, on that day of liberation, will the obituaries in my paper read: *Forever mourning—my wife, my daughter, my unborn son.*

The wounds are so horrible, so deep, that thinking about the future of

Sarajevo—will it ever be the same?—I reach for a simple, affirmative answer and know that to find it will require a tremendous leap of optimism and imagination. Every day in this city of half a million souls, without food, milk, vegetables or fruit to buy, it is a struggle to survive. Every day without electricity, without running water, without heat in destroyed, windowless apartments under constant shelling and sniping, it is a struggle to stay alive. And yet with all the terrible memories of these ten months under siege (I am writing in mid-February 1993) I still believe in the song-writer's prediction: *"Sarajevo will always be, everything else will pass . . . "*

I MUST CONFESS that not very long ago all my own predictions regarding the future of Sarajevo and of Bosnia-Hercegovina proved to be absolutely wrong. I was one of those who simply could not believe that war could ever come to this city. *"Impossible!"* I said to the many foreign visitors—journalists, diplomats, friends—who came to visit *Oslobodjenje*. I had a list of "negative" and "positive" reasons. Under the "negative" factors which I argued would contain the outbreak of violence, I would cite the real fear of what war in the ethnically and religiously mixed Bosnian neighborhoods would be like. Muslims, Serbs, Croats, and Jews not only lived in the same towns but in the same apartment buildings. Throughout Bosnia there was a high percentage of mixed marriages. It was quite obvious that for any ethnic group to begin to shoot at the "other" they would at the same time have to shoot at "themselves," or their own. But, surely, I would insist, still the most compelling and "positive" reason had to be the fact that in Bosnia—and especially in Sarajevo—we had a long and enduring tradition of peaceful cohabitation among the different ethnic and religious communities. A living testament to this fact were the Orthodox church, the Catholic cathedral, the Jewish synagogue, and the Muslim mosque which stood together—as they had for centuries—secure and undisturbed, in the heart of Sarajevo. Today, however, each of these places sacred to Bosnia's multicultural people has come under attack—a target of unrelenting Serbian artillery fire. The one exception is the Serb Orthodox church.

What went wrong with all my predictions? How was it possible for anyone to turn this great cosmopolitan city, where Muslim, Serb, Croat, and Jew had lived together as friends and neighbors, into a living hell? Perhaps, a few explanations are possible. First, let me say that the tragedy of Sarajevo and that of Bosnia was not home-made, it was imported. We became the victims of Serbian President Slobodan Milošević's dream empire—the project of "Greater Serbia"—which was to be built on territory wrested from the neighboring states of Croatia and Bosnia-Hercegovina. Serbia's war propaganda systematically, and over a period of time, set about developing a mentality of *us* (Serbs) against (all of) *them.* Resistance among the Serbs to this "holy aim" of expanding the boundaries of Serbia in order to have "all Serbs in one state" became almost suicidal. Those who spoke out against the project were immediately denounced as "traitors to the national cause"—and silenced.

Second, it is important to recognize that those who organized the aggression and terror against Sarajevo (i.e. the leaders of the Serbian Democratic Party) were never part of the city's tradition of tolerance and accord. They came mostly from remote rural areas, lived in Sarajevo, benefited from its hospitality and possibilities (educational institutions, jobs, careers), but essentially held all others who were different in hatred and contempt. They felt no affinity for Sarajevo and the more urban spirit of coexistence that it embodied in Bosnia-Hercegovina. How else can one explain the extremist Serb leader Radovan Karadžić's unalloyed threat in Bosnia's Parliament? A vote for independence for the republic, he had said, might lead to the "disappearance of the whole nation." He meant, of course, the Muslim population. And, how else is one to understand the statement of Aleksa Buha, the so-called "Foreign Minister" of Karadžić's self-proclaimed "Serbian Republic"? In the presence of television cameras Buha announced, "For us, Serbs, collective suicide is better than living together!"

And, third, I was utterly wrong to believe that no one would start a war in a city where shooting at "others" would necessarily mean killing one's "own." The Serbian aggressors were indifferent. Former Yugoslav army personnel, paramilitary gangs imported from Serbia, and local extremists armed by Karadžić's party overcame this inhibition. Its essence was best expressed by the Serbian army general, Ratko Mladić, in the orders he gave to his artillery units on the hills above Sarajevo. "Shoot at Velešići," barked Mladić, "there aren't too many Serbs there!" His radio message was intercepted and played repeatedly on the public airwaves by Radio Sarajevo. What did it mean? Obviously, that it is all right to kill Serbs too! Just before the war broke out, Stevo Medić, a Serb member in Bosnia's Parliament from Sipovo had threatened the city's "apartment building Serbs" who, in his eyes, had betrayed the Serbian nation by cohabiting with non-Serbs. "Join us," he told them, "because you were not born there." Yet, many still refused the invitation.

The terror and the war that came to Sarajevo, in short, was brought by Serbia and its local collaborators who have been seduced by the "Greater Serbia" dream. And the terror affects the Serbs of Sarajevo in the same way as it affects all others. When shells and snipers hit the citizens of Sarajevo as they stand in the bread or water lines, they do not discriminate; they also kill Serbs. Nearly eighty thousand Serbs have remained in the besieged city and lived through the terror with their neighbors and friends—Muslims and Croats. Having suffered so much for so long, together they have discovered a new sense of solidarity and have helped one another survive the war. This trial by fire, I believe, has strengthened the city's spirit of friendship and tolerance. And so I believe that cosmopolitan Sarajevo will survive. People of different religions and ethnic groups will be sharing the same tables in the city's coffee bars, and all the ordinary pleasures and burdens of life will reappear—on the very first day of peace.

My own personal experience as editor of *Oslobodjenje* is testimony to the spirit that defines Sarajevo. Our newspaper building was one of the most modern in prewar Sarajevo. It was under constant machine gun, mortar, and sniper fire. Serbian extremists from neighboring Nedžarići shelled the building with tanks and virtually destroyed it. Yet throughout the fighting, our editorial staff kept working and publishing the paper each day of the war. They did this despite all the dangers and the very real risks to their lives. The newspaper's staff reflects, almost perfectly, the ethnic picture of Bosnia. We work together on the basis of principles we advocate in the pages of *Oslobodjenje:* a state of equal citizens regardless of ethnic group. Some of the finest journalists on the paper are Serbs—my deputy Gordana Knežević, first columnist Gojko Beri'c, one of three desk editors Branko Tomić, first reporter Vlado Mrkić. One third of our staff, too, is Serb. All of us essentially share the same view on Serbian aggression against Bosnia-Hercegovina. What keeps us working under the worst possible circumstances where our lives are in constant danger is our shared sense of professionalism—and, maybe, an element of Bosnian patriotism too!

Recently one of our most famous soccer stars died in Sarajevo. He had for the last decade been the manager of the city's football club. Svetozar Vujović was a Serb. In spite of the artillery fire from extremist Serbs in the hills above the city, hundreds of people from all nationalities gathered at Sarajevo's Holiday Inn to attend a commemorative ceremony honoring Vujović—a much admired citizen of Sarajevo. Yes, "Sarajevo will always be . . . ," if the terror ever ends.

WHAT OF THE rest of Bosnia-Hercegovina? There are no simple answers. For the healing of the wounds inflicted on the unique character of this land after the war, it might matter whether or not a town was occupied by Serbian forces. In Sarajevo, Tuzla, and Zenica—three of the five largest cities in Bosnia—the chances of preserving a multinational culture are much higher than in Mostar, which was totally destroyed by the Serbian armies, or in Banja Luka, which experienced "ethnic cleansing." The situation is even more grim in the towns along the river Drina, in Zvornik, Foča, Višegrad, or in Bosanska krajina, in Prijedor and Sanski Most—and tens of others. Before the war these towns were largely Muslim, but all have since been systematically, brutally "cleansed"—mass killings, rapes, the burning of homes, the removal of thousands of persons to concentration camps, or their expulsion into exile. In places affected by such genocidal acts—crimes unseen in Europe since the Second World War—it is difficult to imagine how it will be possible to restore the prewar conditions of ordinary, mutually beneficial coexistence.

But, yes, it is still possible. It is *only* possible if those responsible for war crimes are brought to justice, tried and sentenced by international war crimes tribunals in accordance with the strictest standards of international law. If this does not happen, an endless circle of revenge will bring even greater sorrow to Bosnia—violence breeding violence for decades to come.

There is a lesson here for the so-called international community and for all those who have participated in the so far unsuccessful search for a solution in Bosnia-Hercegovina. Regardless of ethnic heritage or religious beliefs, the people in this country can not only live together, but they can live *only* together. Bosnia-Hercegovina is simply indivisible. Those who are cleverly drawing maps, trying to create distinct and separate Muslim, Serbian, and Croatian mini-states within the state of Bosnia may believe this to be the easiest or quickest solution, when, in fact, it might just prove to be the worst possible option.

People in Bosnia still live in very ethnically mixed towns. It is impossible to draw even the tiniest line between them without leaving vast numbers in someone else's ethnic "state." To pursue such a "solution" would turn entire sections of the population into second class citizens. What is even worse, the so-called "solution" along these lines is likely to generate even more victims of violence by encouraging new waves of "ethnic cleansing" designed to create ethnically exclusive Muslim, Serbian, or Croatian mini-states. Division is, simply, no answer for Bosnia-Hercegovina's complexities.

The evidence, already, is staring the peacemakers and the cartographers in the face. The maps of a divided Bosnia-Hercegovina passed around at international conferences have become more a continuing *cause* for the tragedy that has befallen us than a *solution*. When those maps were first introduced into the negotiation process in March 1992, in Lisbon, Serbian forces started an intensive campaign to "cleanse" the territory designated on the maps as "theirs." They embarked upon yet another campaign of killing, raping, imprisoning, and expelling all non-Serbs. When these maps were again re-introduced in January 1993, during the Vance-Owen negotiations in Geneva, incidents of the same type occurred in areas classified as supposedly Croatian—Gornji Vakuf, Busovača, Vitez.

A "solution" based on such maps of division might result in twice as much suffering and bloodshed as we have experienced until now. It is simply impossible to make the town of Mostar into a mini "Croatian capital." Before the war there were more Muslims in Mostar than Croats. It is impossible to make Sarajevo, Tuzla, or Zenica into exclusively Muslim towns without, at the same time, making "others"—non-Croats in Croatian provinces and non-Muslims in Muslim provinces—into second-class citizens. This would virtually replicate the condition experienced by non-Serbs in Karadžić's phantom "Serbian Republic." Thus, what on the surface appears to the map makers and negotiators as the "easiest of solutions" is, in reality, inherently flawed in design. Put into practice in Bosnia, it will foster future decades of conflict, violence, and terror.

WHAT, THEN, IS the solution? In my view, Bosnia-Hercegovina must exist as a state of *all its citizens,* where a constitution upholding the highest standards of civil liberties and human rights will protect each person equally under the law. Bosnia must exist as a nation of free individuals without permitting its territory and its political space to be carved up into ethnic ghettos. Under the terror of rampant nationalism, the rights of the individual have been expunged from political discourse. A deranged collectivism has taken over: the group is everything; the individual is nothing. We can only survive and succeed if we build a state which, while recognizing and protecting the national character and the religious freedom of each ethnic group, upholds and preserves the sovereign fundamental rights of each and every citizen regardless of ethnic or religious origin.

In Bosnia-Hercegovina, to build such a state and society and to recreate the conditions for a lasting peace, it is imperative that the aggressor be defeated. The international community, citing various reasons or excuses, is clearly reluctant to intervene in any meaningful way. The irony is that a firm commitment today to help the Bosnian people defeat and reverse Serbia's aggression would, in the end, not only be the most effective but also the least expensive solution. For if today Serbia's expansionist, Nazi-like military campaign is not defeated or deterred, the consequences tomorrow—certainly for the Balkans, most probably for Europe—are likely to exact a much higher price.

How, then, is Serbia to be stopped? In my view, by a combination of five measures. First, it is imperative that international airstrikes be carried out against specific Serbian military targets, such as the artillery positions encircling Sarajevo and other Bosnian towns. It is these artillery emplacements which—since the beginning of the war—have targeted civilians as their primary, indeed, their exclusive victims. It would take just 24 to 48 hours of aerial bombardment to send a clear message to those in Serbian regime who only speak and comprehend the language of force that the international community, at last, intends to be taken seriously. Second, the arms embargo against Bosnia-Hercegovina must be lifted in order to allow Bosnia the right to defend itself. As an internationally recognized state, the legitimacy of this right to self-defense is undisputed in international law. It is the worst hypocrisy to tell us that there are already too many weapons out there. Indeed, there are, but those weapons are all in one set of hands: those of the aggressor. Third, real, not mythical, sanctions against Serbia must be implemented. If the implementation of sanctions is pursued in its present form, no Bosnian will be left alive long enough to see its effect. Fourth, the international community must be prepared to demonstrate its political will to adopt, and ultimately to impose, a just solution—not a solution legitimizing aggression and acts of barbarism. And, fifth, the world community must prepare an international war crimes tribunal with a solemn purpose equal to the principles established at Nuremberg. Those who are responsible for war crimes and crimes against humanity, perpetrated in full view of the world, must be prosecuted. Justice must not only be done, but must be seen to be done. This is an absolute prerequisite if people expelled from their homes and towns are ever to return—and, above all, if a ravaged country is to be freed from the hunger, the need for vengeance.

Perhaps, one day, then it will be possible to believe again: *"Sarajevo will always be. . . . "*

On Your Knees
with the Dying

DAVID RIEFF

IN THE LION cemetery in Sarajevo, an old man asked me, "Why do the Americans not drop the atom bomb on the Serbs?" A moment later, a mortar bomb exploded about five hundred meters away. The mourners—they had come to bury a fourteen-year-old boy killed by a sniper two days before—ducked, or, rather, went through a kind of pantomime of ducking for cover, since apart from the now battle-scarred statue of the lion and the plinth on which it stood in the center of the cemetery there was no cover there to speak of. Even the headstones in Sarajevo are made of plywood these days, which, the gravediggers will tell you, is of half the thickness it was six months ago. For my part, I stared edgily at two freshly dug graves ten meters down one of the burial rows. From past experience I knew they would be the safest places in which to crouch if the shelling began in earnest, which was a distinct possibility since, as everyone who has lately been to Sarajevo knows, the Serb forces in the hills surrounding the city have made something of a specialty of firing on mourners as they bury their dead.

By Sarajevo standards, the Lion cemetery is safer than other local graveyards, relatively speaking. If it is exposed, it is not nearly so exposed as the soccer pitch nearby, converted into a cemetery by the local authorities in the fall of 1992 to take the overflow from the Koševo hospital morgue. There the chances of being hit are really quite high, which make even experienced photo-journalists think twice before covering a funeral. Every part of Sarajevo is dangerous, almost no place out of reach either of mortar or artillery fire or of the snipers. But the cemeteries are not being fired upon as part of some generalized assault: Sarajevo is a bowl, and small, and the Serb soldiers can see their targets quite clearly, as a visit to their positions will demonstrate. The cemeteries are being targeted deliberately by the gunners of the "Srpska Republika." The proof of this—as if proof were needed—is that there is one cemetery in Sarajevo that has survived completely unscathed through more than a year of war. It is a small Orthodox cemetery, quite near the Delegates' Club where the UN soldiers make their headquarters, and it houses the sepulcher of the heroes of Young Bosnia. The most notable mortal remains here are those of one Gavrilo Princip, famous throughout the world in his day, and now, once again, shudderingly remembered by the world outside the Balkans. The twentieth century, it now appears, began with him in Sarajevo in 1914, and ended in the spring of 1992, in the same city, when a new generation of Bosnian Serb nationalists fired on demonstrators from the upper floors of the Holiday Inn hotel, announcing to a stuporous world the real advent of the post-Cold War era.

The morning before I set out for the Lion cemetery, a French friend, a combat photographer of long experience, told me, "There are two ways of photographing funerals: on your feet with the living, or on your knees with the dead." He might as well have been talking about the ways of thinking about Sarajevo, or the war in Bosnia generally. When one is in the city, its reality is overwhelming. If the press corps there has, as the demeaning phrase has it, "gone native," it is not simply because the reporters here have been frightened half out of their wits but because the situation seems so starkly simple. A European city is being reduced to nothing; Carthage in slow motion, with an audience and a taped record. Nothing, not the complex history of the region, the errors of the Bosnian Muslim authorities, or the sometimes justified fears of the Bosnian Serbs, can mitigate the crime that has taken place, and goes on taking place as I write this. Perhaps the press corps, ensconced in the Holiday Inn (where Radovan Karadžić made his headquarters before decamping to the nearby ski resort of Pale to declare the "Srpska Republika") cannot quite agree with the man in the cemetery who lives in hope of the dropping of an A-bomb, but it harbors its own bellicose fantasies of deliverance. Byron, writing of an execution of three guilty thieves he witnessed in Rome, observed in a letter, "I would have saved them if I could." Speaking for myself (and, perhaps, not only for myself), there have been several times in Sarajevo when I would cheerfully have abandoned notebook for kalashnikov if I imagined that it would have made the slightest difference to the defense of the city.

Such are the puerile fantasies of those powerless to do anything about the horrors they have seen. It was a conceit of journalists—made up partly of corporate self-regard, partly of an unexamined belief in progress and in the idea that Europe, despite its sanguinary history, was a civilized place nowadays—that if people elsewhere could only be told about what was happening in Sarajevo, if they were only to see on their television screens the images of children hit by dum-dum sniper bullets as they played in the safety of their apartments and people massacred as they queued for bread or water, they would want their governments to do something. The hope was that an informed world would urge its governments to prevent not this war—for it is not a war—but this killing, to ensure that, unlike the Jews and the Armenians, the Bosnian Muslims were not either massacred or expelled from their homes. This was an erroneous assumption, as one discovers when one leaves Sarajevo and returns home.

Every journalist who has covered the Bosnian war has had the experience of being told that Bosnia is too complicated. Even one's educated, politically aware friends insist that the whole situation, however tragic, is just *so hard!* Thus do the living reply when one returns, upright, to their kingdom after a prolonged stint in the land of the dead that Sarajevo is fast becoming. And thus are confuted nearly fifty years of liberal assumptions, especially the belief that after the holocaust of European Jewry similar events would not be tolerated, ever. As it turns out though, "never again" simply means that Jews will never again suffer the same fate, not that other peoples will be spared such a fate. Speaking at the opening of the Holocaust Museum in Washington, President Clinton spoke of "deploying memory" to forestall future holocausts. But, of course, memory is no more useful a weapon than information. People can, as we should have known in this age of information, keep all kinds of things in their heads. While knowing what is happening in Bosnia may be a necessary precondition for action, it is anything but a sufficient one. Mostly, I suspect, they switch channels when the images of Sarajevo appear on their TV screens. Had there been television cameras at Auschwitz, or on the plateaux of Anatolia, the viewer response would probably have been the same.

Where information has not bred indifference, it has bred casuistry. Modern people in Western Europe and North America who would not for one second accept the premise that their history should determine their future are pleased to insist that what is going on in Bosnia is a centuries-long civil war that, when all is said and done, must be allowed to burn itself out. This "natural disaster" theory leads ineluctably to the conclusion that nothing can be done for the Bosnians except—am I alone in believing that the image is drawn partly from zoology?—the creation of "safe havens," in other words, reserves for an endangered European minority. To do otherwise, one is told, is to court disaster. One might as well have tried to cap Krakatoa. If this argument does not carry the day, the next to be advanced is that all sides are guilty, and that the only salient difference between them is that the Serbs are the better fighters and have more arms. As David Owen, the EC's principal negotiator, has put it, the Bosnian conflict "is a civil war with elements of aggression." If no side is innocent or guilty then even a decision to lift the arms embargo against the Bosnian government becomes little more than a way of ensuring higher body counts. The obvious conclusion drawn from this "plague on all their houses" argument is that the Bosnian government side—in reality the civilian population of Sarajevo and of the Drina valley enclaves like Goražde, Srebenica, Cerska, and Zepa—must do the lion's share of the dying. To do anything else, one is told, would be inhumane.

Orwell would have a field day watching the world respond to the war in Bosnia. In the name of humanitarian assistance, people are denied the right to defend themselves. United Nations peacekeeping forces (the name itself, in the Bosnian context, is straight out of *1984*), deployed to escort relief convoys to besieged populations, are presented as one further reason why an intervention force must never be considered. To do so would endanger the peacekeepers. But there is no peace, and nowadays people in Sarajevo are dying from Serb bullets, not hunger. This is not to belittle the heroic efforts of agencies like the UN High Commission for Refugees, but, after a year, it is clear that the principal goal of the European powers has not been to intervene, let alone to stop the war, but rather to forestall intervention—all in the name of peace, of course.

Each fresh disaster that befalls the Bosnian Muslims—from the siege of Sarajevo to the fall of Srebrenica, or to the discovery that by the time Zepa had been declared a "safe haven" by the UN, the city had been reduced to rubble and its inhabitants had fled to the Croatian attacks on Muslims in Mostar—has been adduced by Owen and his team as evidence that force is inappropriate and the negotiations must be given further time to work.

"In eight months we've done a lot," a member of the joint UN/EC negotiating team told me. "We got the Croatians to sign on to the Vance-Owen plan, then we got the Muslims to sign, and now we have driven a wedge between the Serbs of Pale and the Belgrade Serbs." In the land of the living, this may be a considerable accomplishment in eight months, but it hasn't done the Bosnians much good, for in the same period the Serbs have succeeded in conquering virtually all the territory of Bosnia-Hercegovina that they covet except the finger in the northeast between Brcko and Doboj and Sarajevo itself. Or that, at least, is the way the picture looks when you are on your knees, with the dead.

For a long time the landscape of Sarajevo was as pitted with dreams as with shellfire. People have grown wearier and more cynical now. Journalists who were once greeted as trusted friends and in whom the Sarajevan placed such hopes are greeted more dispassionately. It is not that the foreigners didn't tell the story of Sarajevo. They did, but nothing happened. So now their presence—our presence, I should say—is as much an irritant to people in Sarajevo as a boon. "Another safari?" an acquaintance asked me when I arrived in the city in the late winter. "What do you hope to see this time, more corpses, more destruction? We should charge you admission." All of this was said with reasonable equanimity, but implacably. The media attention, my friend believed, had done no good. Most of the time (though I continue to return to Sarajevo, and am there in my dreams even when, guiltily, I leave the city for a time) I am inclined to agree with him. A lot of dreams have died there in the past year—dreams that the world has a conscience, that Europe is a civilized place, that there is justice in human affairs as well as sorrow. It should be no surprise that the old millenarian dream that knowledge and truth would set us free would die there as well. Reality, it turns out, is better apprehended in the Lion cemetery than in the Palais des Nations in Geneva or the United Nations in New York, much as we might wish it otherwise.

Return

Francis R. Jones

povratnik (n.) 1. returner 2. one who returns home after working abroad 3. ghost, revenant

FRAGILE, YELLOWED AT the edges, the map splits as I try to open it, along folds the brittle sellotape no longer holds. Felt-tipped on the back, in big red unfaded capitals: SARAJEVO. The letters a little smudged . . .

A MARCH DUSK fifteen years before. Darker clouds are heaping over the range to the east. Drivers from village to village: a few cars turn off the highway for upland farms, but no tourists are taking the pass now, at winter's end whimpering with sleet, as an early night falls.

An hour later, maybe two, a patrol car, green and white in the overhead lights, signals right and slows into the junction. I grope for my passport, readying myself for the inevitable questions: where am I going and why (yesterday, in Germany, the police jittery with the Baader-Meinhof gang on the loose, the interrogation was at pistol point). But the driver—no older than myself—who leans across the empty passenger seat is wearing the green uniform of a border guard.

"*Zur Grenze?*" To the frontier?

"*Ja.*"

"*Steig mal 'rein.*" Climb in.

I was thankful for his lack of curiosity as to why a British hitch-hiker, studentishly scruffy in ex-army greatcoat and earring, should be crossing from Austria into Slovenia, outside the holiday season, so late in the day. The ribbon of road in the headlamp beams lifted and rippled as we left the valley floor, then veered up high to the right. The driver fell silent, peering intently through the sleet-spattered windscreen as he wrenched the car up the hairpin bends, under the massed black Alpine spruce. Cozy with the warmth of the heater, drowsing with the yaw of turn after turn and the growl of the engine, I dozed into sleep.

Unwillingly aware, through closed lids, of arclights ahead and the engine easing as the road leveled off at the summit, I blinked awake. An exchange of thanks and a handshake in the carpark, then off he strode to start his shift.

At the cafeteria table, using my last few schillings on a coffee, I contemplated the night ahead. With luck, I could be well into Croatia by the dead hour—two to four in the morning, before the day's trucks start. Then I could spread my sleeping bag under a bridge. Or maybe it would be better to keep going: that way I might arrive by nightfall. My stomach sank. Another day. Twenty more hours of fighting back sleep, a chain of ten-mile links, every one the same: Where are you going? Why? What's your soccer team?

Why? In Cambridge the summer before, the main appeal of a year's studentship in Yugoslavia had been to stave off decisions (what do you do with a degree in Serbo-Croat and German?). But why Bosnia? Why Sarajevo? Well, the name had a certain oddball cachet: wasn't that where they shot the Archduke? A bit like Serbo-Croat itself—a subject so eccentric (where's Serbo-Croatia?) that I was its only student. And two years before, I had stayed a few days in Sarajevo, entranced by the exoticism of mosques and minarets, of caravanserais and coffeehouses loud with pop sevdalinke, songs of doomed love in aching chromatic scales more Turkish than European. So I had chosen Sarajevo.

But tourists, travelers need no reason—they see, and leave once the exotic threatens to turn into the everyday. To experience the everyday is a slower, deeper knowledge, yet all too soon I realized I needed an aim more pressing than a passive wish for experience. There was precious little exotic, anyway, about the shared two-bed box in Studentski Dom Nedžarići, a tower block on the edge of town, four stories above the tramway and the New Ilidža Road—especially once a grey winter had descended, and with it the smog held in by the ring of mountains.

After two weeks of broken appointments with an alleged supervisor— whom I sighted but once, vanishing briskly round a corridor corner—any notion of serious studies had evaporated. And though a kindly, quizzical professor of English set me essays on Serbo-Croat poetry, with no degree as a goal there seemed little reason for me to be there.

In the end, the reason had come as if by accident. Against all expectation, three handwritten translations, sent with a letter of admiration to a leading Belgrade poet, had returned a week later with enthusiastic corrections. We were talking now of a book-length manuscript to be offered to British publishers.

But then the balance had tipped again. En route to Britain between semesters, a long-distance flirtation with a Dutch friend had exploded into something far more wholehearted than the winter's cautious passion with the girl from Banja Luka. For two weeks in the Hague I had delayed the decision to return. And yet I was returning.

At this moment, maudlin with tiredness and the uncertainty of the night ahead, I had no idea why. But at least I was traveling, postponing reasons. It was then I must have written the sign, attempting to lessen the odds against a long-distance lift. Finding no blank card, I used the back of my street map of Sarajevo. Then, tucking the sign under the top flap, I hoisted my rucksack onto on my back.

Collar turned up, hunched against the swirling snow, I passed the second pole and the snap of its wind—taut tricolor and red star. Inside the customs hall, the Slovenian frontier guard, his face expressionless under the ill-fitting grey cap with its red enamel star, reached for my passport.

"*Englez?*"

"*Da.*"

He flicked through, stopped at a page full of visas: "Student?"

"*Da.*"

"*U Sarajevu?*"

I nodded.

"*Autostop?*"

I nodded again. His face still set, he stamped and returned the passport, then: "*Dodji.*" "Come with me."

At the far end of the hall, a dozen men in open-necked shirts, some middle-aged and grizzled in ill-fitting crimplene suits, others longer-haired and clean-shaven, in the Yugoslav youth uniform of blue jeans and black leather jacket, were standing smoking.

"This Englishman is going to Bosnia. Have you got room?

One of the older men, obviously the group leader, nodded: "*Nema problema.*"

The border guard offered his outstretched hand with a grin: "*Hajde momoče, sretan put.*" "Have a good journey, lad."

As they finished their cigarettes, we exchanged journeys—where are you coming from, where are you going—with the quiet camaraderie of long-distance travelers by night, when the world is no more than a ribbon of asphalt in the headlamp beams.

The men were gastarbeiters, migrant workers returning by coach to their Bosnian villages from the factories of the Ruhr. For this one month a year they would be home: to see mother, father, and sisters again, brothers too young for exile, maybe even wife and children. To work a little further on the tile-clad breezeblock mansion with its wrought iron balconies, which was slowly but surely dwarfing the wood and plaster farmstead where they, their parents, and grandparents were born. Or to sit all day in the kafana, regaling those who did not have the get-up-and-go with rounds of plum brandy and sweet coffee, bragging of blonde girlfriends and Siemens sound systems. The deutschmarks they bore financed an extended network of dependents, supplementing the scant pensions of retired parents, enabling younger brothers and sisters to stay on at school or college. Less apparent but more important, perhaps, they kept the local economy alive, providing work for the building trade, or subsidizing their relatives to run the little farms that patchworked the fertile Bosnian hills.

The leader ground his cigarette stub under his heel, and turned to go. Outside stood the coach, engine revving ready, wipers swishing away the snow. Our group was the last to board; the doors closed with a hiss behind us. As I swung off my rucksack and settled into a free seat, still grinning with elation—all night and three hundred winding miles on a warm coach—the driver hauled out and down into the snowy night, then snapped on the cassette player.

"*Hajde, pij!*"

I raised the proffered bottle to my lips, expecting the searing of pure spirit, but instead a gentle warmth and a taste plummier than the ripest of plums suffused through me.

"It's excellent. What is it?"

"*Mekašlijivovica*—single-distilled. My uncle makes it, up above Tuzla. *Pij još!* Drink some more!"

The driver turned up the cassette, and the agonized lilt of the sevdalinka soared through the coach. Wavering to its climax along the brink of discord, the music reached beyond the words lamenting an impossible love: it sang the bitter sweetness of existence, the pain of life balanced on a knife-edge against the beauty of song as long as the song lasts. As the bus plunged and twisted downwards through the Alpine night, it was the sevdalinka which swept me back, which sang me the reason for my return.

In the early hours, the coach left the Croatian flatlands and began winding into Bosnia's wooded valleys. Between waking and sleep, I had the sensation of coming home: even in darkness, through glass, I could feel the comforting bulk of those fertile hills. The coach stopped every half-hour or so to drop one or two men at a time at a shuttered roadside kafana, at a ramshackle farm with wood shingle roofs and a single light burning in an upstairs room, or at an unmetalled, unsignposted track climbing into the darkness by the rustle of rushing water. Or in a village, where postwar cement-on-breezeblock farmsteads clustered round a few streets of wood-framed claybrick houses with thick-walled courtyards, some of them with overhanging upper stories and ancient slatted windows (designed, in the days of purdah, so that women could see into the street without being seen); where the streets met, there was a whitewashed mosque and a drab glass-and-steel kiosk for bread or newspapers.

Soon after lightfall I too stepped out, a mere hundred miles from Sarajevo. I had heard of Jajce, of course. In this little enclave the medieval kings of Bosnia had been crowned; here, in 1943, Tito's Partisans, yet to take a major town from the Germans, had formed the optimistic government of free Yugoslavia; and it boasted a spectacular waterfall. Grey through the thin, drifting snow, the waterfall may have impressed me, but all I remember, fifteen years on, is the restless fatigue of a night of travel and fragmented sleep. I returned to the roadside, and held out my sign.

NEXT MORNING, BACK in the hostel, my British roommate and I see off our hangovers with a pan of Turkish coffee, brewed thick, black, and sweet on the little hotplate beneath the washbasin. Then we go down to the street. Bob is off to the library, but I stop at the newspaper kiosk by the traffic lights, and come back up in the jerking lift-which I still ride in my dreams, especially of late. I spread the newspaper and the map, still a little damp, on the desk overlooking the flat roof (covered in the shoes and bottles which plummet past our window when the parties on upper floors really get going), and start to star the likely "Rooms to Let."

Time slips. In another March, another room, the same sun breaks between snow-squalls to light the same map's tiny brown-and-yellow mosques, churches, municipal buildings, its parks with their little green trees, its child's train chugging along a railway line. It blends with the shaft of watery light which streams, fifteen years before, from beyond the Ilidža Road, beyond the grown-ups' railway and the distant ridge, to illuminate the street names I've just underlined: Pećina, Panina Kula, Golobrdica, Pirin brijeg . . .

The plan which paved my return had a double justification. By renting a room, Hanneke could join me here (we would probably have to pretend we were married, but intuition told us—even then—that this was less of a lie than an act of faith in the future). And by moving into the old town, I hoped to get closer to Bosnia's people, her past, a way of life missing from the concrete towerblock by the tramline.

THE CLICHÉ PICTURE of Tito's Yugoslavia, then as now, was one of a nation of bridged divides (though no-one could have suspected then how rickety the bridges were): between Europe and Asia Minor, Christianity and Islam, Habsburg Central Europe and the Ottoman Balkans. And yet, to me then, these contrasts, though piquant, were a picturesque backdrop—the stage, perhaps, but not the drama itself. The divides I felt most keenly were not these ancient faultlines of geography, but ones of the mind: between conformity and dissent, materialism and the intellect, modernity and tradition.

On one side of this divide, the unquestioning conformity of most of my fellow students, their lack of dissent from the twin goods of materialism and Party, could be stifling. Their ideal of Party card, flat, fridge, and TV seemed to lack a vital dimension—be it spirituality, political awareness, or faith in culture and tradition.

Yet, on the other side, those who did have higher ideals were possessed with immense creative energy, with a dynamism fed by the country's very diversity, by a faithfulness to traditional roots which avoided the sterile extremes of folklorism and foreign fads. What is more, among intellectuals there was a heady sense of a single community, a community open to any who shared its ideal—even to me, a mere literature student and apprentice translator. This democratic elite—so different from the exclusive and hierarchical cliques of British intellectual life—enabled an enthusiastic cross-fertilization of art-forms, disciplines, and regional cultures. Which in turn helps to explain how postwar Yugoslavia managed to produce a culture out of all proportion to her modest size and material wealth—a Nobel-prize novelist, for instance, world-class poets, a dazzlingly diverse popular music tradition, a unique homegrown school of painting misleadingly called naive.

As for politics, I was touched by the faith, expressed by most I met, in communism as a home-grown revolution, and I shared the universal and genuine admiration for Tito as a wartime and peacetime leader. . . yet I found the unquestioning nature of this faith oppressive.

There were dissenters, of course. But the consenting relationship between rulers and ruled in Tito's Yugoslavia meant that non-conformers were few, and the forces overseeing conformity—such as the widespread network of Interior Ministry (SUP) informers—were many. Some of those unable to follow the herd retreated into depression. Others quietly held their own, for years dodging incentives and threats to join the Party—for it must be said in fairness that, as secret police went, the Yugoslav SUP were more Balkan than autocratic, preferring to look the other way as long as dissidents didn't make too much noise.

(An endearing memory: Bob and I, walking the Miljačka gorge upriver from Sarajevo, are invited by three men picnicking near the roadside to join their meal: "Are you on holiday?"

"No, we're students at the university. How about you?"

"We're SUP officers, but right now it's our lunch break. Have some more chicken.")

Some political dissent, it is true, had ethnic overtones. The leaders of the Croatian Spring six years before had been locked up on charges of separatism. The young Hungarians in Novi Sad, my friends from high-school vacations, saw a stealthy Serbianization going hand-in-hand with attempts at political control. (From one of my monthly visits to the next, the Hungarian student cafe had suddenly become very popular with young Serbian toughs, making free tables hard to find and intimidating to sit at.) Nevertheless, the Croats' real crime had been to advocate democratic reform, just as the Hungarians knew full well that covert Serbianization was not an end in itself, but had the real aim of ensuring political control over a dangerously homogeneous intellectual culture.

Tensions there were, but no worse than the resentments between English, Scots, and Welsh back home. Then the Yugoslav system of guaranteed minority rights in local government, education, and media terms was upheld—rightly, it seemed—as an example to the world. These guarantees, of course, were a matter of vital necessity in a country made up of a patchwork of minorities—as was shown when they broke down only a couple of years later, with the uprising of the Kosovo Albanians and its murderous repression. This put paid not only to the principle of self-determination of peoples within the Yugoslav federation, but also—by making ethnic hatred a respectable vote-winner—it signaled the bloody downfall of Yugoslavia itself. Then, however, in the late seventies, even the most radical or drunken of dissenters never once questioned in my presence the integrity of Yugoslavia as an amalgam of different peoples, nor questioned her borders.

In any case, ethnicity seemed a broad-brush affair, based on language and region rather than ancestry or religion. For the students I knew in Sarajevo, all of whom spoke the Bosnian dialect (about halfway between Serbian and Croatian, but generously spiced with Turkish loan-words), fine ethnic distinctions had little meaning.

Looking back, I can sort Slav from Turkish names, but no further: Snežana, Svetozar; Nermina, Nenad. When I see the ones whose names have faded—the dark-haired, tortoise-shell-spectacled student of English, slinky cabaret singer by night, who took me under her wing; her shy blonde girlfriend, unwitting heart-throb; the languid, penniless poet with ladykilling green eyes and an oft-requited passion for plum brandy, who took over my hostel bed when I left; the glamorous but oh-so-earnest rising Party star—and think of their origins, I draw a blank.

If asked, my friends would have regarded themselves as Yugoslavs. Perhaps also as Bosnians, though all I recall is normal home-town pride: you must come with me back to Tuzla, to Banja Luka. Ironically, however, what I missed among many of these thoroughly modern young Yugoslavs was a sense of deeper heritage, of faithfulness to traditional roots—little suspecting that history would return not as wisdom, but as vengeance.

A recent simplistic revision of East European history, tarring all Communist leaders with Stalin's brush, portrays Tito as an absolute ruler over a misbegotten empire, whose brute force alone kept his citizens from slitting their neighbors' throats. This is a myth; and the fact that former Yugoslavs now spread it (usually to justify the slitting of neighbors' throats) makes it no less of a myth. The cause for the present bloodletting, it seems to me, is rather the opposite. The love for Tito was genuine, but his charisma meant that no questions need ever be asked.

The downfall of the Yugoslav people has been their inability to question the malevolent dictators who followed, preaching not brotherhood and unity but race and blood. Though Tito's Yugoslavia genuinely seemed to have mended the cracks of ancient feud, this, the gap between the complex responsibilities of an exceptionally complex society and simple, charismatic solutions imposed from above, was the fatal faultline it never bridged. When the little Hitlers of today wrenched this gap apart in their lust for power or their fear of the Other, the country shattered along the lines of weakest resistance: religion, language, race. But this is the shape, not the cause, of Yugoslavia's destruction, this land I weep for with her people, this land to which I can never return.

THAT DAY, I hunted houses all over the old town, up and down the streets, alleys, and stairs that tumbled over the foothills of the Miljačka gorge, which held the city in check to the West. The calm jumble of thick-walled, whitewashed buildings seemed a continent, a century away from the city below, the sharp smell of diesel, the clang and screech of trams past department stores and offices; and though as old as the Baščaršija at the city's heart, these ancient suburbs had none of its noise and hustle of cafés and souvenir stalls, hawkers, and loafers.

And to cap it all, it was suddenly spring; a mild sun had enticed children to play in the street, women in flower-patterned pantaloons to gossip raucously in doorways. Two old men in faded-blue work jackets sat side by side, gazing benignly into the middle distance, on a bench by a little triangular graveyard where the turban-capped columns leant higgledy-piggledy and dazzling white in the freshly-washed light.

Golobrdica—bare hillock—was a narrow, cobbled hogback of pantiled single-story houses and flaking courtyard walls, each one almost as high as the houses it joined. I rang at the roofed gate of number 39, its heavy, nail-bossed door long stripped of paint by rain, frost, and sun.

The woman must have been in her forties, with sharp, tired eyes and thick brown hair, streaked with grey, pinned up under a floral cotton headscarf; over her brown-and-ochre paisley pantaloons she wore an old green cardigan.

"I've come about the room. For me and my wife."

She motioned me inside with a downward flick of her hand, through a tiny whitewashed courtyard and the kitchen, where an old man, big and stooped, watery-eyed and wheezing with asthma, examined me intently as I passed.

The room was a white cell with a single bed, an unvarnished spruce chest, a table and chair, and a little round woodstove painted silver; and though the sun shone in through the small square window in the wall a half-meter thick, it still held the cool of winter.

"I'll take it."

The other door off the kitchen led into the main room of the house. She motioned me inside: *"Hajde, sjedi."* "Sit down."

A divan covered with woven rugs ran round three of the walls; the fourth, windowed, overlooked a steep little valley of backyards: vegetable plots, washing lines, chicken runs, and plum trees, their bare branches speckled dark pink and green with opening blossoms. Apart from a low oblong table and a TV set behind the door, there was little furniture; the floor was covered with old, hand-woven celim carpets in three or four different patterns of maroon, indigo, and green, their colors faded and blended with washing.

The woman returned, bearing a copper tray with a brass and copper dzezva—the long-handled can, shaped like an inverted cone, for cooking the coffee—and three tiny gold-rimmed porcelain bowls.

"So when is your wife coming?"

"Not for two or three weeks. She's in Holland. I'll write today and tell her I've found somewhere to live."

The old man nodded, but the woman quickly continued: "But we want to rent the room right away."

"That's fine, I can move in this week."

I handed over the three red hundred-dinar notes; she folded them away in her purse, which she put back in her apron pocket.

Our coffee finished, the landlady took me into the courtyard. Next to
the house door was the toilet—instead of paper, a water tap. Then, off the
kitchen, the partitioned cubicle with its sitting bath. She hesitated in front of
the fridge.

"I could clear you a shelf in here . . . "

She hesitated again.

"It's just that we don't want anything . . . dirty in there, you understand?"

I didn't understand. There was an awkward silence, until I realized she
was talking of pork: "Oh no, don't worry. We don't eat meat at all."

Though her look was as nonplused as mine a moment before, she nodded, at least somewhat reassured.

ELATED, I DESCENDED the flight of steps at the end of the narrow street. Ahead
the sun, sinking in a clear sky, was almost touching the squat, barrel-shaped
minaret of the walled mosque opposite, on the other side of the little built-up
valley leading down towards the center of town. The shadows were suddenly
cold, and I realized I had not eaten since the morning.

Down another flight of stairs, and the twin towers of the Catholic cathedral across the road gave me my bearings. Dolphin-nosed, drab-green trucks
snarled past with baby Fiats in their wake, their sharp fumes filling the narrow
road lined with grimy nineteenth-century buildings. The market had closed
for the day. I turned left along the narrow pavement and into the second door-
way, as a tram clanged past a meter from my shoulder.

The shop had all the allure of a station washroom: white-tiled, with a
light blue formica shelf and mirror along the left-hand wall; at the back, two
steps up to a windowless room with four formica tables and cheap wooden
chairs. On the right, a marble counter with an enormous set of scales, and a
glass cabinet with flat circular tins of burek. But oh, what burek! Vast coils of
brown strudel pastry, warm, crisp, deliciously filling, that oozed melted butter
and sharp sheep's cheese, or fried pumpkin, or spiced apple, or best of all, the
zeljanica—a savory, succulent mix of cheese and spinach that was the next best
thing to heaven on earth.

Halfway through my second plate, I leaned back in the chair and
stretched contentedly. It was good to be back.

PERHAPS IT IS wrong, in these evil days, with Sarajevo under siege, with
Bosnia's enemies shelling bread queues and starving her people out of their
homes, when our TV sets show us emaciated babies with mouths writhed in a
soundless scream, to write of Bosnia as a land of food.

But perhaps it is more important to keep faith with memory: not for my
sake, but for the sake of a land where memory may soon be all we have to cling
to. Invaders down the ages have been drawn to conquest by Bosnia's rich

upland pastures and the orchards of her valleys. Other enemies have burnt her
fields, have put her villages to the knife or sword and slaughtered her flocks.
And yet, fields can be sown again, the blackened plum tree puts forth new
shoots, the massacre's cowed survivors come down from their caves and build
shacks from the rubble.

But the new overlords are not content with conquest, with subjugation.
They mean to obliterate a people; and they know full well that the most effective obliteration comes from within, by setting neighbor against neighbor. To
wipe out a people, it is not enough to harry, to burn, and to kill. Memory itself
must be cleansed—the memory that there ever was such a land, a land where
the living was good, a land that all its people knew as home.

So let these memories exist. The sharp, tangy scent of hot sheep-cheese,
as a dish of burek is flipped from a wooden oven paddle to cool on the marble
slab. A rich, steaming, oily stew, topped with glistening peppers, on a table
shaded by the young leaves of a lime tree in a caravanserai courtyard. Bubbly
coils of hot doughnut pastry and tangy ewe-milk curds, washed down with the
fifth Nikošičko beer of the evening, at the musicians' table of the Hotel Bris-
tol. The scented sepia foam on the coffee in the red-enamel pan that turns
cream-colored as you stir it. Or the cheese market, a vision in white: great
porcelain bowls of curd, soft, glistening slabs of new cheese, stacked wet and
scented on the long marble counters, in front of the starched aprons and head-
dresses of the plump peasant women. And the day the oranges came: after a
winter of carrots and cabbage, pickled or green, the market behind the cathedral suddenly a riot of vermilion, miniature suns piled high on every stall, raucously yelling: Buy us! Eat us! Gorge yourself on summer!

As I STEPPED out of the burek shop into the rush-hour street, I knew that I had
another pilgrimage to make. Turning left along Marshal Tito Street, I crossed
in front of the gated wall that Islamic law had decreed should shield the eyes
of the faithful from the Old Orthodox Church behind.

At least the Turks allowed the Christians to build. Though first-class citizenship was reserved as a perk of Islam, the Ottomans were in fact far more
tolerant of other faiths than most Christian states of their era—a philosophy
born of pragmatism, for bigotry makes inefficient politics when it comes to
ruling a multinational state. When the Jews were expelled from Spain in 1492,
for instance, they found refuge in the Ottoman Empire: for four and a half
centuries, until the Nazi death camps, Sarajevo was one of Europe's great
Sephardic cities. And if one from a subject people embraced Islam, non-Turk-
ish origins were no obstacle to the highest offices of Empire. Such as Gazi
Husrev Beg, the sixteenth-century local boy made good, who invested his
home town with buildings worthy of the Imperial City itself—a university, a
covered bazaar, and the great mosque, to which I was now returning.

In the alley opposite the wall of the church, the souvenir-shop owners
were packing away their copper trays and coffee pots, their factory-woven

celim rugs and peasant slipper pincushions. By the alley window of the strip-light-lit sweetshop down at the corner, a conscript soldier and his girl were huddled, both hands entwined, across a little marble table. The lad behind the counter, back turned to the lovers, sporting the first wisps of a mustache and greasy black hair under his white cotton cap, was staring out through the other window into the gathering dusk.

The metal grille in the mosque wall still stood half-open. Inside was a silence deepened, not broken, by the splash of water. Across the yard, where the corner of the great mosque almost touched the courtyard wall, night was already claiming its domain. An old man, black-capped, the blue of his jacket intense in the half-light, swept dust very slowly into a long-handled pan. Afraid to disturb the silence, I sidled to the stone seat beneath the plane tree, perhaps a lime, whose leaves were beginning to unfold; its smooth white surface was still warm with sun. Water trickled from the brass taps in the side of the high, octagonal fountain, under the ornate cast-iron arabesques of its canopy. The portico of the mosque was lost to shadows, but its arches of carven stone still curved, serene, weightless, and high. Over the dome, the minaret soared white in the dying light, a slender starship waiting for flight.

This was the city's still center, the very essence of Islam: in a walled courtyard, water, a tree, and the warm geometry of stone. In the deep blue velvet sky by the minaret hung a sliver of incandescent silver light: the first moon of spring.

AN ODE FOR SARAJEVO

I sigh when the youth of Sarajevo are
mentioned. I wilt when they speak of
its gardens and waters.

If only you could see,
as I see now,
the city ablaze with its blossoms.

The young people parading on the
Benbasa dam.
Its every corner filled with crystal light.

Beautiful gardens, clear water,
Bright beauties.
All united there.
No fault is found with Sarajevo,
God forbid!

Let the Almighty preserve it
from all evils.
Let the enemy of Sarajevo be
destroyed,
if there be one!

—MEHMET MELLI
Eighteenth Century Bosnian Poet

PART II

Today there are none who wish to die.
That is why we tasted the cruelty of Heaven.
Behold, how many children and uncovered women walk through blood.
[. . .]
Heaven showed its violence over every border.
Many hearts have been roasted over the fires of farewells.
From their homeland they were removed to foreign lands.
In my own homeland I longed for my native land.
We were chastized by the hands of our enemies.
This happened in the year 1697 [. . .]
The sea of misfortune and trouble flooded over and rose above our heads.

—From a poem by an unknown author after Prince Eugene of Savoy's
  burning of Sarajevo in 1697

Remain here! . . . The sun of foreign skies
Will not warm you as warmly as our sun:
The mouthfuls of bread are bitter over there
Where none is your own, where there are no brothers.

Who will find a mother better than one's own?!
Your mother is this very land;
Look across the limestone crags and fields.
Everywhere are graves of your ancestors.

They were the giants of this land,
Radiant examples, who defended her,
You, too, must remain in this land [. . .]

Here your brothers grasp your hand—
Only your wormwood blossoms in foreign lands;
Everything, everything ties you to these crags [. . .]

Remain here! . . .

—From a poem written in 1891 by Aleksa Santić, Serb poet from Mostar,
  Hercegovina, on the exodus of Bosnian Muslims to Turkey after the
  Austro-Hungarian occupation

Serbia's Blood War

T.D. ALLMAN

WE ARE EATING the grapes of the dead, and the grapes are delicious. Juicy, blue-black, sweet and tart, they hang in fulsome ripe clusters in the arbor just behind the house where the Serbs killed the Muslim man and his wife.

It's a glorious late Bosnian afternoon—the seamless sky as deep-blue as the grapes, the warmth of the sun making you glad to be alive, even though snow already coats the hills around Sarajevo.

All day we've been visiting concentration camps, investigating massacre reports, traversing a landscape as pretty and, at first glance, as affluent as the Pennsylvania hunt country. Only up close do you see that many of the handsome chalet-style houses with satellite dishes on the roofs have been bombed out. After a while you can pick out exactly where the Muslims and Croats lived: they're the houses that have been blown up from the inside.

For all the hate and killing that now divide them, the peoples of the former Yugoslavia—the Serbs, Slovenes, Croats, Macedonians, Albanians, and Muslims—are all friendly, family-oriented, and house-proud. A Yugoslav saves up some money and the first thing he does is build a nice house.

This is such a house, or, rather, it was, and that's what makes it seem a crime to spit out the grape seeds onto the little patio, still as neat as a pin except for the dust from the explosion. The shiny glass teacups and spotless, ironed tea towels are still on their shelves in the kitchen, next to the downstairs bedroom, where the explosion crushed the couple to death. The TV sits in the living room, its vacant glass eye somehow intact, and the little red Lada station wagon waits in the garage, its finish still gleaming.

The people who built this house, and lived in it, are gone forever. But in these small mementos you can still see the modest lives of decent, hard work that came to an end five nights ago.

This town is called Prijedor. It's in northeastern Bosnia, a region paradigmatic of what the world has come to call "ethnic cleansing." But except for the rubble and terror, this house could be in Nassau County, New York.

"The Serbs came in the night," a neighbor whispers in German. "The explosion was at one." They put dynamite in the sanctuary of the mosque and around the minaret. When the minaret collapsed, the explosion blew out the back wall of their house. The mother and father were killed instantly. "The children were sleeping upstairs with their grandmother," he adds, "and survived. They fled. No one knows where."

"I suppose he was a guest worker in Germany, like you," I say. "That's how he paid for the house."

"No, he was a salesman—computers," the neighbor answers. "A young man, well-educated, not mixed up in politics. Sir," he continues, "the Serbs come every night. They take two or three people. I am going to be killed soon. Is there some way you could help my children get to Stuttgart? I worked in a bakery there for eight years. My friends there could raise them."

After inspecting the debris of the mosque, which was really just a neighborhood chapel, we drive over to see the Roman Catholic church the Serbs blew up. This, in comparison, was a major edifice, and harder to destroy. The church is a tangle of cement and iron girders now, but the steeple stands—or rather it leans—twisted, pockmarked, scorched by the explosion.

An elderly woman, a Croat Catholic lay worker wearing a medal with the Virgin Mary on it, searches the rubble for relics. "They blew up the church five minutes after they blew up the mosque. The fire station is right over there," she says, pointing to a building behind the church, "but the Serb firemen would not help."

It's getting late now, and people scurry past us into their houses, refusing to answer questions. I knock on several doors. Finally, a Serb opens his door. His house faces the side of the church. Windows in his house were shattered. "Blowing up the church was a bad thing to do," he says. He explains why: "Serbs live around here. Serb property was damaged. Serb people were hurt."

One Serb in his twenties is more than willing to talk. In fact, he starts screaming at me as I walk back to the church. He's wearing tight black jeans, a black T-shirt, dark-brown cowboy boots; he has a gold Orthodox cross on a gold chain around his neck, and an automatic pistol tucked in his belt.

"Get out of here!" he shouts. "You foreigners don't belong here. Prijedor belongs to the Serbs."

UNTIL IT DECIDED to commit suicide, Yugoslavia was on its way to joining the club of affluent European nations. Yugoslavia had tourism, heavy industry; it was a food-surplus nation. Its new freeways linked the rest of the European Community with Greece, Turkey, and the export markets of the Middle East. The totems of an emerging consumer society were everywhere: new gas stations, motels, housing developments, and discos and sidewalk cafés in the villages. Most impressive were the large private houses covering the roadside hills. Before the killing started practically everyone, it seems, was just finishing a new house, or had just bought a new car.

But beneath this surface modernity seethed fierce ethnic hatreds which communism had only suppressed. As the state collapsed and Slovenia, then Croatia, and finally Bosnia seceded from the Yugoslav federation, the Serbs exploded in a frenzy of killing and destruction. First they overran nearly a third of Croatia, committing atrocities unknown in Europe since the end of World War II. Then, last spring, they overran two thirds of Bosnia. Ever since, the world has looked on, horrified, but done nothing to stop the aggression, let alone reverse it.

Later, as I sit in my hotel room in Belgrade watching CNN, the BBC, and SkyNews, peacemakers Cyrus Vance and Lord David Owen dash vainly from Geneva to Zagreb to Belgrade with the latest proposals and cease-fires. The faces of others I've come to interview flash on the screen: Dobrica Ćosić, the novelist who is now president of what is left of Yugoslavia; Milan Panić, the American businessman from Orange County, California, who, from July to December last year, was Yugoslavia's extraordinary prime minister; and, far less frequently, Slobodan Milošević, the president of Serbia, the man many call "Slobo-Saddam" and condemn as the mastermind of "ethnic cleansing," but who, more than any other, average Serbs believe speaks for them, stands up for them, while "the world" gangs up on Serbia.

On the TV screen, all they talk about is peace. Yet afterward the pictures always switch back to Bosnia, especially to Sarajevo—the snipers, the artillery, the old people freezing to death, the children with no names because their relatives are all dead and they are too young to speak. In less than a year, Serbs have murdered more than 100,000 people in Bosnia. More than 100 formal cease-fires have been wantonly violated. According to European Community investigators, Serb soldiers in Bosnia have "systematically" raped more than 20,000 Muslim women in a premeditated campaign to make them flee their homes.

"Everything always goes just as Milošević wants it," an envoy in Belgrade told me. "He is a master at two things: orchestrating the killing, and giving the civilized world just enough cause to avoid military intervention to actually stop these crimes."

Repeatedly, Milošević has strung the international community along, raising hopes for peace, dashing them, and raising them anew. Last autumn, for example, the great expectation was that placing United Nations observers at Serb artillery positions might end the shelling of Sarajevo. After weeks of tortuous negotiations, an agreement was finally reached—and was violated the very day it was scheduled to begin.

In December 1992, hope took political form. After ignoring months of pleas from the outside world for democratic elections in Serbia, Milošević finally permitted his constituents to vote for him. Not only was he re-elected, with a margin of victory that was widened by intimidation and fraud, but he also defeated and drove from office his most important rival, Prime Minister Milan Panić.

Then, in January 1993, hope took another form. International mediators Vance and Owen urged the Bosnian Serbs to accept a compromise peace plan offered in Geneva. Even though the "compromise" would have largely confirmed the Serbs in their conquests, the Serbian response was emphatically negative: as he sat in a UN vehicle at a Serb checkpoint, the deputy prime minister of Bosnia was murdered in cold blood, poisoning this latest prospect for peace.

Even so, Vance and Owen beseeched Milošević to use his "influence" to persuade Bosnian Serbs to accept their latest peace offer—and once again Milošević proved himself the master of events.

Within days the previously intractable Bosnian Serbs demonstrated they had been following Milošević's orders all along by "accepting" the peace plan. Talk of peace was followed by more killing, yet another Serb offensive in Bosnia. Months passed and each passing month confirmed the success of "ethnic cleansing." All the talk of peace had gained for Milošević virtually everything he had sought to gain from the war. Equally significant, the threat of foreign military action was neutralized. Now, with Panić and his other domestic opponents emasculated, Milošević stood alone, more than ever the undisputed leader of "Greater Serbia," as the murderous winter of 1992 melded into the bitter spring and summer of 1993.

The outside world, as always, was too preoccupied with other matters to do much more than dispatch high-profile diplomats. "On every Bosnian's tombstone," a UN "peacekeeper" tells me, "it should be inscribed: 'I died because Helmut Kohl and Francois Mitterrand and John Major were afraid the Maastricht Treaty wouldn't pass.'" He adds bitterly: "And on the children's graves they should write: 'It was also an election year in the United States.'"

But beyond the international community's dithering and cowardice, there's another reason the killing never stops. "We're scared," a ranking UN officer tells me when I ask him why they aren't doing more. "You think this blue helmet protects you? In this country, around every corner, lies death. And no one cares. That's the worst thing about this place. When you die, no one cares."

Belgrade is only 125 miles from Sarajevo, yet the terror there might as well be unfolding on the dark side of the moon—partly because most Serbs never see the reality we foreigners see on our TV sets. Instead, the main television channel broadcasts video versions of Serbian press releases. Thus every night, on the Belgrade news reports, the insatiable hordes of the Muslim-Vatican conspiracy launch new attacks against Serbia. They commit new outrages. And still the world does nothing—absolutely nothing!—to help the heroic Serb people in their lonely struggle against aggression.

One afternoon I meet with a Serb journalist in Belgrade. "You are among the very few people I've met here," I remark, "who don't seem in the grip of clinical paranoia."

"Serbs like me represent nothing," she answers. "The average Serb honestly believes it's Serbia that's under attack. If only every Serb family could get CNN for three months," she goes on, "then maybe there would be some hope for ending the madness."

One diplomat in Belgrade evaluates the phenomenon soberly. "Sure, the

Serbs had certain grievances," he says. "Sure, the others made mistakes. Sure, there's blame on all sides. But the blame is 90 percent Serbian, 10 percent other. Nothing compares to what the Serbs have done, and nothing the others have done justifies it. Did you ever hear of a novel called *The Tribe That Lost Its Head?* That's what we have now in the heart of Europe."

ONE MORNING AT a camp in Bosnia I notice that grown men starve differently from the way children do. We're all familiar with infantile starvation: the spindly legs, the bloated bellies, the heads too heavy for the neck to carry. But past puberty, starvation takes a different course. People come to look like sculptures.

The prisoner who calls out to me, in French, "Mister, do you have a light?" looks like the effigy of a medieval martyr. You can see the skull and cheekbones. It's as though his skin is transparent. He's dying for a smoke. "It's great when you journalists visit," he says. "The Serbs let the Red Cross give us cigarettes."

Some 1,200 men are packed into this cattle shed, located on an unprotected mountainside. They are arranged in six long lines, and each man has only the space of a folded blanket where he can sit or lie down on the floor, which is not really a floor, only gravel. The gravel slopes downward, so when it rains or snows the thin blankets are soaked, chilling the emaciated men, none of whom have coats. There is no heating in this shed, or in any of the other sheds in this camp, where some 5,000 people face winter in the same conditions. As I talk to the prisoners, people whisper, mostly in German, sometimes in English: "Tell the world. Don't let the world forget us."

Red Cross workers are distributing cigarettes. But there are no matches. I give the prisoner who speaks French my lighter and ask, "Muslim or Croat?" Everyone around him laughs. "I'm Serb!" he says. "Baptized in the Orthodox Church. But the day the Serbs rounded up the Muslims in Prijedor I was taking a walk with four Muslim friends, all girls. When I explained I was a Serb, they beat me up." He's 24 and so glad to be able to light his cigarette that he grins broadly, and when he does you can see he's beginning to lose his teeth from the lack of vitamins.

Here, as in the intellectual salons of Belgrade, one encounters the lack of shame or guilt that normally characterizes pathological behavior. To the contrary, the Serbs are proud of this camp. They believe it proves they are treating their "prisoners of war" decently. But aside from the fact that conditions here do not comply with the Geneva convention, there's another noteworthy aspect to these "prisoners of war": none of them are soldiers. They are all still wearing the same light summer civilian clothing they had on when they were apprehended months ago. When I ask the Serb authorities about weapons captured from these "prisoners of war," they say there are none.

Another curiosity: there are no wounded here, or in the camp hospital, which is actually just a small dispensary. They do have men who are suffering, but from disease or malnutrition, not wounds. This raises the question of what the Serbs in Bosnia do with real POWs. "They kill them all," an international relief official who has investigated these matters explains later.

The camp hospital is manned by imprisoned Croat and Bosnian Muslim doctors. When I ask one of the doctors how he came to be here, he says, "I was in my surgery in Prijedor. They burst in, pointed a gun at me, and took me away. I don't know where my wife and children are."

The doctors are terrified—much more terrified than the prisoners in the shed—and later I learn why. In Bosnia it is Serb practice when they "cleanse" a town like Prijedor to terrorize average people, especially women and children, into fleeing after signing over their houses and other property to what is called "the Serbian Republic of Bosnia and Hercegovina." Men capable—even though not culpable—of armed resistance are imprisoned, like the prisoners in this camp. Then they kill the non-Serb elite: the doctors, lawyers, engineers, rich businessmen, and elected officials, like the mayor of Prijedor, who, along with 48 other of the town's notables, was never seen alive again after being seized by Serb gunmen.

"Have there been atrocities? Incidences of torture?"

"Please," the doctor says, "do not ask such questions."

I try to compose a purely technical line of inquiry: "Given the physical circumstances of this camp—the mountain exposure, lack of shelter from the cold, and limited sanitary facilities—what will be the public-health implications of the onset of winter?"

"Forty percent of the people here will die," the doctor answers.

At another camp, not even the Serb militiamen running it pretend the inmates are prisoners of war. This is called a "processing center." The process which the 5,000 people here have undergone is this: they were rounded up by Serb gunmen, their houses were dynamited, and they were taken to the Omarska concentration camp, the camp that elicited worldwide outrage when it was discovered last summer. After international pressure closed Omarska, they were transferred here.

The building's name, written in both Latin and Cyrillic scripts, reveals this camp's former identity: "Brotherhood School." Though there are some women here, the prisoners are mostly middle-aged men and boys. Some huddle in tents in the schoolyard. The rest sleep inside the building; their mats cover the corridors, the staircases, the classrooms. I meet a man and his son who have been sleeping in the latrine for more than a month.

"That's our house over there," the boy says, pointing through the toilet window. Like the home of the computer salesman in Prijedor, it's a very nice house. It would be worth several hundred thousand dollars in the United States—or would have been—before it was dynamited from the inside.

Though most of the houses around here have been demolished, a few remain intact. When you pass them you see women hanging out laundry, men working on their cars, as if nothing were unusual about their surroundings. When I ask why those houses were spared, a guard answers, "They belong to Serbs."

I'm curious about something else. Even according to the official version of events, the people held here are victims. They were kidnapped; their property destroyed. So why are they the ones in detention?

"If they went back to their homes, they would be killed by their Serb neighbors," the Serb answers, as though this were so normal it should be obvious even to a foreigner. At this point our conversation is interrupted by gunfire. A bus full of Serbs is passing the camp, and some of the young toughs on the bus fire their automatic weapons and jeer the camp inmates.

When the shooting ceases I ask about a further point of curiosity. The majority of the prisoners here are Muslims; most of the rest are Croats. But there's also a pathetic little encampment of Ukrainians. Actually, they are Ruthenians: their ancestors came from the region that used to be the extreme eastern end of Czechoslovakia, which was annexed to the Ukraine after World War II.

Ukrainians, Ruthenians, they all look alike to me, as do Serbs, Croats, and everyone else in this dreadful fratricide, and what they all look like, in their prime, are star guards on a championship Indiana University basketball team. The Muslims, especially, seem disproportionately tall, blond, blue-eyed. Of course, Serbs, Croats, and Muslims know how to tell one another apart.

But still, in the midst of these old blood feuds, why arrest the Ruthenian Ukrainians? Why destroy *their* houses?

Again, the Serb officer answers benignly, as though explaining the obvious to a child: "They are not Serbs."

AT BANJA LUKA'S Bosna Hotel, which looks like a Ramada Inn, I sup with the Devil, and it occurs to me that I have neglected to bring a long spoon. Actually, the police chief of Prijedor, seated on my right, is amiable, though didactic. Over cocktails he delivers a long discourse on his specialty, which he describes as "ethnic warfare." By his own account he played a major roll in "cleansing" Prijedor, and helped run the notorious Omarska camp.

As the first course arrives he opines that it's "very mean" of the media to say Serbs have committed war crimes. "You Americans do not understand ethnic warfare," he says, "because you fight only clean wars, like Kuwait and Vietnam. We do not have that luxury. We Serbs are fighting to save ourselves from genocide." He explains, almost pedantically: "In ethnic warfare the enemy doesn't wear a uniform or carry a gun. Everyone is the enemy."

Our host, the police chief of Banja Luka, sits opposite me. We are enjoying his hospitality tonight because at three-thirty this afternoon a fellow dinner guest, Roy Gutman of *New York Newsday*, was arrested while he was walking along a street in Banja Luka after visiting a Muslim source. This was considered sufficient cause for him to be pulled over, manhandled, dragged into the police station, and threatened with the usual consequences. The black humor in all this was that his arrest was going to make him late for our four o'clock interview with the Banja Luka police chief.

By the time I finally found out what had happened, and reached the police station, Roy had been transformed from prisoner into honored guest. Turkish coffee was served. Would we like some slivovitz, the Yugoslav plum brandy?

Human rights are respected in Banja Luka, the assembled officials assured us. It's not as if people can be arrested just for walking down the street, though, of course, misunderstandings can occur anywhere, even in the capital of the Serbian Republic of Bosnia and Hercegovina. The Banja Luka police chief capped our reconciliation by inviting everyone in the room to dinner, including the Prijedor police chief.

Besides Roy and me, another American is present: a Croat-American kid from Chicago named John, who was arrested with Roy. John had come along with us from Zagreb, the capital of Croatia, partly for the ride and partly to help translate. But following his experience with the Serb police, he's still so scared that, even at dinner, he can't bring himself to speak.

Our host, the Banja Luka police chief, plays good cop; the Prijedor police chief is the bad cop. In an early conversational gambit, the Prijedor police chief declares that though the world is against Serbia, this won't stop the Serbs. "We will fight to the death," he vows.

I ask him why the world has turned against the Serbs.

There is, he explains patiently, a conspiracy against the Serbs led by the Vatican, the Muslim fundamentalists, the European Economic Community, and the United States. Like nearly all the Serbs I meet, he believes that Serbia is a great nation, chosen to play a special role in history, and that the world is destined to pay dearly for the folly of not recognizing this fact. "We Serbs forgive, but we don't forget," he says more in sorrow than anger. "We won't forget the West sided with the Muslims and Croats."

"Yes, the world will pay a big price for opposing us," another official agrees.

"What price?" I ask.

"World War I began here," he answers matter-of-factly. "World War III will begin here, too."

This prospect seems to alarm none of our Serb dinner companions. To the contrary, they see it as proof they are right and "the world" is wrong. "You come from a decadent civilization," the Prijedor police chief elaborates. "You have forgotten who your real enemies are."

At this point the Banja Luka police chief, the good cop, breaks in. "Mr. Gutman," he says amiably, "I think you are Jewish."

"Yes," Roy answers.

"We like Jews!" he says, beaming. "Jews understand Muslims. They know how to deal with them."

Roy resumes his questioning without comment. Is it true, he asks, that Serbs killed all the male children in the village of Verbanći? Can our Serb dinner companions enlighten us on the reports that 167 people were crushed to death trying to escape through an air-conditioning duct because they were suffocating in the room where they were being held? And what about the ravine story: how, after a bus full of Muslims was stopped and the passengers killed, the bodies were thrown down a ravine?

There are three official responses to all such questions, punctuated by smiles and toasts to Serb-American understanding: "Muslim lies." "Croat lies." And: "We are investigating."

Still, even in the good cop's smile, there is puzzlement. Why should this Jew care about Muslim bodies thrown down a ravine? Can't he understand we are all fighting the same enemy—or at least should be?

"We don't think of ourselves as Christians and Jews," I interject, attempting to lighten the conversation. "We're just a happy crew of Americans wandering around Bosnia, trying to figure out what's going on. Believe me"— my airy wave includes John, the Croat from Chicago, as well as Roy—"we spend days together in the car"—I realize I'm just getting myself in deeper and deeper—"and the subject of our different ethnicities never comes up. We just think of ourselves as fellow Americans," I conclude, grinning like an idiot because I see the Serbs think I am an idiot. To them, Roy's the Jew, who should be their natural ally in the battle to the death with Islam, but who isn't. I'm the white-bread Westerner who, however patiently they explain the obvious, Will Never Understand.

But now, thanks to my cheery intervention, several of the Serbs are eyeing John. He may have been born in Chicago, but nothing can change the fact that he is a Croat. They know exactly what would have been done to John today when he was arrested if he had not been with Roy and not had a US passport. So does John.

While Roy quizzes the Banja Luka police chief, I converse with the bad cop. "That certainly was a professional job done on the mosque and church," I observe. "Who did it?"

"Not professional enough," he complains. "Vandals did it."

"That's funny," I say. "The mosque was blown up at one a.m. The church was blown up five minutes later. But there's a curfew in Prijedor. Only forces under your command are allowed out that late at night. And you can't just blow up buildings on the spur of the moment. It takes hours, at least, to organize such demolitions."

"We are investigating," he answers. Then he adds, "A Croat sniper was firing from the steeple of the church."

"You don't mean that night, at five past one in the morning?"

"No," he says, smiling. "Before."

"And the mosque? That was an enemy position too?"

"Yes, you are right. The mosque was being used by enemies of the Serbs." The police chief of Prijedor smiles. He is beginning to develop hope for me.

"And all the destroyed houses we saw?"

"They all had bunkers."

"So the fact the Muslim houses had basements meant they had to be dynamited?"

"Yes," the police chief says. "You are beginning to understand."

After a few hours, the debris of the meal lies around us. "A number of the prisoners we saw are starving," I say.

"Because they are Muslims," the official who predicted World War III interjects. "We do everything for them, but sometimes we have only pork grease for cooking, so they refuse to eat." He adds, "They are taking food out of the mouths of Serbs."

"But the Koranic dietary laws are waived in life-or-death situations . . . ," I start to say, but the fatigue and the slivovitz prevent me from pursuing the point.

I begin again. "What did you do to your mayor?" I ask the police chief of Prijedor. "He was freely elected. He was your boss, wasn't he?"

"He was elected by Muslims."

"They say you killed him."

"He escaped."

"Along with the 48 other officials and civic leaders?"

"Yes. Same night. We never saw them again."

"More slivovitz!" the good cop says.

I take another sip and ask, "Do you want your children to be killers or computer salesmen?"

At this point the police chief of Prijedor stands up, looks at me, and says, "I am leaving." There's no anger or hatred in his look, only the realization he's been wasting his time. First he had to be polite to the Jew, who deserved to be arrested for consorting with the Muslim. Now he's squandered the whole dinner trying to talk sense into the American.

Our dinner party goes on for another hour. The good cop wants his sons to be computer salesmen. "When the war is over," he assures us, "American investment will be welcome in Banja Luka."

CROSSING SERB-HELD Bosnia by bus provides a vivid corrective to the notion that tribal warfare at the end of the twentieth century is something only dark-skinned people in tropical countries do. The villages through which the bus passes fall into two categories: Serb villages, which are neat, well peopled, and untouched; and Muslim and Croat villages, which are filled with bombed-out mosques, churches, stores, and houses.

Serb officials explain that the towns were destroyed in "the war." But war is random, and in these villages nothing is random. Every house has been destroyed in exactly the same way—from within, by demolition squads. In fact, there's so little external damage that it's clear no battles were fought here at all.

There is no resentful subject population in the towns the Serbs have seized, because there is no one left. One village remains in my mind long after this bus journey ends. The most beautiful long-stemmed yellow flowers are blooming everywhere. In this village not one house is left unburned. There is not one sign of human life—only those glorious yellow flowers. It's as though the flowers, in spectacular profusion, have moved in to fill the ecological niche once held by people.

I'm the only non-Serb on the bus. My fellow passengers are all neatly dressed, respectable people. As I look out the bus window it becomes apparent my fellow passengers do not see what I see. "Oh, that was a church," I murmur as we pass through one village—it was hard at first to tell from the wreckage.

"Sniper," the man behind me says, the word being the same in English and Serbo-Croatian. When, later, we pass a destroyed mosque, he uses another word which is the same in both languages: "mujahedin."

I begin to see what he sees: every Catholic church is a Croat sniper's nest. Every mosque harbors fanatic Muslim fundamentalists determined to inflict genocide on the heroic Serb people.

"So," the man concludes, "we destroy them."

Why such hatred among neighbors who have lived side by side for centuries? The devastation, the inhumanity you see everywhere in Bosnia is a curious example of the triumph of empire long after empires have disappeared. The Serbs, Muslims, and Croats clearly are an identical people, descendants of the same Slav tribesmen who migrated south into the Balkans during the decline of the Roman Empire. They speak the same language, and look indistinguishable. All that really divides them are the different orthographic and ritual peculiarities they inherited from their former imperial masters: the Croats write their common language in Roman script instead of Cyrillic, and they are Roman Catholics instead of Eastern Orthodox Catholics. As for the Muslims, they bear about as much resemblance to Islamic fundamentalists as Unitarians do to Holy Rollers. Nonetheless, because of these acquired differences they are killing each other.

In the Balkan's history of fratricide, the Serbs are hardly the only villains. During World War II, the Croat Nazis, called Ustaše, killed hundreds of thousands of Serbs in concentration camps. When I tell a Serb in one city recently destroyed by systematic bombing, "It must be tough living here," he replies, "It's fine. No more Ustaše." By which he means no more Croats.

It takes the bus nearly nine hours to pick its way along back roads from Banja Luka to Belgrade, a distance of 170 miles. I pass part of the journey reading the numerous press releases handed out at the Serb military headquarters in Banja Luka. The press releases are the literary equivalents of Prijedor—explosions of rage, paranoia, and madness. An official communiqué, entitled "Lying Violent Hands on the Serbian Woman," reads:

> Under such a hot, Balkanic sky every single demonstrative shape of life, every single demonstrative shape of death have been unmeasurably bloodier, more vehement and rougher drawn than gloved Europe could ever imagine. Whatever the criterion of ferociousness is more venomous the roads of human and death are crueler, by all means. Wherever human bodies are getting buried into tombs, bottom of pit cannot be reached. Anyway, both the dagger and the pit have become here an institution of hatred.

A random paragraph from "Catholicity Keeps Imposing Its Attitudes by Force" reads:

> In this war in Yugoslavia, too, Vatican keeps insisting on a sort of national-religious team because of the fact that, through the medium of the faithful Germans, they have germanized the Croats—as Catholics—and used them as live flesh-meat. That's why Vatican is to be responsible for churches were built to be compared more to military bunkers and armament store-houses than to temples of God.

The bus stops at 11 military checkpoints. Eleven times everyone's identity papers are checked. Eleven times a man with a gun looks into the face of each passenger and each passenger looks back. At first I'm worried. I don't have a visa—for either the Serbian Republic of Bosnia or Serbia itself—and it would be tedious, at the least, to spend the night as a prisoner of these troops. But after the first few checks, I relax. The guys with the guns aren't looking for Americans without visas. They're searching for Muslims and Croats.

BEFORE LEAVING Banja Luka, I visited a scientist who, like the neighbor in Prijedor, had already come to terms with the fact he was not going to live much longer. He was a distinguished scholar and civic leader, but he wasn't a Serb. So he sat in his house every day, waiting to die.

His main concern now was saving the mementos of his life. He was trying to find some way to get his university diplomas and scholarly monographs to his children, who were abroad. "That way," he said, "something of me will survive."

Tending bees had been his hobby; now the bees were one of only three things left that gave him hope for survival. "I have $100, some potatoes, and 70 kilos of honey," he told me before I left him to face the Serbs, the winter, and his fate.

I wondered at the time why, in spite of all the dangers, he didn't make a run for it. Now I understood. He probably would have made it to the bus station, maybe been allowed to buy a ticket and board the bus. He might have made it through a couple of checkpoints. But 11 of them? There was no way. At some point the boys with the guns would have taken him.

Though Banja Luka is Bosnia's second largest city, and the most important part of Bosnia under Serb control, no Croat or Muslim artillery shells fall here, the way Serb shells do on the civilian population of Sarajevo. Still, this too is a dying city. The Serbs have won the war for 70 percent of Bosnia. They've also, already, lost the peace. Our official translator—a blonde, friendly, tireless Serb woman—ran a travel agency before the killing started. No tourist will come here again in her lifetime. Her husband is a manager at what used to be Yugoslavia's biggest shoe factory. Now the market is gone:

Croats, Slovenes, and the others would rather go barefoot than wear Serb shoes.

Like Prijedor, Banja Luka is surprisingly pretty; a handsome tree-lined boulevard runs in front of the hotel. But the trees are plastered with obituary notices of boys killed in the war, and the trees themselves will probably be cut down this winter for fuel.

The Serbs believe that if you just expel or kill sufficient numbers of non-Serbs you can create a 100 percent Serb paradise. But it's as crazy to try ethnic cleansing here in Bosnia as it would be in Brooklyn. This is an alphabet soup country, and this is true of everything else too. Banja Luka's electricity comes from a Muslim-held town called Tuzla. Tuzla's water, meanwhile, comes from Banja Luka. This winter people in Banja Luka are dying from the cold, and people in Tuzla are dying from the lack of safe drinking water—while even more people in Sarajevo are dying from lack of both.

In the Banja Luka hotel, too, you can see the future written. When the Serbs seized control, all non-Serbs on the staff were summarily dismissed. The new, Serb staff—overworked and inexperienced—has no incentive to keep things up: the local dinar in which they are paid is even more worthless than the Belgrade dinar. As I leave the restaurant, I pass the kitchen. Leftover food and unwashed dishes cover the dirty stainless steel counters. The smell follows me as I toil up the eight flights to my room in the darkness. Since there's no electricity, there's no elevator, though the hotel generator provides enough current for a dim light at the top of every other landing. Once busy with tourists and visiting businessmen, the hotel is now nearly empty, though occasionally a local couple will check in for the night.

On the fifth-floor landing I hear an extraordinary sound. It's happened to everyone: unexpectedly hearing the sound of strangers engaging in sexual intercourse on the other side of a thin wall. But I have never heard such violence associated with the act of making love. The screams of pain and rage and the violent thudding follow me up to my room, mixed with the smell of the kitchen and the sound of the automatic-rifle fire punctuating the night.

THE PHONE IN my Belgrade Hyatt Regency Hotel room rings at 6:10 p.m. "His Excellency the President will be waiting for you in the Piano Bar at the Intercon at 6:30," the voice says.

While life constantly diminishes in what was once Yugoslavia, the number of presidents constantly increases. Altogether there are now 11 presidents and nine different currencies in the former Yugoslavia, an area only somewhat larger than Minnesota.

Three hours ago, I met President Karadžić of the "Serbian Republic of Bosnia," who is, by profession, a psychiatrist, and, by avocation, a poet. He was holding what was supposed to be a very important press conference. But when the Belgrade press corps assembled, it became apparent that President Karadžić had once again decided to "prove" an Islamic-fundamentalist intervention in Bosnia. Today, he had some "captured" Arab passports. "If this goes on," he warned in a No-More-Mr.-Nice-Guy tone, "we will accept volunteers too."

"Who would fight for you?" one flabbergasted reporter inquired.

"Romanians," the president answered, "and Germans, lots of Germans."

The listeners scratched their heads. The Romanians are Orthodox, but not Slavic. And the Germans, of course, are neither. But President Karadžić quickly drew a veil of discretion over any more explanations. "I will tell you one thing," he said. "Protestants aren't Catholics. The people in England aren't Catholics, either. People in Scandinavia and many other non-Catholic countries are beginning to understand what is at stake in the battle for Bosnia."

Following the press conference, I spoke with the president, who has been accused by the US State Department, among others, of complicity in crimes against humanity. It was just like the dinner in Banja Luka. President Karadžić had no sense of shame or guilt—that is, of right or wrong. "American investment will be welcome in the new Bosnia," he emphasized as we parted.

In the Piano Bar tonight, no fewer than two presidents are holding court. One is the president of Montenegro—a clean-shaven young Serb whose government, it is said, helps make ends meet by counterfeiting Marlboro cigarettes. But I'm here to meet the president with the eyes and beard of Rasputin. His name is Goran Hadžić, and he's president of the Republic of Krajina, which is the official name for the ransacked, Serb-held areas of Croatia. Waiting with the president are two thugs with shirts open to their navels so you can see their crucifixes, which nestle in the hair on their chests, and the automatic pistols under their jackets. President Hadžić himself is incongruously wearing a cotton-candy-colored suit, which contrasts dramatically with his beard, eyes, and flowing hair, all of which are raven-black.

I'm meeting President Hadžić because, as usual, rumors are buzzing around Belgrade that the Serbian President Slobodan Milošević's days in power are numbered. So far, every prediction of Milošević's political demise has been wrong. But what actually would happen if, one way or another, Milošević were really removed from power?

The optimists see salvation, a way to stop the madness and the killing. But the pessimists fear Milošević's removal could lead to a wider war, including a Serb civil war, with fighting right here in Belgrade. And it may be started by the Rasputin look-alike in front of me who, according to numerous sources, has threatened to invade Serbia should his ally Milošević be ousted.

"Croat lies!" he fires back, eyes flashing, when I ask if Krajina will invade should Milošević ever be deposed. To President Hadžić's title, the introductory epithet "crazy" is usually appended. But, in this instance, he proves to have a far stronger grip on reality than most of the "experts" I've met in Belgrade. "For one thing," he points out with clairvoyant accuracy, "Milošević will stay in power."

Then how will the war end?

As the president of Krajina surveys the future, he begins to earn back his epithet. "The war will continue another two or three years," he predicts. And then "the Russians will overthrow the traitor Boris Yeltsin and rescue us." Hadžić can just see the tanks rumbling south as Mother Russia resumes its role as leader of Slav Orthodoxy in its holy war against the Pope and Islam. "After the war is over," he adds, "we will restore the monarchy. Would you like another gin and tonic?"

Before parting, the president of Krajina kindly offers to introduce me to my third president in four hours, the president of Montenegro, who is still sitting on the other side of the Piano Bar.

IN BELGRADE, I have appointments with two more presidents and a prime minister: Yugoslav President Dobrica Cosić, Serbian President Slobodan Milošević, and Yugoslav Prime Minister Milan Panić, who was soon to be defeated by Milošević in the December election, a prospect which did not dim the brightness of his optimism in the slightest.

"First they called me 'the puppet,'" Panić tells me when met at his official residence, a suburban Monticello with all the ambience of a motel. "Then they called me 'the clown.'" One cannot help wondering how this short, wiry, 63-year-old ex-bicycle racer and California multimillionaire became the prime minister of a country that is only a half-step above Iraq on the scale of bad relations with the United States.

"I bicycled to freedom," he explains in a typically pithy pronouncement. After defecting from Yugoslavia in 1955 during an international bicycle race, Panić arrived in the United States with "two suit cases and $20." He found his American dream in pharmaceuticals, and today he's worth nearly half a billion dollars.

Because of his personal history, Panić is one of those people who no longer have a native tongue. He speaks English with a Serb accent and Serbo-Croatian with an American accent, both at the speed of light. In either language he often says out loud what others are only thinking.

"Ignorant, undemocratic, power-hungry politicians" are to blame for the war, declares Panić referring specifically to President Milošević, whom he once advised to go to work at Disneyland and learn from Donald Duck and Goofy. "I've told Milošević to his face he must go," Panić says. "Several times." Like many small men, Panić has an outsize ego. "I'm not sure how long you'll last as prime minister," I tell him, "but you'd be a natural governor of California."

"Why not president?" he asks. "That's constitutionally impossible," I point out. "You weren't born in the United States."

"The US Constitution has been amended 27 times," he replies with a grin. "It can be amended again for me."

I think Panić is only half joking, partly because of the faith his own life has given him that anything, even Yugoslavia, can be fixed only if talented, practical people tackle it. But his rosy optimism now confronted something terrifyingly dark and intractable: Serb chauvinism.

"They just don't get it," says the prime minister, launching into a more damning critique of the Serb mentality than any that have appeared in the international press. "These guys have got to understand that you just don't accomplish anything by trying to solve problems through force."

But the optimism is irrepressible, and Panić is soon talking about the limitless possibilities of the country if only it were run by live wires like him. "They can learn," he says enthusiastically, "but in order to learn you must be taught." From his press kit, he pulls out his favorite teaching aid, the "Bill of Responsibilities," published by the Freedoms Foundation at Valley Forge, Pennsylvania. He ticks off the obligations of responsibility until he comes to the one that resonates with what I had seen in Bosnia: "To respect the property of others, both private and public."

"But all this is meaningless to such people," I object.

"It must be made meaningful," he insists.

There is nothing hope and hard work can't achieve, according to Milan Panić, as the articles in his press kit demonstrate. THIS IS NOT A WAR OF HATE, argues one headline. NO IDEA IS WORTH KILLING FOR, proclaims another. Panić PROMISES TO CLOSE SERBIAN CAMPS IN BOSNIA, reports a third. And then the most forthright and wishful thought, reflecting his own incredible journey: YUGOSLAVS WILL LIVE LIKE AMERICANS.

A week after meeting Panić, I visit Yugoslav President Cosić, a courtly 72-year-old who is Serbia's most revered living novelist. The president receives me in the same vast salon where Tito received the world's statesmen, and begins the questioning: how sweet do I like my coffee?

The president makes it clear he would prefer to discuss viticulture and literature to warfare; writing novels is his vocation, cultivating grapes his avocation.

"Mr. President," I say, "people tell me your novels are a major source of this catastrophe."

"Please study my books," he replies, his eyes twinkling. "You'll not find one passage in which I condone ethnic cleansing."

Cosić has been described variously as the Solzhenitsyn or the Tolstoy of Serbia. His novels, vast romantic depictions of Mother Serbia's thousand-year struggle for freedom, are certainly not programs for the genocide of non-Serbs. "But," one person who has studied them told me, "they were decisive in creating the intellectual and emotional climate of Serb nationalism in which such outrages came to seem rational. As discontent grew with Tito and Communism, Serbs had a choice between a future on the Western European model or retreating into the mythical heroics of the past. They chose the past, in large part because of Cosić."

Like most presidents in Yugoslavia, Cosić is on his way somewhere, in this case Geneva, where, as always, some breakthrough to peace seems imminent. "Next time," says the president, smiling and shaking my hand, "we'll discuss books, we'll sip wine, we'll get to the bottom of things."

"The president fully understands the dimensions of the catastrophe," some one close to Cosić assures me later. "He understands how his own work has been used to justify criminal excesses of Serb nationalism. Now he is determined, if he can, to write a happy ending. Believe me, if he could remove Milošević and stop the war, he would." But in the end, of course, it would be Milošević who would replace Cosić.

The surreal irony of the situation was that Milošević had created the men who were trying to depose him. In mid-1992, when Serb atrocities in Bosnia first outraged the world, Milošević decided to apply some cosmetics to the face of his regime. So he arranged to have the grandfatherly Cosić made president of what remained of the Yugoslav federation. In turn Cosić, with Milošević approval, appointed Milan Panić, the amiable Serb-American multimillionaire.

But though they turned on him, Cosić and Panić inadvertently served Milošević's grand design very well. The Serbs have spoken with so many contradictory and confusing voices that outsiders could choose to hear whatever they wanted. "Milošević is a genius when it comes to confusing things," a Belgrade realist pointed out. "That's how he stays in power. That's why he's winning." And so, while still controlling everything, Milošević camouflaged himself in a babble of voices.

Later, I remembered what one of Panić's American aides had told me: "I was covered in blood." When he first was named prime minister, Panić had flown into Sarajevo, dreaming he could make peace with a single, dramatic gesture. But neither his courage nor his idealism impressed the snipers. One shot hit his aide's car, and the US journalist traveling alongside bled to death in his arms.

And in the end, Milan Panić would leave office as he entered it—with everything just as Milošević himself wanted it: covered in blood.

I AM LEFT with one president to go, by far the most important—Slobodan Milošević. On the surface Milošević, like Serbia itself, seems modern: he speaks English and dresses like the international banker he once was, representing a Yugoslav state bank in New York. But beneath the pinstripes beat the great, dark themes of Serb nationalism: religion, ideology, death, and bitterness. His father was an Orthodox priest, his mother a devout Communist. Both committed suicide, foreshadowing the double suicide over which their son has presided—first, of Yugoslavia itself; second, and far more important, the suicide of the politics of interethnic harmony it once embodied.

To understand the legacy of Serb bitterness Milošević inherited and exploited, you have to go all the way back to 1389, when the Serbs lost a battle in the southern region of Kosovo to the Turks, who maintained control of the area until 1912. Most national myths are built on victories, but for half a millennium the Battle of Kosovo has been the defining moment of the Serb people, who see themselves, often with reason, as outnumbered victims of barbaric aggression, betrayed by the world.

This chronic Serb sense of aggrievement produced its most tragic result in 1914, when Gavrilo Princip—Serb nationalist terrorist and spiritual grandfather of today's Serb terrorists—assassinated Archduke Franz Ferdinand in Sarajevo. When World War I was over, the victors gathered at Versailles to draw the boundaries of the new Europe. At the cost of millions dead, Princip achieved his objective: the destruction of the hated Austrian and Ottoman empires, traditional oppressors of the Serb people.

But, as Serbs saw it, their dream of a unified "Greater Serbia" had been betrayed once again. The entry of the United States into the fighting, followed by President Wilson's Fourteen Points, had transformed the conflict into "the war to end all wars." Wilson's solution for ending all wars was simple—and, as the future would prove, simple-minded as well. Since wars in Europe were fought over national boundaries, Wilson concluded that the way to prevent future wars was to redraw the map of Europe so that each national group lived, happy and contented, in a nice little nation-state of its own. In some cases it was possible to impose borders that bore some reasonable relation to reality. But when it came to Serbia and its adjacent lands, the demographers threw up their hands. It was no more possible to draw neat national boundaries in the region in 1919 than it would be at the UN today.

So a new multinational empire was cobbled together, called the Kingdom of Serbs, Croats, and Slovenes. It included territories that had previously been parts of Austria, Hungary, Turkey, Serbia, and Montenegro. Though its peoples were mostly Slavs who largely spoke the same language, what really united them was hate.

In 1934, just twenty years after the murder of Archduke Ferdinand, a Croat terrorist killed King Aleksandar Karadjordjević of Yugoslavia, as it was now known, during a state visit to France. This crime was as fateful for Yugoslavia as Princip's original crime had been for the world. It destroyed at a stroke any possibility of Yugoslav cohesion in the era of Hitler and Mussolini. Five years later, when World War II began, the "Yugoslavs" turned on one another with a viciousness that mirrored the collapse of European civilization. From 1941 to 1945, 1.7 million Yugoslavs, more than 10 percent of the total population, were killed—mostly by other Yugoslavs. The Croat Fascists—the Ustaše—treated Serbs the same way the Germans treated Jews, deepening the Serb sense of victimization.

Yet after the war, these disputatious peoples, more divided than ever because of the recent atrocities, were forced to live together again, under the control of Josip Broz, the peasant son of a Croat father and Slovene mother. Like many a Balkan king, he began as a warlord and, even before assuming power, took a reign name: Tito. For thirty-five years the Communist dictator, who dressed in a white field marshal's uniform and lived in palaces all over the country, ruled his strange, hybrid country with an iron hand and a velvet touch. But in the power vacuum left by Tito's death, history was preparing to repeat itself.

The Croats, Slovenes, and others were tired of repression, tired of Com-

munism—most of all tired of living under what they regarded as Serb domination. But as Serbs saw it, they were the victims. Even today Serbs constantly
point out that "Josip Broz" was no Serb—only the latest in a string of foreign
oppressors. And the Serb sense of bitterness and betrayal resulted in a repudi-
ation of Tito that had a typical Balkan twist to it: many Serbs believed Tito
was not a man. "He was a woman," people still say, in all seriousness—a cas-
tration of the dominant Yugoslav leader of the twentieth century that sums up
the Serbs' own sense of having been emasculated by history.

In Tito's Yugoslavia, Milošević was a climbing apparatchik. Within years
of the dictator's death, he had become the acknowledged leader of the Serbs.
In 1987, Serb nationalists started holding demonstrations at the hallowed
Kosovo battle site, protesting the political power exercised by the region's
Muslim Albanian majority. Things got out of hand when the government television channel, which Milošević controlled, showed Albanian police beating
Serb demonstrators. Instead of calming the situation, Milošević turned crisis
into tragedy. He denounced the local authorities, and roused the Serbs to a
fever pitch of indignation. "No one will beat you again," he vowed—a
promise he betrayed soon afterwards when his tanks crushed democracy
demonstrators on the streets of Belgrade.

The faceless apparatchik was now a national hero. By 1989, he had
imposed a police state on Serbia with predictable consequences. As Slovenia,
Croatia, and Bosnia broke away, Milošević took them on in the same brutal
way he had dealt with the Albanians in Kosovo. "If we must fight, then by
God we will fight," he declared in a famous speech. "Because if we don't know
how to work well or to do business, at least we know how to fight well."

My interview with Milošević is set for a Tuesday, three p.m. sharp.
Staffers at the Serb Ministry of Information are amazed. "He never gives interviews!" one exclaims. Diplomatic and journalistic friends are less surprised than
confused. "He never lets himself get caught in a situation where he can be asked
questions he can't answer," one chief of mission tells me. "He avoids responsibility for his actions. That's how he stays in power. I bet he's just diddling you,
just like he diddles Lord Owen and Cyrus Vance, and Panić and Cosić."

"If Milošević doesn't want to see me," I ask, "why wouldn't he just say
no?"

"Milošević is a conspirator," he answers. "He survives by confusing people. That's how he distracts people from what he's really doing."

In the end, of course, the paranoids are right. The meeting is canceled—
though I am assured it has only been postponed. This goes on for a week.

"The game is not completely played out yet," an ambassador in Belgrade tells me a couple of days later. On one of his crested cocktail napkins he
writes down six numerals. "The number in Milošević's bunker," he explains.
When he is in Belgrade, Milošević reportedly spends most of his time in a
windowless, bombproof command center in the basement of the presidential
palace. "Call around five tomorrow afternoon," advises the ambassador. "I
have reason to suspect he'll be there."

The next day, at exactly five o'clock, I dial the six digits. The phone rings once. "Yes," answers a voice.

"President Milošević," I say quickly, "I'm calling about our appointment. The situation is so tragic. Please avail yourself of this opportunity to talk to the American—"

"No!" interjects the voice, and there is a click.

I dial again, but the phone rings 20, 30 times with no answer. I imagine Milošević sitting in his underground bunker, listening to the phone ring over and over again, both the master and the prisoner of the situation he has created.

It is said that one of the Serbian president's principal activities in his bunker is determining just what goes on government television—an important question in a country where there is little other nightly entertainment. One Saturday I watch an entire evening of Belgrade TV. What impresses me the most is not the Serb propaganda on the "news" programs but the brutality of the entire programming package. From Bosnia, there is a report on Muslim atrocities, which may or may not have occurred, but the camera keeps zooming in on a man in a coffin, his face crawling with maggots. Shortly afterward, porno videos—not the sort of bosomy romps shown on American cable but fellatio, cunnilingus, and penetration, all in graphic close-up—came on the government channel.

"You're right to link the government approach to killing with the government approach to sex," an elderly woman tells me later. A Serb by birth and an Italian countess by marriage, she is one of Belgrade's authentic legends. "Nothing Croats or Muslims or anyone else does can excuse your own crimes," she once declared. Her public outrage at Serb actions has resulted in death threats, and recently, on a main street in Belgrade, in broad daylight, this old lady was shot through the hand by a sniper.

In the ensuing weeks, Milošević diddles everybody. He promises to allow UN surveillance teams into Sarajevo, but the shelling of the city never stops. In the meantime, the Serbs begin another major offensive in Bosnia, moving forward, inexorably and brutally, to fulfill Milošević's dark dream.

VUKOVAR IS THE most peaceful city in Milošević's Greater Serbia, and since it is Sunday we visit a church. The church is also very peaceful because it is a ruin, like everything in Vukovar—not almost everything, not practically everything, *everything.* The Yugoslav army systematically destroyed Vukovar—street by street, house by house. The peacefulness of Vukovar is the peacefulness of total devastation, total death. Surveying the ruins, I think of Hue following the Tet offensive, or of Beirut. But they never were as dead as this. In the bright afternoon sunlight Vukovar, demolished in the summer of 1991, is like one of those ghost cities of India, where 1,000 or 2,000 years ago a brilliant civilization flourished, then was extinguished.

Absurdly, money is scattered all over the church ruins like wastepaper, along with catechisms. No one picks up the money, just as no one prays here, because there are no people here anymore. I pick up a First Communion card with a little girl's photo on it and some old Yugoslav dinars to keep as souvenirs.

Vukovar, at least in terms of ruined buildings, is the biggest city in the Serbian Republic of Krajina, the president of which I'd met in the Piano Bar at the Intercon in Belgrade. "Krajina" consists of the parts of Croatia the Serbs grabbed last year when Croatia declared its independence. Everywhere the pattern was the same—the pattern I first observed in Prijedor. Serb terrorists overthrew the local government and killed the local notables. In terror, non-Serbs, along with a lot of Serbs, fled, and "Greater Serbia" gained another province. Only in Vukovar, as in Sarajevo, people resisted. So Vukovar was destroyed, as Sarajevo is in the process of being destroyed right now.

When I ask Serb friends about Vukovar, they answer as they always do: it was the Croats' fault, just as it was the Muslims' fault in Bosnia, and the Albanians' fault in Kosovo. The Croats shouldn't have resisted. Anyway, Vukovar really was a Serb city, and this also gave them the right to destroy it.

In fact, according to official statistics, 84,024 people lived in Vukovar and its environs before the killing started. Of these, 43.7 percent were Croat, 37.4 percent, Serb, and 18.9 percent, "other," which actually means "both"—since most of the "others" would have been either the children of mixed marriages or partners in them. Now not more than a few hundred people are still alive in Vukovar. "I need some footage of life among the ruins," says Tom Aspell, an NBC correspondent, so we go searching. The only signs of life are occasional clumps of men—some armed, some not—sitting out in the sunshine, in front of bombed-out buildings, drinking.

Then we see a lovely old couple working in their garden. May we visit them?

They would be delighted. She rushes to make coffee, while he shows us the garden—tomatoes, pumpkins, plums. After serving the coffee, the old woman sits down in front of Tom's camera and is asked to describe what happened here. Immediately, she starts crying. She tells us that she and her neighbors spent nine weeks huddling in her basement without fuel, water, or sanitation. They survived on rotting potatoes. The nearest water was a hundred yards away. Sometimes, when one of them went for water, she didn't make it back, and the others stayed in the cellar, dying of thirst, too frightened to go searching for water or the body.

Out in the garden the old man has been trying to amass firewood, but the stack he's gathered so far wouldn't last two weeks in winter. As soon as you got a fire started, the heat would rush away through the cracks and holes in the house. The exterior is pock-marked with bullet holes, and the concussion from an artillery shell has knocked off part of the roof, but it still looks like a house. Only inside can you see the real damage. Insulation gone, windows gone, floor boards severed—this house can't shelter human life anymore.

These people, whose house and life were destroyed by Serb artillery, happen to be Serbs themselves. And like most Serbs the old man loves America because he believes America is the natural friend of the Serbs. "America must establish a program to reconstruct Vukovar," he tells me. His own program is quite specific: "Please have the Americans send me a boat," he says. He explains: "My boat was destroyed in the shelling. When the Americans replace my boat I can catch fish in the Danube."

"Was this an entirely Serb neighborhood?" I ask.

"No," his wife replies. "Slovenes next door. A Croat-Serb couple over there, Muslims, Hungarians, but mostly mixed marriages. This was not a Serb neighborhood." She tries to remember what kind of a neighborhood it had been. "It was a Yugoslav neighborhood," she says.

After we say good-bye, Tom decides, "Now I need to do a stand-up, desolation as the backdrop." He picks a crossroads of desolation, what once must have been a busy intersection downtown. Nearby stands the only undamaged building in Vukovar. It's intact because it was built after the fighting stopped. It's called the Donald Duck Café.

The Serb driver and I go in while Tom does his stand-up. Actually, the driver isn't really a driver. He's a physicist, but, as he explains, "there's not much work for scientists in ex-Yugoslavia."

We pass the time talking about the Heisenberg uncertainty principle and the enigma of causality. Obviously there's a reason things happen and, even more important, a reason things don't happen—a reason Vukovar was destroyed, and other cities were not. But what is the reason? In our time, quantum physics and history have converged. We know more and more about quarks and neutrinos, but these sub-atomic particles have turned out to be like Yugoslav history. The more you know, the less explicable things become. Do the Ottomans and Habsburgs really explain why Croats and Serbs are killing each other right now? Was what happened 30 or 1,000 years ago the "cause" of Vukovar's destruction?

"Vukovar should not be rebuilt," the driver-physicist announces. "It should be left as it is, as a monument to human folly." Being a good Serb, he has not said "to Serb folly." He goes on to say, "I would fight and die for Serbia. But what Serbia?" he continues. "Not the Serbia that destroyed Vukovar."

He then describes the mythical Serbia of great artists, poets, and scientists, that magnificent bulwark of civilization in the Balkans glorified in the novels of Dobrica Cosić—the hallucination of which, in fact, was the reason for the death of Vukovar and all the other deaths. Like all Serbs I meet, he just doesn't get it. In Europe at the end of the twentieth century, to believe it is right to kill for any nation is not the source of the madness. It is the madness itself.

The Donald Duck Café is like the bar scene in Star Wars. One guy here is five-five, 350 pounds, and has six fingers on each hand. From the ruins, mutants have arisen. The Donald Duck Café is where they do their deals: currency, cigarettes, VCRs, guns, ammo, anything you want.

"Which is the killer?" I ask the driver-physicist.

"They're all killers," he replies, referring to our fellow patrons.

"No, I'm not talking about snipers and artillery. I mean, which one actually kills people with his own hands?"

"That one," he says, making his choice with the slightest nod of the head. "He looks normal."

"AND THE COLORED girls go—"

"Voulez-vous coucher avec moi, ce soir—"

"Take me to the pilot, take me to the pilot of your soul—"

According to the music, we are lost between the moon and New York City. But we're actually in a disco in Priština, capital of Kosovo, a region also known in press dispatches as "the tinderbox of the Balkans" and "the war waiting to happen." In this godforsaken place, halfway between Bulgaria and Albania, the 1970s, it seems, never ended, at least in this disco. Everyone's wearing blue jeans, some with bell-bottoms.

Priština, like the rest of Kosovo, might be in Asia Minor. Beyond the modern buildings and tree-lined boulevards downtown, Priština is a Levantine city: winding alleys, lamb roasting on spits, mustachioed men gossiping in coffeehouses.

Priština isn't like Vukovar. The buildings are still standing; there's been no war here yet. Nationalism has created a different horror here—the Serb version of apartheid. Albanians aren't allowed in this disco, or into the modern hotel where we are staying, or anywhere downtown.

Three years ago, under President Milošević's orders, the Serbs did here what they later did in Prijedor, and in most places where they've seized power. All non-Serbs were summarily fired from their jobs, which were then given to Serbs. The Albanians' political and economic rights were extinguished. In essence this was the first of all the Milošević-sponsored coups d'état through which the Serbs would try to "cleanse" the parts of Croatia and Bosnia they wanted for themselves.

But how to "cleanse" an area where Serbs are outnumbered nine to one?

There were simply too many non-Serbs to do what was done in Prijedor, so the Serbs opted for making life miserable for the Albanians: their jobs were taken away; classes at the university were taught in Serbo-Croation only; the official use of the Albanian language was prohibited.

Meanwhile, in this disco, the Serbs party. And they smile at you. They are as delighted to see you as the police chief of Banja Luka was, because they believe that, once you see Kosovo, you will see things as they see them.

Various Serbs patiently explain it to me—why Albanians do not have the same rights Serbs do. I can never fully grasp the argument. But in Belgrade, Professor Mihailo Marković, a Serb intellectual who has spent much time in the United States, comes closest.

When Yugoslavia was established following World War I, he reminds me, it was initially called the Kingdom of Serbs, Croats, and Slovenes. "They were the constituent peoples of Yugoslavia," he elaborates. "Therefore they have the right to dissolve the state and to redefine its internal boundaries," which is certainly one way of describing what happened in places like Vukovar. "However, the Albanians are not a constituent people. Hence, they possess no such right."

"But so few Serbs live in Kosovo," I reply, "and it's only been a part of Serbia since 1912. Why shouldn't the Albanians have the same—"

Behind the professor's elegant legalisms glints the madness of history. "Kosovo is Serb," he says. "It always has been Serb. It always will be."

IT'S 6:30 A.M. I'm waiting outside the hotel in Priština with two heavy suitcases. I've lugged them down the street a ways. This is because the Albanian president of Kosovo, Ibrahim Rugova, whom I interviewed yesterday, was kind enough to offer me a lift to Skopje, the capital of Macedonia—the least known and happiest of Yugoslavia's breakaway republics. But Albanians, even presidents, aren't allowed inside the Priština hotel.

What happens if an Albanian does enter one of these Serb preserves? "The first time they beat you up," one Albanian told me when I suggested he meet me for coffee in the hotel. "The second time they kill you."

So the arrangement is this: I'll be waiting as inconspicuously as possible down the street from the hotel when the Albanian car drives up as inconspicuously as possible. As soon as it arrives I'll jump in.

Over in the Albanian section of Priština, the president is waiting in another car. The idea was that this morning we could talk in the car. But now he says, "I don't think you should come in the car with me. You go in the other car."

I ask why. "Sometimes Serb troops stop my car," he answers. "They devise certain humiliations. When we're safely inside Macedonia, you can ride with me, and we'll talk."

We drive south through the glorious autumn foliage toward Macedonia; except for the minarets, Kosovo looks like Vermont. At the border, each car is stopped, then is waved on. Stop, wave, except with the president's car, which gets a long stop before the wave comes.

A hundred yards inside Macedonia the two cars pull over, and I get in the back with the president. Of course, like all the presidents I've interviewed in Yugoslavia, he's not a real president. No one recognizes the Albanian Republic of Kosovo except Albania. But after the Serbs disenfranchised the Albanians, the Albanians went ahead and held their own election, and chose him as chief of state.

"What's your background?" I ask.

"I'm a literary theoretician," he replies in perfect French. "A Constructivist. I wrote my thesis in Paris." He adds, "I never thought I'd be a president, but after the Serbs closed down the university where I was a professor, I emerged as a kind of spokesman. One thing led to another and so here I am today. Did you visit our PEN center?"

Under President Rugova's leadership the Albanians—in contrast to the Croats and Bosnians—have opted for nonviolent resistance. Beside their PEN center, they've got a branch of Amnesty International and close ties with human rights groups around the world.

All this has created problems for the Serbs. If the Albanians were shooting at them, that would provide a pretext for "cleansing." But the Albanians go in for international solidarity, not guerrilla warfare. The president today is on his way to visit England, as the guest of some human-rights-concerned MPs. I'm bemused by this French-intellectual, chain-smoking, Islamic-secularist Albanian president. "A Constructivist president in a deconstructionist country," I remark.

"You could put it that way," he answers.

Knowing how French-educated intellectuals think, I say, "Among American writers, you prefer Hemingway to Fitzgerald, and Faulkner to Hemingway?"

"Most of all," the president answers, "I love Edgar Allan Poe."

AT THE SERB Ministry of Information in Belgrade they give you brown paper shopping bags, complete with the ministry logo on them, to carry the propaganda, the passion, and the hate away. It's all the same stuff I first saw in Banja Luka, only written in correct English and printed on glossy paper.

One expensively produced brochure contains page after page of old photographs of severed Serb heads. "Never Again" is its title, referring to Croat atrocities during World War II. But, of course, it is happening again, and one reason is that in these official documents there's the same revelry in brutalization that's followed me everywhere in the territories Serbs control.

Ostensibly, these raging diatribes I carry back to my hotel in the Ministry of Information shopping bag are meant to show the world how evil all the innumerable enemies of the Serbs are. But this propaganda really shows how successfully the Serbs have poisoned their own minds. The ministry also publishes a monthly periodical, scholarly in format. It shows that self-brutalization takes an intellectual form as well.

The publication is supposedly a compendium of distinguished commentary on the Yugoslav crisis. But the articles bear titles such as "The Evil Deeds of a Slav Pope," "Satanization of Serbia," and "European Hoodlum Democracy Will Not Break the Serbs."

Along with the satanization of everyone else, and the Serb bravado, there is the whining self-pity that runs through all extreme Serb nationalist discourse. "How Lies Travel Around the World," laments one article. "The German Do Not Want Our Mathematicians," complains another.

The ladies at the ministries of information treated me very kindly while I was in Belgrade. I say "ministries" because, just as Belgrade has two presidents, it has two ministries of information: one Serb, one federal. The ladies at the ministries run to a refined, admirable type. They work very hard; they dress very demurely; they are very polite; and they all seem well into middle age. The best word to describe them is "maternal," and certainly they brought a motherly quality to their treatment of me. They answered faxes; they found facts and statistics. They got important interviews for me. They were as kind as they could be.

I wanted to show two of these ladies my gratitude; after some reflection I invited them to high tea at the Hyatt. There's a lovely salon at the far end of the atrium, which looks as if it might be in Back Bay Boston. Exquisite pastries are displayed on an antique mahogany table. Waitresses wearing frilly white aprons pour tea from a silver service into porcelain cups.

My invitation aroused discreet excitement. Finally the great day arrived. As we ordered our tea and selected our pastries, it seemed to me these two ladies had had their hair done for the occasion.

We had an unspoken pact: we would discuss only light, happy things over tea. I diverted them for a time by discussing how difficult it was for foreigners to pronounce Serb names. "Your system of writing is too logical," I said. "It helplessly confuses people who speak languages like English, where the way words are spelled has no necessary connection with the way they are spoken. Take President Cosić," I went on. "I can only get his name right if I first remind myself it sounds something like 'sausage.'"

The two ladies tittered appreciatively at this witticism, and I continued: "And President Karadžić. I can never get that right. Karadžić? Karadžić! Karadžić," I said, trying out several pronunciations.

"Karadžić! President Karadžić!" the young man at the next table called out to us. He rose and rushed over to us. "You know President Karadžić?" he asked in Serbian, the ladies translating. "I have met him," I replied. "Do you know him?"

"President Karadžić is my friend," he said, beaming.

"Please sit down," I said.

"What do you do?" he asked.

"I'm a writer. What do you do?"

"I am a killer," he said.

"Oh, whom do you kill?"

"I used to kill people in Sarajevo," he answered. "Now I kill people in Belgrade."

The young man began pulling out all sorts of documents, which I handed to the ladies to translate. "I didn't just kill people in Sarajevo," he said. "Two years ago I killed many people in Krajina, children and women. Then I killed people in Vukovar."

"But the war hadn't started two years ago in Krajina."

"We had started," he said.

"And what brings you to the Hyatt?" I asked.

"I like it here!" he said. "It's cozy. The service is good. And the ice cream! The ice cream here is wonderful."

"Yes," I said, "I understand that. But what I really meant to ask, if you will excuse me, is how can you afford to eat here? Tea and cakes here cost more than most Serbs now earn in a week."

"Oh, I have no problem with money," he answered. "I have plenty of money."

"Where do you get the money?"

"President Karadžić gives it to me."

"President Karadžić personally?"

"His people give it to me. Also General Ratko Mladić," he added, referring to the Serb officer commanding the artillery attacks on Sarajevo. "Fifty thousand deutsche marks at a time."

"Why do they give you the money?"

"I buy things for them, and then, when I have bought the things, they give me another 50,000 deutsche marks. You can buy anything on the Belgrade black market," he said with a grin, as though it were an ice-cream shop. "But sometimes you buy things and, even though you have paid for them, people don't deliver."

"What do you do then?"

"First I tear out their fingernails, then I cut off their thumbs; if that doesn't work I slit their throats. You're staying here in Hyatt?" he concluded. "What's your room number?"

The two ladies looked at me, curious as to how I would respond.

"As a matter of fact I'm not staying at the Hyatt," I lied affably, trying to smile naturally. "I'm staying at the Moskva, downtown."

"What room number?"

"Three-oh-eight," I replied, praying there was a Room 308 at the Moskva Hotel. "As a matter of fact I have to get back, and I promised these two charming ladies a lift downtown."

"Do you have to leave so soon? I enjoy talking with you. I could buy you some ice cream," he pleaded. "Oh well, I'll look for you at the Moskva. I don't have enough friends in Belgrade."

Very slowly the three of us walked the enormous length of the Hyatt atrium, careful not to appear to be hurrying. Only when we got outside, beyond the enormous glass doors, did our three heads swivel backward involuntarily, in unison.

No, he had not followed us.

According to the documents he had showed us, they told me, his story checked out. Buried among the papers was one advising psychiatric counseling.

"What if he finds you?" one of the ladies asked.

"How can he find me? He thinks I'm at the Moskva."

"You gave him your card." It was true. As a kind of friendship gift, he'd given me an Arkan button—Arkan being the nickname of Zelko Ražnjatović, one of the most notorious and popular terrorists in Serbia, and also an elected member of the Serb parliament. In return, I'd given him my card.

"But it only has my New York address on it." Yet at that moment we all felt the force of it: how the insane can make connections, discover secrets, seek you out.

"Well, in that case, I'm sure it will be all right," she said quickly, grasping my hand in thanks. "The tea was wonderful."

The other lady added, "Had I read about this in your article—and I am sure you will put it in your article—I would not have believed it, even though I know you personally. Except—"

"Except," she went on, "there are boys like him all over Belgrade these days. Only the other morning, while I was waiting in line for the bus, a young man was boasting to everyone about the people he'd tortured in Bosnia."

"I don't understand," she added as we said good-bye for the last time, "what is being done to the Serbs."

After double-bolting the door of my room, I turned on the TV: Sarajevo, as usual; artillery shells falling. I realized I had no idea what artillery shells cost. Could you buy one, several, or many of them for fifty thousand deutsche marks?

That night, when the knock came on the door, I didn't know what to do. Ignore it? Pretend no one was here? But the TV was on.

The knock came again, persistent. I walked to the door and, as silently as I could, moved the little metal cover out of the way so I could look through the little glass eye in the door. It was the night maid, come to turn down the bed.

That moment, walking to the door, was the only moment in Yugoslavia when I felt real terror. But even then, what appalled me most wasn't the boy who had given me the Arkan button but those last words the nice lady from the ministry said to me: *"I don't understand what is being done to the Serbs."*

For as long as I can foresee, all journeys among the Serbs will begin and end as mine began and ended, in encounters with madness. The terror will always be no farther away than the smiling face at the next table—until the Serbs find some way to confront not what "the world" has done to them but what they have done to themselves.

TRANSLATIONS FROM MAK DIZDAR

Sleepers Under the Stone

FRANCIS R. JONES

1978

STUDENTS ESCAPING the smog of Sarajevo, we stepped out into the little valley town late in the afternoon. The driver snapped off the skirling pop-kolo, climbed down the coach steps and headed caféwards. Quiet—lime trees round the square, the rush of a river over a weir.

Just beyond it, Nermina had promised us the finest mosque in the Balkans—which turned out to be a small, white, empty, perfect cube, its interior picked out in mock-solemn green and red arabesques. Outside—chestnut trees, the fruit spiky and green, and cheerful, turbanned gravestones.

Bob and I leant over the bridge as we left, spotting trout against the shingle. Nermina joined us. "Nice place to be buried," I quipped.

She smiled briefly. "You know what happened in the war? Here they drowned the Muslims in the river."

"Who did?"

She shrugged. And then we noticed the inscriptions on the stones—so many with one day in 1942.

Next day, Bogomil cemetery. It was hot; the morning breeze had dropped by the time we arrived at the metal fence. Inside, the stećci: rows of four-foot-high stone oblongs in the straggling, yellow grass, some with pitched roofs like houses for the dead. No guard, no visitors but ourselves. The gate opened and we drifted in different directions. On the near end of the first tomb, I saw a vine heavy with fruit; along its side ran a frieze of crescents and crosses, beneath it a line of stylized, full-skirted women dancing the kolo. About to turn to see the other end, I looked ahead, and found myself face-to-face with a man whose head was the sun and whose enormous left hand was raised palm-first at me—the Heretic Christ. On the next stone, the sleeper under the stone, an armed giant, brandishing a bow in his right hand and his left hand again raised—to do what? A snake as thick as my wrist—no stone dragon this—slithered in panic half a meter in front of me, heading for the long grass round the tomb. I turned and sauntered in feigned nonchalance back to the others.

RAISED TO DO what? No one knows. There are theories of course. To stop the sinful, to halt the holy Crusaders at war with those who worshipped the True, the Heretic Christ. Or to ward off the evil eye. Or in greeting to the stranger. No one knows.

Precious little, in fact, is known about the Bogomil heretics. Except for three religious texts (one of them a version of the Lord's Prayer with one word amended), we only have the tracts and inquisitors' guides of their enemies, whom the Bogomils saw as the servants of the Church of the Whore in Rome.

These tracts tell us that the heresy developed in tenth-century Bulgaria from a mixture of Eastern dualist beliefs. The founder of the sect was a village priest turned itinerant preacher called Bogomil—"Dear to God." His was a dour faith for a harsh world. It taught that the earth was created by the Devil: thus all its hierarchies—bailiff, King, priest, Pope—were inherently evil. As a result Bogomilism appealed strongly to the feudal poor, cropping up in different guises over the following centuries and throughout medieval Europe—as Catharism in France, for instance.

Not surprisingly, the mighty of Church and State tried ferociously to stamp it out: through propaganda—the English word "bugger" is a medieval version of "Bulgar," sodomy being the standard vice imputed to heretics; failing that, through Crusades which offered the righteous the choice of forcible conversion or slaughter.

Many chose the latter, for it mattered little. By dying they renounced the devil's works and turned toward God. Soon, very soon, they would be raised from their graves to sit at Christ's right hand, and their tormentors would be cast into the outer darkness.

Indeed, the Bogomils' cosmology differed dangerously from Roman and Byzantine dogma. Two of their texts—the apocryphal Vision of Isaiah and Secret Supper—tell that, in the beginning, God had two sons, Sataniel the elder and Christ the younger. Sataniel, with his angels, rebelled against God. Sataniel, attempting to emulate his father's sublime act of creation, shaped only grotesque parodies: instead of heaven, this earth; instead of the angels, a thing called man. And even then, his creatures would not move or breathe until he had stolen a flame of divine fire and hidden a spark at each man's heart.

Yet this very act was Sataniel's undoing and man's salvation. For God sent Christ, his younger son, to earth—no man he, but pure spirit, untainted by the excrement of flesh. And, as fire seeks its source, each spark might turn towards the blaze of light that is the undying Christ. But Sataniel's call is stronger. Few, too few, have recognized the light and turned their backs on the two darknesses around them: this earth and this flesh.

But the end is at hand: one day soon Christ will return in glory, destroy utterly all his brother's works, and lead the spirits of the chosen—his father's beloved—into the new Jerusalem.

A DOUR FAITH indeed. Not surprisingly, the Bogomils paid an ungodly price for declaring their spiritual and temporal betters to be the agents of Satan. More surprising, perhaps, is the adoption of the Bogomil faith by the Princes of Bosnia, who sought to build a statelet from the rubble of Stefan Dušan's Serbian Empire after his death in 1355. What form of compromise must have been made, for a faith that spurned the world to become an arm of the state, remains unknown. They left no texts, only stones.

A few years later, in 1389, the brief unity of the Christian states of the Balkans was shattered by the Ottoman Turks at Kosovo, the Blackbirds' Field. One by one, the vassal states were merged into the Empire.

In Serbia, the conquered people clung to their church as a symbol of nationhood. The Bosnian and Hercegovinian peasants, however, had known only oppression and slaughter from Rome and Byzantium. As their own church, founded upon the untemporal, faded into folk memory, the temporal advantages of taking the new state faith weighed all the stronger. And so they turned to Islam.

1993

AND YET, AS the Bogomil said, each state must crumble to the dust of which it is made. The Ottoman Empire is no more, and live-and-let-live pragmatism of Balkan Islam has no place in an age of terrible purity. Twice this century have the Crusaders come again with fire and the knife and the one true faith, to harry the heretic folk of Bosnia and Hercegovina from their homes, to drown and stab and rape and burn.

Over the stones, smoke drifts once more on the wind. Under the stones, the chosen sleep. But the day they shall wake is at hand.

ROADS

1

You have decreed me not to be cost what may
Charging me down
You laugh and weep
On your way
You purge all clean
You wipe all out

You have decided to wipe me out whatever the price
Yet nowhere will you find
The real
Road to me

For
You know roads carved and cleared
But none beyond
(Barren they be and narrow indeed
No matter how broad
And long
They seem
To you
So proud
And strong)

You know only the paths
That rise
From heart
And
Eyes

But that is not all

2

Roads unfold ahead
With no trace of beaten track
No almanac
Departure time
Or tide

Your path to me in my misery
Seems trodden and tried in your sight
The sort
That leads
Left
Or
Right

You fool yourself I can be found
If you follow a course
Like north
Or
South

But that is not all

Hide and seek
Eyes peeled
Come and find me
Beneath the rye rippling in the wind
In the roots of earth where the dark has congealed

3

But from the measureless heights
Above
Might
Must
Crush
The mightiest
Breast

But that is not all

You know no right of way
At the crossroads
Of night
And day

But that is not all

For you know least that in your life
The one true war
The hardest strife
Is at your
Spirit's core.

And so you do not know
That you are the least of my evils
Among a legion
Of larger
Evils

You do not know
With whom you are dealing

You know nothing of this roadmap I own

4

You do not know that the road from you to me
Is other than the road
From me
To you

You know nothing of my wealth
Hidden from your mighty eyes
(You do not know
That fate
Did demise
And deal me
Far more than
You may
Surmise)

You have decided to wipe me out whatever the price
But nowhere will you find the real road
To me

(I understand you:
You are a man in one space and time
Alive just here and now
You cannot know of the boundless
Space of time
In which I am
Immanent
From a distant yesterday
To a far-off tomorrow
Thinking
of you

But that is not all)

A WORD ON MAN

FIRST

Born in a body barred in with veins
Dreaming that seven heavens descend

Barred in a heart bound into brains
Dreaming the sun in dark without end

Bound in with skin ground into bones
Where is the bridge

To heaven's thrones?

SECOND

Barred in a ribcage of silver your chains
Be ye so mighty no whiter than serf

Born in a body barred in with veins
Dreaming a union of heaven and earth

Cast out of heaven you thirst wine and bread
When will your home

Be your homeland instead?

THIRD

Barred in with bones woven in flesh
Soon will your bones poke through this mesh

Cast out of heaven you crave wine and bread
Stone and smoke you all get in their stead

I see your one hand but where is the other
Was it lifted

To kill its brother?

FOURTH

Barred in a heart bound in a brain
Black your cave the sun you crave

Dreaming of heaven near once again
Your body sways drunken through the shoots

Bound in its blood devoured by roots
In this kolo of sorrow

Do you lead
Or follow?

FIFTH

In this kolo of sorrow you don't follow or lead
You're a tavern of carrion a dance of decay

While the tomb acts alone the body will stay
But when will the body

Become just a deed?

KOLO

Hand in hand
                              bound in a bond
Hand on hand
                    salt on a wound

Earth is so heavy
                    heaven so high
Were I a falcon
                    then I would fly

Original poems from *Kameni spavač (Stone Sleeper)*, 1966

TRANSLATED BY FRANCIS R. JONES

Culture Under Fire

Smail Balić

AN INTRINSIC ELEMENT of the bloody drama that is unfolding in Bosnia since April 1992 is the barbaric assault on the cultural heritage of the land. All that is the embodiment of the cultural and religious identity of Bosnia's Muslims has been targeted for destruction; in essence this has meant the destruction of the singular, defining character of Bosnia itself.

At the time of writing (January 1993), Serbian forces had destroyed or grievously damaged nearly one thousand mosques, or two-fifths of the total number of Muslim places of worship in the country. Three significant libraries had also been demolished: the National and University Library in Sarajevo, the Library of the Oriental Institute in Sarajevo, and the National Library in Mostar. The number of schools with reference libraries destroyed or damaged had begun to climb into the hundreds. Whole urban environments of extraordinary beauty and architectural value have been razed. The picturesque towns of Foča, Mostar, Jajce, Old Sarajevo, and others have all but disappeared. As this relentless war against Bosnia extinguishes life and destroys a people, it is also obliterating all records, monuments of the past, creative works, and fruits of the heart written down in books or engraved in stone.

IN BOSNIA, AS elsewhere in the world, the most tangible expression of its cultural heritage was its architecture—monuments built in an earlier time, many inspired by religious commitment. Devout altruism together with personal artistic and creative initiatives gave impulse to a whole range of cultural and humanitarian endeavor. This was particularly true of the Ottoman period (1463–1878). Thus a significant part of Bosnia's cultural and architectural treasure were its many large mosques or *džamija* (from the Turkish *cami*); smaller mosques or Muslim places of worship, *mesdžid* (from the Turkish *mescid*), distinguished by their lack of minarets; theological seminaries, pedagogical schools for dervishes, places for meeting and meditation; mausoleums; and tombstones. To these were added more secular projects such as clock-towers, baths, libraries, hospices or *musafirhane,* charitable kitchens for the poor, bridges, fountains, aqueducts, public toilets, and cobble-stoned streets.

Of great artistic value were the stylishly conceived, counter-balanced, great domed mosques. Until the beginning of the last decade of the twentieth century about thirty of these had survived. The domed mosques were massive structures alongside which slender minarets thrust skyward. Under the influence of the Seljuk building tradition the entrance portals were quite often recessed in the mass of the structure and adorned with stalactites and Arabic calligraphy. The space before the portals was usually vaulted and bounded by arcades. The interiors of these mosques were decorated with arches, capitals, bases, and numerous stalactites. On the flat decorations of the walls arabesques with floral and geometric motifs predominated. A careful allocation of interior space and use of surface decor, imparted a harmonious effect, and made the mosque appear larger and more imposing than it was in reality. And, finally, a well-planned location heightened the beauty of the structure: a river or stream frequently flowed nearby; and if not, then water splashing from a decorative fountain enhanced the serenity of the surroundings.[1]

Far too many of these great domed mosques have now been destroyed by the Chetniks. The Tabačica mosque, which had stood on the bank of the little river Radobolja in Mostar, was one such beauty that like many others was pulverized in the first assaults on the city. Cypress, sycamore, chestnut, linden, acacia, walnut, and other trees grew near most mosques. These natural treasures too are gone now: what the Chetniks had not destroyed fell victim to the axes and saws of the local population during the terrible winter of 1992–1993. Among the more notable mosques that have been turned into ruins as a consequence of deliberate rocketing are the Ustikolina mosque from the pre-Ottoman period; Aladža in Foča, a masterpiece of Ottoman architecture from 1550; the Ali-Paša and Slatina mosques, also in the Foča area; as well as the Foča Emperor's Mosque from 1500, set alight and burnt to the ground. Almost all of Mostar's mosques have been seriously ravaged, among which Karadjozbeg mosque (1557) and Mehmed-Paša mosque (1618) were renowned for their beauty and the harmony of architectural elements.

All Islamic architecture east of Stolac in Hercegovina, especially mosques, has in part been damaged, in part deliberately erased from the earth.[2] Of some seventy buildings housing theological schools or *medresa* (from the Turkish *medrese*) and dating from the Ottoman era, only two had survived to most recent times: Gazi Husrevbeg's *medresa* in Sarajevo and Sišman Ibrahim-Paša's *medresa* in Počitelj. The archetypal old Bosnian medresa was situated around a small, intimate courtyard, from which it was separated by arcaded corridors. In the middle of the courtyard was a fountain from which water cascaded in several small waterfalls. The main decorative element of the building were tall portals with reliefs and stalactites on the flanking walls. The facade was also decorated with an engraved chronogram of the construction, ordinarily in gold Arabic calligraphy, noting the name of the founder of the endowment along with a prayer for his soul. With every twelve or more small cupolas, under which the students' rooms were situated, a chimney in the shape of a miniature minaret reached for the sky. Today, in the war, the Sarajevo *medresa* has been damaged, while the one in Počitelj is still standing.

The first dervish house for meditation or *tekija* (from the Turkish *tekke*) is thought to have been founded even before the medieval Bosnian kingdom fell under Turkish rule in 1463. Of the five remaining old *tekijas*, in Sarajevo, Fojnica, Blagaj near Mostar, Zvornik, and Foča, the latter three have been extensively damaged. The Blagaj *tekija* was exceptionally beautiful, erected on a great cliff overlooking the source of the Buna River. Alongside it was the mausoleum or *turbe* of the founder of the *tekija*.

Muslim burial monuments—enclosed and open mausoleums (with pillars and a roof but no walls)—and tombs with characteristic headstones, or *mezar*, have sustained heavy destruction. Even in the former Yugoslavia numerous Muslim cemeteries were confiscated, bulldozed, and used for new construction or turned into parks. This barbaric practice is being followed in territories under the occupation of the Serbian forces today. Along with graveyards, smaller mosques disappear overnight. Parking areas for vehicles are marked out on their sites, as was the case in Bosanska Krupa and elsewhere in the so-called "Serbian Republic" in the Bosnian land.

The old bridges of Bosnia have also not been spared. Their bold architecture and attractive arches had always drawn great notice from visitors. The most famous were the bridges in Mostar, which gave the town its name (*stari most* meaning "old bridge"); in Višegrad—made famous by Ivo Andrić's monumental novel *The Bridge on the Drina;* in Zepa; on the Bregava River near Počitelj; on the Miljačka near Sarajevo; and Arslanagić's Bridge in Trebinje. The last named was disassembled and transferred to another, inappropriate location during the Communist era. All the rest, to a greater or lesser extent, have been damaged in the war. In the city of Mostar all the bridges were mined and blown up—except the Old Bridge, *Stara ćuprija* (from the Turkish *kopru*), which, instead, sustained a direct hit and was hollowed out by a crater.

The two magnificent *karavan-sarajs* on the flanks of the Višegrad Bridge of Mehmed-Paša Sokolović (the sixteenth-century Turkish Grand Vezir from Bosnia) and the old ćuprija in Goražde have lain in ruins for some time. The two remaining single-roofed bazaars—Brusa-bezistan and Gazi-Husrevbeg-bezistan—both magnificent domed edifices in Sarajevo, had survived from Ottoman times. Today they have been bombarded from the surrounding hills and have suffered heavy damage. Nor have the clock-towers or *sahat-kula* in Sarajevo, Mostar, and other towns escaped the destruction.[3]

Yet another important part of the Muslim cultural legacy were wells (*cesma*) with ornamental decorations, decorative fountains (*šadrvan*), public drinking fountains (*sebil*), and baths—both public (*hamam*) and private or domestic (*hamamdžic*). Aside from the numerous aqueducts and the swimming pool in Sarajevo, the old Bošnjaks also constructed a large number of public bath-houses. The only remaining bath, Gazi Husrevbeg's *hamam* in Sarajevo, has been damaged. The Chetniks also mined the aqueducts to compound the hardship of the cities they have laid siege to—thus making what they least cherish, purity of soul and body, the priority targets.

The development of Bosnian cities is closely tied to the foundation of pious endowments or *vakuf*. (According to the historian Hamdija Kreševljaković [died 1959] a significant number of the pious endowments in Bosnia were the work of ordinary people: tradesmen, small merchants, tillers of the land, women, and so forth.) Most of these cities came into being in the fifteenth and sixteenth centuries, when the Ottoman Empire was at the zenith of its power, and while the Bošnjaks sat on the seats of the Grand Vezirs for fifty-two consecutive years.[4]

In order to assure open vistas, residential buildings in old Bosnian cities were terraced, large spaces separating one from the other. For reasons of health, commerce, and aesthetics, they were constructed in the vicinity of free-flowing water or near lakes. The natural beauty of the surrounding areas was preserved and the residential architecture itself was made to the measure of a man, so that it had human dimensions. Living examples of such urban planning—now already in rather well-advanced stages of destruction—are the cities of Mostar, Blagaj near Mostar, Travnik, and Foča. In old settlements, the waters of rivers, brooks, and fountains splashed from all directions with the scent and freshness of nature (though sometimes the water of drainage canals could be heard as well!). "Who is not enchanted even today," wrote Kornelius Gurlitt at the beginning of this century, "by the urban portrait of the Bosnian capital city? It is incomparable for the force of its contradictions; the city is divided into two sharply distinct sections: the modern European, and the Ottoman-Oriental. But its Europeanization goes relentlessly forward, and there is a danger that the old Oriental quarters may be lost, as was the case in the capital cities of the other, neighboring Balkan countries."[5]

In their drive to extirpate Islam and the Muslims from the region the Chetniks have created a desolate waste and a sort of Balkan leveling in Sarajevo. While the Ottoman quarters of Bosnian cities have been particular targets, in Sarajevo even the Central European legacy of the Austro-Hungarian monarchy has not been spared. Thus the splendid former city hall or *beledija,* which was built by Austria in the postclassical Moorish style, has been rocketed and burned to the ground. Since the Second World War it had housed the National and University Libraries. The entire collection, extremely valuable for the wealth of its documents—letters, Oriental manuscripts produced on the territory of Bosnia, and archival treasures of various sorts—has disappeared along with the building. The chieftain of the extremist Serbs, Radovan Karadžić, brazenly declared after this act of vandalism that the Muslims had destroyed the National Library themselves in revenge against Austria—a country which was well-regarded by the Bosnian Muslims, and which, in recognition of its Muslim subjects, had built the Sarajevo *beledija* in the Arabic-Islamic style.[6]

As for Mostar, Bosnia's second largest city, in a startling account of its devastation Rupert Neudeck, a distinguished German journalist and one of the leading members of the humanitarian working group, *Cap Anamur,* writes:

The left side of this jewel among all cities of the former Yugoslavia
. . . is completely burned and ravaged. This was consciously done
by the Serb militias . . . which used phosphorus bombs to simply
incinerate those monuments most splendid and most deserving of
protection. The Hotel Neretva, one of the reminders of the Habsburg era, constructed on the very bank of the river Neretva; the
Muslim bath, faithfully built according to the example of the most
beautiful bath in Budapest; the School of Music; the mosques; the
Tabačica-mošeja (mosque) in the immediate area of the world-
famous, single-arched Old Bridge, which the builder managed to
erect, after three failed attempts, in 1566 . . . The inhabitants of
Mostar shake their heads and wonder why they were so naive that
in the course of the last two years they did not notice these preparations. The Serb part of the city's population dwelled on the hills
and slopes surrounding the city, from where the Serb militias began
their campaign of conquest and plunder. The bridges which link
the left bank with the right—thirteen of them by number—with
the exception of the unique Old Bridge (Stara ćuprija), were all
hollowed out underneath and plugged with mines two years ago.
Then, in the decisive moment, they were blown into the sky.[7]

The willful destruction of monuments of Islamic culture has a long tradition in
the Balkans. At the beginning of the seventeenth century, according to the travel
writer Evliyma Celebi [died 1684], Belgrade had two hundred and seventeen
mosques, thirteen mesdžidas, seventeen tekijas, nine learning centers for the
study of Islamic tradition (dar al-hadit), eight medresas, seven public bath-
houses, and six roadside inns (karavan-saraj). Only the humble Bajrakli-džamija
in Gospodar Jevrem Street has survived until today. In Leskovac [in Serbia] even
in 1878, when Bosnia-Hercegovina was occupied by Austro-Hungarian troops,
there were six mosques, two mesdžidas, and ten tekijas. Not one of these monuments exists today. At the end of the twentieth century, Serbia's war against
Bosnia is continuing that uncultured, barbarous tradition which, itself, is part of
the long-standing desire underlying the politics of several Balkan countries to
annihilate Muslims and Islamic culture in the Balkan region.

WHO ARE THE Bosnian Muslims? Why is their culture under fire? Contrary to
Serb and Croat mythology the Bosnian Muslims were *not* Serbs or Croats who
converted to Islam. They were a distinct group—they call themselves
Bošnjaks—who have, through the centuries, identified themselves with the
land of Bosnia. Their ancestors in the independent kingdom of Bosnia
(1377–1463), which predated the Ottoman and Austro-Hungarian conquests, were the Patarenes or Bogomils. Nor was the emergence of Islam in the
Balkans a consequence of Turkish expansion alone. In the period from the
ninth century to the thirteenth century, prior to the arrival of the Ottoman

Turks, there were pockets of Muslim population along the course of the middle and lower Danube, the lower Sava, and in the area where the Drina flows into the Sava.[8]

In the fifteenth and sixteenth centuries there were mass conversions to Islam, mainly by the Patarenes or Bogomils, or their Catholic descendants (actually Crypto-Bogomils) who had been oppressed and persecuted by Bosnia's neighbors. The Islam practiced by the Ottomans, who ruled Bosnia from 1463 to 1878, had a strong mystical strain, was endowed with numerous syncretic elements, and, for its times, was quite tolerant. Since the "Bosnian Church"—embodying the indigenous Patarenism or Bogomilism—was organized on lines similar to those of the Islamic mystics order, did not recognize the clergy of the papal primateship, regarded Christ as a spiritual person, and so forth, the Bosnian Bogomils saw themselves as having encountered a spiritual relative when the Ottoman's made their appearance. Furthermore, the main thrust of Ottoman expansion was directed against Hungary, the former oppressor who had conducted veritable crusades against the Bosnians and their state. Therefore, both political and national considerations were at play—and so a large part of the native population, led by the aristocracy, adopted the Islamic faith.

By the end of the ninteenth century, when the Austro-Hungarian empire ruled over Bosnia, the people of Bosnia had defined their separate identities. The Bosnian Catholics defined themselves as Croats, the Orthodox or Pravoslavs as Serbs. And from the very outset, each of these two nationalisms claimed the Muslims for itself. At the same time, surreptitiously or openly, efforts were directed towards eliminating Bosnia and the Bošnjaks from political vocabulary and popular consciousness. In 1971, in Tito's Yugoslavia, the Muslims of Bosnia were recognized as "Muslims in the national sense," a distinct nation at par with the Serbs, the Croats, the Albanians in a decentralizing federation. This recognition and new designation was only a constitutional confirmation of historical fact: the majority of the Bosnians—the Bošnjaks—had been Muslim by faith since the middle of the fifteenth century.

But this, obviously, had no effect on the claims that Croatian and Serbian nationalisms have laid to Bosnia and its indigenous Muslims. Serb political propaganda has not only defined Bosnia's Muslims as converted Serbs (as, among other Serb academics, by Veselin Djuretić), but, by extension of that argument, also as traitors to Serbdom. Bosnian Islam has been the target of abuse and hostility of Belgrade's mass media over the past decade, with the Belgrade sociologist Miroljub Jevtić—former Communist turned fervent nationalist—who poses as an expert on Islam while playing a leading role in this hate propaganda. Together with a number of extremist nationalist Serbian writers and politicians, he has conjured up a new kind of anti-Semitism among his compatriots, a quasi flesh-and-blood archetype of an enemy. The result is "Final Solution–Serbian Version" which we are witnessing today in Bosnia.

The fundamental motive of the aggression against Bosnia lies in the craving for power. The inevitable collapse of authoritarian Communist structures, in favor of the democratic self-determination of the South Slavic nations, threatened the privileged position of Serbdom. The Serbian masses were therefore mobilized by conjuring up historical resentments and mythological stories of a glorious Serb past. The "cosmic disaster" that befell the Serbian people in their defeat by the Turks on the Field of Kosovo in 1389 was revived in memory, together with a call for vengeance. The Muslims, as the alleged descendants of the Turks (the propagators of Islam in the Balkans) were the ready targets. Serbian extremists maintained that the Bosnian Muslims were "fundamentalists" who had dared to want to set up an Islamic Republic in the heart of Europe. For years Belgrade's media had been suspecting any autonomous activity on the part of the Albanians and Muslims as being an act of religious separatism—even a manifestation of the spirit of jihad, wrongly translated into a "holy war."

Numerous books were published. Books about the persecution of the Serbs by the Ustaše regime in the one-time "Independent State of Croatia" (1941–1945) reviving bitter historical memories (some Muslims, as opposed to the majority of their co-religionists, had collaborated with the Ustaše regime); books about the Bosnian Muslims' alleged betrayal of Serbdom through their acceptance of Islam; books about the Serbs' inability to capitalize on their heroism (according to Dobrica Cosić, writer and briefly president of the so-called Federal Republic of Yugoslavia, the Serbs always win the war but lose the peace); books about the jihad as the latent mechanism with which the Muslims threaten the world; books about Islam as the hidden support of Albanian atheism until 1991; and so forth.

Repelled by the frenzied propaganda, intelligent, independent-minded people have been leaving Serbia in droves. "A terrible darkness has already fallen over culture," complains one of the bold Serbian philanthropists, the former mayor of Belgrade, architect Bogdan Bogdanović. "If you have glanced into our bookstores, there are only books about genocide, books about ancient empires and calendars, books on parapsychology, some kind of 'Vava the psychic.' And that is all. I don't know how it is in your country," Bogdanović continues his lament in a conversation with a Croatian journalist, "but we here cannot get away from the priests on television. When you are an atheist, or more precisely an agnostic, you can better see who has faith, and who doesn't have faith in God. I value and deeply respect it, when I see that someone has faith. Sometimes I am even envious. But when I watch that priestly phalanx of ours, except for this wretched Patriarch Pavle who presumably believes in God . . . the rest are all rogues. . . . We do not have historical knowledge, because history was not even taught in the schools. So instead of history it comes down to oral embellishment. Fables and mythologizing begin."[9]

The oral embellishment about which Bogdanović speaks is given shape above all in Serb folk poetry. But for the simple inhabitant of the Balkans, even fictional songs and stories are a source of reporting about the events of the past, and also the basis for a distorted "historical memory" which moves the masses. Besides the *hajduk* songs (songs of the Balkan brigands), for the peasant Serb such a work as the epic poem, "The Mountain Wreath," by Bishop Petar Petrović Njegos of Montenegro (1812–1851), which glorifies the eradication of the *poturice* or converts to Islam in Montenegro at the turn of the eighteenth century, is a sort of Scripture. In this work, which for the entire period of Yugoslavia's existence was required reading in schools, the destruction of Islamic culture ("So tear down the minarets and mosques!") and the slaughter of innocent people are openly urged.[10]

The cumulative result of such adroit manipulation of historical memory through myths and propaganda is that long-nurtured, long-repressed vengefulness has finally overwhelmed the hearts of many Serbs, the majority of whom in Bosnia are highlanders or constitute the peasantry. In the Ottoman period, in large part, they were resettled in Bosnia to till the land for the mostly Muslim landowners. As a consequence the population of Bosnia came to comprise two significantly different groups: the autochthonous (native) urban population and the rural, largely settler population, constituting the peasantry. The assault on Bosnia's cosmopolitan, urban centers and the destruction of their Islamic heritage and character has thus been carried out by those sections of society whose hatred of the city, urban culture (and relative urban affluence) has—under the influence of noxious propaganda against Bosnian Muslims as either Turks or treacherous Serbs—led to the barbarism we are witnessing today.

Part of the propaganda against the Turks—and, by extension, the Muslims of Bosnia—had been the denigration of Turk or Ottoman culture and civilization. In scholarship, the belief that the Turks contributed nothing to the development of culture and were, instead, the representatives of obscurantism (a belief held, among others, by Ivo Andrić) had been eclipsed. Such a view was predominant in Europe several centuries ago, so that scholarship took account of the Ottoman cultural legacy only *extra ordinem*. People spoke of the benighted Turkish era. Under the pressure of such prejudices, numerous Islamic structures of extraordinary artistic value were ascribed to other cultures: the Old Bridge in Mostar to the Romans, Sokolović's ćuprija in Višegrad to the Byzantines, Mehmed-Paša's hamam in Višegrad to the Serbs, and so forth. An oblique approach to Ottoman culture—without familiarity with the three so-called Islamic languages (Arabic, Persian, Turkish) and the underlying spiritual forces that defined public life in that era—was bound to result in truncated notions about the Ottoman period and about Islam. Only in this fashion could researchers such as the Czech scholar Konstanin Jirecek, along with some literary figures, arrive at the conclusion—today hardly supportable—that the Ottomans initiated the darkest period in the history of the Balkan peoples.

Although rejected by serious scholarship, this attitude has been systematically reinforced in certain post-Communist societies which have for some time now been gripped by a fever of irrational nationalism. The drive toward national homogenization and demographic alteration of a hitherto multinational Bosnia can only be seen in this context. In Bosnia-Hercegovina, it has taken the form of "ethnic cleansing," which, in effect, means the expulsion and eradication of the autochthonous population and the violent interruption of its normal development and progress.

NOTES

1. Even though they are not expressly artistic works, all other Bosnian mosques are also largely pleasant and attractive to the observer. The interior architecture is often very beautiful. Carpets woven with much love are spread on the floors, and the hues of the painted walls give the *mesdžids* particular charm.

2. The best introduction to this cultural endowment is provided by Hivzija Hasandedić, *Muslimanske baštine u istočnoj Hercegovini* (Sarajevo, 1990).

3. During the establishment of the old Ottoman urban infrastructure, beside the Bosnian Muslim and Turkish builders, master-craftsmen from Italy and Dalmatian Croatia also participated. Two builders of the Orthodox faith are known as well: Staniša and Tanasije. On the other hand, Islamic architecture influenced the manner of church construction. Islamic miniature painting is reflected in Serbian church painting, as the art historian Zagorka Janc has demonstrated. Despite all of this held in common, Serbian fanatics are ravaging everything that carries an Islamic stamp.

4. Following the battle of Mohacs in Hungary in 1526, the Bošnjaks also administered the conquered areas of Hungary, and so they established urban cores of the Ottoman type there as well. At that time many Serbs were developing a lavish commerce in Hungary under the Bošnjaks' protection, and together with them enjoyed many privileges.

5. Cited in Ernest Bauer, *Zwischen Halbmond und Doppeledler* (Vienna and Munich, 1971), p. 178.

6. See my reply to Karadžić's lie in *Die Presse* (Vienna), September 26, 1992, (Tribune der Leser), p. 15.

7. Rupert Neudeck, "Bosnien—europäische Brücke zur islamischen Welt," *Orientierung,* 56 (Zurich,1992), p. 208.

8. For a start, see my paper "Der Islam im mittelalterlichen Ungarn." U: *Sudostforschungen* 23 (Munich,1964), pp. 19-35.

9. Zeljko Hodonje, "Sešeljeve 'zlatne kašike," *Večernji List,* Zagreb, January 16, 1993, pp. 1-11.

10. While researching South Slavic folk poetry, the Croat linguist Tomo Maretić established that, unlike other folk poetry in the Balkans, the simple folk songs of the Bosnian Muslims contain little brutality, cruelty, or savagery. And those songs are the mirror of the national soul.

TRANSLATED BY PAUL JUKIĆ AND EDITH GERRARD

Winter Idyll

Mirko Kovač

Winter idyll
snow in each yard
swilling death
with swigs of blood
our Serbian bard!

Night foul
  wolves prowl
    winds yowl
      dogs growl
        to church they go
          the folk my foe
            I fire my bow
              winds out-howl
                its whistle of woe

arrow sing
  village below
    evening glow
      bell ring
        bull thunder
          sheep bleat
            hound howl
              cock crow
                times sunder

Christmas fast
  to church at last
    my bones to warm
      to deal out doom
        the pious massed
          munching bread
            my knife I thrust
              deep in their guts
                the blade runs red

blood lapping
  rattle of life
    gelding knife
      balls hacking
        pecker lacking
          I left the brats
            churchbell choke
              pious folk
                flee for your life

knees go faint   each little ass
 curse their saint   on a cushion of glass
  bullets scourging   as a warrior bard
   their blessed Virgin   sows Serbian seed
    their Bosnian hearts   when need be I knife
     their coat of arms   for the good of tomorrow
      and God is Serbian   o lyric of life!
       Saint Sava my guide   my hero is Djogo
        watch by my side   his verse sometimes shocks
         two Catholic wenches   he's unorthodox
          on vestry benches   but he's Orthodox!

                    Winter idyll
                    blest be this day
                    minefields charred
                    a scented bouquet
                    for our Serbian bard!

Translated by Francis R. Jones

Christmas fast: on Christmas Eve one does not eat, only having a Christmas supper when returning from Midnight Mass.

Saint Sava: the patron saint of Serbia.

Djogo: Gojko Djogo, a poet jailed for his verse criticizing the "system" in the early 1980s, became a leading figurehead among the Bosnian Serbs, giving their campaign of dismemberment of the Bosnian state intellectual "respectability"; the poem expresses the contempt which many Yugoslav writers feel for his stance.

Is This Not Genocide?

IBRAHIM KAJAN

Whoever destroys an innocent life is in God's eyes
like one who destroys all humankind. And whoever saves a life
is like one who has saved all humankind.
—THE QUR'AN, V.32

AND THEN THERE is genocide, an innocent word of terrible meaning. To destroy the foundation of a person's existence; to destroy the very seed (the "gene") of a nation; to exterminate that which is "not mine and does not want to be mine"—this is the simplest and most precise definition of the word.

At its third session on December 9, 1948, the United Nations General Assembly adopted the Convention on the prevention and punishment of the crime of genocide. The states that signed this document affirmed that genocide was an international crime which they are obliged to prevent and punish with the full force of international law whether it occurs in the midst of a war between states or within a single state. The Convention considers the crime of genocide "any act committed with the intention to destroy partially or completely a national, ethnic, religious or racial group." It also states that it is a crime to kill members of a group or to inflict grave injury upon the physical existence or integrity of a group. The "intentional subjugation of a group by means aimed at its complete or partial destruction" is genocide. This includes acts where the goal is to prevent births within a particular group or to forcibly transfer children from one group to another.

Vladimir Dedijer, the president of the Russell Tribunal, has noted that there are many shortcomings in the United Nations Convention on Genocide. These flaws have become evident in the era of "new methods" reflecting the dark side of "developed humanism." For example, Dedijer notes that cultural genocide is not considered in the Convention, and finds it curious that "all the great powers were against condemning this form of genocide."[1]

The terrible events in Bosnia have presented the world with one more variant of a war crime which in its systematic method of execution has no precedent. This new dimension is the organized rape of young girls and women which has taken place in Bosnia over the past year. Europe has stood paralyzed before a form of evil which emerged from the borders of its classical Greek and Christian heritage. Sartre reminded us that "genocides happened both before and after the promulgation of the Convention."[2] Yet, for the sake of law, any future revision of the Convention must incorporate these new forms of genocidal activity and codify them as crimes.

In every crime the intent is primary. This is also true where it concerns genocide. Horrific mass murders may still not be considered an act of genocide, if the principal motive is not the destruction of a nation, an ethnic group, or a religion. There exists clear and unambiguous evidence that the violence carried out against the Muslims of Bosnia-Hercegovina represents a process of systematic and intentional genocide. Furthermore, the evidence can be clearly documented.

In the period immediately prior to the 1992 referendum in which the citizens of Bosnia-Hercegovina voted on the question of a sovereign, united, and independent state for them, Dr. Radovan Karadžić, the president of the Serbian Democratic Party (SDS), stated publicly: "If Bosnia and Hercegovina do not remain in Yugoslavia, then one nation will disappear!" Karadžić's statement was carried widely in the press. He made clear in this statement his intent to destroy another nation. From Sarajevo, Alija Izetbegović replied: "There will be no war in Bosnia and Hercegovina. It takes two sides for war."

The Bosnian Muslims did not want war. Even when the massacres began, people thought it would not move beyond the neighboring village. They said to themselves, "It will not happen here. It will stop there." But Karadžić's Serbs did not stop. Many of those who ended up in the concentration camps had thought the terror would stop before it reached their villages or homes.

Although barely a year has passed, it is time to present some of the evidence we have in our possession of known crimes. The first public report against the terror that was to engulf Bosnia-Hercegovina had come in an unnoticed bulletin published by the Party of Democratic Action (SDA), which is led by President of Bosnia, Alija Izetbegović.

> BIJELJINA, APRIL 6, 1992: Except for three members of the Executive Committee of the SDA of Bijeljina, everyone else [in the party leadership] was killed. The worst shooting and most of the killings were carried out in the Great Park in front of the Atija mosque in Bijeljina. As people were coming out of the mosque after evening prayers, the Arkanovći immediately slaughtered two men and then fired on the others, killing them. In panic, people turned back and fled into the mosque. Then the Arkanovći threw bombs into the mosque, killing everyone inside. After this the Arkanovći entered the mosque and committed a loathsome deed:

they relieved themselves on the corpses. Following this massacre, forty thousand Muslims fled from Bijeljina and Janja to Tuzla.[3]

This report has been confirmed in several accounts by refugees who fled Bijeljina. The reports are clear that Muslims were killed in groups. Specifically, Muslim leaders who were intellectuals or professionals were selected for early death as priority targets. There were acts of mutilation and desecration against the dead. The systematic destruction of mosques became an integral part of the campaign by Serbian forces. The cultural heritage of the Muslims of Bosnia-Hercegovina became a target. Furthermore, general panic was intentionally organized through the exercise of systematic terror in order to create a mass exodus.

We have collected testimonies from the first refugees. Most of them are peasants driven out of largely Muslim villages and towns. They are civilians. They were virtually scraped off the surface of the earth they lived upon. For example, the town of Vlasenica and its surrounding region was a predominantly Muslim area that has been swept bare by the iron broom of "ethnic cleansing." Those who were left behind in the panic were packed into camps and their property was stolen.

A selection of the many personal testimonies gathered in the past year are presented here in order that the reader can reflect on whether or not the Convention on the Prevention of Genocide has, in fact, been violated.

I

A REFUGEE FROM ZVORNIK

ON APRIL 6, 1992, members of the SDS put up barricades in Meterize. They were first raised at nine thirty in the evening. The workers who normally work in the Karakaj area were unable to go to work that evening. The next day when I went into the street I noticed that the local Serbs were packing up their belongings and hurriedly moving out of the area. The Muslim community grew uneasy and on that day the Crisis Headquarters of Zvornik was formed. We heard that the city would be attacked if the demands of the SDS were not met.

On the morning of April 8 small-arms fire could be heard from the barricades. The shooting continued until mid-day when an artillery shell was fired on the city. Once the artillery opened up people started to flee toward Kula-Grad.[4] As they ran, snipers from the Serbian side of the Drina at Krecani began shooting at the terrified civilians. This was only the beginning. Tank units of the Yugoslav People's Army (JNA) began firing upon the city. Shells fired by the JNA fell on the town throughout the night of April 8—9. At least four to five thousand people from Zvornik fled toward Kula-Grad. The snipers killed people as they fled with their families. Our own neighbor, Suad Mehmedović was wounded in this manner. The son of Džemal Musić Rokan, was shot in the chest and died.

As we fled to Kula-Grad, I observed a group of twenty-five Chetniks move into the city as they crossed at the hydroelectric dam. This was near to the settlement known as Hrid. According to eyewitnesses with whom I spoke many crimes were committed there. I personally saw Safet and Hajra, two workers at the local gas station, lying dead on the ground. Amir, who we called "The Musician," was also killed.

I know they killed children in Tabaći. Among the dead was Sabit, a local driver, his wife, and two sons. They ordered my neighbor, Rama, to shoot several civilians. When he refused, they killed him.[5]

II
A REFUGEE FROM FOČA

DURING THE BATTLE of Foča most of the Muslims were gathered in the section of the town known as Donje Polje. There was a Serbian sniper position above the barbershop. At one point Rade Elez called upon the Muslims in the fishermen's section of town to surrender. He used the megaphone on top of the tavern known as the Fisherman's Restaurant. A number of people surrendered and when they did the Chetniks lined them up and drove them into Foča's prison. The son of Asim Gogalija, whom I knew, was among the prisoners. After three or four days of fighting Foča fell.

It was then that I heard the Chetniks took the Isanović family for a "medical examination" and when they reached the hospital they killed them. Durak Saban was staying with us in our house at this time. When there was a lull in the battle he would go out and gather up people's belongings so they would not be lost. It is for this reason that Milanović, the police official from Gradinic who lived beside the dam at Gornje Polje, had Saban hauled off to the prison. Saban had seen how the Chetniks were looting people's homes. He had also seen how Asim Hadžiahmetović's store had been looted. Hadžiahmetović had already fled.

I saw how twenty Chetniks crossed the meadow above the prison and set Hadžiahmetović's house on fire. This was the beginning of the burning of Muslim Foča. I watched as they burned Hasan Pilav's apartment. He was the director of the sawmill. I saw them burn the houses of many Muslims in Aladža and Donje Polje. When Radio Foča fell into Serbian hands, Velibor Ostojić declared over the radio that the township of Foča was Serbian. He said that Muslims would no longer be permitted to live in Foča. And he added that every Serbian woman would have to bear seven children.

I also saw three young Serbian men break into and rob the apartment of Reuf Tafra, the director of Foča's medical center. I heard that during their first attack the Chetniks killed ten young Muslim men from the families of Djuderija, Silajdžić, and Vojević. They were all from the village of Susješno. The Chetniks claimed they had killed ten Ustaša, not ten Muslims. Using the Fisherman's Restaurant as their base, Serbian snipers killed people throughout the Surkovac area. After one Serb was shot they took revenge on the entire area.

They set fire to the Emperor's Mosque and danced the *kolo*. They sang, "Well, men, shall we build a church in the center of Foča!"[6]

III
A REFUGEE FROM THE VILLAGE OF KOSMAN

THE VILLAGE OF KOSMAN is an hour's walk from the village of Perovići. A Chetnik group led by Ratomir Mastilović took twelve people away from our village. Mastilović's unit included Tihomir Aćimović, Zeljko Majdov, Radmilo and Sreta Mijović, Luka Tomović, Zdravko and Milenko Pavlović, Mile Majdov, Djoko Vuković, and Ljubo Kavocević. The people they abducted were from the Lagarija family. This included Nazif, Abida, Salih, Fadil, Semso, Ibro, Ekrem, and Serif. From the Vejo family they abducted Fehim, Hasib, and Nermin. They also took away the Albanian called Halim. None of these people came back.

The same Chetnik group crammed a large group from our village into Meća Deleuta's house. I know that from the Deleuta family there was Meša, Latif, Umija, Safet, Mušan, and Mulija. Salima and Paša from the Vejo family and Saha and Semso from the Lagarija family were among those pushed into the house. The Chetniks doused the house with gasoline and burned everyone alive. Everyone was burned to death. After this the Chetniks set the entire village of Kosman on fire and burned it to the ground. They drove off all the livestock. It was May 4, 1992, when all of this happened.[7]

IV
A REFUGEE FROM THE VILLAGE OF JELEĆ

EVER SINCE THE MUSLIM HOLIDAY of Bajram our life has become a nightmare. It all began on April 4, 1992, when the first shots rang through our village and Chetniks from the Serbian village of Vodice began shelling us incessantly. The villagers hid in the canyon of the Bistrice river. We had already prepared some shelters. These were small huts about a meter high built from stones and covered with boards. The shelling of the village lasted about three days and fourteen Muslim houses were destroyed. When the shelling stopped the Chetnik infantry entered the village and began killing people. They targeted men, women, and children.

They killed my husband and his brothers Omer, Asim, Mustafa, and Zulfo. These were all the sons of Jusuf. Our relatives and their sons were also killed. There was Hakija Srnja, son of Sućro; Hajika's son Enver Srnja; Zulfo's son Evledin Srnja; Asim's son Nedžad Srnja; and Edhem Sljivo, the son of Ibro. All these people were shot. Five days after they were killed, survivors from our village were able to bury their corpses during the night. They are buried at the scene of the crime, beside the Krupice river, near Zulfo and Hakija's house.

I know the Chetniks also killed the following people: Osman Zametica, Jusuf Džinic and his wife, Mustafa Tuzlak, an Albanian called Nasuf whose corpse was terribly mutilated, Edhem and his wife Fata and one daughter, Uzeir Hadžić and his son Enver and daughter-in-law Jelena, and Haso Hadžić. They were all killed in Hamdo Hadžić's weekend house. They are buried now beside the house.

I saw who committed these crimes. They were our Serb neighbors who were teachers from the elementary school in Jeleć. All were members of the SDS. Particularly prominent among them were the Chetnik leaders Zoran Miljanović and Pero Elez from Miljevina.[8]

V

A REFUGEE FROM THE VILLAGE OF KOSOVO POLJE

THE CHETNIKS CAME into the village on June 3, 1992. It was not hard to recognize them with the badges on their caps. They went into my brother Sefket's house. They began kicking his wife Fatima. They demanded money and all her jewelry. My sister-in-law brought them what they wanted. They then locked her up in the house and raped her. After they had finished they set the house on fire with Fatima in it. The remains of her hair and bones were found.

On the same day they burned down the house of Hakija Kos. They then burned down my father Abid Jamak's house and slaughtered him. They began their genocidal work in Kosovo Polje at ten o'clock at night. They had warned the villagers that they should move out of their houses by the morning. With megaphones they ordered everyone to hand over their arms and bring their cars to the crossroads. If they did not do so, they were told that their houses would be burned to the ground. My father did not want to follow their orders to abandon his home. Milan Lukić is among the most infamous of the Chetnik leaders who came to Kosovo Polje. He, among others, is responsible for these criminal acts. It was Lukić who sang the Chetnik song, "Muslims, you yellow ants, your days are numbered."[9]

VI

A REFUGEE FROM THE VILLAGE OF ZLATNIK

ON MAY 27, 1992, the Chetniks surrounded the house of Islam Kustura in the village of Zlatnik near Dobrun. They drove the people out of the house to a stream which was three hundred meters away. They took everyone's identity cards and burned them. Nikola Kavačević and his two sons, Petar and Budimar, killed my brother Ahmet Mutapčić, who was twenty-one, and my brother Ibra Kustura, who was twenty-seven. Their corpses were then mutilated by those who murdered them. My father watched all this. Afterwards they drove him into the woods toward the village of Boglice.

Milos Sikirič was among these criminals. The Chetniks' headquarters were located at his house. The Chetniks looted and burned the Muslim villages of Zlatnik, Turjak, and Zanožje. Everyone who could fled these villages to save their lives. In Zanožje I know they killed Nezir Kasapović. They burned him in his stable. At the end of May they also burned down the village of Smriječje. In one incident six women were burned alive in one house. The Celik family was killed in the same way.[10]

VII
A REFUGEE FROM THE VILLAGE OF KOSTJEREVO

MY NAME IS TIMA DAUTOVIĆ. I am an eyewitness to unimaginable crimes which took place in the villages of Kostjerevo and Drinjača in the Commune of Zvornik. The crimes were carried out by members of the Serbian Chetniks. Some were from this region and others had come from Serbia. The village of Kostjerevo no longer exists. The houses of Muslims were looted and burned. Women were dishonored, and they were taken way with their children in the direction of Tuzla.

Using force and violence, the Chetniks drove the entire population out of our village and sent them in the direction of Drinjača. We knew the leaders of the Chetniks. One was Dragan Ingjatović who was a former employee of Zvornik's municipal administration. There was also the policeman, Ljubisav from Zelinje. I knew another of their leaders—Mile Mijatović who was also known as Cornpone.

It was these Chetniks who took our men to the auditorium in the cultural center of our town. It was there that they beat them for hours. The women and children could hear the screams and moans of these helpless people. Blood covered the walls. The Chetniks then took thirty-five men out of the center and shot them. They slaughtered them all. The men to die were seventeen to seventy years old. No one survived.

The women's turn came next. The Chetniks raped them and molested them in other ways. The Chetniks kidnapped the remaining people. They took away about a dozen boys up to the age of fifteen. Their fate is completely unknown. On May 31, a Sunday, they packed 150 women and children into two buses and drove them toward Tuzla. In order to prove that my account is true I will name the thirty-five victims in Drinjača who I personally knew . . . I am prepared to repeat this statement before any international court.[11]

VIII
A FORMER INMATE OF THE CONCENTRATION CAMP AT KARAKAJ

I WAS IMPRISONED in the Serbian concentration camp at Karakaj in Zvornik from June 1 to 10. They had turned the Technical Museum at the school in

Karakaj into a camp. There were about seven hundred prisoners from the Muslim villages of Sestići, Klisa, Djulići, Sjenokos, Kaludran, Celišmanu, Lupe, and Bijeli Potok.

The camp authorities were relentless in their brutal treatment of the inmates. We were kept in overcrowded rooms without sufficient air or water. Many people died in this suffocating atmosphere. They beat us with their fists, rifle butts, and planks of wood. I saw people covered with blood. After the beatings many never got up again. We were ordered to pick up those who had fallen and to load them onto trucks. Although many were still alive, they were driven off. I do not know where. I know of more than twenty people who died from suffocation. Among them was Hrustan Avdić who was director of the elementary school in Petkovci.

The number of prisoners kept declining. There was only one reason. They would come and take away a new group. They would tell us they were taking them to Pale for a prisoner exchange. Immediately, however, we could hear rifle shots, screams, and the moans of the dying. My group's turn soon came. There were many with me including Nurija Jašarević and Avdo Jašarević from the village of Klisa. The others included Sejdo Hasanović, Muradif Hasanović, Asim Hamzić, Smajo Smalović, Ramiz Sinanović, and Osman Samjlović. All these men came from the village of Sestići. They made us stand against the wall and the began firing immediately. I took my cousin Sejdo's hand. It was a miracle but I survived and hid like a dead man among my dead neighbors. When the Chetniks went off to get a new group of prisoners, I crawled away from the killing ground.

Before I arrived at the camp about four hundred people had already been killed. The other three hundred inmates were exposed to many kinds of torture. I doubt they were allowed to live. They would have been inconvenient witnesses to the horrific crimes which were committed. Among those who committed the murders were a number of men who were the neighbors of those they killed. I can identify Vlajko Ivanović from Petkovci who previously was an executive at the Gorenje factory. I also saw Božo Vidović from Malešići who had been a member of the town council in Zvornik. The man who killed the most was Miladin Gojkov Todorović from Tršić. I am prepared to repeat this statement before any international court or commission if requested.[12]

IX
MERSUDINA HODŽIĆ FROM THE VILLAGE OF ZAKLOPAČA

IT WAS SATURDAY, MAY 16, around four o'clock when a van arrived in the village with reservists. They surrounded the village. Time passed. Nothing happened, except occasionally we heard distant shooting. About five o'clock two police cars arrived with reservists, and the policeman, Miomir Milošević, from the neighboring village of Milići. Five Lada Niva cars which were full of Chetniks also arrived. One of the cars had the word "massacre" written on it. There were at least fifty Chetniks. All the cars were full and some of the Chetniks were sitting on the roofs of the cars. Several were wearing camouflage uniforms and some had disguised their faces with nylon stockings or sunglasses. Some of them were dressed as civilians.

They had beards, Chetnik badges, and other Chetnik symbols. They came into the village and asked where we kept our weapons. They said that if they found any weapons we didn't have a chance. In fact, no one in the village had any weapons because we had handed them over much earlier when we were given an ultimatum. Two people tried to run for it, but they were caught. One of them was my uncle Haso Hodžić. They brought him over to where we were. First, they shot him in the legs. And, then they shot him in the head. Ilija Janković's brother from Rajići killed him. Mujo Hodžić, Bećir Hodžić, Raif Hodžić, Salko Salahović, and Bajro Salahović had been working in the fields. The Chetniks took them away. They included another of my uncles and five other men. They were all killed. The Chetniks began to shoot all over the village. My mother and the other women tried to hide in their houses. The Chetniks fired on our houses for fifteen or twenty minutes. We lay on the floor for about an hour until it was quiet. We then began to escape from the village. It was then that I saw the dead eyes of my brother.[13]

X
SENA HODŽIĆ FROM THE VILLAGE OF ZAKLOPAČA

WHEN THE CHETNIKS came into the village, I was at home with my husband Ibrahim who was thirty-nine, my sons Halid, age twelve, and Amir, age eight. When the Chetniks began to shoot, we tried to run away. My husband tried to get out of the village, but I stayed in the house with the children because I was afraid to go out. The Chetniks were all around. Milorad Milošević told my husband to come closer. When Ibrahim approached, Milošević shot him right in the stomach. From the window I saw my husband fall to the ground. He was dead. Just a few meters from where my husband was killed, they held two young men, the unmarried brothers Osman and Bego Hamidović. The Chetnik Brano shot them just as he walked up to them. Osman died right away, but Bego still showed signs of life. He asked for help and some water. We were afraid to go out and help him.

As soon as the Chetniks left, killing everything in their way, we went out and tried to help Bego. But it was too late. He was dead. While the Chetniks were busy killing the Hamidović brothers, three other men, Salim Abdić and Murat and Muradif Hreljić tried to escape from the village, but the Chetniks caught them and brought them back to the village, and killed them ruthlessly. After that, the Chetniks went into Salim's house, where his older brother Musto Abdić, his father Saban, his mother Mevla, his daughter, his sister-in-law Zulfija, his son Samir, age seven, and his one-year-old baby were. The Chetniks killed them all at the same time. When we got to them, they were lying in blood, heaped one on top of the other. When we saw what had happened to the Abdić family, I took the children and fled with the others in a truck. I left my husband lying on the ground with all the other dead people in our village.[14]

XI
AN EIGHTY-FOUR-YEAR-OLD REFUGEE FROM MILJEVINA

THEY CAUGHT MY HUSBAND and slaughtered him. And then they threw his body on the fire. I saw them set seven houses on fire. They left and then returned. This time they packed all our animals onto tractors and trucks and drove them toward Miljevina. They said they were taking it all to Serbia and Montenegro. Everything was burned to the ground. Nothing was left. Nothing but ashes. Yes, they caught Abid Vukara. They threw him into the fire and burned him alive. There was one girl. I remember she was retarded. They killed her father and also threw him into the fire. They took her away and raped her.[15]

XII
THE TESTIMONY OF ALIJA LUANOVIĆ FROM BRČKO

THEY DROVE US LIKE A HERD into the hospital in Brčko. They constantly used their rifle butts to beat us. One old woman fell under the blows and never got up. They divided the people whom they had gathered into groups. About 180 or 200 men were taken off to the mosque. I was among this group. Most stayed at the mosque for four days but I was transferred to another place. In the mosque we had no place to relieve ourselves. We were forced to make use of the *avdestana*.[16]

We were given food for the first time after two days. The slightest remark would elicit a range of punishments. They beat people on the palms with a club. I saw them cut off a man's ear and another's nose. They also would jump from a table onto a man's breastbone. All this took place at the hospital where we were first held as prisoners. One young man who was known in town as Sarajka was crucified in the town center.

After two days they took a group of about two hundred people to the restaurant at the Laser plant. On that night a young Chetnik they called Ranko arrived. He was about thirty years old. He called out people by their last name and slaughtered them in front of the factory building. The guards made them lie on the ground so that they were out of our sight. Only when they had gone away and we could manage to get up to the windows did we see these people with their throats cut. In the room next to the restaurant there were a dozen women of various ages. Ranko raped a woman who was the mother of two children. I know this from the cries I heard.

They called out the names of people who belonged to the SDA, and many others, by their last names. They called them out in sets of three. We would hear three shots. Of course, they never came back. They did everything in sets of three. It was all part of the symbolism. They crossed themselves with three fingers and they killed people in groups of three. I could see what happened through a crack in the door of the shed. They laid people down on their sides with their heads on the sidewalk beside the gutter. This way the blood flowed away. They killed twenty-five to thirty people every night until May 16. The last one killed was Avdo Karić who lived in the same house as I did.

After the 16th the direct killing stopped. We saw the corpses of people they brought in from other locations. Until the 16th they threw the naked bodies of those they had been killed into the Sava river. They then started burning them in the dog pound where stray dogs had been killed once. At one stage they were bringing dead people in cars from the city and packing them into mass graves in Potočari. Later they switched methods and drove them in refrigerator trucks and burned them at the dog pound. This is on the road out of Brčko towards the Interplet factory. One day they brought ten or twenty young men, aged eighteen to twenty-five, naked, with their genitals torn out. Many also had their ears and noses cut off. Out of the total of 1,500 prisoners, 120 were saved and got out only by some kind of intervention or bribery.[17]

WHILE THE WORLD watches in silence, the Muslims of Bosnia are being exterminated or driven from the land they always called home. And this genocide—if one may use the word—is taking place in the heart of "civilized" Europe. The question Danilo Kiš once raised still needs to be answered: "Who are we? Where are we from? Where are we going?"

NOTES

1. Vladimir Dedijer and Anton Meletić, *Genocide Against Muslims, 1941-1945: Collection of Documents and Testimony* (Sarajevo: Svjetlost, 1990).

2. Cited in Dedijer and Meletić, p. viii.

3. Arkanovći are the followers of Zeljko Ražnjatović who is better known as "Arkan." This is one of several Serbian paramilitary formations the members of which are now frequently called "Chetniks" after the World War II units led by Draž Mihailović. Fiercely anti-Partisan, the Chetniks, who opposed the Germans at the start of the war, ultimately collaborated with the Nazis in a common but futile effort to defeat Tito's Partisans. [Editors' note.]

4. Kula-Grad is a suburb of Zvornik.

5. Ibrahim Kajan, *Muslimanski danak u krvi* (Zagreb, 1992), pp. 29-30.

6. The full text of B. I.'s testimony is in the Zenica Center for the Investigation of War Crimes and Genocide.

7. The full text of H. S.'s statement is in the Zenica Center.

8. The statement of S. N., a housewife from the village of Jeleć, is in the Zenica Center.

9. The testimony of K. B. from the village of Kosovo Polje in the Commune of Višegrad is located in Zenica, in the records of the Council for the Protection of the People of Bosnia from Genocide and the Effects of War, September 25, 1992.

10. The full text of the testimony of K. S. is located in the records of the Council.

11. The full testimony and the list of names given by Tima Dautović can be found in Kajan, pp. 38-39.

12. The statement of the survivor from Karakaj was recorded in Tuzla on June 18, 1992. See Kajan, pp. 38-39.

13. Mersudina Hodžić's testimony was recorded in Zagreb at the end of May 1992. She arrived in Zagreb with about fifty women and children from the village of Zaklopača. Not a single male from their village is known to have survived the May 16 massacre. Her testimony was reported by several European journalists who met her shortly after her arrival.

14. Kajan, pp. 46-47.

15. This account was recorded on videotape in Jablanica, July 1992.

16. The *avdestana* is a facility used for the ritual ablutions before prayers.

17. Kajan, p. 63.

TRANSLATED BY DOROTHEA HANSON

DIALOGUE IN THE DARK

The Harsh Song of the
Circular Saw

BALÁZS ATTILA

BUDAPEST, NOVEMBER 1992:

So you fought with the Serb irregulars?

I was an officer in the Serbian Liberation Army.

What's your name?

It's not important.

Your rank?

Leave it, okay?

Don't get me wrong, it's just that I've been told you were involved in, how shall I put it, atrocities. I mean . . .

Atrocities? Tough situations, maybe. I'm a fighter for the Cause. Me and my gun. That's all.

So what are you doing in Hungary, if you don't mind my asking? I thought you guys hadn't got all you wanted yet.

The fight goes on.

Without you?

Sure, it'll go on without me. To the bitter end. There's more than one person running things.

What are their names then?

Don't push me, right? You know if you need to.

Well, I don't . . . At least, I'm not sure. Milošević seems to be getting out. You mean Karadžić and the other guys?

Milošević, that's a long story . . .

Are you angry with him?

I'd rather not say.

Or with Karadžić?

Nor with Karadžić.

Why not?

Never mind.

So are you the one running things?

Come off it! I'm just a little cog in a great machine.

Even now, without your gun?

Sure.

So you're not going back to fight?

Probably not.

Why not?

I've had enough, that's why.

But the Cause still exists . . .

I did what I did. What I could.

So you did what you could and now you're getting out while the going's good . . .

What are you muttering about?

Okay, so you were an officer in the Serbian Liberation Army. The struggle contin-

ues. And you've had enough for some reason. Someone in this bar—their name's not important—told me you were involved in ethnic cleansing round Zvornik.

Who told you that?

I don't know the guy. He's gone.

Yeah, it's true, except that "cleansing" isn't the right word. Anyway, I was just an onlooker. I didn't take part as such.

So what actually happened there?

Why are you so interested? You're not one of those fucking journalists, are you?

Course not. I'm just interested, that's all. You don't have to tell me if you don't feel like it.

Why shouldn't I?

I've heard those Muslims aren't exactly innocent either.

You've got to be joking, mate. They go around raping and scalping Serb women, they cut the dicks off Serb men, and you know what they do to young boys? They circumcise them with rusty knives!

Really?

Yeah, believe me. I've seen it with my own eyes.

Sure, I believe you. But what happened round Zvornik? You were there?

I've already told you, I wasn't involved. Except when my unit took a village. We'd lost a lot of men. Everyone was sort of mad and it got hard to keep the lads under control.

Which village was it?

It doesn't matter. What difference does it make? Anyway, the lads were really mad. They tied the Muslim prisoners with wire to a long cable. All men. About two dozen of them. The order was to take them to the sawmill and lock them up in some sort of store. But when we arrived, we found the store had been shelled to bits—you couldn't have kept a blind cow in there. Half of it was blown away. We'd no idea what to do next, so we lined the Muslims up in the yard and waited. And then one of the lads noticed this huge circular saw and had the bright idea of making firewood out of the prisoners. It was meant to be a joke, but then it got serious. And then it started . . .

Did no one try to stop it?

I told you, the boys were out of control. One of them in particular, he'd been spreading the tale about his kid being eaten by the Muslims.

You can't believe that . . .

Well, who am I to say? The fact was that the kid really had disappeared and his dad had flipped his lid. He was egging them on.

So they really cut the Muslims into bits?

Yes, a few of them.

How many?

I don't remember exactly. A few. There was blood all over the place in no time and the lads gradually lost interest. I didn't see it all. I left before it ended. I walked off. I'd had my bellyful.

So that was when you decided to get out?

Look, there are some things you don't go around telling everybody. But I'll tell you, it's not a pretty sight to watch a circular saw go through human flesh. The way it snarls through the bones . . .

Even if it's a Muslim or a Croat?

Well, we've all got red blood.

Were they screaming?

As if they were being skinned alive, some of them. Some were yelling that their fathers were Serbs and they'd tell everything, if only we'd spare their lives. And let them go.

Did you let them go?

No. How did we know they wouldn't cheat on us? Anyway, who cared what they had to say? It was no time for talking. We'd bottled up our anger far too long.

I bet.

Too fucking right. That's how it was. There they were, screaming and yelling, throwing themselves on their knees, some of them fainting. Not all of them, though. Some of those Muslims didn't make a sound. Just waiting to die. Not saying a word . . .

That must have been hard. I mean, to cut one of them up . . .

Exactly. It was when they were sawing up one of the quiet guys that the lads decided to call it a day.

What happened to the rest?

They shot them. It's okay, at least it's quick. The party has to stop sometime.

So how does this little tale end?

Look, my conscience is clean. There's no blood on my hands.

I hope so. What are you going to do next?

Just get off my back! I've told you, there are things you don't blab about to everybody. No offense meant—you stood me a round. But you see what I mean?

Sure.

But I'll tell you this: one thing's for sure. I'm heading for the West.

You reckon you can make it?

Come on—we've got connections, you know that. We always have done and we always will.

I wrote down this dialogue as soon as I had left the smoke-filled bar. It was hardly the time and place for a cassette recorder. The bar is on what is known as Tram Corner, on Budapest's Great Boulevard, and is run partly by an ex-Yugoslav army officer. Most of the clientele are Serbs, who gather there to talk and listen to Serbian music. The instructions for the pinball machine are in English and Serbian (though not in Cyrillic). There is plenty of drink from ex-Yugoslavia—drink which all too often puts people in a fighting mood. The conversation was in Serbian. I lived for thirty-six years in Serbia. Though an ethnic Hungarian, I know the majority culture inside out, and speak good enough Serbian to pass for a Serb. For awhile, at least.

And this story? Let us hope it was the product of a sick mind. But there are few grounds for hope nowadays.

TRANSLATED BY FRANCIS R. JONES

The Road to Manjača

ORHAN BOSNEVIĆ*

I AM A SURVIVOR of Manjača concentration camp, near the Bosnian town of Banja Luka. I survived—though some wished me dead—though many others have ceased to exist. Now, looking back, I tell myself how lucky I am to be alive. Or should I feel guilty? Perhaps my body should feel guilty, for enduring all that was done to me. Or perhaps my spirit, for never letting me lose all hope. Or perhaps life itself, for not having cosseted me.

War has engulfed my country. People are dying there now, in their hundreds, from bullets, famine, and fear. I have lived through part of my people's suffering, and now my greatest need is to tell it to the world. We used to know little of the evils of the past, for we had not been told about them: perhaps this ignorance of our own history is one reason for the evils of today. But now I must speak out, to my people and to others, so they may know what is happening in Bosnia.

When I think back now, after a few months of freedom, I am haunted by questions: Why? How? Why did it happen? How could neighbor turn against neighbor, friend against friend, relative against relative? In Bosnia-Hercegovina we are so intermingled that there is hardly a single family which does not number Muslims, Serbs, and Croats among its members. We have lived together for centuries amid the matchless beauty of our valleys and hills, surviving all the vicissitudes of time.

Such was my life in Sanski Most, a town in northwestern Bosnia. No longer a youngster, I had all I wanted in life: a family of my own, a decent job. I loved my home town, with its rivers, its valleys, its people. The thought of leaving it never crossed my mind, and almost everyone I knew was content with life there.

But then, in the spring of last year, the Yugoslav army came. Following

---

* Orhan Bosnević is a pseudonym. Names of Serb policemen and military officers have also been changed. (The actual names are being provided to Helsinki Watch and the UN War Crimes Commission.) In all instances, identities have been disguised in an effort to protect the author's relatives still living in Serbian-controlled Bosnia-Hercegovina from any reprisals. Since war came to his country, Bosnević counts thirty-nine relatives among the dead.

the usual pattern, their first act was to seize power from the local council; Serbian flags were hoisted on official buildings, and machine-gun posts appeared at key crossroads.

In 1992 Sanski Most had sixty thousand registered inhabitants: 47 percent Muslim (of whom I was one), 42 percent Serb, and 7 percent Croat, the rest declaring themselves to be Gypsies, "Yugoslavs," and the like. From one day to the next, all the Muslims and Croats were turned out of their jobs. The factories stopped working and freedom of movement was restricted, turning Sanski Most into a ghost town.

From May onwards we would normally spend all our free time in the countryside, tending our animals, orchards, and market gardens. But, this time, with the spring, the army came and no one was allowed to leave their home. A tension was in the air, as if the town were waiting for something.

Finally the storm broke. On May 26th, the Muslim areas of Sanski Most were viciously shelled from the surrounding mountains. Then the Serbs attacked. We were defenseless. In an orgy of shooting, smashing, burning, and murder, the Chetnik irregulars destroyed everything Muslim or Croatian in the town: for two days the streets echoed with gunfire, and entire neighborhoods were razed—the houses burnt down with families still inside.

And then the arrests started. People were taken through the streets to the sports center and local schools. Old men, women and children, youths and girls—some in slippers, some clutching a plastic bag or a blanket grabbed in haste. Disbelieving, bewildered eyes stared from their pale, exhausted faces.

LOCK-UP

EVERY DAY MORE and more people were brought in from the surrounding villages and towns, as others were taken away. I waited for my turn to come. People tried to reassure me that the notorious "special prisons" were a thing of the past—and yet I grew more and more fearful, as if things were coming to a head.

When it happened, it was a beautiful summer's day. I stepped out onto the balcony to breathe the warm air, then went back into the bathroom to shave. My wife was preparing lunch, mange-tout peas, the first of the year: I could hardly wait. As I came out of the bathroom, my wife said: "It's the police." It was just after twelve.

I was standing by the door, my son sitting on the couch, my daughter to his right, and my wife in front of them. Time had stopped.

Two sharp knocks echoed through the flat (the doorbell did not work, as our electricity had been cut off). Two policemen stood outside, with automatic rifles. "Get yourself ready. They want a chat with you down at police headquarters."

I got into their car, a red Mercedes with two more policemen inside. I knew the driver: he used to come round for a coffee now and again. "What have you done wrong then?" he asked. "No idea," I answered.

They took me to Betonirka, the local concrete works, where I was locked up in one of three garages. In each garage, between twenty and forty men were confined in a three-by-five-meter space.

I was summoned to the factory office at about eleven o'clock on the second night. "Hands up against the wall, spread your legs," someone ordered.

Seven men laid into me. Martić, the worst of the Sanski Most police thugs, started hitting me in the chest with his fists, while someone else, who must have been left-handed, beat me with a stick on my left arm and leg and across my back. Suddenly Martić hurled himself at me, driving his knee into my left kidney. Another, Kravić, tried to kick me in the genitals with his boot, but I managed to grab his foot. "Off my fucking leg, you bastard!" he swore.

Someone hit me on the head, and I lost consciousness. They threw a bucket of water over me. Lying huddled on the floor, unable to stand, I could see three men in camouflage fatigues. "Where am I? What's going on? I must have died and gone to hell . . ." I told myself.

I was hauled back onto my feet, only to be beaten senseless again—three times in all. When they finally let me go, drenched and beaten like a cur, I had no idea who or where I was. Unable to stand on my left leg, I somehow dragged myself back. While Kravić was opening up another garage, I leant against a pile of concrete blocks stacked in front of my garage. Broken, scarcely breathing, I struggled vainly to come to my senses. The guard in front of me released the safety catch on his rifle, snarling: "One move and you're dead!" At last my garage was opened, and somehow I managed to crawl to a sleeping space.

All that night men were taken out and beaten. I became feverish, shivering with cold, while outside it was a fine, warm summer's night. My left leg below the knee had swollen to twice its normal size.

Suddenly the order rang out: "Everyone stand!" When they saw I could not stand up, I was given permission to lie down. The others stood all night and all the following day.

It rained during the night, but the next morning was sunny. Until midday, conditions were bearable, but as the temperature climbed outside—it must have reached 35 degrees—and the rainwater which had leaked in through the roof began to evaporate, they became intolerable. The garage had just one tiny window about forty centimeters square; to make matters worse, our Chetnik jailers had piled concrete blocks against it to foil any attempts at escape. As a result, little, if any, fresh air could enter the garage. The garage roof was no more than an inch above our heads; when you put your hand against it, it was like touching the inside of an oven. And so we were baked and steamed alive all afternoon.

Suddenly the door was opened. "Outside! You! Interrogation time." Though still limping, I found I could walk again. Anyway, it was only a hundred meters to the police headquarters and, accompanied by an armed policeman, I had little temptation to dawdle.

In the entrance hall I was greeted by an old acquaintance, police chief Mirko Trtić. As I was standing there, Branko Prtić, a criminal investigator and another old acquaintance, came up to me. "I didn't recognize you from behind," he said. It's hardly surprising, I thought, after the beauty treatment your thugs gave me.

I followed Prtić into the interrogation room. As question followed question, it turned out that I was guilty of every crime under the sun, the worst of all being the fact that I had been born a Muslim. The man who had once been my friend demanded: "What is it you Muslims want? Both banks in town have got Muslim managers, the finance office boss is a Croat, and there's hardly a public company in the area without a Muslim in charge. All the shops, bars, and private firms are in Muslim hands. You've gone too far, let me tell you. What is it you want?" This guy's off his rocker, I thought. For a Muslim to make it to managerial level anywhere in former Yugoslavia, it took hard, honest work—no more, no less.

A thuggish hulk of a policeman entered, probably according to a pre-orchestrated plan. The interrogator asked me something, and I answered that I did not know. In words curiously similar to those of his boss, the policeman yelled: "What is it you Muslims want? We're going to get rid of the lot of you, you'll see! Any of you who're left behind will have to wear badges on their shoulders like the Yids in the war, so that whenever we see you we can kick you in the arse and say: 'Quick march, Turkish cunt!' "

I just stared at him. I could not believe my ears. These people had been my neighbors, my friends. Had I really been so blind? But why look for reasons? They hated me for what I was—a Muslim—and that was that.

CARGO OF DEATH

WHILE I WAS HELD in the Betonirka garages, people were taken away for beatings at every hour of the day or night: I was convinced they were going to kill us all in the end. But worse was to come.

On the evening of July 6th, the food they gave us was rotten. Anyone who ate even a couple of spoonfuls fell sick. All night long men had to relieve themselves in the garage, where they crouched or lay.

Morning came at last, bright and warm; but July 7th, 1992 will long be remembered as an evil day for the Muslims and Croats of Sanski Most. After breakfast, the beatings started again: by midday, almost every prisoner had been done over. Then we were called out for a roll call beside a waiting truck. "Into the truck, at the double!" came the command.

By late that afternoon, we had been traveling for several hours. What little water we had brought with us was gone. Sixty-five beaten, sick, dehydrated men in a hermetically sealed truck with scarcely room for forty. And it was hot, dreadfully hot. Some stumbled frantically round the truck, some stripped off their clothes, some cried out to Allah. The heat was unbearable. Drops of condensation spattered down from the tarpaulin.

I was sitting in the upper section of the truck, beside a chain which linked the sides together. Gazibara Hajrudin had been lying beside me all journey, and Jakov Marin across my knees. From time to time I would bend forward, for there were two small holes in the truck floor which let in a little air. Afraid I might not otherwise be able to get up again, I struggled to my feet and turned my head toward the side of the truck, searching for air.

I dreamt I was by the River Sava with my wife and children. The kids were jumping into the water, and I jumped with them. It was so beautifully cool. . . .

At one point I felt a searing pain in my chest, but it went again. The water was long gone. A bottle was passed around. People urinated in it, then drank the contents. The heat was relentless. My eyelids drooped. We had been traveling for five or six hours. Someone slapped my face, I heard my name called, but I could not summon the energy to answer. To this very day I have no idea who it was, or why.

My neighbor Zika Mujadžić was lying across my back. I pushed him off. Dževad Muhić was making incomprehensible sounds as his brother Nedžad tried to comfort him: "Not far now, brother, we're almost there." Neither of them reached Manjača alive: they both suffocated.

A horrible silence had crept over the lower half of the truck. It was about seven o'clock now; the heat of the day had passed, and the air was breathable again. The truck stopped: we had arrived at Manjača. The tarpaulin was opened. "Out!" came the order. I hauled myself towards the back of the truck. I was one of only two or three men to get out unaided—crawl out, to be precise, for none of us could stand.

Ivo Tutić was a young man, big and muscled; he stumbled round the lorry, blood pouring from his mouth, nose, and ears. The rush of fresh air when the tarpaulin was lifted must have burst every vein in his head. His was no death for a man: it was the death of a wounded beast.

At midday, sixty-five men had entered the truck. Eight hours later, having traveled a mere forty miles, eighteen of us were already corpses. Drenched with sweat, we survivors shivered feverishly in the early evening air, as six more, their limbs writhing in pain, struggled in their death-throes beside the truck. We asked for water. There was none.

"Heads down, hands behind you!" We were lined up with the five hundred others who had survived the journey from Sanski Most, and marched toward the gates of Manjača Camp.

KONCENTRACIONI LOGOR MANJAČA

LOGOR MANJAČA, a concentration camp for Muslims and Croats from all over Bosnia-Hercegovina, lies on the Manjača plateau just above Banja Luka. Once a Yugoslav army farm, its six animal sheds housed about four thousand men—if the inmates of a concentration camp may be called men.

If only we had been treated as well as the cattle and sheep that the sheds had been built for! Six to seven hundred of us, ranging from high school pupils to men in their eighties, were crammed like sardines into each seventy-by-twelve-meter building. At night we slept on the bare concrete or on fern leaves. In the day we were allowed to move a meter to the right of our sleeping position, a meter to the left, and to go to the latrine—in columns of ten men at a time. When it was hot outside, conditions were unbearable; when it was cold, they were worse.

In this camp of fear and horror, where the next moment might summon us to our deaths, we had two "meals" a day. Breakfast was a cup of a warm, colored liquid they called tea, a slice of bread (we were given one loaf between twenty-two to thirty of us), and a piece of bacon the size of a boiled sweet. For lunch, a third of a bowl of unsalted potato or bean soup, with or without a small piece of bread. On this grand diet we all lost ten, twenty, thirty kilos or more, and we were light-headed with hunger.

Logor Manjača was really two camps in one. The first consisted of three sheds where the inmates lived, a hay barn used as a kitchen, a first-aid post, and a solitary confinement block. The second camp was similar, except that it had no first-aid post or isolation cells. Barbed wire and minefields separated the two camps and surrounded the whole complex.

At first, all movement was restricted to the shed. After two months, groups of twenty men at a time from each shed were allowed twenty minutes' fresh air in turn. With six to seven hundred prisoners in each shed—or "pavilion," as we were forced to call them, probably because it sounded pleasanter—it is not too hard to calculate how much fresh air we actually got. Some of us never went out at all.

After the beatings and the hunger, our biggest problems were lack of fresh air, water, and hygiene. Suffocation and thirst had already killed some of us. As for hygiene, it was virtually non-existent. Our heads were shaved immediately on arrival, and I had two baths of two or three minutes each during my whole imprisonment. Our last bath—by courtesy of the army, who ran the camp—was on August 18th; the first inmates left Manjača on November 14th, in a state that is perhaps better left to the imagination.

Field latrines had been dug between the sheds. When it rained, the contents overflowed into the sheds, for the ground was sloping: then we were forced to walk and sleep in human excrement. The only comfort was that in the beginning—until the International Red Cross brought food—there was little need to use the latrines anyway. Some only went every twenty to thirty days, and one man did not go for seventy-three days.

The all-pervading filth meant that we all had cold sores and dysentery. Later we managed to get a little water, contaminated with diesel fuel, from a nearby lake where the vehicles were washed. Then we were able, after a fashion, to wash our clothes.

We did our washing at the back of the sheds, next to the minefield. Once, when I was inside the shed, there was a massive explosion, followed a few seconds later by the thud of something black hitting one of the transparent roof panels. A murmur went round the shed: "Another man gone."

A prisoner—Ramadan Skorić from Kotor Varos—had stepped on a mine. Screaming, blood pouring from the jagged stumps of flesh and bone where his feet had been, he dragged himself to safety. None of us dared help him.

THE DEATH OF EMIR MULALIĆ

AND THEN THERE were the constant interrogations, which we all had to go through, especially when a new group arrived. One day it was the turn of Emir Mulalić, a former policeman from Sanski Most, and two of his ex-colleagues, Ibrahim Begović and Esef Zukić. Afterwards Begović told us what happened.

At a wink from the interrogator, three cops started laying into Emir. The interrogator started firing questions at him, each one more ridiculous than the last, but didn't stop beating him. Emir couldn't take any more and begged: "Water, give me some water—piss in my mouth, anything!"

They ignored him and carried on beating him. God knows how many times he went down. The last time, he just lay there on the floor. They tried to get him up again by kicking his legs, but he didn't budge. "On your feet," they shouted, but he couldn't get up, so two of them hauled him onto his feet while the third kept hitting him. "Give me some water, I can't take any more!" Emir groaned, but he got a fist in the belly instead.

One of the cops said to another—Spaga it was, who used to be a waiter in Banja Luka (and who later became camp commandant)—"What d'you call that? Tickling?" That got Spaga really mad. He yelled: "Can't take any more, can you? You think I'm scared or something?" and laid into him like a maniac. Just to show he wasn't scared of a helpless, dying man too frightened to move.

Emir didn't open his eyes again. The two cops held him up like a sack of potatoes as Spaga kept beating him. When they let him go, he just slid to the floor and lay there, not moving.

Then the bastards got scared, all right. They tried to kick him awake, cursing and swearing, but it was no good—he was dead.

So another life was gone, for no reason. Back home we say that when someone dies, a star goes out. That year, a lot of stars went out over my country. One of them belonged to Emir Mulalić, but at least his suffering was over.

A doctor was called, but what good was a doctor now? His death certificate, issued by the camp authorities—and signed by a doctor—stated that Emir Mulalić had died of sunstroke. There are many such certificates, though fewer than those who died in the camp. They are all false.

THE DAY OF THE LIVING DEAD

ON THE EVENING of Thursday August 5th, Chetnik songs and growling engines, interspersed with bursts of gunfire, could be heard in the camp: sounds that chilled the spine. Next day we heard that prisoners were being shipped in from Omarska—an iron-ore mine near the town of Prijedor that had become a concentration camp for Muslims and Croats.

They brought them in all day. Living corpses, 1300 of them. Lice-ridden, many too weak to stand. There was not a crust of bread for them in the camp, though they had not eaten since Wednesday. They carried water bottles, red ones; later we heard that all they had had to drink was waste water from the mine, heavily contaminated with iron.

And they had horrific stories to tell. Every night a list of names was read out; if your name was called, you never came back. One prisoner, Muharem Hrnčić-Silja, told us that he once had to load a tractor with thirty-nine corpses. All in all, it seems that about one thousand five hundred men were murdered in Omarska. Just because of their names.

The interrogations in Omarska followed the same pattern as everywhere else: whatever you said, they beat you senseless. Except that their brutality had a creative touch—such as forcing prisoners to bite off each others' testicles. Our hair stood on end as witnesses told us of the deaths of Emir and Jasko—of the sound of a man's screams as his genitals were bitten off.

Every war in the history of the world has had its torturers. But compared to the Chetniks, they are all mere apprentices; this work goes beyond bestiality, for no animal could do what they do.

Take Meho Kapetanović, for instance, an elderly, well-respected man from Prijedor. They brought in a little girl and ordered Kapetanović to rape her. He burst into tears. "Please, for humanity's sake," he begged them, as if they were human beings: "She's young enough to be my granddaughter!" They forced him to do it, as he wept.

The Omarska prisoners spent their first night at Manjača in their buses. During the night, many of them were called out to be beaten and killed. These are the men who died at Manjˇca that night: Nihad Bašić, Nezir Krak, Zvonko Tokmadžić, Senrd Džužin Babić; and Jama Jasmin Ališić and Munja Dedo Crnalić, who were no more than youths.

VISITORS

WE HAD NO shortage of visitors. The first to arrive were the International Red Cross, who later returned with food and blankets: it is thanks to them that many of us are still alive. There were numerous visits by journalists. Bernard Kouchner came, the French Minister of Health and Humanitarian Affairs, and Colin Doyle, the United Nations Protection Force commander. Tadeusz Mazowiecki, UN Secretary-General Boutros Boutros-Ghali's human rights investigator, got as far as the main gate but was refused entry by the camp authorities.

In August, however, they did let in Vojo Kuprešanin, a deputy in Bosnia-Herzegovina's prewar Assembly and now a high-ranking official in the self-proclaimed "Serbian Republic" of Bosnia-Hercegovina. He delivered a speech; we were his captive audience: "We Serbs, Muslims, and Croats are all one nation. We must and shall live together in harmony." It was a fascinating speech, a real gem. Though we were his prisoners, he spoke of living together in harmony; though we were being murdered by his men, he spoke of one nation.

SONGS

THE CAMP INMATES sometimes worked in the prison workshop or outside. Making pistol and rifle butts, digging ditches, forestry work. They were also building a church: the mosque in Ključ had had its roof stripped, and now prisoners from a concentration camp were putting it on a church.

One team of inmates was building a boat for Lieutenant-Colonel Milutin Ratić, the camp commandant. A retired army officer, it seems that he had jumped at the chance of promotion plus a little excitement in his old age. During the numerous visits by journalists, he never missed the opportunity of telling them of all the atrocities we civilians had committed, and of how the Serbs, as a peace-loving people, treated us with utmost correctness.

This inspired my fellow-prisoner Ibrahim Begović to make up a song, which he called "We Keep to Geneva Here," after the convention which the commandant was so fond of referring to. "We keep to Geneva here: one loaf's plenty for twenty-two, we break their ribs and keep them thirsty, we do them in and pinch their wedding rings—we keep to Geneva here, as I'm an officer and a gentleman!"

Some officer, some gentleman, lieutenant-colonel! But oh, how greedily we eyed your loaves, lieutenant-colonel! Each of us could have eaten three of them, even if we perished in the attempt. Have you ever had to share a loaf with twenty-one others, lieutenant-colonel? Have you ever seen your own body melt and vanish before your eyes? Have you ever fainted with hunger? Have you ever panted with thirst like a dog, only to be beaten like a dog? Have you ever been to the brink of death from thirst and heat? Have you ever seen your comrades suffocate beside you, or heard the death-rattle in their throats? Have you ever looked evil in the eye?

Begović's other song was called "Guilty." "I'm guilty because I'm a Muslim, I'm guilty because I'm a Croat, I'm guilty, that's why I've got to die . . ."

SURVIVAL

THERE WAS NO rank or hierarchy in the camp, whether of education, knowledge, or age. We were equals in the eyes of guards and inmates alike, though some had a special role: the day's general-duties squad, sweeping squad, and water squad, or the unofficial entertainers and wags. But the struggle for sheer survival dominated everything.

The Chetniks were not content with daily beatings and killings, with keeping us in animal sheds, with stealing everything we owned down to our watches and shoes, with seeing us live in mud and die of hunger. Every day they gave us a show of strength: one of their planes would buzz the camp, less than 50 meters above the sheds. We would look up and mutter: "Go on, crash, even if you take us all with you!"

Our daily news was provided by the Camp Press, a non-existent news agency. In the morning the news was bad, in the afternoon so-so, and in the evening it was good, to wish us sweet dreams. I suspect that this news was actually spread by the camp authorities via the grasses, or camp informers. But not all news was official: there was always some tale to alleviate the monotony of camp life or to give us the strength to carry on.

All the time my only thought was how to survive, assuming I had the good fortune not to be killed outright. I am convinced that it was only some inner stability that saved me. I created this island of stability by singing (to myself, or with a fellow-prisoner—and then only just loud enough for us to hear each other, for singing was forbidden), by keeping my sense of humor, and by thinking of my family.

In the end, a man needs to realize that he is alone in the world, and that the only one who can help him is himself. This thought often went through my mind. There wasn't a square meter of space I could call my own. In my shed, six hundred men: acquaintances, colleagues, friends, neighbors, relatives. Two thousand in our camp, and as many across the dividing wire. And yet I felt alone, just as others told me how they felt alone. Under such conditions, we had to create a calmness within ourselves, for in the end everything came down to individual experience. Our fear was our own, our beatings were our own, our physical endurance was our own—only our suffering was shared.

From the moment we arrived in the camp there were rumors of our impending release. But days became weeks, and weeks became months. Summer came and went, autumn wore on and winter loomed, but we were still in the camp. Rumors started circulating that they would be releasing the older prisoners, those aged forty-four and over; then it became those over forty-two.

To our surprise, the rumors came true. November 14th was a chilly autumn day. Snow had fallen overnight and it was slushy underfoot. Representatives of the Red Cross and UNPROFOR appeared; under their escort—and that of the camp guards, of course—we old-timers were herded out into buses.

But the kids were left behind the wire, three thousand of them still. They clung to the wire, weeping as we wept for them.

We were given cigarettes: everybody was eagerly pressing cigarettes on friends and relatives. And a bar of chocolate lay on every seat. Good God, after all we've been through, to see chocolate again!

But the wire, the barbed wire tore our hearts apart. How is it that we can go, and our dearest not come with us? Zijad Zukić the father could leave, but his three sons had to stay; Muhamed Biogradlija left two sons behind. How many sons, how many fathers, how many brothers, how many kinsfolk had already disappeared or perished, how many were being torn apart right now, how many hearts were breaking!

Can the world not see what is happening to people, to families, to entire nations? People of reason, can you not see the broken adults, the bewildered children and grandparents, the youths turned gray-haired overnight? Can you not see their miserable, tear-stained, haggard faces? Surely you cannot be blind, surely something of this must touch you. Why do you permit the strong to torture and exterminate the weak, and yet forbid the weak the means of defending themselves? Can we really have sinned so deeply against God and man that we must suffer all the evils of mankind?

The sky's tears mingled with ours. Our years were all we had left: our hearts, our souls remained behind in Manjača, to shield our children from their Chetnik captors.

The buses were moving. We could not believe it: we were leaving. We passed a barracks, then Serbian villages where the children taunted us with the three-fingered Chetnik salute. Everywhere, ruined houses. The busy traffic of Banja Luka was no more—only the odd truck or bicycle.

In Bosanska Gradiška our guards got out of the bus. We crossed the bridge over the River Sava, which separates Bosnia-Hercegovina from Croatia. In the Croatian village of Novska, the blue helmets of UNPROFOR. Is this freedom? Can it really be true? We disembarked from the Serbian buses and crossed the road to where the Croatian buses were waiting.

"Excuse me, driver—is there any chance of the news?" The first radio news for five months, as we drove into the town of Karlovac.

Freedom at last! Rebirth! But where are our families, where are our dear ones? Where will this madness end?

—*April 1993*

TRANSLATED BY FRANCIS R. JONES

Bloody Morning

Džemaludin Latić

1.

Morning. The mountain breathes. The clearing shines.
Wind conducts the forest choir.
Sunlight trickles down the pines,
Stretching the shadows ever higher.

Beside a thorn tree, all alone,
a roe-deer grazed, not yet full-grown!

Lovely it was, like a gift only dreamed,
this pastoral scene—a wonder it seemed
and yet it was smashed by a frantic roar,
setting a pack of hounds on her spoor!

She pricked alert in less than a breath
She felt her skin shiver and start—
such shouts and howling threatened death,
From birth she'd known it in her heart!

On slender legs she turned to flee,
the little princess leapt down the scree.

Through forest and clearing, sun and dark,
she bounded, tall and scratched by the bark,
through bushes, harried by the pack
who snuffled out her twisting track.

2.

Why did you run so wildly away?
Why didn't you linger, why didn't you stay
and graze a while—surely you knew
a friend indeed would rescue you?

Or, loving the itch of antler tines,
the whinny of sisters, the belling of hinds,
did you want no foes a-slaver for blood
with snouts fit only for snuffling in mud?

3.

How may these slender legs endure,
this supple body, fiery grey?
Long, too long have streams and moor
echoed loud with the hunters' bay . . .

4.

If you don't make it by the night,
bursting between us high on our hill,
heads will rise and ears will thrill
at every rustle, however slight . . .

We'll know that, legs too shattered to leap,
exhausted, you're at peace, asleep,
we'll know that now the straining ears
of one of our own are deaf to all fears.

TRANSLATED BY FRANCIS R. JONES

Women Hide Behind
a Wall of Silence

SLAVENKA DRACULIĆ

T HE ROOM IS tiny, with one small window letting in
almost no light on a gloomy winter morning. Outside, it's bitter cold, minus fifteen degrees centi-
grade. Stiffly frozen pieces of hand-washed clothing are hanging on lines
stretched between the barracks.

This is my first visit to Rešnik, a camp near Zagreb housing nine thousand refugees, mostly Muslims, from Bosnia-Hercegovina. They have lived
here for months now, ten to fifteen in one room. They are not allowed to
cook, they have to fetch their water from outside faucets, and the nearest toilets are fifty meters away. In the room of the Kahrimanović family there are six
bunk beds, one tin stove, no table, no chairs, no closet. All they possess is laid
out on the beds: clothes, toys, cans of food, two or three pots. Yet these people, from a village near Kozarac in Bosnia, consider themselves lucky because
they have survived.

The crowded room smells of freshly brewed coffee, of dampness, and of
unwashed bodies. Eight men, five women, and four or five children are sitting
in a circle, eager to talk. They have nothing to do but wait. When I ask them
what they're waiting for, they are not certain. Three of the men are waiting for
a foreign country to accept them as immigrants; the others do not know what
they are waiting for. One woman waits for a sign that her husband is alive,
another just cries.

The women prefer to talk about the war, how much land they once
owned, how many cattle, how big their houses were. The men talk about how
they survived Omarska and Trnopolje concentration camps. None of them
will mention the subject they know I've come here to talk about. Finally, I ask
them if they have heard about mass rapes. Have they seen any? At first there is
a silence; even the children are quiet for a moment, as if that horrible word
leaves them speechless. I sense it is the wrong way to ask this question, or the
wrong time or context, but it is too late—I feel the doors are closing. Then I
get an answer: "There were no women raped in our village. We were just
lucky, I guess," says one of the women. "We heard that it happened in other
villages," cautiously adds Smail, the oldest man in the room. The conversation

suddenly stops. People get up and start leaving, a sign that I should do the same. As I am walking out the door, an old woman, Hajra, says in a low voice, "Come tomorrow, my child. Then we'll tell you what we know. We can't talk about these things in front of men, you know."

I expected this kind of reaction. I was warned by colleagues who have tried to talk to rape victims. Since September, when news stories, eyewitness accounts, and official reports began appearing in the press, it has been clear that mass rapes are taking place in Bosnia. Now refugee women are questioned almost every day. A reporter gets off the plane at Zagreb and, like the old American journalists' joke, barges into one of the five or six refugee camps nearby, asking, "Anyone who was raped and speaks English?"

But most of the time one runs into a wall of silence. This silence is driving everyone crazy: reporters, feminist activists, UN officials, European Community delegates, Human Rights Watch, and Helsinki Watch and Amnesty International envoys—all of them enter small and crowded rooms in this or another camp in Croatia, hoping to get closer to the real picture, to hear eyewitness testimony. But in vain. The likelihood is that they will leave empty-handed or hear the same stories from the same few women willing to talk. If they are persistent and patient, they will eventually find a victim who will tell her story. Or they will go to Bosnia—to the towns of Tuzla or Zenica, where women and doctors are a bit more open, perhaps because they are in the war zone. Otherwise, they leave confused and disappointed that, after all the fuss that the rapes have caused in the world media, the women are reticent. Why won't they talk? Don't they know it is good for them?

The matter is more complicated than outsiders realize. That their cases might provide evidence against war criminals is not the main concern of these women. They barely survived the terrors of the war; many have lost family members or have husbands and sons who are still fighting there—or are held in concentration camps or have disappeared and it's not known if they are alive or dead. If the women talk, they could jeopardize the men's lives. Besides, once they are safely out of Bosnia, they want to forget what happened to them as quickly as possible. The third, and perhaps the most important, reason is that they want to hide it. Even though each woman is one among the many victims of a mass rape, what happened to them is in the domain of unspeakable things, the ultimate humiliation and shame. The invisible scars are never going to heal, but it is better if they can hide their hurt and shame from others, even relatives and neighbors.

A doctor told me a story about three sisters. One of them was raped but didn't dare to tell the other two until her pregnancy became evident. After all, under normal conditions only one out of ten rape victims reports the crime. Why would women who are raped in wartime be more forthcoming? Most of the victims are Muslims from strongly patriarchal communities; they simply do not want to revive the pain they went through. I asked one if the women talk about it among themselves. No, she said, they prefer to face it all alone.

Still another problem is that it is extremely difficult to gather solid evidence under wartime conditions, with daily shelling and lack of food, water, and electricity. In Bosnia, governmental commissions are investigating war crimes and are compiling affidavits. Such documentation is also collected by local clubs of exiles, the police, the Interior Ministry, hospitals, individual doctors, and social workers. But these are random efforts and the results are not made available to the public. In fact, the barely functioning Bosnian government is not using rape reports as propaganda. If it were, the evidence and documentation would be more available. But all the officials have been able to do up to now is publish a few bulletins containing estimates of the number of victims and excerpts from victims' testimony; one report was submitted to the UN. It's almost as if they prefer to hide the information rather than go public with it.

And yet, by now there is sufficient evidence to conclude that tens of thousands of women in Bosnia-Hercegovina have been raped. The European Community recently put the number of rape victims at twenty thousand. The Sarajevo State Commission for Investigation of War Crimes estimates that fifty thousand women were raped up to October 1992. The numbers are highly controversial, and it may be that the truth will not be known until after the war, if ever. It could well be that, because of the wall of silence and the difficulty in documenting actual cases, the number is far greater than the world is ready to believe.

When I returned to Rešnik the day after my first visit, there were only five women in the room. The youngest one, seventeen-year-old Mersiha, who just the day before strongly denied that she'd ever seen any rape, spoke up: "Yes, I knew that five of my school colleagues were raped and killed afterward. I saw them lying in a ditch. They were there for days and each time I passed by I didn't want to look, but I did. It was in June. Their clothes were torn off them and I could see that they had been tortured. I saw knife wounds on their breasts, on their stomachs. Then, one afternoon, when we were coming back from a concentration camp where my brother was imprisoned—there were about fifty women walking back to our village through the woods—we saw that armed Serb Chetniks were waiting for us. We knew what was going to happen, but it was impossible to escape. They stopped us and chose two women. Then about ten Chetniks raped them in front of us. We were forced to stand and watch. It was dark when they released us, and I still remember how one of the women shivered when I took off my jacket and put it over her naked shoulders."

When Mersiha talked, the other women didn't comment. They stared at the floor as if they were guilty, as if they were to blame. I asked Mersiha, "But what about you?" She looked at her mother, sitting there and listening, as if asking her for permission to say more. "No, it did not happen to me," she said, but I doubted her. Maybe, if I came on another day, she would decide to tell me her true story. That is how it works; only patience and empathy can break the wall of self-protection.

But Mersiha did tell me about a cousin who was raped. Her story led me to a refugee camp in Karlovac, as if she had given me an Ariadne's thread leading to an underground network—a secret, silent, frightened network of women who know about one another's misery but prefer to hide it. The thirty-year-old cousin had been raped by four Serbian boys who looked perfectly normal, barely over twenty—not drunk, not crazy, not beasts. In fact, they were the boys next door; she knew them because they were from a nearby Serbian village. "After all these months," she said, "I cannot get rid of a feeling of carrying some kind of visible stamp, of being dirty, physically dirty, and guilty." When I asked her if she would go back, she said something that I heard over and over from many Muslims—and not only from rape victims or even women: "Under no condition would I return to live in the same village with Serbs as before. I would never let my children go to a school with their children. I would not work with them. In fact, I would not even live in the same state with them."

These words reveal the role that mass rape plays in the Serbian program of "ethnic cleansing." As Susan Brownmiller and other feminists have pointed out, women have been raped in every war: as retaliation, to damage another man's "property," to send a message to the enemy. Rape is an instrument of war, a very efficient weapon for demoralization and humiliation. In World War II, Russian and Jewish women were raped by Nazis, and Soviet soldiers raped German women by the hundreds of thousands. Chinese women were raped by the Japanese, Vietnamese by Americans. What seems to be unprecedented about the rapes of Muslim women in Bosnia (and, to a lesser extent, the Croat women too) is that there is a clear political purpose behind the practice. The rapes in Bosnia are not only a standard tactic of war, they are an organized and systematic attempt to cleanse (to move, resettle, exile) the Muslim population from certain territories. Serbs want to conquer in order to establish a Greater Serbia. The eyewitness accounts and reports state that women are raped everywhere and at all times, and victims are of all ages, from six to eighty. They are also deliberately impregnated in great numbers, held captive and released only after abortion becomes impossible. This is so they will "give birth to little Chetniks," the women are told. While Muslim men are killed fighting or are exterminated in about one hundred concentration camps, women are raped and impregnated and expelled from their country. Thus not only is their cultural and religious integrity destroyed but the reproductive potential of the whole nation is threatened. Of course, Croats and Muslims have raped Serbian women in Bosnia too, but the Serbs are the aggressors, bent on taking over two-thirds of the territory. This does not justify Croat and Muslim offenses, but they are in a defensive war and do not practice systematic and organized rape.

Women who have been raped have almost no future. Besides the psychological damage, and in spite of a *fatwa* issued by the highest Bosnian Muslim authority, the Imam, that men should marry these women and raise the progeny of the rape in a Muslim spirit, each of them knows that this is unlikely to happen. It may seem very abstract to speak of rape as a method of "ethnic cleansing," but it becomes quite clear and understandable when one talks to the victims and witnesses. One woman told me that if she were raped, she would kill herself, even if her husband did not reject her. She could not stand the shame and humiliation, she could not face her children afterward. "I would prefer to be killed than raped"; "I thought about killing myself so many times"—this is what they say. One of the most disturbing and painful things to hear is their attitude toward the children born of this violence. All the women I have spoken with or heard about or whose statements I have read— whether or not they are victims or eyewitnesses—with no exception said they would kill such a child ("I'd strangle it with my own hands," as Hajra put it) or abandon it.

To hear such statements from women, many of them mothers, gives an idea of how strongly they feel about rape, what intense negative emotions mass rape has stirred in them. In their view, the rapes are only one of the things the enemy is doing to them and are directly linked to other kinds of aggression, from shelling and attack to imprisonment, torture, killing, depor- tation, and, finally, exile from their own homes, from their own country. They are suffering not only a loss of pride but also the loss of their identity and of their country—the loss of everything they ever had. This is why the mass rapes of women in Bosnia cannot be discussed without taking into account the political context.

What the rape victims care about most is the reaction of their immedi- ate social group—their husbands, fathers, brothers, and other relatives, their neighbors, their village, their compatriots. Their lives are strongly rooted in community, and any help they might receive individually will be inadequate. As one of them who declined psychiatric care said to me: "I refused the doc- tors' help because I cannot see how they could help me. I need the under- standing of my relatives. I need to go back home." The most important therapy is reintegration of the victims into normal life, but this is almost impossible. Reintegration is not going to happen soon; people cannot go home because of the war. And integration into the few countries that have accepted some half-million refugees is problematic. Western Europe is closing its borders because of a rising tide of xenophobia and racism and because of the recession.

About half of the nearly two million Muslims who lived in Bosnia are now in exile. Europe has no policy on what to do with the greatest migration of refugees since World War II, on how to stop the bloodshed in Bosnia, and bring about a sensible political solution that would be acceptable to all three sides. Without a political solution, rape victims are left to themselves and to partial solutions that offer only short-term relief. It is easy to invoke the famil- iar feminist argument that rapes in wartime only draw wider attention when they are used as propaganda. If this is so, in Bosnia the propaganda hasn't been working. The mass media have mainly focused on the sensationalistic aspect and have treated it as a woman's problem only, without considering the wider context, in terms of arousing public pressure for a comprehensive political set- tlement.

But even if the rapes were used for political propaganda, this could be justified because of the Serbian policy of exiling and destroying the Muslim population. If an entire ethnic group is systematically destroyed to the point of genocide, it is legitimate to "use" accounts of rape (or anything else, for that matter) as a means of getting attention and influencing public opinion.

Strangely enough, the women themselves—the five in Rešnik camp, for example—are fully aware of this, much more than are the many politicians, humanitarians, feminists, activists, or journalists who are taking their side and trying to help them. They also know something else, of which Europe is not yet aware: if there is no political solution soon, the Muslims will turn to terrorism as a last resort. Bosnia's Muslims are the Palestinians of Europe, and they will not willingly give up the right to their land.

As I was about to leave the little room in Resnik, a boy entered and listened to the end of our conversation. "I will slaughter Serbs with a dull knife," he said, matter-of-factly. I asked him how old he was. Thirteen, he said. In two years he will be doing just that, if there is no other future for him. But he won't kill just Serbs. There will be a price to pay for those who prefer to close their eyes now. It was easy to see it on that boy's face.

EXTRACT FROM A SUFI CHRONICLE OF 2092

The Land of Inexhaustible Inspiration

ENES KARIĆ

FOR ALMOST TEN centuries, until 1992, Bosnia had been a land of rich and wonderful inspiration. Countless poets had sung of her landscapes. One writer even won the Nobel prize, thanks to Bosnia's virtues. Many scholars of comparative religion praised Bosnia and its heritage of Abraham, and recorded in their books how its sons prospered more than they suffered. Four ages of the children of heaven were counted in Bosnia. Almighty God in his grace scattered rich treasures over Bosnia. A great part of this world's religious mosaic was spread out before you in Bosnia. Verily, Bosnia was then a land of many streams, beautiful springs, and sweet flowers.

And then in the year of our Lord 1992, for the first time in its history, Bosnia became the home of great evil and the seat of misfortune. From that year, one could drink one's fill of evil in Bosnia. Without any effort or impediment one could find hundreds of evil inspirations. Instead of spring waters and clear brooks, the Bosnian earth burst forth with the most diverse hydra-headed evil. It was then that the whole world said that they carried this evil on their own shoulders, and that the sons of Abraham who called themselves Orthodox had sown this evil in Bosnian soil with their own hands. But why it was so, and whether it was so to the end, shall be discussed on other pages of this chronicle . . .

I AM NOT ALONE in recording how the Muslims of Bosnia were in that time long besieged in many cities; other chroniclers record this as well. Thus one can read truthfully of these things. It was in those days that the Orthodox sons of Abraham became the unsurpassable masters of evil. Imagine the position of a small ant which is placed at the center of a ring of fire. The only thing which keeps it from death is to stay forever in the center! Moving anywhere, especially if it rushes to one side or the other, puts its existence in peril. Truly, such was the grievous position of the Muslims in those days . . .

TRAVELERS FROM the Western end of the Earth wrote many books about the tragic fate of the Muslim women of Bosnia. The author of one such book said, when asked how he managed to produce such an excellent work, "Go to Bosnia! Even one who has never felt inspiration will find it there!" (This writer sold tens of thousands of copies of his work. They say that once, when he was drunk in some Parisian café, he gave thanks to the disaster that befell Bosnia's Muslims: were it not for this, he never would have become such a good writer!) Many Western theoreticians of the *War in Bosnia* asserted that the war was not all bad, that it also had its positive dimension. Hitherto, the very idea of warfare by rape was unheard of. If there had been no war in Bosnia, and the Orthodox sons of Abraham had not crafted this strategy of military bestiality, the theory of warfare would have been the poorer!

Before the Bosnian calamity of 1992, offensives against the honor and integrity of women were unknown. The conquest of a country was familiar from pre-Bosnian wars—it was done by Napoleon, Genghis Khan, Kutuzov—but a high-level command for an attack against the women of one nation and against their honor, that we have only in Bosnia. It was after Bosnia that many instigators of war spread this strategy to the ends of the earth. The discovery of a single evil, which had been unknown in that form to mankind, led to the multiplication first of that evil and then of other, similar evils. The rape of a mother in front of her children led to the rape of that mother in front of her parents, and then in front of her husband. The generals said: "Rape her first before the eyes of those whom she bore, then before the eyes of those who bore her, then before the eyes of her husband who fathered children with her!"

Inscrutable, indeed, are the paths of human inspiration in evil.

TO THIS DAY, which is to say just decades after its completion, the tragedy of Bosnia has inspired hundreds of learned doctoral dissertations. A particular problem, analyzed and discussed from many points of view, is the question of the *water torture*. This has been one of the most coveted topics, fought over by young scholars—the Bosnologists.

Thus, one French student sought to prove that the water torture was the result of religious atavism in Bosnia. Although the West introduced the washing of one's backside with water in its modern hygienic code, some nations still do not practice it simply because the washing of the backside is enjoined by some religions, such as Judaism and Islam, to which those nations hold strong aversions. To adopt such a practice was to become, for a moment, a Jew or a Muslim, even if only in the bathroom! (They say that this doctoral candidate was praised by the Chairman of his examination committee. The tragedy of Bosnia, the Chairman said, must be thoroughly researched. Not even the backside may be overlooked.) In any case, my friends, the problem of Bosnia is indeed on that level.

For months, and for years, people defiantly carried canisters through the streets of Sarajevo in the stampede for water. The Orthodox sons of Abraham poured out from the hills hot shards of iron, which sliced off legs, arms, heads. My friend from Ciglana told me that not long ago, they spent hours looking for a man's hand. A fragment of hot iron tore it off as though in jest, sliced it off and threw it somewhere into a park. They found it only the next day, barely chasing away a hungry dog who had also found the hand. This man too was looking for water, thereby losing his life, and his dead body losing its hand.

MY FRIENDS, THIS is simply fantastical—the art of dying in Bosnia in 1992—in Sarajevo, Goradže, Mostar, Jajce, Bihać, Gradać, Srebrenica. After 1992, the European scholars of death (thanatologists) began making expeditions to Bosnia. One of these scholars has alone published three immense volumes on the skillful methods of killing in Bosnia. (At the time, he noted that he still had three-fifths of his material in unpublished notes, which he would ulti-mately present to the public: he was waiting for the reaction to the first three volumes. Bosnia has yielded such a wealth of material to him that he is unable to express himself in just three volumes.)

In Bosnia people die by the unbearable lightness of the creativity of evil. Here you can see, almost as a joke, the deaths of two children in a bus hit by the bullets of an anti-aircraft gun. The killer asked himself at the time, *Did the children's eyes fall out?* Yes, yes, this would be interesting to know, for experts say that in 93.27 percent of these cases, the victims' eyes fall out and land in their own laps.

There exist, they say, many theological reasons why the Orthodox sons of Abraham killed tens of thousands of Sarajevans in the first seven months of slaughter alone. Consider, for example a dilemma presented to one Orthodox son of Abraham in a dream: "Can God Almighty raise from the dead people whose bones are mingled in the grave?" In Sarajevo, you see, there is no room for cemeteries, and people are buried with strangers in common graves. There-fore nowhere, my friends, nowhere will the Day of Judgment be as interesting as in Bosnia! When the divine command is heard, "Awake!", then bones from the crowded graves will fly to their owners, colliding with the bones of strangers. The resurrected will marvel at one another and ask: "How was it that so many of us were gathered in one grave, my friends? Why this crowd-ing, my people? Which three of us came first, and which last, killed by hot iron from the hills?"

Such conversations on the Day of Judgment are only possible in Bosnia! For Bosnia is the land of inexhaustible inspiration on the unbearable lightness of dying. You see, not long ago, even the theologians fell into a dark quandary over the question of how to bury a man who had been reduced to a greasy stain on the pavement after a direct hit by a piece of hot iron, 120 millimeter caliber, from the hills! Yes, yes, Bosnia is a theological inspiration as well, my friends. This is a theology of new elements and new definitions of death, the grave, the funeral. Some theologians already promise volume upon volume of learned answers.

BUT ABOVE ALL else, as I write in my chronicle, it is interesting to note how the Orthodox sons of Abraham taught the besieged Muslims of the all-pervading presence of God. More precisely, they made the Muslims realize that the dear Lord is closer to one than one's own carotid artery! And so death takes a house-wife while she cooks her stew! It happened the other day in Dobrinja! There are many such cases. In this respect Bosnia is a very rich country, my friends.

It is said in a certain Islamic tradition that the dear God holds the human heart between his two fingers. When one strolls along the streets of Paris, New York, and Munich, one would do well to believe this, because in Bosnia, my friends, it is quite easy to believe. When you see so many places where molten iron rains down from the hills and still you stretch out in one piece in your skin, then you do know that the paths of the Lord are inscrutable. And you understand that Bosnia, the land of inexhaustible inspiration, is held in the palm of His hand.

On Nationalism

Danilo Kiš

NATIONALISM IS FIRST and foremost paranoia. Collective and individual paranoia. As collective paranoia it results from envy and fear, and most of all from the loss of individual consciousness; this collective paranoia is therefore simply an accumulation of individual paranoias at the pitch of paroxysm. If, in the framework of a social order, an individual is not able to "express himself," because the order in question is not congenial and does not stimulate him as an *individual,* or because it thwarts him as an individual, in other words does not allow him to assume an entity of his own, he is obliged to search for this entity outside identity and outside the so-called social structure. Thus he becomes a member of a pseudo-masonic group which seems to pose problems of epochal importance as its goals and objectives: the survival and prestige of a nation or nations, the preservation of tradition and the nation's sacrosanct values—folkloric, philosophical, ethical, literary, etc. Invested with such a secret, semi-public, or public mission, A.N. Other becomes a man of action, a tribune of the people, a semblance of an individual. Once we have him cut down to size, isolated from the herd, and out of the pseudo-masonic lodge where he had installed himself or been installed by others, we are faced with an individual without individuality, a nationalist, Cousin Jules. This the Jules that Sartre wrote about, a zero in his family, a man whose only distinction is that he can blanch at the mere mention of a single topic: the English. This pallor, this trembling, this "secret"—to be able to blanch at the mention of the English—constitute his social being and make him important, existent: do not mention *English* tea in front of him, or the others will start winking and signaling, kicking you under the table, because Jules is touchy about the English (and loves his own fold, the French), in a word, Jules is a personality, becomes a personality, thanks to *English* tea. This kind of profile, which fits all nationalists, can be freely elaborated to its conclusion: the nationalist is, as a rule, equally piffling as a social being and as an individual. Outside the commitment he has made, he is a nonentity.

He neglects his family, his job (usually in an office), literature (if he is a writer), his social responsibilities, since these are all petty compared with his

messianism. Needless to say, his is *by choice* an ascetic, a potential fighter bid-
ing his time. Paraphrasing Sartre on anti-Semitism, nationalism is a comprehensive and free choice, a global attitude not only toward other nations but
toward people in general, toward history and society; it is at once a passion
and a world-view. The nationalist is by definition an ignoramus. Nationalism
is the line of least resistance, the easy way. The nationalist is untroubled, he
knows or thinks he knows what his values are, his, that's to say national, that's
to say the values of the nation he belongs to, ethical and political; he is not
interested in others, *they are no concern of his,* hell—it's other people (other
nations, another tribe). They don't even need investigating. The nationalist
sees other people in his own image—as nationalists. A comfortable standpoint, as we noted. Fear and envy. A commitment and engagement needing
no effort. Not only is hell other people, in a national key of course, but also:
whatever is not mine (Serbian, Croatian, French . . .) is alien to me.

Nationalism is an ideology of banality. As such, nationalism is a totali-
tarian ideology. Nationalism is moreover, and not only in the etymological
sense, the last remaining ideology and demagogy that addresses itself to the
people. Writers know this best. That's why every writer who declares that he
writes "about the people and for the people," who claims to surrender his individual voice to the *higher* interests of the nation, should be suspected of
nationalism. Nationalism is also kitsch: in its Serbo-Croatian variant it takes
the form of squabbling about the national origin of GINGERBREAD HEARTS.*

As a rule the nationalist doesn't know a single foreign language or any
variant of his own, nor is he familiar with other cultures (they are no concern
of his). But there is more to it than this. If he does know foreign languages,
which means that as an intellectual he has an insight into the cultural heritage
of other nations, great or small, they serve only to let him draw analogies, to
the detriment of those others, naturally. Kitsch and folklore, folkloric kitsch if
you prefer, are nothing but camouflaged nationalism, a fertile field for nationalist ideology. The upsurge of folklore studies, both in this country and in the
world at large, is due to nationalism, not anthropology. Insisting on the
famous *couleur locale* is likewise, outside an artistic context (i.e., unless in the
service of artistic truth), a covert form of nationalism. Nationalism is thus, in
the first place, negativity; nationalism is a negative spiritual category because
it thrives on denial and by denial. We are not what they are. We are the positive pole, they the negative. Our values, national, nationalist, have no function
except in relation to the nationalism of those others: we are nationalist, but
they are even more so; we slit throats (when we must) but they do too and
even more; we are drunkards, they are alcoholics; our history is proper only *in
relation* to theirs; our language is pure only *in relation* to theirs. Nationalism
lives by relativism. There are no general values—aesthetic, ethical, etc. Only

* Biscuits in the shape of hearts, or people, or things, decorated with colored sugar, and sold by bakers
  in Vojvodina, Serbia, and other parts of ex-Yugoslavia. (Translators note)

relative ones. And it is principally in this sense that nationalism is reactionary. *All* that matters is to be better than my brother or half-brother, the rest is no concern of mine. To jump not very high but higher than him; the others do not count. This is what we have defined as fear. Others are allowed to catch us up, even to overtake us; that is no concern of ours. The goals of nationalism are always attainable, *attainable* because modest, modest because mean. You don't go jumping or shot-putting to reach *your* own best but to beat the only others who matter, so similar and so different, on whose account you took the field. The nationalist, as we noted, fears no one but his brother. But him he fears with an existential, pathological dread; for the *chosen* enemy's victory is his own *total* defeat, the annihilation of his very being. As a shirker and a nonentity the nationalist does not aim high. Victory over the chosen enemy, the other, is total victory. This is why victory, victory that is guaranteed and defeat that is never final. The nationalist fears no one, "no one save God," but his God is made to his own measure, it is his double sitting at the next table, his own entity, the conscious and organized section of the family and the nation—pale Cousin *Jim*. To be a nationalist is therefore to be an individual with no obligations. It is to be "a coward who will not admit his cowardice; a murderer who represses his murderous proclivities without being able to master them, yet who dares not kill except in effigy, or in the anonymity of a crowd; a malcontent who, fearing the consequences of rebellion, dares not rebel"—the spitting image of Sartre's anti-Semite. Whence, we wonder, such cowardice, such an attitude, such an upsurge of nationalism, in this day and age? Oppressed by ideologies, on the margin of social changes, crammed and lost between antagonistic ideologies, unequal to individual rebellion because it is denied to him, the individual finds himself in a quandary, a vacuum; although he is a social being, he takes no part in social life; although he is an individualist, individuality has been refused him in the name of ideology; what is left but to seek his social being *elsewhere?* The nationalist is a frustrated individualist, nationalism is the frustrated (collective) expression of this kind of individualism, at once ideology and anti-ideology . . .

TRANSLATED BY IVANA DJORDJEVIĆ

This brief text "On Nationalism" appeared in 1973 and quickly became the focus of much controversy. Kiš himself, relishing the scandal it provoked, called the text "notorious." It is included in this collection with the kind permission of Kiš' literary executor, Pascale Delpech, and by the courtesy of Mark Thompson.

The Seventh Day
The Book of Genesis

MAK DIZDAR

. . . And I saw the water eating away the earth
The sun drinking the water
The earth belching out fire
I saw beast attacking beast
Man spilling man's blood
I saw evil deeds on all sides
I saw the evil deeds thou didst create
For I had tasted of the fruit of the tree of knowledge
I saw for my eyes were opened
And I cried out
It is not good It is not good It is not
This thy earth
Is good only for the stones . . .

TRANSLATED BY ANNE PENNINGTON

PART III

A word has come to my kingdom that the Turkish tsar Muhamed intends to attack me with his army during the forthcoming summer and that he has prepared everything necessary. I cannot by myself resist such Turkish power. I amiably prayed the Hungarian and Venetian lords and Gjerj Kastriot to come to my aid in this misfortune. I pray you, my all-honorable, powerful, serene lord and father, the same. I do not ask for golden hills, but would be glad that my enemies and the people of land know that your help will not be wanting. Because if the Bosnians see that they will not be alone in this war and that others will help them, they will go into war and fight with greater bravery, and the Turkish army, too, will not enter into my possessions without fear and forethought. Approaches to my land are very difficult and many fortresses are invincible, permitting none to penetrate deeply into my kingdom. [. . .] If you believe me and help me, I shall be saved, otherwise—I shall perish. And my ruin will not be mine alone—it will pull down many others, like a torrent.

—From the letter of Stjepan Tomašević, the last king of Bosnia, to Eneas Silvius Piccolo-mini, Pope Pius II, in 1461 AD

In the era of the ruler of the world Murat-khan, the son of Selim
the most high benefactor Muhammed-pasha,
who was the grand vizier to three rulers,
made his greatest endowment; may the Lord count it among his good deeds!
In pure intention he built with his gracious sight the great bridge over the river
    Drina.
It was so beautiful that he, who sees it,
holds that a pearl stands in the water, and the firmament is its shell. [. . .]
Muhammed-pasha built this bridge across the water in the year 985.

—The inscription on the bridge of Mehmed-pasha Sokullu (Sokolović) over the Drina River at Višegrad, 1577 AD

Separating History from Myth

AN INTERVIEW WITH IVO BANAC

*Professor of History and Master of Pierson College,
Yale University*

RABIA ALI: The war in Bosnia-Hercegovina has been generally perceived in the West as a civil war or a tribal blood feud—the product of centuries-old enmities between the Serbs, Croats, and Muslims. In the media and in the pronouncements of statesmen and political commentators, the conflict is described as a "typical" Balkan convulsion which cannot be understood, much less mediated or settled by any international intervention. One finds much confusion about the war, its causes and likely consequences, even among many educated, normally well-informed people. As a historian, how would you define the war and its historical roots in Bosnia?

IVO BANAC: Let us discuss first "what it is," and then, perhaps, "what it is not." I view the war as essentially a war of aggression conducted by Serbia and Montenegro, in tandem with the Yugoslav People's Army which was taken over by Serbia and used for its own purposes. It is a war of aggression against an internationally recognized independent state with a democratic constitution that guaranteed rights to all citizens, including Serbs.

In the process of waging this war, aggressive forces had to instrumentalize the Serbian community in Bosnia-Hercegovina: they had to turn a relatively peaceful population—however large its prejudices about the nature of Bosnia and its role in Bosnia—into a group that would become auxiliary to the aims of the aggressor. This was one of the reasons the instigators of the process had to proceed very slowly, gradually implicating the Bosnian Serb community in their project of aggression and expansion. This could not be done overnight; it had to be done in stages. First, they had to isolate those who were opposed to their plans and had struggled against them. Then they had to implicate all the others in what initially were small acts of repression against the other communities and, ultimately, in very large and horrid crimes.

If one wishes to think in terms of historical analogies (which are sometimes helpful, though not always), the Serbian war policy in Bosnia-Hercegovina resembles to a great extent the approach adopted by the German administration against Czechoslovakia in the late 1930s. Therefore, one could view Radovan Karadžić as being Konrad Henlein and the Serbian Democratic Party as the Sudetendeutsche Partei. Thus, in pursuit of Serbia's war aims in Bosnia-Hercegovina, one community—the Bosnian Serbs—was essentially subverted and presented with a reinterpretation of its own history: namely, that it had always been on the receiving end of Muslim domination in Bosnia-Hercegovina and that its future and security lay within a "Greater Serbia." In this reinterpretation, of course, the Croats are accorded a very negative role as auxiliaries to the Muslim aim of domination.

The position of the Croat community was somewhat more complicated. Initially, and to a considerable extent even now, the aims of its leaders were to join with the Muslim community in the defense of Bosnia-Hercegovina, but the dominant party among the Croats went through several changes. There were purges of its leadership which turned it into an instrument of [President Franjo] Tudjman's own aspirations in Bosnia-Hercegovina.

LAWRENCE LIFSCHULTZ: Are you referring here to the purge of Stjepan Kljuić from the leadership of the Croatian Democratic Union of Bosnia-Hercegovina [HDZ] and his replacement by Mate Boban?

BANAC: Yes, the purge targeted Kljuić—and Davor Perinović before him—and it proceeded in several stages exploiting the differences among the Croats of Bosnia. The Croat community in Bosnia-Hercegovina is split between the Croats of Central Bosnia who are greater in number, and the Croats of western Hercegovina who represent about a third of the total Croat population of the country. This latter group has emerged as the politically dominant force principally because of the physical and military control it exercises over significant territory and, most importantly, because of the backing its leader Mate Boban receives from Zagreb.

Stjepan Kljuić represented the point of view of the Croats of central Bosnia for whom the defense of Bosnia-Hercegovina was the paramount requirement, as opposed to many Croats from western Hercegovina for whom the defense of western Hercegovina was all that mattered; what happened elsewhere was of little or no importance. Their point of view was well summarized in the statement of one of Kljuić's political enemies who said, "What is Cajniče to me?!" (Cajniče is a town in eastern Bosnia that has no Croats among its population.) This, of course, is a narrow view focused entirely on local interests and is part of the tendency among the Croats in western Hercegovina and adjacent areas of Bosnia, such as Tomislavgrad, to see the areas inhabited by them as suburbs of Zagreb.

These are the forces which, today, are trying to draw out other Croats from more ethnically mixed areas of Bosnia-Hercegovina into the exclusively Croat cantons that have been legitimized by the Vance-Owen plan. The Croats in central Bosnia are under tremendous pressure from these elements to leave their areas—to get out of Sarajevo, Travnik, Tuzla—and to migrate to the so-called Croat cantons. Boban's objective is to create on the Croat side the equivalent of what the Serbs have achieved through military force in Serb-populated areas: a nationally homogenized entity. There is significant resistance to these developments, and great division over the issue in Croatia, where it is probably the most important internal issue in Croatia at the moment.

In sum, I see what has happened in Bosnia as a form of aggression clearly instigated and directed by Serbia, which has succeeded in creating an entirely different political climate in Bosnia-Hercegovina to the point where the defense of the Bosnian state has, today, come to be centered largely around the Muslim community. And for things to have reached this stage, the world, too, bears a great deal of responsibility: it has not allowed Bosnia-Hercegovina the right, and thus the arms it needed, to defend itself.

To define the war as a tribal feud or a civil war is simply an easy way of dismissing the whole thing. The argument then is that if something has been going on forever, presumably, it will continue forever and hence nothing need be done to alleviate the situation. The best thing to do, therefore, is simply to sit back and watch as this hellish situation plays itself out. The assumption on the part of the outside powers-that-be is that these sub-humans will get tired of killing one another, and then, perhaps, those outsiders can step in and do something to patch up the situation in one way or another. It all adds up to a combination of political opportunism and intellectual laziness.

LIFSCHULTZ: Related to the question of definitions is the question of the validity of Bosnia-Hercegovina as a political entity. Many pundits and politicians continue to describe Bosnia as an artificial construct that has never had a distinct identity or presence in history. Notable among these for example, is A. M. Rosenthal, former editor and currently a regular columnist of *The New York Times,* who has attempted in his columns to "inform" the debate by suggesting on several occasions, in different ways, that Bosnia has no historical legitimacy and the Muslims no national rights since they are a community of converts. "As for the Muslim leaders," he writes, for instance, in the *Times* of April 16, 1993, "they had declared the independence of a Bosnia which had not existed as a nation and in which they did not have a majority. There are no 'Bosnians'—just Slavs who call themselves Serbs, Croatians or Muslims." The corollary of this position is that since Bosnia-Hercegovina has never been an independent state or the national home of any particular people, its defense as an independent state is not imperative.

Influential commentators like Rosenthal thus reflect not only a disregard for history, but also a blithe contempt for facts which are still part of the current record. For example, the vote for independence by a large majority of Bosnians in a referendum which the European Community had asked for, and the joint decision, therefore, to declare independence by a multinational Bosnian government composed of representatives, in equal numbers, of all three of the country's constituent nations (as well as the representatives of the Jews and other minorities) is presented as an irresponsible and undemocratic act, as it were, of "Muslim leaders." How do you respond to such statements and interpretations of Balkan—and Bosnian—history?

BANAC: This is all sheer nonsense. I do not know how to account for such statements and arguments except to say that they reflect the great—at times, willful—ignorance which surrounds this matter. If this were all true, I would be the first one to join in support of the partition of Bosnia-Hercegovina, but this is not the case. The historical fact is that Bosnia-Hercegovina has a profile which is unique, and distinct from the identity of the neighboring countries. Its existence goes back to the Middle Ages.

The Bosnian state was the last of the major South Slav states emerging in the fourteenth and fifteenth centuries. It was a major regional power which, at various moments, included sections of present-day Croatia and Serbia. During the period of the Ottoman Empire its structure was maintained in a peculiar, local way precisely because it was a frontier area for the Ottomans. Therefore, the maintenance of a landed nobility which was hereditary and, as such, unique in the Ottoman Muslim state gave Bosnia a very clear regional distinction which set it apart from other central Ottoman provinces.

For example, in the nineteenth century, this feudatory structure of Bosnia did assume leadership in a struggle to maintain Bosnia on what was an anti-*Tanzimat* program. The objective was to assert Bosnia's uniqueness and to seek a greater measure of autonomy, which, in the nineteenth-century Ottoman Empire, was as good as independence. Indeed, many of the national movements in the Ottoman Empire argued initially for autonomy. In the declining Ottoman state this was one way to maintain the unity of one's own area which was always subject to the irredentist dreams of others. So the continuity of Bosnia as a distinct political entity was preserved in the Ottoman Empire.

During the Austro-Hungarian period, Bosnia-Hercegovina was a separate province which did not fit very comfortably into the dualist system established under Ausgleich in 1867. Nevertheless, in a complicated sort of way it did fit into the structure. It was administered both out of Austria and out of Hungary through a joint Minister of Finance, an arrangement which, of course, was not at all logical but which became an ad hoc solution. The political program of Benjamin von Kállay, who was that joint minister of finance and thus the dominant figure at this stage in Bosnia, as well as Kállay's ideology of Bosnianism effectively denied the region to both Croatia and Serbia.

This sense of autonomy was maintained during the early years of the first Yugoslav state even though, in royal Yugoslavia, Bosnia did not exist as a formal entity. While it was not divided as some other areas were, its unity consisted essentially of a collectivity of smaller entities. The denial to it of the formal status of a province in the interwar period fed into the national program of the Communist Party during the 1930s. The autonomy of Bosnia-Hercegovina became an objective of the Party. Its position was codified at the end of the war as one of the constituent republics of the Yugoslav Communist federation, but it was constituted on a non-national basis. It was the only republic that was a not a matrix republic, for it was, in fact, a republic that was multinational by definition.

Thus, from the medieval period to Tito's federalism there has been a Bosnia. It is a land which has its own distinct cultural flavor. An important influence, of course, has been the presence of a very large Muslim community. With the exception of Albania there is no comparable group in the neighborhood. Furthermore, when one examines the national cultures of the non-Muslims there, the Serbs of Bosnia-Hercegovina, and the Croats of Bosnia-Hercegovina, one can find unique and distinctive features that are not identical to the national cultures of the matrix countries. The literature of the Bosnian Croats is distinct from that of the Croats in Croatia. Similarly, the literature of the Bosnian Serbs is quite distinct from the literature of the Serbs in Serbia proper.

LIFSCHULTZ: Arguments which are based on the false premise that Bosnia has no real cultural or historical identity, perhaps, represent something more invidious. They legitimize the idea of the fragmentation of Bosnia-Hercegovina by its division into smaller ethnic entities as proposed by the Vance-Owen plan or some other device which the Western intelligentsia will, in the end, rationalize as the "best" of all the "bad" solutions.

BANAC: Of course, this is the direction in which this type of argument leads. If the Western powers want to abandon Bosnia and do nothing, then let them be frank about it and not twist the historical record to rationalize their positions. The rich history of co-existence between these communities is also part of that record.

ALI: The fact that Bosnia, through history, has existed as a separate and unique entity long before it became part of Yugoslavia still leaves open the question of its viability as a sovereign state under the present political circumstances. If Yugoslavia failed as a multinational state, what legitimacy would an independent multinational Bosnia-Hercegovina, often described as a Yugoslavia in microcosm, have? The constituent nations of Yugoslavia—the Croats, Serbs, and Slovenes—sought their affirmation, identity, and progress in new states defined by or based on ethnicity. Was it not inevitable that Bosnia, too, would disintegrate as the Serbs and Croats of Bosnia-Hercegovina sought, or were encouraged to seek, the union of "their" Bosnian territory with their "mother" countries?

BANAC: If Bosnia were a collectivity of separate entities, then it would have been a mini-Yugoslavia. But it is not that. Bosnia is a historical entity which has its own identity and its own history. In other words, it is not a Yugoslavia; it cannot be construed to be a mini-Yugoslavia. There is a temptation to do this precisely by people who seek to divide it. The argument goes more or less the way you put it: Yugoslavia disintegrated as a multinational state and so, too, must multinational Bosnia. This is basically a Serbian argument.

I do not see it that way because I view Bosnia as primarily a functioning society which Yugoslavia never was. My question is how does one keep a complicated, complex entity like Bosnia-Hercegovina together? Undoubtedly the answer presupposes an interest in the maintenance of Bosnia-Hercegovina by its neighbors. This is something that makes the situation extremely complex. Precisely because Serbia does not wish to have an independent Bosnia-Hercegovina, the project becomes immensely more difficult. And precisely because the present Croatian leadership would like to settle all the historical issues with Serbs by the division of Bosnia-Hercegovina, the project is made still more difficult.

LIFSCHULTZ: So for the Croats of Hercegovina to throw their support behind the idea of a united Bosnia-Hercegovina would require the Croatian state to take a clear stand on the sovereignty and indivisibility of Bosnia?

BANAC: Yes, a different policy in Zagreb would have a tremendous effect especially on the thinking of the Croats in western Hercegovina. Furthermore, I am certain that had the unity of Zagreb and Sarejevo been maintained in a sincere way, Serbian aggression would have been defeated a long time ago.

ALI: Wouldn't one also say that Tudjman and others who sought the division of Bosnia might have contained their own expansionist ambitions had the West—instead of settling on the partition of Bosnia-Hercegovina as the best and quickest solution—sent a very strong and clear message that it would not countenance the carve-up of a sovereign member of the United Nations? In the end, or rather from the very beginning, by putting an international seal of approval on the policy of an ethnic carve-up of Bosnia-Hercegovina the Vance-Owen plan had the immediate effect of encouraging both the Serbs and the Croats to secure their share of Bosnian territory.

BANAC: There is no question that the Vance-Owen plan did precisely that, and the consequences in their fullness are there for all to see. The horrors of Vitez and the escalation of the war between the Croat and the Bosnian government forces, which are now fighting on two fronts, are a direct result of the Vance-Owen plan. It was interpreted by the Croats in the way that was, in fact, logical: "This is our canton, which means we exercise power here. You do not agree with us? Well, ship out, or submit!" All of the disputes about the use of language in schools, about the flying of national flags in the so-called Croat cantons are all aspects of the logical interpretation of the Vance-Owen plan.

As a result, you have the current situation which, in my view, can be solved only in one of two ways. The first would involve a change of heart in the neighborhood. For the present this is improbable. The second would involve the determined support of the international community which has been sorely lacking. And there are many reasons why the international community should act.

To my mind, if Bosnia did not exist, it would be necessary to create it—precisely because it mitigates the hostilities between Serbia and Croatia. Many of the contradictions can, in fact, be resolved through a policy of equality inside Bosnia-Hercegovina. There is another very important reason why Bosnia should exist as an independent state. It has to do with the Bosnian Muslim community itself which has no other national home. This is why the Muslim community has, to a very large extent, become the cement of Bosnia-Hercegovina. It would be wrong to say that this community is uniquely Bosnian and the others are not—because there is a great danger that this argument, too, would undermine the unity of Bosnia-Hercegovina. As I mentioned earlier, the Bosnian Croats and the Bosnian Serbs have distinctive cultures that distinguish them from their mainstream cultures that obtain, respectively, in Croatia and Serbia. They are distinctively Bosnian. It is this element which sustains the cultural unity of Bosnia-Hercegovina and explains why so many Bosnian Croats and Bosnian Serbs have supported the Bosnian government.

LIFSCHULTZ: While we are on the subject of multinational states, would you elaborate a little on your argument in *The National Question in Yugoslavia* that democracy and Yugoslav "unitarism" were incompatible phenomena. In other multinational states such as Pakistan and India, for example, precisely the opposite position has been argued. Thus Pakistan's disintegration in 1971 has primarily been seen as a consequence of the extinction of democracy under an increasingly authoritarian state. Can any broad conceptual propositions or conclusions be made regarding multinational states and democratic structures?

BANAC: My argument is not that multinational states and democratic systems are necessarily at odds in all instances. What I have said is that this was the case in the Yugoslav experience. The reason has to do with the nature of the South Slavic national ideologies, specifically the Serbian national ideology. One way to illustrate this is to consider how Yugoslavia was viewed conceptually by the different constituent nationalities. For example, I think that for the Serbs—especially Serbs from Serbia—the entire territory of Yugoslavia was seen as something which was theirs. For a Serb, being in Slovenia or Macedonia was not a qualitatively different experience from being in central Serbia. This was exactly *not* the way the non-Serbian national groups viewed the country. A Croat or a Slovene who, temporarily, by way of business or otherwise, was in central Serbia knew that he was in a different area that was not the same as his home ground. The possessive nature of Serbian national ideology has on occasion expressed itself through the ideology of Yugoslavism. It matters very little what the effluvia are if the content is possession. This was unique and prevented any sort of democratic agreement from the very beginning.

I would argue that the first Yugoslav state failed, not in 1941 when it disintegrated, but in 1921 with the adoption of the centralist constitution. And it went from bad to worse. In 1929 there was the introduction of the royal dictatorship when King Aleksandar tried to do by force that which he had failed to do through the pseudo-parliamentary system of the 1920s. This led to tremendous dislocations and, basically, to the failure of Yugoslavism as any sort of integrative ideology.

The Communists tried to resuscitate this ideology in the guise of a Soviet-style federation, and they had some success with it. But they were more successful when they argued for the clear identity of all the constituent parts—a key element of their program during the war. They did not win the war under the banner of Yugoslav unitarism; they won under the banner of the national liberation of Slovenia, Croatia, Serbia, Macedonia, and so on. But then, of course, they went through many new phases in the definition of that particular concept, and the particularly negative phase coincided with one of the more open periods of the postwar Yugoslav socialism. In the 1950s, when Tito argued for integration of all these different identities within a supranational Yugoslav identity, he provoked tremendous opposition among the Communists of Slovenia, Croatia, and so on, who saw this as an opening for the revival of Serbian hegemony. This conflict came to a head in 1962–63 with Tito's change of position. He abandoned the idea of Yugoslav integration, becoming increasingly aware of the harm this would do to the unity of Yugoslavia. He then tried to give greater rein to the genuinely federalist tendencies inside the Party and the state.

LIFSCHULTZ: So in 1962 he essentially reversed himself?

BANAC: Yes, Tito reversed himself. He adopted the position of Edvard Kardelj, who was the number two man in the Yugoslav leadership in the postwar period. Kardelj was always extremely critical of Yugoslav unitarism; in this instance, he became the winner in an intraparty dispute. A footnote, however, should be introduced here: everything was happening within an essentially dictatorial structure; what was different after the war was the fact that a minority party was the dominant, the *only*, political organization on the scene and, therefore, all the debates about the nature of the Yugoslav political system and Yugoslavia's federal form of organization took place principally within the legal ten percent of the whole political structure. It was not terribly representative. I stress this because there is a notion that nationalism was revived after the collapse of communism. This is not accurate. The reality was that since nationalism was repressed, or, more exactly, the politics of identity were repressed, during the Communist period, all issues dealing with such matters were debated inside the Party. By the 1970s, sections of the Party itself had become exponents of the specific national interests. The Communist Party itself became federalized—and its federalization meant the end of its effective unity and the beginning of the crisis that led to the downfall of the second

Yugoslav state. With the introduction of multiparty democracy, the entire structure withered away.

Now, it is true the Slobodan Milošević, and the Serbian party leadership even before Milošević, accelerated the demise enormously. They made reform extremely difficult. I would say they made it impossible. It is very likely, however, that the end would have come anyway. The key point was 1971 when Tito, for pragmatic reasons, shut the door to national communist policies that were being championed by the League of Communists of Croatia. At that stage Tito was supported by the Belgrade "partiocracy" for reasons that had less to do with pragmatism than with questions of supremacy and caste interests.

The movement of 1971 resembled structurally the Dubček movement in Czechoslovakia where the reform effort was attacked as politically suspect and made to appear illegitimate. And with that, you had the end of a possibility of reform of the Yugoslav federation. Although, in the Constitution of 1974, Tito formally incorporated many ideas of the Croat reform movement, these ideas were not adopted on a democratic basis. Tito imposed the constitutional structure from above. The unity of the country was entirely dependent on the domination of the Party which was itself increasingly fragmented. It lasted as long as Tito was on the scene. As soon as he was gone, the whole house began to crumble and Milošević pulled it down.

ALI: What was the alternative program advanced by the Croat Communists in 1971? What did they want and what difference would the adoption of their proposals have made?

BANAC: The Croat Communists were essentially in favor of a confederation. First, on the economic plane, they proposed a system of what they called "clean accounts." They argued that the industrialized republics such as Croatia were at a disadvantage within the federal system. There are counter-arguments to this view, but the Croatian leadership wanted to make these issues the subject of an open political debate. They proposed that the question be discussed freely with a sense of give-and-take. This was new. On the cultural level this meant a legitimation of national cultures and the clear recognition of the existence of such cultures as an alternative to the dominant cultural paradigm of Yugoslav unitarism. With respect to political democracy, the Croats were advocating the opening of the media to voices of opposition. As was the case in Czechoslovakia, the proposed changes were all admittedly within a Communist structure. In fact, these developments really did lead to a period of considerable free speech and relatively free political expression.

ALI: In other words, what you had was what is sometimes referred to as the "Croatian Spring," similar in some respects to earlier developments in Prague? But why was Tito determined to oppose these developments?

BANAC: Yes, the term "Croatian Spring" is frequently used. Of course, there are many differences in the developments in Prague and those in Yugoslavia—and, again, these center on the national question. I believe Tito opposed these developments because he considered them to be premature and subversive of his own aims of restructuring the federation. One of his close associates once put it to me in the following way. He said here was someone (Tito) waiting in an ambush to shoot the dangerous unitarist bear, when, all of a sudden, someone else started jumping in front of him and prevented him from carrying out his operation the way he intended. Perhaps, this explanation is too simple. In my own view I think that Tito, who was a master of political balance, came under tremendous pressure in 1971 to stop the Croatian movement from accomplishing its political aims.

LIFSCHULTZ: Where was the pressure coming from?

BANAC: There was pressure from Serbia but also from abroad. There were, in this case, tremendous pressures bearing down on Tito from the West. Nixon was not terribly happy with these new developments in Yugoslavia. He viewed them as possibly weakening a strongly established Western front in Yugoslavia. There were threats from Brezhnev as well. On several occasions during that year Tito cited Brezhnev's warnings. The Soviets had said that if the Yugoslav leadership could not keep order in their own house, the Soviets would be only too happy to perform the job on the basis of Soviet "fraternal assistance."

ALI: You are saying that both the Soviet Union and the United States had an interest in maintaining the status quo in Yugoslavia?

BANAC: Yes, but for different reasons. The special status of Yugoslavia was part of the Cold War system.

ALI: However, Tito in 1974 essentially adopted—from the top down—many of the proposals of Croatia's Communist leadership as part of his own program.

BANAC: This was never admitted. The Milošević camp frequently uses this as a polemical weapon against Tito. But, it is true that many of the ideas the Croatian leadership advanced in 1971 were incorporated into the 1974 Constitution. Nevertheless, this was done under a slightly different guise. The distinctions are perhaps somewhat esoteric. What constitutes sovereignty? In 1971 sovereignty for the Croat leadership was essentially "national." In the 1974 Constitution sovereignty was defined within the nomenclature of "self-management." In other words, the question was not addressed in terms of the sovereignty of national republics within Yugoslavia but of socialist entities operating in a framework of self-management.

ALI: Jelena Lovrić in her article in this book tells us that shortly after the purge of the Croatian liberals in the Party in 1971, Tito had also moved against the Serb liberals. These Serbs, in Lovrić's view, were seeking to separate Serbia from its total identification with Yugoslavia. In other words, Serbia, in its self-perception, was entirely synonymous with Yugoslavia and saw itself as its principal, if not sole, defender and guardian. People like Latinka Perović, for instance, sought to alter Serbia's view of its position and its role in Yugoslavia. In their view, it was more important for Serbia—a republic with vast backward areas in its hinterland—to focus on its own development and modernization. Would you agree with Lovrić?

BANAC: I think that she is absolutely right. Although this is probably going to sound somewhat exaggerated, I would argue that in the history of Serbia, starting with the period of the uprisings early in the nineteenth century and continuing to the present, the most outstanding political leadership Serbia ever had was precisely that of Marko Nikezić and Latinka Perović in the late 1960s and early 1970s. Because they wanted to emancipate Serbia from the federation—which was very unusual—they entered into conflict with Tito. And the conflict arose because they were perceived by Tito as fighting against his predominance—his extra-systemic role within Yugoslavia. This certainly contributed to their downfall. In addition, when Tito removed the Croatian leadership, he upset the political balance in the country very dangerously. He had to rebalance it somehow. So in 1972 he struck against the Serbian liberals. And he also struck against liberals in a number of other republics. This "rebalancing" had extremely deleterious effects. It was after this that the political leadership in Serbia fell into very bad hands. Although, by comparison, the new leaders were infinitely better than Milošević who later succeeded them, they nevertheless constituted an opposition of sorts against Tito which became evident even in his lifetime. The first attacks against the Constitution of 1974 emerged precisely from this quarter at the end of the 1970s.

LIFSCHULTZ: There are different views, among the contributors to this volume and others, regarding European and American policies toward Yugoslavia in the last days of its existence. Some like Mark Thompson argue that the delay in recognizing Slovenia and Croatia, and then Bosnia-Hercegovina, only laid the groundwork for greater violence on the part of Serbia. Thompson insists that the ineptness of European diplomacy in 1990–91 virtually abetted the "Greater Serbia" camp. Mihailo Crnobrnja has argued that the West's failure to support Marković's attempt to negotiate a new federal arrangement left the field open to Milošević and his supporters. John Newhouse in *The New Yorker* of June 28, 1993, has argued that American assurances to Milošević in 1991 that the United States supported a united Yugoslavia led Milošević under the pretext of Yugoslav federalism to carve out the boundaries of a "Greater Serbia" in Croatia and Bosnia.

How do you analyze European and American diplomacy in the

1988–92 period? Was the dissolution of Yugoslavia inevitable? Would it have occurred regardless of European or American policies? And, if so, would other policies on the part of the international community have led to a less brutal form of dissolution? Or, was all of this irrelevant in the end to the internal dynamic of the expansionist project of a "Greater Serbia"?

BANAC: In my view American policy was the most important factor. The Europeans were not really involved in the Yugoslav crisis until the spring of 1991. The essential point to understand is what the principal contours of American policy were in this period. The dominant note was the belief that Yugoslavia was capable of surviving as a unitarist state. This view misunderstood fundamentally the nature of the deep cleavages in the country and the stage of disintegration that had already been reached. By 1991 such a position was not a plausible one.

I agree with Newhouse's argument. By stressing the unity of the country in the way the United States did at that juncture, it effectively helped Milošević. This was precisely the argument he used to put pressure on all the forces that were opposed to him in the various republics. Perhaps the most negative moment was in June 1991 when Secretary of State Baker visited Belgrade. Baker delivered exactly the wrong signal at the wrong time to Milošević and the Yugoslav People's Army. By declaring itself in favor of Yugoslav unity at precisely the moment Milošević was preparing to undertake military action on behalf of his "Greater Serbia" project, the United States essentially encouraged him.

Why did the United States act in this way? There are several possible explanations. Clearly, the disintegration of the Soviet Union was an obsession of American policy at this stage. American diplomats judged both situations as analogous and concluded that the break-up of Yugoslavia would be extremely dangerous and destabilizing. The difference, of course, was that in Yugoslavia the Americans were encouraging precisely the figure who more than any other was himself responsible for the political agenda that would finally destroy Yugoslavia. As the political sponsor of a resurgent and aggressive Serbian nationalism, Milošević had made co-existence impossible for others. After the Soviet Union disintegrated in the summer of 1991, the analogy continued. The obsession now became the question of maintaining Russia, and, specifically, the Yeltsin regime. And, in the former Yugoslavia, Serbia, like Russia in the Soviet Union, was seen as the principal successor state.

There is another reason why the United States was deeply committed to the maintenance of Yugoslavia. This commitment had everything to do with the role of Yugoslavia in the Cold War, but nothing to do with the notion that Yugoslavia was a democratic alternative to the Soviet Union. Yugoslavia was viewed as an acceptable alternative to the Communist regimes of Eastern Europe because it existed as a power that was not subservient to the Soviet Union. This is what Tito symbolized for the West. The enormous amount of economic aid and political support that successive American administrations committed to Yugoslavia became second nature to the American political establishment. It simply could not conceive of this area without the sort of state structure that Tito had maintained so successfully for so long. This underlying attitude encouraged Milošević along his own path. When the United States did not react to the mini-war in Slovenia, this opened the gates for Milošević's war in Croatia. The crisis grew during the summer of 1991 and was transformed into open war in the fall of 1991.

LIFSCHULTZ: So, in your view, the Americans could have stopped events from taking the turn that they did?

BANAC: Absolutely. I think that they could have stopped it anywhere along the line. I'm not saying that nothing was done. There are indications that by the spring of 1991 Washington had acted to prevent a total military takeover in Belgrade. This happened, probably in January 1991, during extremely dramatic negotiations between Tudjman and the military leadership in Belgrade. Perhaps the United States also intervened on another occasion in the spring of 1991. But all these actions were within the framework of Yugoslavia. In Washington it was simply inconceivable to imagine that Yugoslavia had been shattered, and irreparably so. But I think that the real test of American and European inaction came in the fall of 1991 during the bombardment of Vukovar, Dubrovnik, and many other places in Croatia. At that point, a clear message could have been delivered to Belgrade to stop these attacks. This was not done, thereby opening the way to the German initiative in favor of the recognition of Slovenia and Croatia. For this the Germans have been called to considerable account. From my point of view, not only was that the right thing to do under the circumstances, but the demoralization in Belgrade that took place *after* the recognition shows how much more effective such a move could have been had it come even earlier.

LIFSCHULTZ: You are saying that the German initiative to recognize Slovenia and Croatia came only after the bombardment of Croatian cities. Would the Germans not have acted regardless of Belgrade's aggression?

BANAC: I do not think so. The German recognition of the independence of these republics at this stage was more a knee-jerk response; the bombing precipitated considerable activity on the part of the Germans, which, of course, would have been far more effective had it come earlier. Again, the whole Western alliance was still operating under the unspoken idea that Yugoslavia could be preserved. I cannot see how this was realistic, considering the nature of the events. How could one imagine that after Vukovar—after many, many other things had happened—that this country could be held together?

ALI: During this period wasn't Izetbegović of Bosnia-Hercegovina trying to persuade Germany and the Europeans not to be hasty with their recognition of Croatia and Slovenia, but to hold off so that some arrangement could be worked out for a final resolution of the Yugoslav crisis? Apparently, the Bosnians were worried that they would be left to the tender mercies of the Milošević regime should Slovenia and Croatia abandon the federation and, to preempt exactly this, Izetbegović and Gligorov, the leader of Macedonia, had drawn up certain proposals for the restructuring of Yugoslavia?

BANAC: Both Bosnia and Macedonia were in an extremely precarious position. On the territory of both Bosnia-Hercegovina and Macedonia, there were very heavy concentrations of the Yugoslav People's Army. In Bosnia, especially, there had already been a very heavy mobilization of the Serbs, and this was extremely serious because the Serbs constitute one-third of the Bosnian population (they are not very significant in Macedonia). Both Izetbegović and Gligorov tried to find some sort of a third way between Milošević and the already self-proclaimed independent republics of Slovenia and Croatia. This was unrealistic: their position was absolutely hopeless at this point. I must say that both of them did not try to complicate matters for Slovenia and Croatia, as is sometimes claimed. Their hands, especially Izetbegović's, were tied.

At this point precautionary, or preemptive, measures, especially in Bosnia-Hercegovina, were crucial, but these were not taken. If at this stage, contingents of United Nations troops—or, perhaps, troops from that Sleeping Beauty, the European Union—had been introduced into Bosnia, it is possible that many of the things that happened later on would never have occurred. We are talking about the summer and especially the fall of 1991. Remember, one of the problems for Izetbegović was precisely that the citizens of Bosnia-Hercegovina, which had now become a sovereign republic after having proclaimed itself sovereign in the fall of 1991, were being recruited into the Yugoslav People's Army in order to fight in Croatia and he was telling them: "Do not go. This is not our war." That was a significant challenge to the Yugoslav People's Army given the army's overwhelming presence in the republic. All the same, he really had less and less maneuverability.

LIFSCHULTZ: Was there anyone in the West who saw the necessity for such preemptive or protective action in Bosnia at the time?

BANAC: Not really. No, this is quite remarkable, isn't it?

ALI: Would you say that, in France and Britain, considerations of their historic alliance with Serbia were operating at some level which led them to balk continually at any decisive international action against Serb aggression? I recall listening with some fascination to a British member of parliament on television referring to the Serbs as "our allies" while arguing against any intervention against Serbia.

BANAC: It is difficult to believe that these could be political considerations at the end of the twentieth century, but there is probably something to it. I think this has not so much to do with Serbia as it has with fears of the future role of a united Germany. Historical memory in Western Europe is not as insignificant as many Euro politicians pretend, and a united Germany did change the political landscape of Europe. Moreover the cost of uniting Germany has created a number of difficulties for Western European economies. So I think that the problem of Germany was then transferred to the Balkan situation, and in a curious way. European actions or decisions were less a response to the question of what path to find for the successor states of Yugoslavia and more a part of the political fencing that went on between the Germans and their Western allies. Perhaps these divisions would have come over other issues, but they came precisely over the issue of Yugoslavia, and demonstrated amply, in 1991–92—the year of European unity—the extent to which Europe was not really united and not really a political entity.

LIFSCHULTZ: So the fencing that occurred was, in part, determined by the fear that the German initiative toward the recognition of Slovenia and Croatia in 1991 heralded the extension of German hegemony in the Balkans. Are you saying that this was a fear that, for instance, worried France?

BANAC: I am being extremely cautious because, of course, they knew better than that. Germany was playing a very limited game, and after it pushed for the recognition of Slovenia and Croatia it basically pulled back, and since that time has really done extremely little. There are many extenuating circumstances, of course. Germany is a diplomatic and an economic power but it is not a military power. It is restrained also by the memories of the Hitler period. But, all the same, I think that many of these issues that go back to the First World War do have a certain resonance on the West European scene, where Serbia is a recognizable entity and many of the other South Slavic republics are not. Now, of course, the Belgrade regime—I think not as successfully as it hoped—tried to capitalize on these feelings, and in its very crude propaganda it was essentially saying to London and to Paris that they were abandoning an ally to an increasingly aggressive Germany, which, I think, is easier to believe in Belgrade than in Paris or London. After all, there are certain restraints that the Alliance imposes on all of its partners. Nevertheless, to a very large extent, the disputes over what course to take in the Balkans destabilized Western Europe and are an opening to a dangerous process that is probably going to widen as, not just the Balkan, but the international crisis sharpens.

ALI: Let us turn again, then, to the subject of Bosnia-Hercegovina. If it did not exist, you said, it would have to be created. Well, since it does exist, the question becomes how can it be saved from extinction? How can it be defended? In this context, perhaps we can discuss the policies the international community has pursued in seeking to secure peace in Bosnia-Hercegovina. How do you assess their actions and their thinking?

BANAC: There has been a contradiction in the behavior of the international community. First, before the Bosnian government declared independence a set of rules and criteria were established as the basis on which Bosnia-Herce-govina would receive international recognition as an independent state. It met these criteria. The international community then abandoned this policy by treating the government of Bosnia-Hercegovina—at this point, still multina-tional—as if it were merely one of several contending factions.

This was an extremely interesting sleight of hand, a device that took the international community off the hook. The correct and logical thing was for the international community, having once recognized Bosnia and its territo-rial integrity, to have then intervened on behalf of a very weak and essentially unarmed state that was suddenly faced with the most brutal forms of aggres-sion. When it became independent, Bosnia had on its territory all the units of the Yugoslav People's Army withdrawn from Slovenia and Croatia and the military units which were already there. Bosnia had been one of the centers of Yugoslavia's military industry and there had always been a large garrison of it's military there during the Cold War. Thus, when independence came, Bosnia was especially vulnerable to attack if these units were deployed against it.

The only solution ever was to suppress and then to defeat aggression. This could only have been done with a significant investment of military power, but no one wanted to do what was required. So all sorts of excuses were found, including the ones we have talked about. It is an "ethnic war"; these are "eternal problems" which cannot be solved; and more recently the so-called "Russian problem" where Bosnia could not be permitted to "undermine" Yeltsin—and on and on.

There is always some reason not to do the only logical thing, which is to intervene. In the process this could not have been done without a cost to inter-national organizations, all of which, to a very large extent, have already been badly compromised in Bosnia. The United Nations has seriously compro-mised its integrity and its mission; the European Community, obviously NATO, and, of course, the United States, all of them appeared to be paper tigers. Utterly toothless, they followed up each phase of Serbian aggression with continuing expressions of joy at any minimal sign of "good will" on the part of the Serbian leadership. For example, when Karadžić signed the Vance-Owen proposals in Athens in May 1993, this was accepted as a significant advance, but for those who could see, it was clear that before pen was put to paper it amounted to nothing. Nevertheless, the Europeans and the Ameri-cans heaved a great sigh of relief as if things were suddenly going to improve. It was not clear why. Meanwhile, Bosnia has had to pay a tremendous price for promises which were not kept and actions which were not taken. At the moment the full dimensions and price of this tragedy cannot be counted.

ALI: When you call for international action, what precise form of intervention are you calling for?

BANAC: First, I think the Bosnian state must be permitted to arm itself. The notion that one is neutral by preventing Bosnians from arming themselves is political dishonesty. In fact, one is acting on the side of the aggressor by preventing the lifting of the arms embargo. This is the first and most essential action the international community must take. There is a great deal of evidence that not only Bosnian Muslims but other Bosnians, including many Croats and Serbs, were ready to fight for Bosnia against the aggressors. But this resolve to mount a multinational defense was essentially undercut by the international community. The Bosnians could not fight with slingshots; they had to be armed with the requisite weapons, for they were up against an extremely well-armed and relatively well-trained army.

LIFSCHULTZ: Are you saying essentially that if the United Nations, the European Community, and the United States had not wanted to get "off the hook" and find any excuse to compromise with Serbia, they would have lifted the arms embargo right from the start?

BANAC: Yes, and we can speculate on why they refused to lift the arms embargo. The refusal represented in part an element of wishful thinking by the Western powers, and in part the belief that the entire matter was not very dangerous. They chose to believe, therefore, that Milošević—as awful as he was, and as deeply implicated as he was in the bloodiest of crimes, since 1945—could not create the conditions for a major international conflagration. I can only say that their analysis really demonstrates a failure of imagination.

Perhaps, Milošević cannot trigger a Third World War, and perhaps this is impossible in a post-Cold War situation, but what Milošević has done, and with greater effectiveness than many realize, is to demonstrate that there are no real restrictions on aggressive behavior. This will simply give carte blanche to Miloševićes everywhere, of whom there are and will be quite a few.

LIFSCHULTZ: The principal—in fact, the only—solution the international community has insisted on has been the Vance-Owen plan. David Owen called it "the only game in town." Critics have argued that the plan was deeply flawed. While it required a Serbian withdrawal from some territory, it still validated the seizure of significant areas by the Karadžić-Mladić forces. The plan was built on the notion of partition along the lines of ethnicity which the government of Bosnia has consistently opposed on the grounds that it wants to maintain a multinational state. Kemal Kurspahić, the editor of Sarajevo's *Oslobodjenje,* refers to it as an "apartheid" solution. What do you feel were its fundamental flaws? Or, could it have been a basis for peace?

BANAC: It was a seriously flawed plan and some of the flaws were mentioned in your question. The Vance-Owen plan divided Bosnia-Hercegovina on the basis of national cantons where it would be difficult, if not impossible, to guarantee the rights of minority groups, and it would ultimately lead to a partition of the country. The plan presupposed that the Mladić-Karadžić's forces would withdraw into those areas which the plan had reserved for the Bosnian Serbs. But who was going to compel them to do that? Let us, for argument sake, say that this were to happen in one way or another. Who was going to protect the democratic liberties of, say, Muslims in Banja Luka? Who was going to make certain that people who had been driven out of Bileća would be able to return to their homes? The Vance-Owen proposals put forward an extremely complicated set of requirements with absolutely no means of implementation. In reality, they were proposing a "solution" on the lines of the division of Cyprus which is a permanent partition with no means of ever unifying the parts. The Vance-Owen plan was basically a placebo meant both for the Bosnians and for the international community, and nothing more. In the real world, it would be more difficult to enforce the Vance-Owen plan than to mount military operations against the aggressor.

In backing the plan, though, the West had decided to do the very minimum, that is, to make a show of protecting the Bosnian Muslim community, if necessary through the sort of policies that were attempted on behalf of the Kurds in Iraq by the creation of inviolate zones, perhaps protected by UN or NATO forces. As for the rest of Bosnia-Hercegovina, the thinking is that different parts of it will simply gravitate to the centers of national attraction—Serbia and Croatia. And this has been the unarticulated aspect of the Vance-Owen plan. The Washington agreement of May 1993 [between the United States, Britain, France, Spain, and Russia] on the creation of six Muslim "safe havens" merely takes this to the final logical conclusion. The "safe havens" are no longer Muslim cantons but reservations for the maintenance of a moribund Muslim people. The plan for the partitioning of Bosnia-Hercegovina put forward by Milošević and Tudjman in June—backed once again by David Owen—follows on the heels of the Vance-Owen plan and the Washington agreement legitimizing Serbian and Croatian victories in Bosnia-Hercegovina.

LIFSCHULTZ: In other words, the apparent flaws in the proposed solutions are not flaws at all but logical elements of what the West sees as a realistic settlement of the conflict? Of course, it would be a settlement that destroys Bosnia as an independent state.

BANAC: The Vance-Owen plan as it was publicized was not going to accomplish the purpose that was ascribed to it. It simply postponed any sort of resolution of the Bosnian question, perhaps in the fond hope that somehow from somewhere other forces would stitch together what was unstitched by the Vance-Owen plan. The backers of the Plan have always been vague because they have no real answers to these questions. Instead, they talk in terms of "economic forces" or "political forces" or, perhaps, "common interests" against some as yet undefined "third outside element" which might undo what their plan has sought to do.

LIFSCHULTZ: What is the alternative? Is the full arming of the Bosnian government the only means to equalize or more than equalize the military balance? Are you saying that a well-armed Bosnian government could re-establish control over the areas now held by Serbia and Croatia and then grant rights of equal citizenship to all? Is this the only alternative scenario?

BANAC: I can think of nothing else. Of course, along with military assistance there would also have to be a mechanism to verify the good intentions of the Bosnian government. Because of the horrors that are happening inside Bosnia-Hercegovina, there is considerable bitterness which could lead perhaps to a repetition of some of the most damaging aspects of Serbian aggression. A mechanism needs to be established to prevent this. In my view the most effective measure would be the apprehension of war criminals whose identities are quite well known. This would deter vigilante efforts. However, it is rather difficult to establish a genuine mechanism when one is negotiating with people like Karadžić, Mladić, and Milošević.

LIFSCHULTZ: Zoran Pajić and Anthony Borden have advocated a revival of the trusteeship system under UN auspices for Bosnia. Is this really a way forward?

BANAC: I have many reservations about revitalizing the UN trusteeship system in this situation. It was used principally in parts of the colonial world and has ceased to function with the independence of most of the trusteeships. I have reservations also because I doubt a trusteeship of Bosnia would be carried out in an appropriate manner given the policies of the leading members of the Security Council. Could one, for instance, really expect the Russians to contribute to the growth of consociational democracy in Bosnia-Hercegovina? However, if the alternative is the dissolution of Bosnia-Hercegovina, I am perfectly willing to take the risk.

ALI: How would this work?

BANAC: Frankly, I have difficulty visualizing how this would operate. It would effectively mean the lessening of the sovereignty of an elected government which is a member state of the United Nations. This is unprecedented. At best we could view a trusteeship as an effort to provide a service in revitalizing the political system of Bosnia-Hercegovina which has been sundered by war. It would be an extremely complicated task and inferior to assisting the government of Bosnia militarily in securing its authority over its sovereign territory. Our dilemma in discussing all these possibilities is the fact that during the past year many of the sinews which held this country together have disappeared. One always faces the question as to what extent we are dealing with a moribund entity. And I hope against hope that it has not come to that.

ALI: In order for the UN to take over trusteeship power in Bosnia and provide in some form the type of "service" which you have proposed, it is clear that the war would first have to stop. In order to repair, rebuild, and restore the sinews which once held Bosnian society together, there would have to be peace. The Serb war machine would have to be dismantled, perhaps all parties will need to be disarmed. This would have to be the precondition for any trusteeship to have any hope of reconstructing and rebuilding a state. So we are back to square one: how to stop the war? how to convince the Serbs—and, now, the Croats as well—that Bosnia is indivisible?

BANAC: You have answered your own question. Without international military support in defense of Bosnia-Hercegovina there can be nothing. This seems plain to everybody except the Western diplomats.

LIFSCHULTZ: Among the many who oppose any military action against the Belgrade regime is Misha Glenny, the BBC's Eastern European correspondent. In his April 1992 Op-Ed piece in *The New York Times,* for instance, he states that "for those of us who live and work in the Balkans, things look a little different. We know that a bombing of the Serbs will let loose a sea of blood in which Southeastern Europe will drown." As someone who has a long history of involvement in Balkan affairs, what do you make of Glenny's position (and his more general perspective on the conflict in his book, *The Fall of Yugoslavia).* Glenny also advances the view that "only the Vance-Owen plan has recognized the complexity of the situation." What is your view of Glenny's assessment?

BANAC: Mr. Glenny is not a very reliable reporter on the Balkan conflict. This is because he sticks to the appearance and never delves deeper. He truly believes in all these myths of Balkan savagery and imagines that Milošević has the resources to withstand a well-directed blow. He claims, for example, that should Serbia be attacked she would spread the war to Kosovo. But Serbia *already is* at war in Kosovo. It is a silent war, a desperate war, but war all the same. This war cannot be negotiated away. Certainly not by Milošević.

Glenny is representative of all the good partisans of civil rights who find resistance to national inequality more distasteful than the causes. Time will not work wonders. Only struggle against Serbian aggression will change the Balkan battlefront. The Vance-Owen plan is no substitute for the defeat of Milošević and Karadžić, nor has this plan accounted for any special complexities. It has created some by tempting the "owners" of the national provinces to full possession of their mini-states. But this is not an advantage.

ALI: We have already touched on the issue of the resurgence of nationalism in former Yugoslavia and Eastern Europe as a post-Communist phenomenon. We talked about how this was not just a phenomenon which had suddenly materialized after communism, but it was always there—repressed, contained, inhibited—and the forms that it is taking now were, perhaps, partly determined by the way it had been contained and repressed and not allowed to find expression within the political system of the time. To return to that discussion again, how would you define or analyze this whole phenomenon across Eastern and Central Europe which we are witnessing after the collapse of the Communist states? Hobsbawm, for instance, makes a distinction between the project of nationalism in the nineteenth and the early twentieth century as it was taken up by the anti-colonialist movements in Africa and Asia, and the kind of nationalism that we see now, certainly in Eastern Europe, and in other parts of the world.

According to Hobsbawm, the earlier brand of nationalism sought to expand the human social, political, and cultural unit; it subsumed various ethnicities, various regional, parochial, linguistic differences within a larger nation, so to speak. That particular nationalism had a project, a program, a wider vision; it was building a particular kind of state. (Whether it succeeded or not, of course, is a different matter.) On the other hand, the nationalism that we see today is exclusionist, seeking more sharply to distinguish "us" from "them," focused almost entirely on ethnicity, race, language, and not having, therefore, a larger, overarching ideological, philosophical, or political project. How do you respond to Hobsbawm's view?

BANAC: First, I think Eric Hobsbawm is singularly ill-prepared to deal with this particular issue because he sees nationalism as basically the revenge of society for the failure of socialism in Eastern Europe. He then goes as far as to question the Leninist project of national self-determination, which he sees as the Original Sin of the Communist movement that basically brought about its downfall. All of this is wrong. Leninism could not have succeeded had it not taken into account the most serious problem of the Russian Empire which was a collectivity of unequal nations.

Second, there is this notion of the "icebox effect"; namely that communism froze all discussion of nationhood in Russia since the Revolution in 1917, and in Eastern Europe, more or less, since 1945, and all of a sudden, now, with the collapse of communism we are going back to 1939, or to 1917; that we are witnessing the return of history, and so on and so forth. There are many other metaphors that are being thought up to describe the supposed "revival" of nationalism. I repeat once again: the national question never disappeared in any of these countries except that it was debated under adverse circumstances, and, basically, within the ruling Communist parties.

I was amused, for example, by what a Russian participant at a conference I recently attended in Istanbul had to say. In his view (and we are now going back to Hobsbawm) there are essentially two possibilities: on the one hand there is the nationalism of Jefferson, which is constructive, civic nationalism, a state nationalism devoid of any sort of ethnic bias; and on the other hand there is the nationalism of Adolf Hitler. Now, this is, of course, a gross vulgarization because it excludes all types of phenomena, possibilities, in between—including such things as were happening in the Soviet Union under Stalin who demonstrated that you could be a nationalist under the label of proletarian internationalism. You could exile whole national groups to Central Asia simply because they were somehow suspected of undermining your war effort, however true or untrue this might have been.

So the national issue did not disappear. It did not disappear in the Soviet Union, certainly, and, needless to say, it did not disappear in Yugoslavia or in any of the multinational countries of Eastern Europe, and even in those that were uninational. There was the problem of Soviet hegemony in such places as Poland, for example, and one cannot forget to what extent that was a stifling influence from the point of view of the system itself, and one that could not be corrected.

Now, as my third point, I would like to introduce, perhaps, a more sensible way of looking at nationalism, which to me is always an ideology. This is very important because under the term of nationalism Hobsbawm confuses any number of entirely different phenomena. To him it is a political movement, an ideology, a civic project, an identity—all of these things which are not necessarily the same. Nationalism *is* an ideology and, moreover, is an extremely adaptive ideology as opposed to, say, socialism, which has a very basic, firm, and clear structure. Nationalism is adaptive, and it adapts to the intellectual concerns of the center. (Here, again, we go to the issue of center and periphery.) It reflects the principal intellectual concerns of any given historical period; it cannot assume the characteristics of a particular historical period in another age. I think that nationalism in Europe, in its different manifestations, has reflected a whole series of intellectual changes in Europe. For example, there was a nationalism of the period of the Enlightenment; of the French Revolution; of the period of Romanticism; and there was a nationalism of the Positivist period at the end of the nineteenth century—integral nationalism, a particularly unwelcome form that had many deleterious effects in Eastern Europe. Integral nationalism viewed national conflict as war in which the weaker group inevitably would suffer losses. During the interwar period in Eastern Europe the dominant concern was that of national independence. To some extent it resembled the problems of the post-1989 period. Then there was a nationalism of the period of fascism, and also a nationalism of the period of socialism, of communism.

In each one of these cases, what was important was that the existing form of nationalism reflected the dominant concerns of the center, albeit with some exceptions. For example, the split in Europe after the Second World War created two centers, and this was unusual. Now, once again, Europe is being reintegrated basically around the West European center. Bearing all of this in mind, given the adaptive nature of nationalist ideology, you cannot have the fascist type of nationalism in an era of Enlightenment. Should present-day East European nationalisms turn fascistic, it will be because of the changes in Western Europe. Therefore, worry about fascism in Eastern Europe, when Mr. Le Pen comes to power in France; worry about it when Solingens become commonplace in Germany or in Britain. Extreme, rabid nationalist movements are not yet—perhaps, they will not be—significant in European politics. This is a surmise. Still, we do see in some countries the growing political importance of extremist nationalist movements. When Šešelj wins eighteen percent of the vote in Serbia, that is a very dangerous sign because it is the first time in post-war Europe that a party that is fascist by anybody's definition is in possession of almost one-fifth of the electorate. But I don't think that even under the circumstances of isolation in Serbia, politics can take a direction that would be totally dissonant with the developments in Western Europe. I think that Serbia is an isolated case, a case of a country that is undergoing a tremendous internal crisis. But I don't think that this particular movement can sustain itself forever as long as it is at odds with the dominant ideological currents in Western Europe.

Now, is this reassuring by itself? This doesn't, in any sense, foreclose the possibility of tremendous reversals in this very soft area of post-Communist Europe—economically, politically, ideologically. All the same, there is some room for optimism. The turn of events in the former Yugoslavia, the establishment of an extreme chauvinist regime in Serbia, and the war that it has imposed on some of the other successor states of Yugoslavia—that sort of a phenomenon has not happened anywhere else. That is why it is still an isolated tendency. Yeltsin could have, with equal logic, conducted operations against the other successor states of the Soviet Union, moreover with the same arguments: Russians are in danger in the Baltic states, in the Ukraine, in Kazakhstan, everywhere! We have to defend them; we have to create a new Russian state; we have to re-gather the Russian lands! In other words, a Russian version of the Milošević program. But this has not happened.

ALI: Not as yet. And let us hope that it will not.

LIFSCHULTZ: How, then, do you actually characterize Milošević?

ALI: That he is an aberration?

BANAC: Milošević's fascism is aberrant, yes.

LIFSCHULTZ: Nevertheless, in terms of ideology how does one characterize the Milošević regime in Belgrade? Šešelj's movement in Serbia is clearly a reflection of fascist ideology. Milošević and Šešelj both stand behind the program of "ethnic cleansing" and the "Greater Serbia" project. Is the Belgrade regime a fascist formation reminiscent of Mussolini with a few technical borrowings from the Nazis vis à vis "ethnic purity" and the targeting of civilians?

BANAC: I did not mean to exculpate Milošević by calling Šešelj a fascist. There have been arguments that Milošević's regime resembles the early Mussolini regime in Italy. Indeed, if one looks at what is possible and what is not possible in Serbia, one can argue that the Milošević regime, too, is a fascist regime. In Italy, in the early 1920s, you did have oppositional deputies in the parliament. Terror was conducted against them—for example, the assassination of Matteotti. You had an oppositional press, which you also have in Serbia, but it is marginalized—*Vreme, Borba, Ekonomska Politika,* and so on. These are newspapers that are not widely read, and I don't think they have any influence on the behavior of the masses in Serbia. So one can have pockets of opposition within certain types of fascist regimes. From every other point of view, I would say that the Milošević regime is a fascist regime. Yes, I have argued that. There are many people who see this as not terribly significant. To me it is, because it helps us understand the social nature of this phenomenon.

LIFSCHULTZ: But Mussolini also had an economic project, did he not? It is not quite clear what economic project the Milošević regime seems to be pursuing.

BANAC: Yes, this is true, there is no equivalent economic project in Serbia, of any sort. What is confusing about the Milošević regime is its origins, of course, because it emerged from the shell of the ruling League of Communists of Serbia. But it is entirely misleading to say, as is frequently said, that Milošević is some sort of an unreconstructed Bolshevik. He is certainly not that. There is no connection with his origins that is obvious to me. His is a sort of a mixed system that has not yet fully defined itself, and probably prefers not to do so, leaving all sorts of possibilities open for itself. But I think that the basic defining element is fascism.

ALI: Would you say that this fascistic element in Serbia today reflects any kind of continuity, in the historical sense, to the political current represented by the Chetniks in the earlier part of the century?

BANAC: The Chetniks are an interesting lot, but I would very much hesitate to call them fascists, and not simply because they arose in the context of opposition to the occupation of Serbia. The Chetniks were, essentially, a premodern phenomenon whereas fascism is a modern phenomenon. The Chetniks were premodern in the sense that they were a continuation of the armed bands that operated in Macedonia in the period before the Balkan wars, at the time when all the interested neighboring states—Serbia, Greece, Bulgaria—were trying to develop their own insurgent groups in Macedonia. There was a tradition of this non-political, nationalistic activity that existed in the interwar period in Yugoslavia where the Chetnik movement existed in two forms: as state-sponsored and independent clubs, and also as guerrilla units inside the Yugoslav Royal Army which were then very easily rejuvenated after 1941.

But in all of this you do not see the presence of any modern political ideologies. What you see is Serbian nationalism, and during the Second World War, the program of "ethnic cleansing." Stevan Moljević, who was one of the ideologists of the Chetnik movement during the Second World War, wrote a document that is extremely interesting from the point of view of what is happening today. He, too, wanted to get rid of Muslims and Croats in all areas where there were Serbs, to create a mini-Croatia on the fringes of an expanded Serbia as a sort of colonized entity, and to have a somewhat larger Slovenia in alliance with Serbia on the northwestern extremities of Yugoslavia. Moljević's program can easily be detected in the ideas of Milošević, Šešelj, or other ideologists of Serbian nationalism in the 1980s and 1990s. So there is that continuity. But, all the same, the Chetniks are really a hoary Balkan phenomenon—an armed band that has its roots in the Hajduk movement during the Ottoman times.

ALI: One of the reasons I brought that up is because there has been a tendency on all sides to define one another by terms that conjure up an unsavory historical past. The Croats refer to the Serbs as Chetniks, while the Serbs use the blanket term, Ustašas, to describe all Croats (and both have labeled the Muslims, the Mujahideen, a term of more recent vintage in Western discourse). How would you explain the resurgence of this sort of rhetoric? As cheap, manipulative propaganda which has no connection with any reality on the ground?

BANAC: It is sad to say that the term Chetnik is no longer considered pejorative in Serbia. And there are actual Chetnik units with all the paraphernalia. It is very interesting to analyze the iconography. For example, the beard—which in the peasant culture of Serbia is a sign of mourning: somebody dies, one does not shave. This was something that happened in times of war and times of mourning. Then the fur hat, usually with symbols of skull and crossbones—intimidating symbols—and the black flag, again with skull and crossbones with such inscriptions as "For King and Fatherland," and so on. This is a throwback to premodern forms of consciousness. The Ustašas, on the other hand, had an element of this Balkan primitivism, but they were also a modern movement in the sense that they were a fascist movement. So the two groups were entirely dissimilar in their origins, although, in fact, in everyday encounters during the Second World War they probably were not all that much different—very similar methods, very similar types of organizational and behavioral forms.

ALI: What is the strength and the significance of the Ustaša element in Croatia right now?

BANAC: Formally nothing, but there is a certain nostalgia for it which I find extremely unpleasant and dangerous. There is a certain suspension of critical reading of this period which did enormous damage to Croatia. It is not an exaggeration to say that the legitimacy of the Croatian state, to a very large extent, was compromised precisely because the very idea of a Croatian state after 1945 was seen as necessarily a revival of the Ustaša experience in the Second World War. So it upsets me enormously when I see these graffiti in Croatia that essentially glorify Ante Pavelić's fascist dictatorship of the forties or when I see that some Croat units in Bosnia-Hercegovina have the names of the Ustaša commanders of the Second World War. I think that this is an extremely negative and self-defeating development. On the other hand, the reason why this is happening is precisely in the context of Serbian aggression, and also in response to the Serbian version that all Croats are, in fact, Ustašas. There is a certain bravado element which turns that around, and says, "They want to call us Ustašas. So that's what we are. By God, we are Ustašas!" It is infantile, it is primitive, it is dangerous, and I think not enough is being done to suspend it.

LIFSCHULTZ: What proportion of the Croat population separates itself from this, and makes the distinction?

BANAC: An overwhelming majority. Parties that play up these symbols are politically marginal.

LIFSCHULTZ: In light of our earlier discussion on the nature of the Milošević regime in Serbia, how would you characterize the Tudjman regime? What would you say is the project of this regime and the forces which support it?

BANAC: To begin with, the Constitution as it stands today gives excessive powers to the president and, in addition, the role of the parliament is limited almost to that of an extra in the political system. This is precisely what Yeltsin has proposed for Russia, and it is an extremely dubious proposition which can be defended only in light of the nature of the current Russian parliament. I would hope that one would get a better parliament in Russia and limit the powers of the president. That is precisely the formula I would like to see applied in Croatia as well.

Despite all the bad aspects of the Tudjman government, Croatia is not a dictatorship and it is not a state in which civil liberties are systematically suspended. I think that Croatia has many problems. There is an attempt on the part of the current government to monopolize the political scene, but, on the other hand, this has to a large extent been successfully resisted. The elections for local government in February 1993 show a great loss of influence on the part of the ruling HDZ. In many localities, including the three most important cities outside Zagreb, the opposition won. There is a real mobilization on the part of the opposition that is channeled within the legal and constitutional grounds. There is no attempt to fight the weaknesses of the government on the extraconstitutional plain—which is good, despite the fact that one would wish the opposition were more successful under the current rules of the game. I think that one should not worry about the consolidation of democratic institutions in Croatia, provided there isn't an upsurge of the right-wing forces. This, of course, is a real possibility. The strength of the right will be determined by a very, very threadbare situation on the fronts, and the fact that Croatia is in real danger of losing significant portions of its territory—ironically, precisely because of its policies in Bosnia-Hercegovina. For there is an analogy at work here: by backing Croatian claims to the "Croat" regions of Bosnia, the Croatian government strengthens the Serbian claims to the "Serb" regions in Croatia.

So it is a precarious situation, and there is much to be worried about. But it is by no means as precarious as may appear from many of the reports on Croatia. The economic situation is extremely difficult; production is down to half of the prewar period; markets have been lost; integration with Western Europe has not been accomplished; there is a certain embargo, as it were, against Croatia. But I think that all these difficulties can be surmounted if one could reach a lasting peace and, with it, see the decline in the influence of the HDZ, which is inevitable given the fragmentation of this party into several factions.

Ali: Do you feel that people like Jelena Lovrić are exaggerating when they say that certain elements among the Croatian nationalists were mirror images of Milošević; that, in a certain sense, they welcomed the emergence of the particular extremist brand of Serb nationalism we are seeing today because it provided them with the rationale to secure their own project. She is referring, in particular, to Bosnia-Hercegovina when she says that Milošević and Tudjman were in agreement on a number of things, whether implicitly or explicitly. "The division of Bosnia-Hercegovina was the subject," she says, "of their deepest mutual understanding."

Banac: There is a problem with this particular argument because it does not take chronology into account. Milošević was an established political fact in Serbia in 1987. It was during this time that many errors were committed— not just by the West, but also by the Communist leaderships of Slovenia and Croatia. I was recently discussing this with an Albanian intellectual who was "differentiated" in 1991, which is to say that he was essentially expelled from his teaching position because he would not agree with the new pro-Serb line in the League of Communists of Kosovo. And what were the errors committed by the Slovenian and Croatian leadership—and I would also say the leadership in Bosnia-Hercegovina and Macedonia? They did not take advantage of Tito's Constitution of 1974, which could only be changed by complete unanimity. They were so frightened by the phenomenon of Serbian nationalism under Milošević's leadership that they were only too willing to appease him. In fact, everybody was appeasing Milošević. They were prepared to grant him all the leeway to reintegrate Kosovo and Vojvodina into Serbia—and this was done by some of the best people on the Yugoslav political scene! Some of the worst things in Kosovo were done while Janez Drnovšek was the chairman of the collective presidency and Ante Marković, the premier of Yugoslavia. It was Marković who was breaking bread with Milošević in 1989, at a time when Milošević was about to give a new Constitution for Serbia. They were all convinced that if only the Kosovo issue was resolved to Milošević's liking, he would stop. That was not the way it worked. Milošević expanded pressure, took on Montenegro, showed every sign of trying to subvert not just Bosnia-Hercegovina, but also Croatia and even Slovenia. And while this was happening, the so-called Croat nationalists of the Tudjman type were not permitted to participate in any political dialogue. They emerged precisely because the Croat society felt tremendously threatened by Milošević, and the issue in the election of 1990 in Croatia was precisely what to do in order to escape from the deathly grip of Milošević's policy. Tudjman, initially, tried to resolve these dilemmas by bringing about the confederal proposal. One can argue whether independence was his principal aim all along, but one should not underestimate how popular that demand was in Croatian society—particularly in light of Milošević. But I think that it is quite unfair to equate the phenomenon of Milošević with the sort of defensive mechanisms that developed in Slovenia and Croatia to try to withstand it. No, it was Milošević who was the active force; everybody else was constantly reacting to him. And this is happening even now.

LIFSCHULTZ: The Slovenian and the Croatian Communists walked out of the Party at the last Congress in 1990. Could they not even at that stage have attempted to secure adherence to the 1974 Constitution?

BANAC: No, by then the Constitution was already a dead letter. That Congress marked the end of the Party. It was too late by then. The time to stop Milošević was earlier, precisely on the issue of Kosovo. And it was the Croat and Slovene Communists who betrayed Kosovo.

LIFSCHULTZ: Finally, now with the disintegration of Yugoslavia, how do you see the economic prospects for the successor states? Will the severe narrowing of the national market and a cautious European Community concerned about cheap imports from low-wage countries lead to the new states being relegated to the economic periphery? In other words, is Slavoj Žižek correct when he suggests that the new states might not make it into the ranks of those who are allowed "inside" as opposed to those who are condemned to remain "outside," like most countries of the Third World, for instance?

BANAC: The economic prospects for the successor states are grim. There is no question about that. Much depends on western Europe's willingness to invest and to integrate these countries. It would be difficult in the best of circumstances because there is a competition, not just among the successor states of Yugoslavia but among all the former Communist countries of Eastern Europe. Now who can blame Western investors if they concentrate on stable countries, such as Hungary, the Czech Republic, perhaps Poland? In this competition one has to demonstrate certain attractions for the Western interests, and this is, among other things, a political question—the ability to create a stable state, one which is in accord with the rules of the game of Western Europe. Those who can manage it, do have a future; those who think that they can pursue some sort of a separate, "third" road are very likely to go into isolation and autarchy which is no solution at all. So there is going to be a certain natural selection.

I think that Slovenia has taken several steps which have put it in the most favorable position among all the successor states of Yugoslavia. Žižek's commentary, of course, is probably more metaphorical than real, although I am not underestimating the problems of Slovenia. Croatia, on the other hand, has a tremendous problem because it has become three islands, really. It has a precarious geography even in the best of circumstances, which is now further threatened by the fact that the unity of the state is essentially cut in two very important areas. Dalmatia has become an island, and the connections between north-western Croatia and Slavonia are also very tenuous at the moment. For Croatia it is essential to regain the occupied territories. This is going to be extremely difficult. I do not see any serious effort on the part of the European Community, the United Nations, and others involved, to extend to Croatia the realistic prospect of reintegration in spite of the fact that there are some efforts on the parts of the Serbs in the occupied territories to get out of their isolation by making local deals with the Croat authorities—something which is continuously obstructed by the more extreme forces in the occupied territories. So, this is an issue upon which Croatia's future, to a very large extent, depends. If one wishes to marginalize Croatia, the best way to do it is to deny it any prospects of reintegration with its occupied territories. And, I am afraid, to some extent this is happening; there are some forces in the West who see the separation of these lands from Croatia as a long-range project. This is extremely dangerous and helps only the most reactionary forces in Croatia at the moment.

LIFSCHULTZ: This situation, of course, is similar to the situation in Bosnia itself.

BANAC: Absolutely. I think this is one reason why Bosnian policy is the most controversial and acute internal issue in Croatia today. The stand one takes on Croatia's Bosnian policy will, to a very large extent, determine one's position on the further development of Croatia.

ALI: In effect, then, would not the best way forward be the actual military defeat of the Serb variant of fascism in Serbia? Both in Germany and Italy it was only military defeat that brought fascism to an end.

BANAC: The military defeat of Serbia would be good not only for everybody who was subjected to Serbian aggression, but it would be good for Serbia too. However, one thing that one would not wish for is the total collapse of Serbia because this would engender unnatural appetites in the neighborhood, including in Croatia and Bosnia-Hercegovina. What one wants to have is a "normal"

Serbia which would give up its imperial ambitions, not just in Croatia and Bosnia-Hercegovina but also in Kosovo and Vojvodina. But this is a very tall and difficult order, something that is at the moment entirely unacceptable not just to Milošević and those to the right of Milošević, but even to those forces in Serbia which are considered sympathetic from the Western point of view. The one thing that unites all of them is the notion that Serbia cannot exist unless it realizes its integration with all the communities across the Drina and Sava rivers. This is a belief which is shared by a whole spectrum of Serbian political parties with very few exceptions. Those who resist it are the most positive forces in Serbia, and they are the most isolated forces in Serbia. So, in the end, I think the military defeat of Serbia is the only way out.

ALI: Returning, at the end, to the theme with which we began—of the "wild Balkans" in general, and of Bosnia-Hercegovina as a land in the grips of millennial hatred and blood-letting—let me ask you about Ivo Andrić, the celebrated writer of Yugoslavia. He has been resurrected lately as a witness to the insensate savagery of Bosnia by some among those who warn darkly against coming to the aid of the Bosnians. Passages from his writings have been cited, among others, by Milovan Djilas's son, Aleksa Djilas (quite recently in a letter to *The New York Times* of April 16, 1993), to demonstrate that the people of Bosnia are imbued with an organic hatred—something which they are almost born with, or absorb from the earth they walk on, the air they breathe. How do the writings of Ivo Andrić, the Nobel laureate, lend themselves to this sort of anti-intellectual, mystical stuff?

BANAC: I do not think that there is a more contradictory figure in the Balkans than Ivo Andrić. Here was a man who came from the Bosnian Croat community; no writer has written more positively about the Bosnian Franciscans than Ivo Andrić. He entered into literature as a participant in an anthology called *Young Croatian Lyrics,* published in 1914. At that point, he was still thinking of himself as a Croat, but he belonged to the Yugoslav Nationalist Youth, specifically to Young Bosnia, and as a result was arrested by the Austro-Hungarian authorities during the First World War. He then came into his own in interwar Yugoslavia. He was picked up by one of his mentors, again a Bosnian Croat who was a minister in the early post-World War I Yugoslav governments. He entered into Yugoslav diplomatic service and, in the 1930s, became very much of a fascist fellow traveler. His political articles in the journal *XX vek* (Twentieth Century) justified such things as the Munich Pact, and so on (he wrote under the psuedonym of Patrius). He was the Yugoslav envoy to Berlin at the time of the signing of the Tripartite Pact, and if one looks carefully at the photographs of the signing of the Pact in Vienna, behind Ribbentrop and Cincar Marković, one will see the silhouette of Ivo Andrić. During the war, he was in Belgrade under the occupation. He did not participate in any of the political activities during that period. He was invited into the Chetniks but, to his credit, he resisted. And it was during the period of the occupation that he wrote his major novels, *Bridge on the Drina* and *Chronicle of Travnik,* and started some others.

After the war, the Yugoslav Communist regime needed a cultural icon, and there were, really, two candidates. One was Andrić, politically compromised during the interwar period, and especially vulnerable as a result, and welcome, too, as a result. The other was Miroslav Krleža who was a Communist from 1919, but had two problems. He was in conflict with the Party from 1937 onwards and was expelled in 1939. He was a critic of Stalinism, a covert critic, and did not participate in the Partisan resistance. The other problem Krleža had was that he was entirely too Croat—his themes are Croat themes, themes of cultural alienation within central Europe, obsessions with the Habsburg heritage, obsessions with marginality, and so on. This did not lend itself to the sort of Yugoslav synthesis that the regime needed in 1945. So they settled on Andrić and very quickly made him the pinnacle of the Socialist cultural establishment, ending with his joining the Party very soon after the war. He became the first president of the Yugoslav Writers Association, and so on. He was always a political conformist, although he had absolutely no common ground with the Communist ideology. If one reads his diaries and his reminiscences, one can see this perfectly clearly.

Andrić had one problem which makes it possible to misuse him in the context of the current situation in Bosnia. He saw the Ottoman period—and the Muslim community, as a consequence of the Ottoman period—as a particularly negative element in the history of Bosnia-Hercegovina. His doctoral dissertation, which he defended at the University of Graz in 1924, and which was published soon after Tito's death in 1982, is an explicit anti-Muslim document. I became aware only recently of the debate about *Bridge on the Drina* in the exile Bosnian Muslim publications from the 1960s after Andrić won the Nobel prize. The famous dramatic scene of impalement of a Serb Hajduk by the "Turks" in the novel was seen by Muslims as a commentary on the whole Ottoman period and, indeed, on the Muslim presence in Bosnia-Hercegovina. The notion that Bosnia is a dark *vilayet,* the land of hate, and so on, is something that accords with his general temperamental disposition—he was not a very happy man, or an optimist—but also accords with his vision of Bosnia-Hercegovina which then justifies all these notions about the incongruity of Bosnia-Hercegovina. So, perhaps, one of the most important writers from the land of Bosnia has, posthumously, become an inspiration for those who are destroying it. His views have become part of the thesis—advanced, among others, by Robert D. Kaplan [author of *Balkan Ghosts: A Journey Through History*]—that the people of Bosnia—Serbs, Croats, Muslims—are the best haters around. These are banal half-truths. There is no sane reason to believe that in this particular corner of the world there is some sort of a special concentration of hate. Human beings are human beings everywhere.

The Final Solution of
Bosnia-Hercegovina

MARK THOMPSON

Bosnia, that exotic country in the heart of Europe . . .
DANILO KIŠ[1]

S INCE APRIL 1992, the Republic of Bosnia-Hercegovina has been assaulted with extreme violence and
absolute barbarity. Its people are massacred: perhaps
100,000 have been killed, perhaps twice that number; no one knows. Men are
herded into prison camps to be executed, beaten, tortured, or if they are lucky,
humiliated, starved, expelled abroad. Women are systematically raped, children are slung under the tracks of advancing tanks, old people are chased from
their homes at gunpoint, abandoning whatever chattels they cannot carry.
Cattle wagons deport thousands of these people northwards, away to countries that don't want them: Croatia, Slovenia, Italy, Hungary, Austria—anywhere.

The aggressors control two thirds of the republic, and one Bosnian in
three is a refugee. Those who dare to stay in the "liberated" areas are subject to
tyrannical controls upon their freedom of association, communication,
mobility and employment.

A spokesman for the United Nations High Commission on Refugees
(UNHCR) likened these controls to Nazi restrictions against Jews. The same
organization estimated that Bosnian homes were destroyed through the spring
and summer at a rate of 200 per day. Villages are razed; towns and cities are
laid waste with mortar, phosphorus, napalm, and cluster bombs; bridges are
blown. Fields and roads are sown with mines. Outposts of resistance are blockaded and starved.

It is an attempt to obliterate Bosnia-Hercegovina as living entity and
idea. One might say that, from the point of view of those who mastermind the
aggression, so many people must be killed and terrorized and so much property must be destroyed to persuade the Bosnians themselves, and the onlook-
ing world, that Bosnia-Hercegovina was a false or impossible entity glued
together by hatred and violence and communism, that the idea of Bosnia-

Hercegovina is anachronistic, sectarian. In short, that it deserves to die. And if it, perhaps, didn't deserve to die quite like this, anyway it is definitely finished now, smashed beyond repair.

This is what the aggressors want their victims and everyone else to conclude. Many of the victims are convinced, and seek nothing but the chance to restart their lives elsewhere—anywhere. Others refuse to accept defeat, and fight back. But the really significant audience at the Bosnian theater is the outsiders, because they alone have power either to restore Bosnia-Hercegovina or to ratify its abolition.

The outsiders fall into two unequal parts. Crammed into the front rows is the Serbian and Montenegrin public. Behind sits the crowd of Western governments, public, and institutions. Mostly the Western publics boo and hiss the ghastly spectacle, sometimes they check their watches, yawn discreetly, wring their hands. Their governments and institutions riffle through wads of documents on their laps, conferring in low voices, looking up now and then to add a hasty boo, wagging a finger at the stage and devoutly wishing the entire scene to disappear.

The Serbs and the Montenegrins down in the front seats, meanwhile, are making a minor pandemonium of their own. Some scramble over the footlights to join the slaughtering, egged on by others with war-whoops and patriotic cries. A tiny number rounds on the enthusiasts, denouncing the assault. Others again have turned to face the larger foreign audience, and stand yelling madly that the aggressors on stage are really the victims and the victims really the aggressors. The majority, though, scratch their heads, looking confused and very grim, sunk in a stupor of introversion as the corpses pile up before their half-averted gaze.

THE CONTINUUM OF European and US failure in former Yugoslavia has been ruptured only by rare bursts of tough-minded realism. The West's failure over Bosnia-Hercegovina is more unpardonable as well as more spectacular than that over Croatia, because the Bosnian government, unlike its Croatian counterpart, did everything in its power to heed the advice of the European Community (EC) and the US State Department, removing causes of conflict and refusing to arm its people; because EC and UN dithering has wrenched an even higher price from innocent people; and because the EC and UN have no excuse for not learning in Croatia how to distinguish the genuine causes of conflict from ostensible causes and pretexts, and framing their strategy on that basis.

While Europe bears most responsibility, the United States has been no better. Miffed, apparently, at misreading the events which led to conflict in Slovenia and Croatia, the Bush administration spent the autumn of 1991 sulking in its tent. Then it barged back into the limelight by taking up the cause of Bosnia-Hercegovina's independence, only—like the Europeans—to abandon Bosnia-Hercegovina utterly when the assault came.

In the course of the late summer and autumn of 1991, as the Serb and Yugoslav People's Army (JNA) signed and broke cease-fire after cease-fire in Croatia, the EC mediators seemed finally to learn that the alleged genocidal peril facing the Serbs in an independent Croatia was not the real cause of aggression there. The turning point, in this respect, was Serbia's rejection in October of the EC's proposal, accepted by the other five republics, to re-form Yugoslavia into a loose confederation of sovereign states.

Whether the EC and UN grasped that the twin-engined motor of war was JNA's drive to preserve as much of the old federation as possible, plus Serbian President Milošević's imperative need for national conflict outside Serbia to divert the country from chronic internal discontents which the regime cannot tackle because tackling them would mean ridding Serbia of the incubus regime itself—whether the international mediators grasped this, was not clear at the time. The endless sequel of mistakes suggests that they didn't and still haven't.

Consider the crucial matter of recognition. The conclusion begging to be drawn from the chronology of events in November, December, and January 1991–1992, is that the EC's threat to recognize Croatia imminently as an independent state in its existing borders acted as an unignorable constraint on the aggressors; their maximal goal of toppling Croatia's government and keeping most of its territory inside "Yugoslavia" became patently impossible to achieve. The level of violence fell; Serbia returned to the negotiating table; the January 2 cease-fire was brokered by Cyrus Vance, the UN special envoy.

There were other reasons too for Belgrade's new pliancy: the military stalemate after the fall of Vukovar, the unpopularity of the EC's economic sanctions, the face-saving possibility of negotiating with the UN instead of "capitulating" to the "Fourth Reich," and above all the advantageous terms of the Vance Plan. But the coercive threat of recognition was indispensable. The EC had insisted for months on preserving the inter-republican borders; but words are words, after all, while recognition was proof positive that a land-grab would not be acknowledged yet again in Balkan history by the watching powers.

Yet even this lesson was being ignored next door, in Bosnia-Hercegovina. At a meeting held on December 16, 1991, the EC foreign ministers established a mechanism for republics to gain recognition as independent states. Candidates had to apply within five days; if they satisfied five criteria concerning human and minority rights and territorial claims against other republics or non-Yugoslav neighbors, they would be recognized on January 15, 1992. Each candidacy would be examined by an Arbitration Commission chaired by Robert Badinter, a French constitutional lawyer.

Devised for the benefit of Bosnia-Hercegovina and Macedonia, this mechanism failed them both. The applications of Slovenia and Croatia were a formality. Serbia and Montenegro would certainly not apply, because their entire stance necessitated persisting in the fiction that they were Yugoslavia, however many republics "disassociated" themselves (the judicious term used by Slovenia and Croatia to define their decisions of June 1991).

The four republics duly applied. Slovenia, Croatia, and Macedonia satisfied the Commission, despite doubts about Croatia's provision for its Serb minority. As for Bosnia-Hercegovina, Badinter reported that it was difficult to know what the people wanted; he proposed a referendum.

Now the EC committed a cardinal error. It recognized only Slovenia and Croatia. If this was ominous for Macedonia, for Bosnia-Hercegovina it was a disaster. The Community's loss of nerve—falling back from the realism of December 16—can only have encouraged the forces that would shortly unleash a carefully prepared assault.

The proper judgment for a constitutional lawyer to reach was not a proper decision for the Community to enact. In the conditions of that moment, and in the light of the Bosnian Serb leadership's campaign since 1990 to preempt any move toward independence by the republic's government by threats and bullying, the function of such a procedure—with its utterly predictable outcome—would be to buy time for that leadership and for the JNA, then amassing men and material in the republic, and to hand them a propaganda tool.

Sixty-three percent of the electorate voted on March 1, 1992. Of these, 99 percent opted for independence. The great majority of Serbs (31 percent of the population) boycotted the referendum, and Radovan Karadžić[2], their self-proclaimed leader, has described the result ever since as Muslims and Croats ganging up against the Serbs.

Did the Western mediators even anticipate this outcome? The main value of the referendum in their eyes was, one must suppose, that it allowed them to relapse into verbalism and procrastination. They seemed to assume that the mere threat of recognition would serve in Bosnia-Hercegovina as in Croatia—as if the outcome in Croatia had not upped the ante for the Milošević regime, the JNA, and the Bosnian Serb leaders, giving them all more cause to start a war in Bosnia-Hercegovina, not less. They had no incentive to cancel their assault and no motive to join any "peace process" except to dissemble their aims, deny their atrocities and defer intervention, so buying time until they were ready to sue for peace—on their terms. Which was all motive enough, of course! And the longer the war goes on, the more the aggressors need something to show for their expenditure of Serbian life and welfare. This vicious circle cannot be broken by "remonstrance after remonstrance, protestation after protestation."[3]

Looking back, the mediators might plead that recognition of Bosnia-Hercegovina in January 1992 would have risked antagonizing the Serbs so much that the January 2 cease-fire in Croatia might have collapsed, thus aborting the UN Protection Force (UNPROFOR) deployment in Serb-held regions of that republic.

This imaginary plea is the best I can think of in the mediators' defense. And it doesn't stand up. Not because the situation in Croatia was not finely poised, nor because the Vance Plan—weighted against Croatia though it is—was not worthy of implementing. (A year later the plan was still worth implementing, but the UN proved incapable of even this.) It doesn't stand up because it evades the deeper EC and UN motives and misunderstandings underlying the negotiators' approach to the conflicts in both Croatia and Bosnia-Hercegovina.

The UN's and EC's goal for Croatia was peace as soon as possible or something that resembled peace, even at the cost of appeasing the aggressor by freezing his land-grabs, which cover fully a quarter of the country, as UN Protected Areas. Never mind the causes of conflict: wrap up a deal now! That was the priority, and it maximized the chances of aggression in Bosnia-Hercegovina.

Beneath this lazy, self-defeating priority lay several key misunderstandings. The most significant of these—apart from blindness to causes—was historical and cultural as much as political. It concerned the idea and reality of Bosnia-Hercegovina.

The mediators proposed that a sovereign Bosnia-Hercegovina could be divided into "three constituent units, based on national principles and taking into account economic, geographic and other criteria." Such was the crucial wording of the Statement of Principles for New Constitutional Arrangements for Bosnia and Hercegovina, drafted by the EC and signed on March 18, 1992, by the government and the leaders of the Serb and Croat communities.

This document, which also upheld the republic's existing borders, was as worthless as the previous autumn's cease-fires; within a month, the assault had begun.

The point is that Western mediators should never have supposed that their fudging Statement offered any firm ground for "further negotiations" ("A working group will be established in order to define the territory of the constituent units . . . " Indeed!). For the nations in Bosnia-Hercegovina were fairly thoroughly mixed, like the colors in a Jackson Pollock painting, as President Izetbegović has observed.

Some statistics are in order. "According to the census of April 1991, Bosnia-Hercegovina's population was 4,354,911. Of the 109 municipalities in the republic, 37 had an absolute Muslim majority, 32 a Serb absolute majority, and 13 a Croat absolute majority (the combined population of these 82 municipalities was some 2.7 million). A further 15 municipalities had a simple Muslim majority, five a simple Serb majority, and seven a simple Croat majority (the combined population of these 27 municipalities was about 1.7 million)."[4]

No viable system for the republic can be derived from "national principles," whether that system is to be the infamous cantonization (carving up by a classier name) or a three-way partition of political and administrative powers with no territorial carve-up. A member of Lord Carrington's office in London advised me that the March 18 Statement intended the latter. However, I would defy anyone to deny that such a plan was not a utopian delusion or a cynical stop-gap, an almost explicit invitation to separatists to persist with their violence. Any carve-up would leave large numbers of any nation in the "wrong" units, unless, of course, coercion is used to purify the units, preferably before these are recognized as autonomous or sovereign; hence, the genocidal onslaught that goes by the euphemistic name of "ethnic cleansing." Once the principle of national units is admitted, Bosnia-Hercegovina is on the slippery slope. For if nationality is the constitutional basis of these units, members of the "wrong" nation would be treated as an encumbrance, a danger.

Did the mediators bother to discover how unpromising the concept of "units on national principles" was in Bosnia-Hercegovina? It had dominated, indeed paralyzed, the political agenda since the 1990 elections.

Taking its cue from Belgrade, where almost all political parties demanded the cantonization or abolition of Bosnia-Hercegovina, the Serb party in Bosnia-Hercegovina—the Srpska Demokratska Stranka, or Serb Democratic Party (SDS), led by Karadžić—wanted a cantonized Bosnia-Hercegovina as a "confederation of three national communities" inside a Federal Yugoslavia. In autumn 1991, when it became clear that the Bosnian Muslim and Croats were being driven towards independence with all its perils, the SDS raised the stakes by forming six "Serb Autonomous Regions" and holding a referendum for Serbs. Ninety-eight percent of an 85 percent turn-out backed the formation of a Serb republic inside Bosnia-Hercegovina, if the republic of Bosnia-Hercegovina tried to break with Yugoslavia. In an independent Bosnia-Hercegovina, Serbs would allegedly be reduced to minority status, and this could not be allowed—especially as the Muslims (43 percent of the population) were allegedly bent on turning Bosnia-Hercegovina into an Islamic theocracy. This farrago has remained SDS dogma.

Of course, a Serb republic within Bosnia-Hercegovina would destroy Bosnia-Hercegovina in all but name, and soon in name also. But that was the Muslims' and Croats' problem; Karadžić wasn't offering proposals for discussion, he was delivering an ultimatum.

In December 1991 and January 1992, the SDS's maneuvers to forestall independence became yet more explicitly threatening. (It appears a model of the ending of Yugoslavia itself, with Serb radicals in power saying "Just you dare secede!" while doing everything to intimidate and heighten the insecurity of the other nations.) According to the self-styled "Assembly of the Serb People of Bosnia-Hercegovina," the Bosnian Serb republic would comprise the six regions plus other areas and municipalities with a Serb population. The Assembly promised rather demurely that "territorial separation . . . will be conducted in a peaceful way and by agreement," though without explaining how this agreement would be gained or what might happen if it proved unobtainable. In short, this was as close to a charter for "ethnic cleansing" as anything could be. It was issued on January 9, 1992, and no Western mediator had any right to suppose that the March 18 document supplanted it.

Croatia's attitude, and that of the politically organized Croats in Bosnia-Hercegovina, has been consistently perfidious. In Croatia, only the extremist Party of Right (PR) is openly opposed to Bosnian integrity and independence—because all Bosnia-Hercegovina rightfully belongs to the great Croatian state. But the PR gained under 7 percent of votes in the 1992 elections; in contrast with Serbia, there is no mass support for annexing any of Bosnia-Hercegovina.

Public opinion is rational; any tampering with Bosnia-Hercegovina would set a dangerous precedent: it would strengthen the secessionist demands by Serb rebels in the UN Protected Areas. Besides, it would be insane for Croatia, which is so dependent on EC and UN goodwill, to challenge their recognition of Bosnia-Hercegovina's sovereignty.

Yet Croatia's rulers are not ruled by rationality. West Hercegovina, which has the highest concentration of Croats, stands to Croatia as Montenegro stands to Serbia: a fountainhead of national spirit. An addiction to fantasies of annexing these barren uplands is part and parcel of Croatian nationalism. So when the "Hercegovina lobby," which for reasons of Yugoslav and Croatian history came to power and influence in Zagreb after the first free elections in 1990, presses the claims of its native land upon President Tudjman, it meets little resistance.

Tudjman's advisors must have told him that cantonization would prolong the travails of Croatia itself, because the Bosnian Serbs would get east Hercegovina, from which they could hold Dubrovnik and Konavle to ransom; and north-west Bosnia, from which they could supply the key rebel enclave in Croatia. But nationalist leaders always tend to believe they can have everything, achieve all their goals, if only they persist. Tudjman cannot relinquish the dream. He refused to support the Bosnia-Hercegovina government's project for a state of citizens with guarantees for national rights.

Although Croatia had done more than any other country to resist the Serb onslaught—especially in the first months when Bosnia-Hercegovina government forces hardly existed—and to succor the refugees of the onslaught, it is patently hanging on for the EC and UN to let Bosnia-Hercegovina be partitioned.

Nothing proved this more than Zagreb's sponsorship of hard-liners among the Croats. Soon after the SDS founded its Serb Autonomous Regions, the Bosnia-Hercegovina's branch of Hrvatska Demokratska Zajednica (HDZ), Croatian Democratic Community, the ruling party in Croatia, created two "Croat Communities" in majority-Croat regions. The HDZ presented these "Croat Communities" as defensive territorial insurance against Serb attack and the possible future disintegration of Bosnia-Hercegovina. While they did not challenge Sarajevo directly, they eroded its authority and fostered separatist fantasies.

Nevertheless, Stjepan Kljuić, the party leader, was an invincible believer in Bosnia-Hercegovina's integrity and independence—like many other Croats in Sarajevo, Tuzla, Travnik, and elsewhere. Under pressure from his own hard-liners and from Zagreb to entertain the cantonal option, he resigned on February 2, 1992, a month before the fateful referendum, telling his party that "many of you who are sitting here and supporting cantonization will actually be living in Greater Serbia. I'll leave for Australia . . . and then you'll realize that I was right all along."[5] Wise words. (Kljuić went to Sarajevo, where he joined Izetbegović's cabinet.)

Presumably the new leadership then worked out the March 18 formula with the SDS, or else agreed when the SDS mooted it, leaving the government isolated and constrained not to obstruct what Lord Carrington (chair of the EC conference on Yugoslavia) and Mr. Cutilheiro (responsible for negotiations about Bosnia-Hercegovina) doubtless liked to think was a respectable interim solution.

As for the Muslims, and the government which represented them without rivalry from another power-center (though it also, of course, represented the Serbs and the Croats who didn't see the SDS and HDZ as their champions), they always saw cantonization as a disaster. They were bound to lose out in any territorial shareout, for two reasons: they were the most dispersed nation, and they lacked a neighboring state to sponsor them politically and militarily. Serbs and Croats cohabited in relatively few districts, whereas Muslims lived with both throughout the republic. Muslims were the cement in Bosnia-Hercegovina (which was the main reason why Tito elevated them in the 1960s to the status of nation). Izetbegović insisted during the first half of 1991—when the SDS was already making his republic ungovernable and rumors abounded of secret deals among the three national leaders—that he would never negotiate cantonization.

Thus, even in conditions of general peace, it would have been careless of the EC to suppose that the March 18 formula could hold for long without very vehement and practical international support for the government; and there has been no sign of that, before or since.

In light of actual events in Croatia and the dynamics of war that prevailed in Serbia, and given the sheer quantity of JNA troops and weaponry that had withdrawn into Bosnia-Hercegovina from Slovenia, Croatia, and latterly Macedonia, the EC's tactic was criminally irresponsible. All the more so because the government of Bosnia-Hercegovina had done everything to accommodate the mediators, the Serbs, and JNA. The worst that can be held against Izetbegović and his team is gullibility. They believed in both the JNA's promise not to force a military solution in Bosnia-Hercegovina and the letter of international law regarding sovereign states. Against their wishes and better judgment, they even accepted the absurd Statement of Principles—effectively breaking the promise of 1991—for the sake of a peace in which they and their people wanted so desperately to believe.

IN JANUARY, FEBRUARY, and March of 1992, as the government of Bosnia-Hercegovina jumped tamely through the EC's legalistic hoops, the SDS and JNA continued to arm the paramilitary forces, while Serbs and Montenegrins pulled back from Croatia. The SDS and JNA secured strategic vantage points, ready to act as and when recognition of Bosnia-Hercegovina was imminent—and all in the knowledge that the West was neither equipped to prevent a swift land-grab, nor willing to react forcefully when the land-grab came.

It came, and a year later the West has still done nothing to puncture the aggressors' confidence that they can do what they wish in Bosnia-Hercegovina with essential impunity. A degree of diplomatic isolation; the bluster of world-wide condemnation; the farce of an economic blockade of Serbia and Montenegro, imposed by the Security Council on May 30 and violated daily; the equally farcical no-fly zone, proclaimed by the same body and resolutely unenforced despite hundreds of violations: these measures bring little or no benefit to Bosnia-Hercegovina, because they do not alter by a whit the bedrock truth that the aggressors have more reason to continue than to halt.

The aggressors' only serious worry has been about the chance of military intervention stopping the massacre before they are ready. But they have been nimble enough to defuse that possibility whenever it has arisen, not that much nimbleness is needed: that will to intervene has just not been there, and Western leaders have been doing the Serbs' propaganda work for them by dredging up every argument and pseudo-argument against escalating political and economic coercion into military coercion. We learned, for instance, the unlikely news that Prime Minister John Major of Britain is haunted by the specter of Dien Bien Phu, where Vietminh forces defeated the French army in 1954. We are told that intervention might get Western forces embroiled in Bosnia-Hercegovina for decades—another Northern Ireland.

More credibly than Mr. Major but no more creditably, the Bush administration invoked the precedent of Vietnam. Many experts, from Henry Kissinger to "the Lord" himself (as Peter Carrington was wryly known in the Slovene and Croatian press), warned how many German divisions were tied down in Bosnia-Hercegovina during World War II. The same people warned that intervention would have no clear objective and remind us how the terrain is tailor-made for guerrilla operations, how much "the Yugoslavs" love fighting, etcetera. No one has explained why the objective could not be to support the legitimate government of Bosnia-Hercegovina and its blueprint for the republic. Had this objective been allowed to steer the diplomatic initiative, some real progress might have been made at the negotiating table.

The false analogies and unwarranted pessimistic warnings are proffered alongside selective revision of current events. Politicians and commentators opine sagely that panicky "premature" recognition of Slovenia, Croatia, and Bosnia-Hercegovina was responsible for the assault or, at least exacerbated it. Often this is merely a coded attack on Germany for hustling the other EC states in December 1991. Perhaps these politicians and commentators realize that this unhistorical argument originated in Belgrade and Banja Luka (headquarters of the SDS). Perhaps they don't. It is the opposite of the truth, and its function is to blacken the most realistic and adequate moment of Western diplomacy. It implies that the fake cause of war was the real cause: if the Bosnian Serbs had not felt threatened, they wouldn't have taken up arms.

Just as spuriously, the argument implies that recognition aborted the chance of a solution acceptable to all sides. But if so, why had the SDS signed the March 18 Statement along with the government and the Bosnian Croat leader? In truth, the Serb-JNA position against statehood for Bosnia-Hercegovina was non-negotiable. (Karadžić had warned that a referendum would mean war.)

Another piece of wisdom fast becoming received is that the EC also blundered by insisting from the outset that only peaceful changes to borders between republics would be recognized. It is difficult to say whether this opinion is more arrogant than ignorant, or vice versa. It takes its cue from Serbian propaganda that these borders are "administrative," invented by Tito, no basis for statehood. It assumes that the peoples and governments of former Yugoslavia do not themselves know very well that these borders define national, historic, and cultural entities, and would not resist tooth and nail any forced border changes, regardless of the EC's approval.

Both these arguments carry a further implication: that the assault on Bosnia-Hercegovina, like its predecessor on Croatia, can be "understood," and to some extent condoned, because the aggressors were provoked. Thus the aggressors' own excuse for committing genocide is draped with diplomatic gravitas and a touch of humility (after all we shouldn't have let the German pressure cloud our better judgment).[6]

A further lie underpins these. It is the claim, repeated daily by a thousand journalists, that this is an ethnic war. This notion, too, originates in Belgrade and Banja Luka. It is a misnomer, because the Serb, Croat, and Muslim nations are ethnically indistinguishable. (The number of Bosnian Muslims of Turkish descent is minuscule.) And it is pernicious, because it disguises a consequence as a cause and mystifies the conflict as orgiastic free-for-all, far removed from political calculation: a spontaneous Balkan combustion—an outbreak of Balkan violence, endemic and insensate, that must be left to burn itself out. Not hard to understand because moderately complex—incomprehensible because irrational. Karadžić never misses a chance to explain in his good English that cease-fires keep being broken because ethnic hatred runs so deep. He knows his audience, and the message he sends is seductive: "Don't intervene! You can't do anything about an ethnic conflict except stand well back. Outsiders would be attacked by everyone, they'd never get out alive." Music to the ears of Europeans and Americans who don't want to intervene anyway.

As well as revision, there has been suppression. In early August 1992, the first pictures of a Serb concentration camp in northern Bosnia were broadcast on Western television. The sight of skeletal, half-naked men milling around behind a barbed-wire fence was deeply shocking. Several days later the shock was compounded by the revelations that the UN peace keepers had known in detail since May about the full gamut of "ethnic cleansing," including camps, home burnings, deportations, and summary executions. No action had been taken to publicize or investigate those early reports, of which Security Council members swiftly denied all knowledge. Pending a full account, suspicion of cover-up at some senior level must remain.

What is the upshot of all this? Outrage has been dulled, doped with fake fatalism. Sober appraisal of military options to stop the horrors has been swamped by trumped-up alarmism. While Western opinion polls showed support for military action, governments intoned that the public would not tolerate the likely price. The triumphant noise about Western technology delivering air-to-ground missiles down Iraqi chimney pots was nowhere to be heard; instead we were told solemnly that Britain and the United States (for instance) would never commit ground troops to Bosnia-Hercegovina.

In fact, Britain did commit troops, to protect humanitarian supplies. But troops for peace-making action are not (yet) the issue; the Sarajevo government hasn't even requested them. What was needed was a UN resolution, reached by consultation with the government of Bosnia-Hercegovina (a UN member state, after all) to forbid further use of heavy artillery, armor, and strike aircraft. Violations would be answered with air strikes.

The nature of the Serbian assault gives reason to suppose that this measure would suffice to transform the conflict and infuse the so-called peace process with new plausibility. (If it failed to do so, the next step would be to lift the arms embargo for the government of Bosnia-Hercegovina.) With the soldiers (54,000 of them) and arms donated to the "Serb Republic of Bosnia" by the JNA as it "withdrew" across the river Drina to Serbia in mid-May, it was a simple matter for Karadžić's Einsatzgruppen to drive hundreds of thousands of defenseless people from their homes. By the end of April 1992, some two thirds of Bosnia-Hercegovina was under Serb control. But as in Croatia, the Serbo-Yugoslav military machine is not up to the job. Again, destruction and rapine are ends as well as means for too many of its hoodlum soldiers. Terrorizing unarmed peasants is one thing; taking towns and cities is quite another. The aggressors' only method is to blockade a town, set up artillery on the surrounding hills, call in air strikes, and unload shells on the citizens day after day, month after month.

This, the Vukovar Technique, bespeaks an oafish, cowardly army without brains on top, discipline below, or morale anywhere. Apart from its barbarity, the method doesn't work. Karadžić boasted on May 17 that "we could take Sarajevo any time. We could finish them in five days." Sarajevo is still untaken. On July 14 he told UN negotiators that Goražde would fall within two days. Goražde has not yet fallen. Tuzla, Zenica, and Bihać still resist.

The aggressors have paid a scant price for their gains. What would happen if the spell of impunity were broken? What would the impact be on the morale of government forces, on public opinion in Serbia, and among the Bosnian Serbs, a proportion of whom has never seen the evil Karadžić as its spokesman?

THESE ARE QUEUING to join the great unanswered questions of our era. The Europeans and the Americans do not judge the destruction of Bosnia-Hercegovina sufficiently threatening to their interests to warrant a military response; and only a military response could have halted the destruction. It is precisely these powers' conception of their interests which defeats every effort of enlightenment, every insistence that more is at stake than stopping "one of the great crimes of twentieth century Europe";[7] namely, the stability of southeast

Europe for the next generation, the future of European integration and of the United Nations, the viability of Helsinki principles, the prospects for non-aggressive solutions of territorial disputes everywhere, above all in the former USSR. A conception of interests that dismisses these certain dangers for an illusory "quiet life" is quite as irrational as, and perhaps less principled than, Franjo Tudjman's yearning for Hercegovina or Dobrica Cosić's dream of "Greater Serbia."

Instead we have watched the peace negotiations fail, month after month, to make any headway whatever, while the conquerors extend and tighten their grip, and Western public pressure for action to defend the Bosnians dissipates. After the Hague, Brussels, Lisbon, London, and Geneva, the circus reached New York, where a "political solution" for Bosnia-Hercegovina seemed close in January and early February 1993. But this prize eluded the outstretched fingers of the mediators. At time of writing, this "solution" grows more remote and implausible with every passing day. The mediators, though, have no patience with fainthearts; Cyrus Vance and David Owen, co-chairmen of the International Conference on Former Yugoslavia, are devoted to their plan, and nothing can discourage them from trying to persuade the Serbs and bully the Bosnians into signing on the dotted line.

Their solution is, of course, no solution. The Vance-Owen plan would reconstitute Bosnia-Hercegovina as a confederation of ten largely autonomous regions. Each nation would control three regions, with Sarajevo remaining neutral. The central government would possess very limited powers, and there would be no army. The regions would "not have any international legal personality" (in the words of the Constitutional Principles); nor would they be allowed to take national names, or to control movement across inter-regional borders.

"At the same time," comments Srdjan Dvornik of the Anti-War Campaign of Croatia, "there is nothing in the foreseen power-structure of the state and the regions that would provide for positive and preventive protection of human and minority rights: no provision for minorities within regions to be fairly represented in regional organs, and no guarantees in advance against national bias by the authorities. Nor is there anything to make the authorities abide by state legislation, to prevent regions uniting on national lines or forming unions with the "mother countries" [i.e. Serbia and Croatia]. For instance, all "uniformed and armed police will be controlled by regional authorities." There would be "demilitarization" without disarmament; thus military hardware would, as in Serb-occupied Croatia, be merely resprayed and transferred to the local "constabulary." In sum, argues Dvornik, "there is nothing to prevent armed conflicts between regions, as there is nothing to prevent penetration by neighboring countries (note that control of the international borders would be exercised by the regions)."[8]

Promoting their plan, Vance and Owen denied that nationality was decisive in demarcating the regions and would dominate their governance. This was dishonest; the "bait" for Serb and Croat forces was precisely that the plan conceded their fundamental claim: that Bosnia-Hercegovina is an artificial patchwork of national territories which must be nationally governed.

The Croat side signed with alacrity, no doubt amazed that the forbidden fruit was about to drop into their hand. (The plan would give them 25 percent of the republic.) President Izetbegović and his government—relegated to the status of Muslim leaders—were dismayed; unfortunately their response was weak and confused. (Their inability to sustain an alternative loudly and clearly is tragic but, given the colossal pressure on from every side, hardly to be wondered at.) As for the Serb side, it has flirted with Vance, Owen, and their employers as blatantly and profitably as everyone knew it would. Karadžić is often very hopeful that real progress is being made at the talks; and he is often very doubtful that his side can keep making concessions. Meanwhile, week after week, his forces bomb, kill, starve, and rape the Bosnians hanging on in northern and eastern Bosnia.

Perhaps Karadžić and company were genuinely tempted by the plan, which grants them 43 percent of territory, including a huge tract in northwest Bosnia. Yet the cost has proved too high; Vance-Owen required the Serbs to renounce their maximal war-aim of winning recognition for their self-proclaimed state within Bosnia-Hercegovina. (This entity would duly annex itself to Serbia as the third unit of "Yugoslavia.") Possession is nine tenths of the law; and if recognition were never to come, so what? They would survive unrecognized.

Serb forces have conquered some 70 percent of the republic, after all, and the arrangement of regions would break the all-important "corridor" connecting the Serb stronghold in northern Bosnia to Belgrade in one direction and, in the other, to the key Serb enclave in Croatia. As this stronghold would not be contiguous with Serbia proper, de facto annexation would be impossible.

Why should the Serb forces accept these conditions in return for mere acceptance by Europe and the UN of the regional (cantonal) principal? Cantonization was only ever a stalking-horse. They only motive to swallow the Vance-Owen pill would have been a fear of intervention to impose another settlement worse for Serb ambitions. The perceived likelihood of military action to realize the no-fly zone over Bosnia-Hercegovina alone accounted for the Serbs' willingness to entertain in December a form of settlement which they had rejected wholesale as recently as November 2. But the fearless British campaign waged in the Security Council chamber against enforcing the no-fly zone carried the day; the Serbs concluded there was still no will to enforce anything. Karadžić kept flirting, his forces kept killing, while Lord Owen kept grittily insisting that his plan was the only game in town.

It has been a nadir of diplomacy. Like their predecessors, the Geneva and New York sessions were a nightmare of make-believe, compounding injustice with bad politics. Karadžić emerged from one session to remark that talks were progressing "as if there hasn't been a war." A typical sneer and an awesome truth. No wonder he and General Mladić, who just a fortnight earlier had been accused by Secretary of State Eagleburger of complicity with crimes against humanity, beamed shiftily at the press like cats which had eaten the cream and could hardly believe they were getting away with it.

Or were they marveling at the double incoherence of European and American policy? The Vance-Owen plan is untenable on several levels. First, the plan cannot work in its own terms. The 1.5 million or 2 million refugees and displaced persons will not be able to return home. The fragile jigsaw of autonomous regions would need permanent protection on a massive scale, because two nations would dispute their portions; the third would be embroiled in the ensuing conflict.

So much is obvious. Yet the plan is proof against all such criticism, because it is not meant to succeed in its stated terms. Its true purpose is very different: to forge a settlement which pays lip-service to the sovereignty of Bosnia-Hercegovina, while fencing it off and carving it up, ensuring that central government lacks the means to constrain any regions which decide to go their own way. Thus the plan contains a barely-veiled promise that much of what the Serbs would not get in the short term could be theirs in the medium term.

The plan is also incoherent at the regional level. Regionalism was always a means to an end for the Serb and Croat forces; by drafting a regional settlement without any commitment to making it stick, the international mediators repeated their error of March 18, 1992, and compounded it by doing so as if the intervening nine months of slaughter and occupation had not occurred. The Croat side has signed, the Serb side has not, but neither shows any readiness to play the Vance-Owen game by calling a cease-fire and allowing a respectable interval of "peace" to elapse before pursuing its goal again more discreetly. No wonder Vance's and Owen's patience is sorely tried: the rank ingratitude must be hard to swallow.

Their plan should be ditched forthwith, and the Security Council should enact a resolution of the kind suggested above. This will not happen, of course. The mediators have given too many hostages to a most dubious fortune; military intervention may yet come by degrees and incidents. An UNPROFOR commander might decide to fulfill his mandate by really using "all necessary means" to deliver aid; or he might tire of assisting at the extermination of the Bosnians, and decide to exceed his mandate. A Serb commander might call the UNPROFOR bluff once too often and trigger a punitive response which shatters the make-believe beyond repair.

Security Council nightmares are made of such stuff. What the mediating powers want is for the situation on the ground to resolve itself until a revised version of the plan, proposing three regions and expanding the Serb territory at the Muslims' cost, proves acceptable to the Serbs. (The Muslims will sign—what option will they have?) It will be another fake solution, guaranteeing a perpetuation of war and, in Serbia and Croatia, the supremacy of radical nationalist politics.

The liberal conscience, however, is flexible and inventive. The mediators will console themselves that such an outcome is inevitable. Only a few will detect a clandestine bond between themselves and the aggressors, both Serb and Croat; for the latter always knew that progress is impossible without dismembering Bosnia-Hercegovina, while the former let themselves be persuaded that progress is impossible without letting Bosnia-Hercegovina be dismembered. Post-Communist Balkan atavism hand in glove with the laissez-faire geopolitics of the democratic West—a deadly partnership.

NOTES

I am indebted to James Gow, Bojen Bujić, George Kenny, Srdjan Dvornik and Zarko Puhovski for insights offered in conversation. *Peace-making and Peace-keeping: European Security and the Yugoslav Wars* by James Gow and James D.D. Smith was useful to me, and can be commended.

1. From "O Andricevej Gospodjic" in *Zivot, literatura* (Svjetlost, Sarajevo, 1990).

2. A Serb from Montenegro, Karadžić, has no feeling for Bosnia and sees Bosnian integrity as nothing other than an obstacle to the fossilized Great Serb project. Rasim Kadić of the Democratic League of Bosnia-Hercegovina recalls a meeting with Karadžić in mid-April 1992, when the assault and genocide were underway. "I am willing to sacrifice this entire generation," he told Rasim, "if it means that future generations [i.e. of Serbs] will live better." (*Mladina*, 14 July 1992.) No doubt he is more discreet with Lord Owen and Cyrus Vance.

3. From William Gladstone's speech upon the "Eastern Question" to the House of Commons, May 7, 1877. In the light of European treatment of the Bosnian Serbs, the relevant passage of Gladstone's superb oration is worth quoting at length: ". . . Necessary guarantees, something beyond mere promises, adequate securities, consisting in something beyond and above the engagements or ostensible proceedings of the Turkish government constituted indeed the pith of the extracts which were read by the Chancellor of the Exchequer on the first night of the Session from the Instructions to Lord Salisbury. Well, what has now become of those necessary guarantees? They are all gone to the winds. We are told in the despatch published this morning that we are to found our hopes on the fact that the Porte has promised certain things, and that as it has promised we cannot be sure that it will not perform. This is the vital point; it lies at the root of the whole matter. We are now told to rely on those promises. But, for my own part, I would repeat what I said on a former occasion, when we were trying remonstrance after remonstrance, protestation after protestation. Those protestations, and those remonstrances, and those representations which have been lavished on the Porte by Her Majesty's Government, are all very well up to a certain point; up to the point at which there remains a semblance of a reasonable hope that they may possibly attain their end. But it is not so, when we have found by long and wide experience that they produce no substantial result whatever . . . "

In 1992 no one expected a Gladstone to arise and reverse single-handedly the Western governments' contemptible appeasing of Bosnia's destroyers (who for their part imagine that they are still fighting the same Turks whose atrocities so outraged Gladstone; an instructive irony). But did we—did the Bosnians—deserve the leaders we got? As the latter's gems of insight risk being lost beneath the torrent of killing, I have rescued three average sparklers for posterity—all British, but they could be American, French, Russian . . .

Prime Minister Major on May 26, 1992: "I have reached the conclusion, not without some consideration, that Serbia bears the greatest responsibility for the present situation." Lord Carrington on June 22, 1992, after talks with Serbian leaders in Belgrade: "I got nowhere, I find this very disappointing." Foreign Minister Douglas Hurd, returning from a visit to former Yugoslavia in mid-June, 1992: "One of the things one learns from actually being [in Bosnia-Hercegovina] is that the fears and hatreds which have been unleashed are absolutely formidable."

4. *Radio Free Europe/Radio Liberty, Inc. Research Report on Eastern Europe,* February 28, 1992.

5. *Ibid.* See also the Reports for July 5, 1991, October 25, 1991, and July 31, 1992.

6. The government of Bosnia-Hercegovina was plainly asking for trouble. "Contributory negligence" is the judicial term; a tendency to blame the victim, evident in Croatia's case, became compulsive in the case of Bosnia-Hercegovina. The Bosnians have been pitied as victims, but their government is rarely, if ever, seen as the proponent of the only viable future for the republic and the region. There is a correlation between the innocence of an embattled victim and the urgency of an onlooker's need to deny that innocence, if the onlooker wants not only to stay uninvolved but to justify non-involvement.

7. David Rieff, "Letter From Bosnia: Original Virtue, Original Sin," *The New Yorker,* November 23, 1992.

8. Srdjan Dvornik, "How To Stop The War In Bosnia-Hercegovina," *New Politics,* 4 (Summer 1993).

A Question of International Solidarity

THOMAS HARRISON

IN EARLY MARCH 1993, John Burns of *The New York Times* described the besieged, mainly Muslim town of Goražde in eastern Bosnia: nearly every building had been hit by Serbian shells, the average weight loss among adults was twenty-five to thirty pounds; and in spite of having watched Serbian heavy armor smash through lightly armed Bosnian forces for almost a year, and having seen two-thirds of Bosnia's territory occupied by the storm troopers of the psychiatrist-warlord Radovan Karadžić, the people of Goražde still refused to follow the advice of Cyrus Vance, David Owen, the United Nations, the United States, the European Community, and nearly everybody else to "face up to reality"—in other words, to give up.

Under the Vance-Owen plan, Goražde would be in one of the three "provinces" that supposedly would have a Muslim majority. However, since most of the province has already been subjected to "ethnic cleansing," there may no longer be a Muslim majority. And even if there were, Burns explains that "the issue among most Muslims in Bosnia is not whether the community they live in would fall into a province that would be governed by Muslims, but the kind of society that would emerge from a peace agreement that has divisive principles at its heart. The point is made often here: most people, certainly most Muslims, but also many Serbs and Croats, want nothing to do with constitutional arrangements that divide power on the basis of nationality and creed."[1]

Nevertheless, most of the Western news media and public opinion persist in thinking of the war in terms of "ethnic strife" and "ancient blood feuds," suggesting a symmetry among all sides that is patently false. Bosnians are fighting to preserve a culturally diverse society in which Muslims, Serbs, and Croats have lived, if not in complete harmony, at least peacefully. They are also defending the idea of a democratic republic founded on universal rights rather than those based on ethnicity. The Serb insurgency, on the other hand, has been inspired by a fascistic ideology of blood and soil; its supporters will not tolerate coexistence with non-Serbs under any circumstances. A Bosnian militia commander spoke the truth when he told *The Times* that this war is "about civilization. It's not an ethnic war, it's a war of ordinary people against primitive men who want to carry us back to tribalism."[2]

It is the Muslims whom the Serbs have singled out for especially savage treatment. If genocide is the word for physical extermination of a national group, there should also be a word for what is happening to the Bosnian Muslims. It shows how the aggressors have been allowed to define the very terms of the discourse on former Yugoslavia so that the world has adopted the Serbs' own obscene coinage—"ethnic cleansing," so reminiscent of the Nazis' "final solution"—to refer to the policy of systematic and extreme mass terror aimed at driving the Muslims into permanent exile and permanently erasing from the map a Bosnian Muslim nation occupying specific land. This policy may not qualify as genocide in the strictest sense, but it is surely a crime against an entire people as such. Despite years of ritually repeating "Never Again," the leaders of the world's democratic states have not only permitted this to happen, they have actively helped to make it possible.

Serbian expansionism initially was regarded in most Western capitals as a lesser evil than a perceived epidemic of secessionism and general "instability" in the Balkans. For a time, Western leaders quietly seemed to desire a speedy and not too cruel victory for Milošević and his protégés, while ostensibly maintaining strict noninvolvement. It was only when Serb aggression began to "get out of hand"—that is, when its almost unprecedented viciousness began to have an effect on public opinion, and when the security of neighboring European states began to seem threatened—that the West was forced to deliver some humanitarian aid while vigorously deploring the atrocities (by "all sides," to be sure) and even hinting, with a total lack of plausibility, at military intervention to "save" Bosnia. Meanwhile, the arms embargo deprived Bosnians of the only means by which "ethnic cleansing" could have been stopped. And a "peace process" was initiated with the basic aim, as Leslie Gelb put it, to get "the Bosnian Muslims to recognize that their cause is hopeless; come to the bargaining table, and accept defeat."[3]

Condemning Serbia and imposing sanctions seems inconsistent with preventing Bosnians from fighting back and simultaneously trying to force them to accept defeat in the guise of "peace" and "realism." These goals, however, are more consistent than they appear. Western policy has been guided not so much by sympathy for Serbian aggression as by contempt for and annoyance with its victims, as well as by the cynical assumption that Milošević, as the "strong man" of the Balkans, eventually would have to be accommodated in the interests of realpolitik and global stability.

The United States and Western Europe have always feared a power vacuum in the Balkans and further east. For this reason, and despite their hostility to Communism, they favored the maintenance of strong multinational states like Yugoslavia and the USSR. The "captive nations" policy of the State Department and the CIA was a useful Cold War propaganda tactic, but was not meant to be taken too seriously; the last thing Western leaders wanted was a host of newly independent Lithuanias, Croatias, Moldovas, and so on.

As far as Yugoslavia is concerned, the West long tolerated—and thus encouraged—massive human rights violations. It essentially turned a blind eye to the Serbian authorities' appalling treatment of the Albanians in the province of Kosovo. When democratic forces in Yugoslavia demanded greater autonomy for the republics, the West generally backed Milošević's hard-line centralist position. On a visit to Belgrade, Secretary of State Baker told Milan Kučan and Franjo Tudjman that the United States would not extend recognition if either republic declared its independence, and he threatened them with international economic isolation if they broke away. Western governments were obviously hostile to Slovenia's and Croatia's exercise of their right to self-determination. And in response, Serbia and the Yugoslav People's Army (JNA) concluded that they had been given a green light to attack the breakaway republics. The Economic Community's (EC) sour reluctance to recognize the new states, and the furious denunciations leveled at Germany for doing so "unilaterally," further encouraged Serbian aggression.

For months, while the killing and "ethnic cleansing" went on, while Dubrovnik was bombarded and Osijek and Vukovar reduced to rubble, the West, including Germany, feigned helplessness, while actually showing little sign of sympathy for Croatia's desperate resistance. In fact, Croatians were more or less accused of having brought it all on themselves. In stark contrast to the international campaign it organized against Iraq in 1990–1991, the Bush administration took a particularly low key approach to the Serbian onslaught. Not until the Lisbon conference in May 1992 did James Baker call for punishing Serbia. By "tilting" toward the Serbs, Western governments and the UN helped ignite the conflagration which has now engulfed Bosnia-Hercegovina and may soon spread to Kosovo and other regions.

Had they immediately recognized Slovenian and Croatian independence and made serious efforts to deter Serbian aggression—both through diplomacy and through material aid to Croatian defense forces—Belgrade might have been too demoralized and uncertain to pursue its plans for conquest and mass terror. Of course, we will never know for certain. But what is clear is that the West, whether wittingly or not, signaled encouragement to Milošević and his allies. Further, the imposition of a blanket arms embargo on the whole of ex-Yugoslavia only ensured that the JNA and its Serbian clients would possess and maintain an overwhelming military advantage over their victims in Croatia, and later Bosnia-Hercegovina.

The Zagreb government committed grave offenses against the rights and sensibilities of the Serb minority in Croatia, and it continues to do so; but these simply cannot be equated with the massive campaign of murder, expulsion, and destruction of whole cities which was inflicted on hundreds of thousands of innocent Croats. Croatian Serbs had, and have, as much right to self-determination as Croats or anybody else. But the war in Croatia was not about Serb self-determination—any more than Hitler's invasion of Czechoslovakia was about the self-determination of the Sudeten Germans. It was a war of Serbian expansion at the expense of Croatia.

Moreover, to defend Croatia's right to resist this aggression does not necessarily imply any political sympathy for Tudjman or approval of his government's treatment of the Serbs. Indeed, the West might have played a very constructive role by showing concern for both the right of the Serb minority to security and autonomy and the right of Croatia's majority to establish an independent state. Instead, the United States and the EC made it abundantly clear that their main concern was to hold Yugoslavia together at all costs, even if this meant blatant Serbian domination. As a logical consequence, Serbian leaders believed that they might attack Croatia with relative impunity. Despite the sanctions, this is more or less what happened. When a cease-fire finally came, the Serbs were left in possession of one third of Croatia's territory. UN troops have so far failed to disarm the Serb militias or guarantee the safe return of Croatian refugees.

For all the differences between Croatia and Bosnia-Hercegovina, the politics of the war have been essentially the same in both republics. But where in Croatia the aggressors simply aimed to carve out Serb territory, which could then be ethnically "cleansed" as necessary, in Bosnia the goal of attaching great chunks of the country's ethnic mosaic to a "Greater Serbia" required the destruction of the republic itself and the massacre or expulsion of most of its Muslim population. Bosnia, like Croatia, declared its independence in order to escape from a Yugoslavia under the domination of Milošević, a domination even more certain after the departure of Slovenia and Croatia. The West responded in the same way as it did in the case of Croatia: not Serbian aggression but Bosnian independence was seen as the problem. The Bosnians, like the Croats and Slovenes, were regarded as somehow responsible for the attacks directed against them.

Far from receiving Western protection, Sarajevo was immediately relegated to the status of just one of the "warring parties," instead of the legitimate elected government of Bosnia-Hercegovina. The EC's special conference—with the United States going along—endorsed negotiations based on "cantonization," carving up the republic into separate ethnic enclaves. This, in effect, conceded the demands of the Serb insurgents and encouraged them to grab as large an enclave as possible. Croatian forces, directed by the Tudjman regime, also moved to slice off large bits of Bosnia-Hercegovina for themselves. Throughout the war, Croatia has continued to play an ambiguous role, sometimes acting directly against the Bosnian resistance, but at other times providing crucial military help. And while extreme Croatian nationalists have demanded a "Greater Croatia" at Bosnia's expense, there has also been broad popular sympathy in Croatia for Bosnian Muslims and the Sarajevo government. Politically, however, the Croatian authorities have continued to support an "ethnic solution" and have thus effectively lined up with Belgrade, the UN and the Western powers against Bosnia. Meanwhile, the EC sponsored a series of meaningless "peace talks" which simply provided time and cover while Bosnia's enemies created "facts on the ground."

Bosnians cheered the arrival of UN troops in March 1992, but it soon became clear that the Blue Helmets, consistent with the policy of the Western powers who dominate the Security Council, had arrived mainly to stabilize the status quo through a cease-fire—which came to mean accepting, to a greater or lesser extent, the results of "ethnic cleansing." Like the EC "peace talks" before them, the UN negotiations simply provided more time and cover while the Serbs seized great swaths of terrain, which then, of course, became the *fait accompli* upon which any "pragmatic" solution had to be based.

In Sarajevo, UN officials were careful to make "even-handed" statements to avoid alienating Serb leaders. The UN commander, General Lewis MacKenzie, went beyond the requirements of neutrality by repeatedly blaming both sides for the bloodshed—outrageously equating the Bosnian fighters, who were defending their homes and families, with Karadžić's legions, who shelled bread lines and maternity hospitals, shot up buses carrying orphans, herded refugees into sealed railway cars, ran brutal concentration camps, and carried out a policy of mass rape. The last tactic had few if any precedents in the long annals of wartime atrocities against women.

As the Sarajevo government continued to reject "pragmatism," the West's pseudo-evenhandedness gave way to increasingly open impatience with the "recalcitrant" Bosnians. With the Serbs, in stark contrast, the West was inexhaustibly patient; they, in turn, were happy to cooperate in any deal that allowed them to keep most of their conquests. This phenomenon could be observed in a *Financial Times* interview with David Owen, who said of his colleague Cyrus Vance, "Cy's relationship with [Milošević] is a very important one. There is trust there, at a level of man for man." The reporter added, "Lord Owen, too, has considerable respect for Mr. Milošević's capacities, though not for his past policies."

No need to worry too much about these past policies, however; having won the Serbian elections, the butcher of the Balkans is, Owen assured us, "now prepared to take on the hard right, he is prepared to deal with [Bosnia] and he is heading towards leading Serbia back into the European family. I have no doubt of that." He goes on: "Serbia and Montenegro have also understood . . . that they have the capacity to be very powerful players in this part of Europe, and that, as the pariahs of Europe, they have no chance of achieving this." His credo as a mediator? "You have to be objective and fair-minded and genuinely seek a negotiated settlement and leave the moral judgments to others."[4]

The Vance-Owen plan reflects this approach perfectly. It has nothing to do with morality and everything to do with accommodating power and brute force. The plan is simply the latest version of cantonization—the operating assumption of the "peace process" since day one. It is based, in fact, on the same premises as the cease-fire agreement in Croatia: while Serbian tactics are to be deplored, the truce lines are to reflect Serbian conquests. While the plan alludes to the need to reverse "ethnic cleansing," it contains nothing that would make this enforceable. This is because the Western powers who are supporting the pact have no intention of rolling back Serbian gains and no serious desire to see them rolled back. The Vance-Owen plan simply endorses the geopolitical status quo created by the Serb (and Croat) offensives. To be "objective and fair-minded" means to understand that justice must always be subordinated to order and stability. If "moral judgments" seem to be at odds with this fetishized order, they must be set aside and ignored. The "powerful players" in the Balkans must be appeased.

After initially making some sympathetic noises about the Muslims getting a bad deal—and cruelly raising hopes in Bosnia—Secretary of State Warren Christopher has also abandoned the Bosnian government and given assurances that the United States will work within the Vance-Owen framework. This is consistent with the new administration's systematic abandonment of the "pro-democracy" foreign policy promised by Clinton during the electoral campaign—as seen in its reversals on Haiti and China. Kissinger-style realpolitik has now frankly taken over the agenda. For one thing, Russia, a very powerful player, naturally takes priority over little Bosnia. Washington has apparently decided that even showing a slight partiality toward the Bosnians is to be avoided because it might strengthen Boris Yeltsin's nationalist opponents and thus threaten stability in Russia. This is a game all too reminiscent of the cynical, and grotesquely short-sighted, "tilt" which rocked back and forth between Iran and Iraq in the Persian Gulf during the 1980s. Just as at one stage a US tilt toward Iraq was intended to weaken the "greater evil," Iran, now a tilt toward Milošević is supposed to weaken the chauvinist Right and thereby strengthen democracy in Russia. But, as in the Gulf, US policy will be utterly self-defeating. Allowing the Serbs to emerge semi-victorious in Bosnia will only encourage nationalists on the right in Russia—as well as all the other friends of the Belgrade regime, like the Securitate elements in Romania.

GIVEN THE ROLE played by the United States, the UN, and the other Western powers thus far, it makes no sense for progressives and democrats to continue to look for any kind of just solution under the aegis of these powers. Instead, alternatives for organizing support for the Bosnian resistance must be pursued. The idea of a "negotiated solution" naturally has great appeal because it seems to offer the best hope for stopping the bloodshed. However, a negotiated solution which is basically imposed on the Bosnians will not bring peace. And those who advocate such a solution as an alternative to Bosnian self-defense risk conceding too much to the aggressors.

In a fundamental sense there is nothing to negotiate in Bosnia. The Serbs have rights, of course, but Serbian expansion has no legitimacy. Karadžić and his henchmen have committed crimes against humanity on such a scale that they have lost their right to speak for Bosnia's Serbs or to take part in any legitimate discussions about Serb self-determination. Their military defeat should be the paramount objective. But if Milošević and Karadžić retain, through negotiations, even a portion of what the Serbs have already occupied, they will have achieved a victory, one which can only encourage further aggression and "ethnic cleansing" in Kosovo, the Sandjak, and Macedonia. It is one thing for the Bosnians to enter into negotiations by their own decision for practical reasons, and from a position of military strength, but another thing for them to enter negotiations while at a political and military disadvantage. Under Bosnia's present circumstances any accord that benefits the Serbs is inherently unjust. The proper role for Western governments is not to force the Bosnians to sit down at the negotiating table, but to help them rectify the balance of power on the ground so that, if a negotiated solution is finally necessary, they will be in the strongest possible position. Since this is not really in the interests of Western governments—as they perceive their interests—they will only provide this help in response to pressure from democratic opinion. Democratic opinion, unfortunately, has until now largely accepted the Vance-Owen plan as the only means of achieving peace.

But the point is, that neither Vance-Owen nor any other kind of agreement based on ethnic cantonization—even one which is supervised by UN troops for many years to come, as the United States now proposes—has much chance of succeeding even on its own terms. Serbian forces have made it clear that they consider any peace agreement to be merely a strategic pause on the road to consolidating a "Greater Serbia." Bosnian refugees are no more likely to accept permanent exile and statelessness than the Palestinians have for almost 45 years now. In short, a peace agreement that recognizes Serbian conquests will not bring peace; it will instead create a kind of UN-sponsored Cold War in the Balkans, probably with constant low-level violence and an ever-present threat of major irredentist conflicts.

Nor would direct military intervention in support of the Bosnian forces (the most unlikely scenario of all), by the United States alone or under UN auspices, bring about a just and democratic resolution to the conflict.

First, even a "limited" intervention will probably escalate because of Western governments' fear of a drawn-out war. Given this fear of becoming bogged down in an unpopular "quagmire," there is a great danger that if the United States or Western Europe send in troops, they will be tempted to shorten the war with some brutal acts of over-kill—like the slaughter of 150,000 Iraqis in 1991. A "Balkan Storm" would probably include bombing attacks on Serbian towns and infrastructure, which would criminally victimize Serbian civilians. And second, it is politically naive to regard UN forces—let alone US troops—as some sort of neutral instrument of fairness and peace, a kind of international "911."

Under whatever command arrangement they are sent in, foreign troops in Bosnia would be the soldiers of existing states, not of some mythic "international community." These states neither cease to be politically self-interested nor begin to operate on the basis of democratic principles merely because they agree to act under UN auspices. UN troops would intervene to impose the political agendas of the states which sent them, and there is more than enough evidence to say that these agendas have nothing to do with self-determination and democracy in ex-Yugoslavia; on this subject there has been, indeed, all too much "international community." A US-led intervention, in particular, would be an extremely bad precedent for peace-making, mainly because it could not be separated from Washington's ongoing desire to assert its "right" to police other countries. If anything like democracy and civil society have a chance in Bosnia, they can only be built through the efforts and under the political control of the Bosnian people themselves. "Waiting for Clinton" (or the UN) would be understandable, if illusory, for the desperate Bosnians; but for those in the West who care about human rights and democratic values, it is a moral dead-end.

The most disturbing aspect of much progressive opinion on the Bosnian war is the progressives' willingness to see the elected Sarajevo government simply dissolved. Vance-Owen would do this not only by constitutionally decentralizing the Bosnian republic, but by effectively disarming Bosnian government forces while allowing Serb and Croat forces to simply change uniforms and become the armed police of their respective "provinces." Lurking behind Vance-Owen, as well as other proposals for "safe havens" and UN trusteeships, is a thoroughly anti-democratic vision, recently articulated by a "senior State Department official" who told *The New York Times* that Bosnia, like Cambodia and Somalia, is a state that is "not capable of governing itself"; in all three cases, the United States and the UN have begun to "take government out of the hands of indigenous peoples."[5] The prospect of the UN acting as a new global colonial power should give pause.

We need to question the assumptions expressed by this American official, assumptions which pervade international discussion of Bosnia and the Balkans generally: that only certain peoples are fit for self-government, while others—the collectively incompetent—need to be tutored in the mysteries of democracy.

This notion has been around since modern democracy began. Even John Stuart Mill declared, "Despotism is a legitimate mode of government in dealing with barbarians, provided the end be their improvement, and the means justified by actually effecting that end."[6] In his critique of Mill's defense of benevolent despotism Michael Walzer has observed, "Whatever plausibility such arguments had in the nineteenth century, they have none today. International society can no longer be divided into civilized and barbarian halves; any line drawn on developmental principles leaves barbarians on both sides."[7] Of course, this view had no plausibility in the nineteenth or any century, beyond providing a pretext for colonial pursuits that usually took barbaric forms by the "effecting" powers.

It is the arrogance and chauvinism of those who live in wealthy, powerful nations that makes it possible to divide up the human race in this way. But it is no more legitimate to deny self-government and self-determination to the Bosnians than it would be to deny these rights to Americans, British, French, or any other supposedly advanced nations. Moreover, how can anyone know that Bosnians are incapable of governing themselves if they have never had an opportunity to do so? Bosnia's tragedy is that, first, communism and, now, Serbian aggression, both with the complicity of the West, have effectively denied its people the opportunity to acquire democratic experience. Bosnia's efforts to create a democratic, multicultural independent state and to defend it against armed attack have been dismissed and undermined from the start by those who should have been its staunchest friends.

Sending in foreign troops to impose a UN trusteeship or some other form of supposedly benevolent domination might serve the interests of Western leaders, but it would not be in the interests of Bosnia. As a matter of fact, a kind of military intervention by the West has already taken place—in the form of the arms embargo—which has crippled Bosnia's ability to defend itself and left it virtually helpless. If the West were to lift the embargo on Bosnia and allow it to acquire heavy weaponry to match Serbian armor, the Bosnians might have a fighting chance to reconquer the occupied territories, disarm the Serb militias, resettle those who have lost their homes, and put the war criminals on trial.

During the Spanish Civil War world democratic opinion denounced the Western powers' hypocritical policy of "nonintervention" and called for arms for the Republic; similarly, the international human rights and peace community should demand that all restrictions on arms transfers to Bosnia be suspended immediately. The Bosnians need to know that democratic opinion in the West is with them, is on their side, and will help them acquire the means to win back their country. They do not need the condescension of those who can only pity them as hapless victims, as pitiful creatures who cannot be trusted to organize their own legitimate armed self-defense, but, sadly, must accept their fate and be crushed.

Bosnian military victories would not only weaken—or even stop the Serbian war machine—they might also decisively undermine the Milošević regime and the far right in Serbia. Serbia needs a revolution, and military defeat may be the shock required to open the way for radical change. There has been massive and growing opposition to Milošević ever since the war began. Already an estimated hundred thousand young Serbs have refused to serve in the army.

It is often argued that arming the Bosnians and raising the stakes for Serbia will only strengthen the extremists—the fascists and gangsters who follow Šešelj and Arkan. However, these elements thrive precisely because Serbian aggression has encountered only the most feeble resistance from its victims. Serbian citizens suffer from the embargo and are offended by the rhetoric of the West, of course; but at the same time, the fact that Serbia has been winning encourages many of them to believe that a "Greater Serbia" is both necessary and achievable. Milošević, Šešelj, and Arkan assume an aura of invincibility. On the other hand, if Serb forces began to suffer reverses in Bosnia, opposition would grow in the army and in Serbian society as a whole. Those Serbs who are sickened by the butchery being carried out in their name and who long for democracy and peace would take heart. Others who are hesitant and uncertain, who chafe under Milošević and his thugs, but are reluctant to challenge them because they seem so powerful, will begin to realize that these "leaders" are the ruin of Serbia—and that real security can come not through expansionism and "ethnic cleansing," but only when Serbs learn to live in harmony with the other peoples of the Balkans.

The place to begin, then, is in active solidarity with the despoiled and persecuted victims of Serbian aggression—the Muslims of Bosnia, the Albanians of Kosovo, the Croats of eastern Slavonia and Vojvodina, and others. In Bosnia, there are still strong multicommunal defense efforts in the towns, while guerrilla groups are proliferating in the countryside. Croatians are determined to win back the Serb-occupied territories. The Kosovars have stood up to ferocious repression, maintaining an entire alternative society and government with nonviolence (for how long?) and immense dignity.

When Americans and Europeans think about the shameful betrayal of Bosnia by Bush, Clinton, Major, Kohl, and Mitterand, we should try to imagine how governments truly committed to democratic principles might have responded to the crises in former Yugoslavia. During the Spanish Civil War, one nation, Mexico, acted with courage, generosity, and adherence to principle, fully supporting the Spanish Republic with arms and food from the first days of the fascist uprising. Mexico refused to play the game of power politics, refused to participate in "business as usual." The whole policy of the West toward Bosnia and the other successor states of Yugoslavia has been immoral and catastrophic—in other words, business as usual.

NOTES

1. John Burns, "Besieged Muslims Place Their Dignity Over Life," *The New York Times,* March 7, 1993.

2. John Burns, "Hearts Heavy, Arms Light, They Are Fighting On For Sarajevo," *The New York Times,* June 27, 1992.

3. Leslie Gelb, "False Humanitarianism," *The New York Times,* August 6, 1992.

4. "Bosnia Negotiators Count Considerable Achievements: Robert Mauthner Talks to Lord Owen About the Peace Process," *Financial Times,* February 1, 1993.

5. David Binder and Barbara Crossette, "As Ethnic Wars Multiply, US Strives For A Policy," *The New York Times,* February 7, 1993.

6. John Stuart Mill, "On Liberty" in *Great Books of the Western World* edited by Robert Maynard Hutchins (Chicago: Encyclopedia Britannica, 1952), 43, p. 272.

7. Michael Walzer, *Just and Unjust Wars* (New York: Basic Books, 1977), pp. 89-90.

THE WESTERN RESPONSE TO THE
WAR IN BOSNIA

A House Built on Sand

MARKO PRELEC

T HE WAR IN Bosnia has presented the world with a powerful challenge—and the world has failed, spectacularly, to meet it. It was not for want of effort, as various Western nations and international organizations strenuously have exerted themselves to rescue the Bosnians from their desperate plight since the war began over a year ago. The failure has been more a failure of understanding: the Western world did not, or would not, fully come to grips with the nature of the war and its combatants, and therefore has been unable to craft a constructive response.

Western policymakers saw Bosnia as a country riven by long-repressed nationalist passions, peopled by ethnic groups that would rather kill than live together. Imposing peace on such a cauldron of hate was beyond any outsider's means, and so they set their as their task reducing the human cost of war and easing the victims' pain. By applying pressure on the warring factions, they hoped to shorten the war and mediate a settlement tolerated by all, if loved by none. The Western response thus boiled down to a careful balance of pressure, mediation, and relief.

In distancing itself from a more direct engagement with the conflict, the international community ignored the singular character of the Serbian leadership which had brought the war to Bosnia. While all the players could be accused of truculence, the Serbs alone refused to compromise on any of their major demands. Furthermore, their demands alone imperiled the very survival of their neighbors. Most importantly, the power of the Yugoslav People's Army (JNA) gave them, exclusively, the ability to take it all and fulfill these demands. And, in doing so, they alone awakened Europe's memories of genocide.

The unique nature of the Serbian regime—its rigidity, enormous power, and fanaticism—made nonsense of the Western response of neutral mediation. Any such policy led, one way or another, to disaster. It also gave the Serbs a monopoly of initiative in the conflict; all the other groups involved, both within the former Yugoslavia and without, formed their policies in reaction to Serbian moves. Any sound analysis of the Bosnian war had to begin, therefore, where that war itself was born—in the heart of the Serbian leadership and of its autocratic guide, Slobodan Milošević.

THE WARS IN the former Yugoslavia did not spring full-grown from Serbian nationalism. To be sure, Serbian society was replete with the usual mix of *ressentiment,* injured national pride, irredentism, bigotry and fear. But these alone failed to explain the wars attending the demise of Yugoslavia; they merely created the potential for violence. After all, this stale amalgam of nationalist excess was hardly uncommon. Many nations had confronted this syndrome before, giving up expansionist ambitions in return for the benefits of peaceful coexistence. The Serbs could have done the same. Instead, they allowed their leaders to fan this sense of grievance into an all-consuming fire.

Milošević came to power in 1986. It was plain that the next few years would be crucial both for Serbia and his own political career. Yugoslavia's gradual demise had ushered in a short period of profound flux in the region's political order. State structures, internal borders, and political systems were dissolving into a fluid mass that would soon coalesce into new, permanent shapes. Repression, civil war, and conquest merged into a seamless fabric of unrest, encouraging the outside world to keep its distance. This presented him with an urgent and uniquely promising opportunity to define the size and shape of Serbia for the twenty-first century.

Furthermore, by becoming the patron of the national cause, he invested himself with an enduring legitimacy that eluded nearly every other pre-1989 head of state in Eastern Europe. He retained the formidable strengths of the Communist regime, its organization, security apparatus, media monopoly, and so on, while replacing its ideological content with nationalism. And by convincing the people that they were in a struggle for survival, he prevented any serious challenge to his authority. Once the wars began, any attack on Milošević appeared an attack on Serbdom itself.

Belligerence became an enduring and necessary aspect of the Serbian regime. Milošević's strategy became extortion—winning concessions by the threat of overwhelming violence. Serbia's pressure on its neighbors had to be constant, as any lengthy interval of peace would allow the region's anarchic condition to solidify into a stable and recognized order, making further aggression far more costly. Moreover, Serbia's overwhelming advantage in firepower could not be sustained for very long; by 1993 it had declined in Bosnia and disappeared in Croatia. For these reasons, Milošević had to ignore all of the constraints that bind statesmen in normal times. He used any means necessary. He bore sanctions, isolation, war, and ruin as the price of success.

A master at manipulating the peace process to serve his own ends, he cultivated the Serbs' image of dangerous unpredictability, violating countless agreements and committing spectacular outrages. The result of this was that the United Nations mediators ceased being surprised or angered by the Serbs' failures to live up to their promises and came to see keeping them at the peace table as a valued goal in itself. Milošević could therefore negotiate at no cost, dragging out the peace talks and buying valuable time to complete the work of "ethnic cleansing."

By cloaking his actions in the hoary myths of Balkan nationalism, he convinced much of the world that his aggression was merely part of an ancient, obscure, and intractable ethnic conflict. Observers of the Bosnian war were often shocked by its brutality, which they explained as a product of resurgent irrational ethnic hatred and savagery. The brutality was, in fact, Milošević's means of ensuring the durability of his gains. The point of the Serbs' campaign of terror was to eliminate any prospective challenge to permanent Serbian rule in the occupied territories, regardless of the outcome of the peace process. Everything the Serbs did in Bosnia was aimed at this goal.

Pressing the attack on Bosnian cities, therefore, served a dual purpose: driving out Muslims, and presenting the government with a choice of surrendering its legitimacy and accepting Serbian rule, or losing more of its people. Systematic atrocities—the massacres, the rapes, the camps, the mutilations—were meant to traumatize refugees into permanent exile and destroy the possibility of coexistence. By routinely killing all captured Muslim community leaders, the Serbs aimed at turning the Muslim people into an incoherent refugee mass lacking the will or ability to make demands. Finally, they destroyed Muslim homes and villages and burned property records, so there would be no place to return to and no way to prove ownership of land. It took a certain distance from the horror of war to see the design in this mosaic of woe, but it was crafted by a master with cool reason, not atavistic passion.

The price Milošević has paid for his extraordinary power has been dependence on wars and enemies. People readily tolerate the privations of a war economy if they feel threatened, but when the threats pass they demand more. Serbia is afflicted by deep social and economic troubles that the wars and international sanctions have exacerbated. There is no indication that Milošević can even begin to resolve them. Furthermore, he has created a substantial expectation for total victory, and were he to conclude peace short of this goal, other nationalists would raise the cry of treason. He has become the prisoner of his own cunning, incapable of surviving in normal times.

Peace would shake the Milošević regime to its core; it remains much easier for him to keep uncovering new enemies to fight. Of course, Milošević does not so much find enemies as create them. He uses the pliant national media to stir up hatred, vastly exaggerating the threat posed to Serbs by his newest target. Through this lens, even minor offenses appeared as examples of genocide. He also provokes his targets into responses that then serve to prove the original accusation, paving the way for violence.

And the supply of potential enemies is nearly endless. He can terrorize the Albanians of Kosovo or Serbia's other minorities; he can stake a claim to Macedonia or reopen the issue of the Serb-populated regions of Croatia; he can purge the domestic opposition or sponsor terrorism aimed at Serbia's imagined enemies abroad. While he remains in power, Serbia is trapped in a cycle of self-delusion and violence, in which new threats to Serbdom are discovered and attacked to justify yesterday's horrors. The Balkans will find peace when this cycle ends, and it will end only when Milošević's regime falls.

THROUGH ALL ITS twists and turns, Western policy in Bosnia never came to grips with the persistently aggressive nature of the Serbian regime. Instead, Western leaders and mediators assumed that by applying diplomatic pressure they could bring Milošević to accept a solution far short of his goals. While Milošević steadfastly refused to buckle under any threat short of force, he gave the impression of being on the brink of compromise, thus dragging out the peace process and winning concessions from the mediators.

The Western world formed its policy during the summer of 1991, when Yugoslavia fell apart. At that time the EC led the Western response, and chose to mediate the emerging conflict as honest brokers. The European effort depended on neutrality, for mediation was impossible if any of the Yugoslav republics suspected European favoritism for one of their rivals. The mediators accordingly pressured the republics' leaders to negotiate a solution to the crisis, and themselves offered several models of such a solution. Western diplomats said, loudly and often, that their governments would never reward unilateral actions (such as land grabs) with recognition, and that the Yugoslavs had to reach a negotiated solution.

In practice, Western policy was exactly the opposite of what it claimed to be: the West would recognize whoever ended up in control, however they got there, and everybody knew it. So Slovenia and Croatia defied the West by declaring independence, and after six months of huffing and puffing the EC recognized them. The Serbs continued their war in Croatia, and the UN mediator, Cyrus Vance, negotiated a settlement that let them keep most of the land they had taken.

While this was going on, Bosnia was the darling of the West: always ready to negotiate and compromise, the Bosnian government took every Western suggestion to heart and committed no unilateral acts. They refused to arm themselves in the face of growing danger, believing the West would save them. And after Serbs brought war to Bosnia in April of 1992, a war far worse than the previous year's in Croatia, the Bosnians were reluctant to fight back. The government hoped its restraint would make Western intervention more likely. They were, after all, doing just what the West had asked them to do.

The West, of course, did intervene, but not in the manner the Bosnians hoped for. The international community did nothing to protect them from the genocidal warfare waged by the Serbs, now known as "ethnic cleansing." Instead, led by the UN, the West launched a two-pronged effort, aimed at providing humanitarian relief and brokering a negotiated solution. This effort suffered from the same gulf between statement and practice that had made a sham of Western mediation in Croatia. Despite its promises to the contrary, the UN consistently deferred to Serbia's mastery on the ground.

The massive humanitarian relief operation was an object lesson in the dilemmas of Western engagement in Bosnia. The UN chose to operate only with Serbian consent, giving besieging forces and paramilitary units a veto over any particular activity. The Serbs blocked deliveries to outlying towns, far from the view of Western media coverage, and confiscated about a quarter of everything the UN brought into Bosnia. The American air-drop operation, originally meant as an end-run around Serbian obstruction of aid deliveries, was extensively modified in deference to the Serbs, effectively vitiating its usefulness. The Serbs threatened to massacre huge numbers of refugees, thus forcing the UN to remove them from Bosnia, completing the process of "ethnic cleansing." At every step, the Serbs extorted compliance with their wishes from the UN by threatening violence, and without exception the UN gave in.

In similar fashion, the United Nations Protection Force (UNPROFOR) in Bosnia became a kind of hostage to the Serbs. These troops were to guard aid deliveries from wholesale looting and to clear obstacles, such as mined roads and barricades. With their limited mandate, they did not actually "protect" anyone, nor did they prevent attacks on convoys. They did, however, prevent aggressive action by the West, since any such action was likely to bring reprisals by the Serbs against the lightly-armed UNPROFOR. The West's hands were tied.

The United Nations' diplomatic efforts played by similar rules, pressuring the Serbs verbally but appeasing them in substance. The Security Council imposed a trade embargo and a no-fly zone, and approved the creation of a war-crimes tribunal, but it took months before the Council agreed to enforce its decisions. Indeed, the UN could not enforce its decisions strictly and at the same time maintain its credibility as an honest broker. The clearest example of this dilemma was the embryonic war crimes tribunal: was it to arrest the Serbian delegation before, or after, it signed the Vance-Owen accords? Strict implementation of UN resolutions also depended on the cooperation of countries which were, for various reasons, reluctant to comply: Greece, Romania, and Russia, out of sympathy for the Serbs, and Britain and France, out of fear of Serbian reprisals.

In any case, the heart of Western diplomatic engagement in Bosnia lay not in UN actions, but rather in the negotiations led by Cyrus Vance and Lord Owen. The stated aim of these negotiations was to find a political settlement for Bosnia acceptable to Croats, Serbs, and Muslims, as well as to Croatia and Serbia, and then to implement and police this settlement with the help of peacekeeping forces drawn from the international community. For any such arrangement to work, the costs of noncompliance had to exceed its benefits for all parties concerned, at each step of implementation. Since the plan left no local party with enough strength to deter the Serbs, the UN had to present them with a believable threat of intervention in case they failed to comply.

There were several problems with this. Serbian forces could obstruct implementation in dozens of ways, some trivial, some grave. They could impede the return of refugees to their homes by veiled threats, procedural delays or outright prohibition, in isolated villages or in whole regions. They could delay withdrawal of their forces, refuse to pull them out altogether or simply appoint paramilitary units as police. They could obstruct the central government, refuse to work with it, or deny its legitimacy altogether. They could gradually introduce the institutions of the Republic of Serbia: its currency, passports, and laws (as, in part, they have already done), or they could declare annexation to Serbia openly. They could also blame noncompliance on unruly subordinates, a tactic they played to the hilt. At the same time, Serbian leaders could threaten to abandon the plan if the peacekeepers punished them over some incident.

Western officials would be reluctant to risk a fragile, hard-won peace by confronting the Serbian leadership over seemingly minor issues; the temptation to overlook violations would be great. But the effects of tolerating episodes of noncompliance would be cumulative, because each successful breach would establish a precedent. Eventually, the enforcers would have nothing left to enforce.

If gradual subversion failed, the Serbs could start shooting at peacekeepers. Peacekeeping troops occupy static defensive positions that are inherently impossible to protect from terroristic attacks. Casualties suffered in such attacks are especially demoralizing: they appear random and meaningless, soldiers killed for no purpose by an invisible enemy. In any case, Western societies are understandably reluctant to accept serious casualties unless their own security is threatened. Peacekeepers seldom stay long when there is no peace to keep.

Moreover, much of the justification for using force would disappear. The failure of a peace agreement is less momentous, less clear-cut than the destruction of a country; failure violates no borders, and the UN can safely stay out. Successful implementation is always relative; it would be hard to declare the plan an unequivocal failure.

Nearly all of these problems plagued the UN's effort to administer its peace plan in Croatia. This plan, also negotiated by Cyrus Vance, was considered a success until January 1993, when Croatian forces moved to reassert control over several UN protected areas. The Croats were prodded into action by frustration over UNPROFOR's failure to secure any of the terms of the peace plan: return of refugees, an ethnically mixed police force and so on. The stakes in Croatia were relatively low, since the protected areas are sparsely populated and cover only a quarter of Croatia's territory. The Vance-Owen plan in Bosnia carried a much heavier burden; the survival of the state and of the Bosnian Muslims as a people depended on its faithful implementation.

The fragile constitutional order envisaged by the Vance-Owen plan would not survive without a major, long-term international commitment. The Serbs and Muslims were both deeply dissatisfied with it; the Serbs were adamant in their refused to accept the plan, while the Muslims were compelled to sign on under severe international pressure. Any new government thus established would lack the support of more than three quarters of

Bosnia's people and would consequently be entirely dependent on Western support. Even if such support were forthcoming, the government would suffer from a paradox: the more it relied on the West for its survival, the more damage it would do to its legitimacy at home. The burden on the West to sustain such a state and government would, therefore, only grow. The Vance-Owen plan thus imposed great demands on the countries charged with implementing it, while eroding the political will needed to meet those demands. This is the classic recipe for a quagmire, and the West walked into it with open, but apparently unseeing eyes.

THE WESTERN RESPONSE to the war in Bosnia that culminated in the Vance-Owen peace plan has been a house built on sand. Its architects took little account of the treacherous ground on which they built, and this failure has had profound implications for Bosnia and for the West itself. On paper, the Vance-Owen plan preserved the unity of the Bosnian state, albeit in decentralized form. This gave the mediators' a rebuttal to the charge of appeasement: they argued that they had forced the Serbs to forswear secession and accept Bosnian sovereignty. By defining Bosnia as a loose federation of provinces, however, they paved the road to its dismemberment and granted the Serbs their main objective. The Serbs' problem was that nobody recognized their right to keep what they had taken. They had enough power to hold onto most of Bosnia for a long time, but only as international pariahs. Western states had promised, many times, never to recognize gains made by force; reneging openly on that promise would have been humiliating. The Serbs needed legitimacy, and until the Vance-Owen plan, that goal seemed forever out of reach.

The plan assigned most state functions to the newly-drawn Bosnian provinces, and recognized Serbian control in three of them. Once the plan was in place, these provinces could secede unilaterally, just as the Yugoslav republics had done two years earlier. In this way, the Vance-Owen plan transformed the Serbian project from an issue of aggression to one of self-determination. The plan transferred a measure of legitimacy from the Bosnian government to the Serbian leadership—a transfer that was to persist after the plan collapsed. It was, clearly, the death knell of the Bosnian state.

The plan was also fateful for the Western powers, presenting them with a choice of unhappy endings. The mediators had pressed the Serbs to sign on to a peace plan that, if faithfully implemented, would mean giving up many of their goals. There were, of course, countless ways the Serbs could obstruct implementation after signing on; it was truly vain to hope that they would meekly renounce the victory they had achieved in the field. The ball would thus be back in the West's court: the enforcing powers could either make a halfhearted attempt at implementation, or back up their promises with serious effort.

In the former case, the price would be humiliation. Failing to stop the fighting, bad in and of itself, would be seemingly impossible to achieve without a massive military intervention, which no Western country had contemplated. However, the really pitiful aspect of the world's actual response was its inability to carry out the policies it chose instead. The Serbs flouted every Western sanction—the no-fly zone, the trade and arms embargoes, the delivery of humanitarian aid—with glee and impunity. The West looked impotent.

Moreover, in their search for a negotiated solution, the mediators stooped to disgraceful levels. They leaned hard on the Bosnian government, a member of the UN, to accept its own demise. The mediators' pronouncements degenerated into fantastic absurdities: the plan did not appease the Serbs, but it did accept and ratify their victory in Bosnia; Slobodan Milošević was the architect of Serbian expansion but would pressure his Bosnian proxies to reject that expansion; the Bosnians' refusal to surrender to the Serbs was to be condemned because it was against peace. Statements with such egregious disregard for truth and consistency cheapened those that made them.

The option of meaningful enforcement entailed making more palpable threats, for it meant fighting the Serbs. Out of the many military options open to the West, fighting for enforcement was surely the worst. It lacked any clear definition of success and completion, aiming instead at staving off the collapse of the peace plan. Serbian forces could choose where and when to engage Western troops; moreover, they could have a protected homebase across the Bosnian border in Serbia. Finally, the whole thankless burden of propping up the unloved Vance-Owen system would fall on Western troops.

The choice between these baleful options is bound to take a good deal of time, during which important things will happen. The toll of the dead will keep mounting, of course, through the summer of 1993 and into another awful winter. Already frayed by a year of fighting and trauma, Bosnia's social fabric might be rent beyond repair. The apparently endless list of atrocities could strengthen the world community's will for forceful action, while making such action more difficult and risky. Worst of all, the Serbs' "ethnic cleansing" could acquire the patina of inevitability and permanence, passing into history as only the latest in a long series of Balkan enormities.

At the core of all these problems rests the Serbs' unwillingness to go along with a fair peace except under duress, with no Western country willing to compel them. The Vance-Owen plan could thus ever only be a fig-leaf for appeasement or a ticket to quagmire. Even if Serbian victory was inevitable, Western countries did not have to humiliate themselves by blessing it and investing it with the prestige of the UN. The final irony, however, is that this victory was not inevitable, even as late as the spring of 1993. The West debased itself—paying dearly for the privilege—for nothing.

MILOŠEVIĆ'S SERBIA IS a rare thing in history, a state that by its nature cannot live peacefully with its neighbors, and as such it merits extraordinary attention from the world community. Any policy on the Yugoslav crisis that rests on obtaining Milošević's agreement for a postwar order is bound to fail. The only way to deal with such a regime is to cripple, as far as possible, its ability to cause trouble and, ultimately, to speed its demise. But by the spring of 1993 the West was deeply committed to the neutral approach, which both encouraged the Serbs and made confronting them impossible. The West's first task, therefore, is to disentangle itself from neutral engagement.

Such disentanglement will require ending the Vance-Owen debacle. The United States could once have done this quite neatly, merely by insisting that the Serbs comply with their present commitments, such as allowing the delivery of food to eastern Bosnia, as a condition for continuing the peace talks. The only reason the Serbs negotiated initially was to buy time by making promises they didn't have to keep. Had this changed, they would have walked out, and the talks would have collapsed. The Clinton administration's move toward military action in the spring of 1993 bore out this dynamic. The Serbs gauged Western resolve carefully, defiant when the West vacillated, conciliatory when it seemed that bombs might be on the way.

The UN also needed to stop allowing UNPROFOR to act as hostage to the Serbs. The UN troops' only real function, providing minimal security for relief convoys, could easily have been taken over by the Bosnian government with some logistical help from the UN. The troops could then have been moved out of reach of Serbian guns, either by pulling them out entirely or by withdrawing them to defensible locations.

The Vance-Owen process and UNPROFOR were the two pillars of neutral engagement: cutting them off would have had two great benefits. First, the fog of confusion would have lifted from the issue of who was to blame; guilt would have settled squarely on the Serbs, where it belonged. If the Serbs themselves wrecked the peace process, their traditional friends could have more easily acquiesced in punitive action. And second, the chief obstacles to such action, namely fear of offending the Serbs and of Serbian retaliation, would have been cleared away. Constructive engagement could begin.

The starting point here needed to be unambiguous support for the Bosnian government, not merely as the representative of the Bosnian Muslims but as the legitimate government of the whole republic. The United States should have leaned hard on Croatia to stop fighting the Muslims in central Bosnia and to stop undermining the Bosnian government. Croat aggression was encouraged by the Vance-Owen plan, which the Croats understood as leading to the eventual dismemberment of Bosnia. The Croats were opportunists, not fanatics; they would fall into line under sufficient pressure from the West. As for the other European states, the United States should have pressed them to help or, failing that, to stay on the sidelines.

Ultimately, the West will have to rescind the shameful arms embargo on Bosnia. Much could be accomplished at the outset by merely relaxing the enforcement and pressing Croatia to reopen its arms pipeline to the Bosnian army. Croatia managed to procure enormous quantities of weapons for its own use while the embargo was still in place: their weapons supply could help the Bosnians to get around the embargo, at least until the UN mustered enough support for its formal revocation.

What might come of all this? The Serbs might respond by going for broke—an all-out offensive to secure victory before time ran out—but their hopes would be slim. They had won against only unarmed opponents, in siege warfare against civilians; every effort to take a major city defended by Croat or Bosnian troops has failed. They might fight on for months, but only on the defensive, taking heavy losses, terribly overextended, relying on vulnerable supply lines from a Serbia squeezed drier by the trade embargo. In such circumstances the Serbs could never hold onto three quarters of Bosnia; nor could they keep terrorizing Bosnia's cities and civilians with impunity. Eventually they would have to pull back.

For the first time, it would be in the Serbs' strategic interest to sue for peace. The settlement emerging from these events would be strong, resting on the actual balance of power and policed by the parties themselves, not by the distant and implausible threat of Western intervention. And unlike the Vance-Owen plan, it might have the added benefit of being just.

WESTERN INTERVENTION in Bosnia has borne an uncomfortable resemblance to its archetypal foreign-policy disaster of recent times, the war in Vietnam. The analogy quickly has become a commonplace, with comparisons being made between the two countries' dense forests, fanatical warriors, and potential for suffocating, hopeless, endless conflict. No one, least of all the American leaders, many of whom had been directly involved, wants to repeat Vietnam's painful history. And so they have approached the Bosnian war from a distance, beginning where Vietnam ended, at the peace table.

But beneath this superficial resemblance run deeper similarities that have carried Western policymakers, unwittingly, to make the same fateful errors of policy in both situations. As in Vietnam, Western leaders never fully understood the people they were dealing with in Bosnia. Having failed in understanding, they set themselves impossible goals and adopted ineffectual means to reach them, while staking their national prestige on success that would prove forever out of reach. They ignored the obvious and mounting signs of defeat, and pressed on deeper and deeper into the mire of a botched and hopeless engagement.

Similar motives drove policy forward in both cases: notably the fear of admitting mistakes and changing course, as well as confidence in Western power; the conviction that a little more effort and time would lead to the light at the end of the tunnel. The great powers exercised the same arrogance in their tendency to dictate to local parties and their reluctance to work with local allies, preferring to do everything alone, in both situations. And most painfully, the dilemma has proven to be the same—a Hobson's choice of humiliation and destruction.

Woven together, these similarities form a cord of kinship that links the wars in Vietnam and Bosnia. The essence of that kinship lies in the attempt to impose an artificial, Western-tailored order on a troubled country, without regard either to the West's resources or to local conditions. There never has been any good reason for such irresponsible, overreaching projects. Of course, Western nations cannot save every life or extinguish every fire; but that does not exuse them from the obligation to make constructive use of their limited resources, helping friends, discouraging enemies. In Bosnia the West has hurt the weak and encouraged their victimizers, and for that there is no excuse. No one with certainty can predict what the outcome would have been had the West chosen a wiser policy, but surely it would have been better than the Western-abetted genocide we now have in Bosnia.

The Degradation
of the Bosnian
Peace Negotiations

Kasim Trnka

THE WAR IN Bosnia-Hercegovina is the tragic consequence of an extremely unfavorable confluence of
international and internal developments. The end
of the division of the world on the basis of confrontational blocs had coincided with the first steps toward the establishment of democratic institutions
in Bosnia. However, the process of establishing the basic integrative elements
of a democratic society had only begun when war overwhelmed the new state.

The journey of Bosnia-Hercegovina from a Yugoslav republic to independent statehood had been shadowed by the transformation of nationalist or
ethnic consciousness in Yugoslavia from its previously assigned role as a
marker of private and cultural identity into a larger political project exercising
its hegemony over a people as a group or collectivity. In this context, the resurgence of Serbian nationalism was a particularly disquieting development.

As a historical constant, nationalism had been carefully constructed and
nurtured among the Serbs. Since the middle of the last century, it had been
defined as a political program sanctioned and sustained by the Orthodox
church and Serbia's intellectual and political leadership. Yet, as an ideology,
Serbian nationalism has often taken fundamentally anti-democratic forms.
The equality and liberty of individuals or other communities are sacrificed to
a grand irrational myth surrounding the uniqueness and superiority of the
Serbian nation, which is presumed to be threatened by hostile forces and thus
in perpetual danger of extinction.

The modern variant of Serbian nationalism, therefore, refused to accept
the independence of other Yugoslav republics even though the new states had
been established in accordance with democratic norms with the support of the
citizens of the seceding republics. In Bosnia-Hercegovina a referendum was
held in which nearly two-thirds of the electorate participated, and voted in
favor of the independence, sovereignty, and indivisibility of the multinational
state. Following the referendum the international community concluded that
all the necessary preconditions for the establishment of an independent and
sovereign state existed. There followed a process in which Bosnia-Hercegovina
was recognized by many nations and was accepted into the United Nations,

the Conference on Security and Cooperation in Europe (CSCE), and other international associations.

The Serbian nationalist program, on the other hand, was incapable of solving the Serbian national question by democratic means. The authorities in Serbia rejected all proposals for securing the rights of Bosnian Serbs within an independent Bosnia-Hercegovina; the acceptance of these proposals would have thwarted their nationalist objective of "protecting" the Serb nation by establishing a "Greater Serbia" through the annexation of all territory where Serbs had settled outside Serbia. Since the Serbian nationalist leadership exercised decisive influence over the Yugoslav army, it opted for war against Croatia and Bosnia-Hercegovina as a means of territorial conquest.

The aggression took on forms of extraordinary brutality. The entire policy of "ethnic cleansing" enforced by specific attacks against the civilian population certainly approached the standard of genocide. In those areas occupied by Serbian forces, the Serbs set about destroying everything which was "not Serbian," which, in effect, meant the destruction of the historical and cultural heritage of the Muslim people of Bosnia.

The international community had a moral, political, and legal obligation to stop the war and to prevent its consequences. A clear legal basis existed for the international community to take action. The articles of the Helsinki Conference and the Paris Charter take as their starting point the position that the defense of human rights is not just a question of national sovereignty but it is also the prerogative and responsibility of the wider international community. On the question of Bosnia, the European Community and the United Nations have demonstrated their incompetence at implementing principles they spent decades developing and drafting into charters.

The EC and the UN initiated two conferences on the war in Bosnia. The first, the London Conference of August 1992, recognized the territorial integrity of Bosnia-Hercegovina and implicitly identified the aggressor by imposing sanctions against Serbia and Montenegro.*

Although the London Conference and a series of Security Council reso-

---

* Editor's note: The London Conference was organized by UN Secretary General Boutros Boutros-Ghali, and British Prime Minister John Major, acting on behalf of the EC. The London Conference adopted seven measures pertaining to Bosnia-Hercegovina: "1) A cessation of all hostilities in the Republic of Bosnia-Hercegovina; 2) An end to all outside involvement in the current conflict either in terms of material or human support; 3) The gathering of all heavy weaponry under international supervision; 4) The demilitarization of large cities with oversight by international observers; 5) The establishment of refugee centers and centers of humanitarian assistance for citizens of Bosnia-Hercegovina who have been driven from their dwellings, or whose dwellings have been destroyed, until such time as their return can be assured; 6) The expansion of humanitarian aid to all areas of Bosnia-Hercegovina where it is needed, in cooperation with local participants; 7) The establishment of peacekeeping forces under the auspices of the United Nations in order to maintain the cease-fire, the supervision of military movements, and the establishment of other confidence building measures." (See "Sedam Tocaka za Bitt," *Novi Vjesnik*, August 28, 1992, cited in Alan F. Fogelquist, "The Break Up of Yugoslavia: International Policy and the War in Bosnia-Hercegovina" [Whitmore Lake, MI: AEIOU Publishing, 1993] pp. 41–42)

lutions defined in principle the acceptable tenets for a resolution of the crisis, no effective mechanism of implementation was developed as a means of either halting hostilities or actually resolving the crisis. Instead, Bosnia became an experiment in the structuring of international policy and action for a new era. By overplaying its "fear" of Bosnia-Hercegovina becoming a dangerous precedent for international engagement and the use of force in all future crisis points in the world, the international community ultimately tied itself in knots and failed to act effectively on the most essential principles of the UN Charter and the Helsinki Conference.

The London Conference of August 1992 was followed in September 1992 by the so-called Geneva Conference, which was convened under the joint chairmanship of David Owen, representing the EC as its new appointee, and Cyrus Vance, representing the UN Secretary General. The mandate of the Geneva Conference was very clear: its sole task was to find mechanisms for the implementation of the London Principles. Unfortunately, the Geneva Conference deviated from its mandate and in so doing significantly degraded the entire peace process.

The formulations advanced at Geneva by Vance and Owen introduced two fundamentally flawed assumptions. These are responsible for all the subsequent weaknesses of the peace negotiations sponsored by the EC and the UN. For all practical purposes the Geneva Conference abandoned the starting position of the London Conference. In London, it was established without ambiguity that Bosnia was a sovereign state which had the legal right to defend itself against the aggression of another state. In Geneva, Vance and Owen altered the formulation and thus abandoned their mandate. Instead, they imposed the formulation of "three warring factions" upon the negotiations. They brought delegations into the negotiation process which they, as mediators, chose to identify as representatives of the three largest nationalities in Bosnia-Hercegovina.

The implications of this change were to prove tragic. The new formulation ignored the fact of aggression which the London principles had recognized. By ignoring the element of aggression the EC and UN mediators gave preeminence to the view that the war was essentially a civil, interethnic, and religious war. Although the Bosnian government reflected a multi-ethnic, cosmopolitan, and pluralistic constituency, it was now designated a "faction." This formulation placed the legitimate and legally elected organs of state power on a par with illegitimate self-proclaimed structures which were engaged in acts of aggression backed by external forces.

Thus, the Geneva Conference accepted, as legitimate representatives of the three nationalities, the leaders of three particular national political parties. None of these individuals had ever been given any mandate in an election to negotiate away the existence of Bosnia-Hercegovina as an integral, undivided state. They represented parties which had been elected to the parliament of the country, but they could not even pretend to represent the entire community to which they belonged; there existed several other parties representing other political tendencies and drawing support from varied, national, and multinational constituencies. In addition, in the last elections, more than one-fourth of the electorate did not support any of the three political parties which Vance and Owen elevated to the status of the national representatives of the "warring factions."

The Geneva Conference, which ultimately moved to New York in February 1993, advanced a second unacceptable premise. It insisted that the negotiations must first reach a compromise political solution in order to bring about an end to hostilities. This provided an enormous advantage to the aggressors who were militarily twenty times stronger than the defenders. The aggressors simply kept the negotiations going while they proceeded with their attacks, their violence, their "ethnic cleansing," and their genocidal acts. They used their daily military advances as a means of exercising pressure on the negotiating position of those who were defending themselves. Instead of demanding a cessation of hostilities as a first principle and a precondition for negotiations, the Geneva format actually prolonged hostilities and immeasurably increased the suffering of the civilian population.

At this stage the international community could have taken firm action to stop the war. It could have advanced a plausible military option to deter the ongoing aggression. Instead, the international community relentlessly applied pressure on the representatives of the legal government of Bosnia to make even further concessions. Not only did the world community not fulfil its obligation to defend a member-state of the United Nations, it compounded its failure to act by denying Bosnia-Hercegovina the legitimate right of self-defense by maintaining an arms embargo. This was not only a morally and politically reprehensible position, it was also contrary to international law which guarantees a nation the right to self-defense.

Several international forums, including the General Assembly of the United Nations, have declared that aggression has occurred against the Republic of Bosnia-Hercegovina and that genocidal acts have been committed. Therefore, the legal requirements for the initiation of international action against both aggression and genocide have been fulfilled. Furthermore, a state under attack has, in accordance with Article 51 of the UN Charter, the right to self-defense. The exercise of this right requires arms. The international community has frustrated this right by asserting, without legal grounds, that the embargo on arms imports imposed on Yugoslavia in 1991 extended to Bosnia. The effect has been to contradict Article 51 by denying a victim of aggression the means of self-defense. Besides being politically and morally indefensible, such a position is perilously close to collusion with aggression. Ultimately, the International Court of Justice in the Hague will have to review these facts and draw the relevant legal conclusions. However, it appears self-evident that it is legally untenable to apply an arms embargo to the Republic of Bosnia-Hercegovina which was imposed on another state.

The Vance-Owen talks at Geneva gave the highest priority to forms of political compromise which fused pragmatism with expediency. The result was a proposal for a settlement of the conflict which is at variance with the principles of international law and the traditions of a juridical system based on democratic principles. The Vance-Owen plan is conceptually flawed and inconsistent. In practice it would only prolong instability and create new conflicts with unpredictable consequences. It is a proposal which favors an existing balance of forces that has been established by aggressive acts. Whatever minimal territory it asks be given up, it still makes significant territorial concessions to the one side which enjoys military superiority. This is not a proposal which democratic states that oppose the seizure of territory by force can accept without abandoning fundamental principles. The relinquishment of such principles is evident in every aspect of the Vance-Owen plan.

Instead of advancing a plausible solution based on democratic principles which could ultimately lay the foundation for long-term stability in Bosnia and in the region, the plan makes enormous concessions to one specific nationalist program which has pursued its objectives with forms of violence that have not been seen in Europe for half a century. Perhaps the most egregious element of the Vance-Owen plan is a projected constitutional order which essentially fulfills one of the most important aims of the aggression—the destruction of Bosnia's state structure.

Bosnia-Hercegovina has a long political and legal history. It began as a state in the early middle ages at a time when many Balkan and European states did not yet exist. Its multicultural, multi-ethnic, and multireligious character has survived throughout its history. Even when it lost its formal independence it retained its territorial and administrative integrity within the Ottoman Empire, the Austro-Hungarian Empire, and lastly in Yugoslavia.

The Vance-Owen plan would bring an end to this long history. Formally, the plan declares itself in support of Bosnia being a democratic state. However, the plan deprives Bosnia-Hercegovina of all the normal elements of a democratic constitution. The requirement that all decisionmaking be on the basis of unanimity among ethnic groups would clearly lead to a situation where the state structure would simply be unable to function. A formula for permanent constitutional gridlock is a formula for instability. The Vance-Owen plan provides no framework to construct a democratic consensus capable of governing the state. In fact, it can only interfere with the development of democratic structures and processes. In pursuit of what appeared to them to be a pragmatic solution, the mediators consistently gave much greater heed to the incompatible nationalist agendas of particular political parties than to the formation of real democratic institutions which could stand above sectional interests.

Under the plan the equality of all citizens is also brought into question. The central government is denied even a minimal authority to guarantee basic rights and liberties to its citizens. It would not be permitted to have at its disposal any kind of military or police force. The central government would not have the means to implement its decisions. Such a government would not even possess the basic mechanisms to conduct a rational economic policy for making use of the country's national resources.

Finally, the formation of ten provinces as advocated under the Vance-Owen plan would permit each province to establish its own constitution. The provinces would not be states under international law. Nevertheless, each provincial authority would be able to exercise a broad range of powers. This, in itself, is not necessarily a bad thing. However, when one considers that the specific borders of the provinces favor Serb and Croat national interests, it becomes clear that the confrontation between the national elites will continue indefinitely. Under the plan, existing armed units will pull back to the provinces where each respective nation is in the majority. If one adds to this the fact that provincial police forces will be exclusively under the control of the provincial governments, it becomes apparent that the Vance-Owen plan is a scheme for the permanent ethnic division of Bosnia.

There is nothing contained in these proposals of a future constitutional order which will halt the process of "ethnic cleansing." Under such an arrangement it is only realistic to expect the process to continue and intensify in both disguised and overt forms. By granting "ethnic control" over provincial territory it will become impossible for refugees who have been dispossessed to return to their homes. Thus, the suffering of the country's population will continue and the prospect of new flare-ups will remain.

Furthermore, the transitional arrangements which the Vance-Owen plan proposes are not founded on basic principles of legality and democratic legitimacy. In the period between the cessation of hostilities and the holding of new elections, the plan requires the formal suspension of existing state structures which are anchored in a democratic constitutional order. It is an order which was confirmed and supported in free, democratic, and multiparty elections.

In its place the Vance-Owen proposals, once again, make a significant concession to aggression by providing for a single governing body composed of three appointed representatives of each nationality (Muslims, Serbs, and Croats). It is proposed that this body assume the combined powers of the head of state, the legislature, and the executive. This creates an absurd situation in regard to constitutional law. Organs which were directly elected by the citizens are suspended while other organs which have no legitimacy, nor any democratic foundations, are established. The elected members of the Presidency of Bosnia-Hercegovina and members of its parliament are deemed irrelevant while an unelected authority with unspecified responsibilities is empowered. With all its faults and flaws, it is also quite evident that there are simply no means specified by which the various provisions and guarantees of the Vance-Owen plan can be implemented realistically.

These are just a few of the many shortcomings of both the conceptual and practical character of the Vance-Owen proposals. All the weaknesses of the plan are a direct consequence of the failure of the world community to stand behind the basic principles of international law. There remains in the end, as in the beginning, only one legitimate and practical solution—the lifting of the arms embargo imposed upon the legal government of the Republic of Bosnia-Hercegovina. By removing the embargo the world community merely recognizes the legal principle that a country under attack has the right to defend itself. There is no third option.

In the case of Bosnia, the international community has failed to demonstrate resolve in defense of the most fundamental principles of democracy and international law. The incompetence of its diplomacy and its hesitancy to act effectively on behalf of established principles has only increased and prolonged the suffering of Bosnia's people. In the long term, it has also created the possibility of new armed conflicts throughout the world and the further destabilization of the international political and legal order.

TRANSLATED BY DOROTHEA HANSON AND MARKO PRELEC

How Not to Divide
the Indivisible

STJEPKO GOLUBIC
SUSAN CAMPBELL
THOMAS GOLUBIC

A S THE WAR in Bosnia-Hercegovina enters its second year, the world's peacemakers continue their efforts to develop a peace plan which would be acceptable to all parties to the conflict. A central component of all the proposals on the table has been the division of the country on the basis of "ethnic dominance," whereby a given territory belongs to and is governed by the ethnic group which is most numerous.

The creation of cantons in Bosnia-Hercegovina on the Swiss model was among the earliest proposals for such a division and was promoted by Peter Carrington and José Cutilheiro within the framework of the Lisbon and Brussels conferences on the future of Bosnia-Hercegovina in February and March 1992. The most recent version of the "cantonization models" for the country was presented in January 1993, in Geneva, by David Owen and Cyrus Vance, as a part of a comprehensive peace plan of the International Conference on the Former Yugoslavia (ICFY). Regardless of any differences or refinements, all such proposals for Bosnia-Hercegovina—defined by the principle of a carve-up on the basis of ethnicity—are inherently unworkable attempts to divide the indivisible.

Our study employs a demographic analysis of the prewar population of Bosnia-Hercegovina, derived from the official census data of 1991, to assess the feasibility of subdividing the country on the basis of several different criteria: ethnic dominance, distribution of minorities, topographic features, and the management of natural resources. The prewar demographic status of the country represents the only legitimate and objective basis for discussions about a just peace settlement and the future administrative structure of Bosnia-Hercegovina. Our underlying assumption is that violence should not be rewarded, and cannot be used as a means for territorial gain. Therefore our study began by concentrating on the demographic composition and distribution in Bosnia-Hercegovina prior to the outbreak of hostilities.

The data used in this study were extracted from the official 1991 Yugoslav population census of Bosnia-Hercegovina. An older census, taken in 1981, was compared to assess general demographic trends. Bosnia-Hercegovina is divided administratively into 100 districts. The 5 districts of the capital city of Sarajevo, that is, Sarajevo-Center, Hadzići, Ilias, Pale, and Trnovo, are treated as a single district in the 1991 census. The census data used in this study consisted of the total numbers of inhabitants by districts, and the percent distribution by four groups based on the declaration of ethnicity of those counted by the census (see *Table 4*). The three major ethnic and religious categories include Muslim Slavs, Orthodox Serbs, and Catholic Croats. The category "Other" includes other nationalities, as well as persons registered as "Yugoslavs." The latter identity has been used most frequently by children of mixed marriages or as an expression of ideological opposition to any narrower ethnic or national identity. The category "Yugoslavs," as an expression of self-identification, has declined in the course of the past ten years, paralleling an increased awareness of nationality. Other changes can be explained by normal demographic dynamics and mobility.

A map outlining the 100 districts was used as a basis for construction of territorial subdivisions using different criteria (ethnic dominance, minority distribution, topographic features, and so forth). The surface areas were measured on these maps using Sigma-Scan measuring software. The census data were entered in a spreadsheet for sorting and further processing. The census districts are not of a uniform size, either by surface area or by population. They are identified in the map in *Figure 1,* and listed alphabetically in *Table 4*. Thus, the "resolution power" of the "ethnic maps" generated in this study is limited by the sizes of each of the 100 census districts.

IN EXAMINING THE plausibility of a regional subdivision of Bosnia-Hercegovina into "cantons" based on ethnic dominance, the census districts were sorted and ranked according to their most numerous ethnic group. Plurality (relative majority of less than 50 percent) and absolute majority (greater than 50 percent) were used as criteria for sorting. The resulting aggregate districts were mapped to determine where the dominance of each of the three ethnic groups occurs. From this information, outlines of "ethnic cantons" could be derived. Two such models are compared. The first model is based on plurality ("relative dominance" by districts, regardless of percentage), resulting in three "ethnic cantons." The second model is based on ethnic majority of greater than 50 percent ("absolute dominance"), resulting in four "ethnic cantons." The fourth "canton" is comprised of districts in which dominance is shared, since none of the groups exceeds 50 percent.

In constructing the "Three-Canton Model," the districts with an absolute dominance of more than 50 percent (by the respective ethnic groups) represent the "core districts," which comprise the darker shaded areas in the map in *Figure 2*. The districts showing dominance by plurality, with less then 50 percent dominance by a particular ethnic group, represent the "marginal districts" in this model, and comprise the lighter shaded areas in the map. The table accompanying the legend in *Figure 2* compares the distribution of the three major ethnic groups in Bosnia-Hercegovina as a whole with that for each of the three "ethnic

Figure 1. Bosnia-Hercegovina Census Districts

cantons." This information is summarized in the upper part of *Table 1* and placed in the context of absolute population numbers and surface areas.

Muslim Slavs are the most numerous ethnic group in Bosnia-Hercegovina. They have an "absolute majority" (more than 50 percent) in 31 out of 100 districts, *(Figure 2,* dark gray). These are, in descending order of dominance: Cazin, Velika Kladuša, Zivinice, Kalesija, Breza, Olovo, Srebrenik, Srebrenica, Bosanska Krupa, Visoko, Kladanj, Banovići, Gračanica, Tešanj, Jablanica, Goražde, Lukavac, Bihać, Bratunac, Višegrad, Rogatica, Gradačac, Zavidovići, Zvornik, Gornji Vakuf, Donji Vakuf, Vlasenica, Zenica, Kakanj, Konjic, and Foča. In addition, Muslim Slavs dominate by plurality (less than 50 percent) in an additional 14 districts *(Figure 2,* light gray). Of these 14 districts, 5 are shared with Serbs as a co-dominant group: Sarajevo, Sanski Most, Maglaj, Prijedor, and Doboj. The remaining 9 districts are shared with Croats as the co-dominant group: Fojnica, Tuzla, Zepće, Travnik, Stolac, Brčko, Bugojno, Jajce, and Mostar. A region outlined so as to include all the above Muslim-dominated districts, representing the "Muslim Slav Canton" of the three-canton model, would include 64.3 percent of all Muslim Slavs of Bosnia-Hercegovina. Accordingly, 35.7 percent would be left outside that region. The Muslim Slav majority in this entire region is on the average 56.5

percent, whereas 43.5 percent of the population are non-Muslim minorities. The region covers some 22,000 square kilometers, or 43 percent of the total surface area of the republic (see *Table 1*). This is the most densely populated region of Bosnia-Hercegovina, which includes the capital city of Sarajevo. About 2.8 million people, or 64 percent of the republic's total population lived in this region, amounting to an average density of 127 inhabitants per square kilometer. Even if the urban districts of Sarajevo are excluded from calculation, the population density of the area would still exceed 100 inhabitants per square kilometer (*Table 1*, numbers in parentheses).

A similarly mixed ethnic composition existed in the Serb-dominated districts. Serbs are the second most populous ethnic group of Bosnia-Hercegovina. They, too, are represented by a greater than 50 percent majority in 31 out of 100 districts (*Figure 2*, bold stripes): Titov Drvar, Bosansko Grahovo, Sekovići, Ljubinj, Srbac, Celinac, Laktaši, Bileća, Glamoč, Sipovo, Mrkonjić Grad, Bosanski Petrovac, Nevesinje, Prnjavor, Rudo, Skender Vakuf, Trebinje, Bosanska Dubica, Sokolac, Gacko, Kalinovik, Bosanski Novi, Bosanska Gradiška, Bijeljina, Han Pijesak, Ugljevik, Lopare, Teslić, Banja Luka, Cajniče, and Kupres. Serbs dominate by plurality in an additional 4 districts (*Figure 2*, fine stripes). Two of these are with Muslim Slavs as the co-dominant group: Ključ and Modriča. Two are shared with Croats as the co-dominant groups: Derventa and Kotor Varos. A region outlined so as to include all Serb-dominated districts would include 48.5 percent of all Serbs of Bosnia-Hercegovina, leaving 51.5 percent distributed outside that region. This would represent the "Serb Canton" of the three-canton model. The Serb majority in this region is on average 61.5 percent, vs. the 38.5 percent of non-Serb minorities. This region is about the same size as that dominated by Muslim Slavs, covering almost 22,500 square kilometers, or 44 percent of the total surface area of the republic. The region is less densely populated, with slightly more than a million people, amounting to 25 percent of the republic's population. The average population density was, accordingly, much lower, about 48 per square kilometer (see *Table 1*).

Croats are the third most populous group of Bosnia-Hercegovina. Croats constitute more than 50 percent in only 13 out of 100 districts: Grude, Posušje, Duvno (Tomislav Grad), Lištica, Citluk, Ljubuski, Neum, Orašje, Livno, Kreševo, Prozor, Odžak, Capljina, and Kiseljak. Croats hold a relative majority in an additional 6 districts. Four are shared with Muslim Slavs: Busovača, Vitez, Vareš, and Pučarevo (Novi Travnik). Two have Serbs as the co-dominant group: Bosanski Samac and Bosanski Brod. Areas outlined so as to include all Croat-dominated districts (*Figure 2*, checkered), or the "Croat Canton" of the three-canton model, would include 41.5 percent of all Croats of Bosnia-Hercegovina. The remaining 56.5 percent of Croats would remain distributed outside of that region. Croats would hold a 65.7 percent majority vs. the non-Croat minorities of 34.3 percent in a region covering 6,642 square kilometers, or 13 percent of the republic's surface area. Somewhat less than a half million people lived in this area with an average density of 72 inhabitants per square kilometer (see *Table 1*).

The three cantons defined by the combined criteria of ethnic dominance (absolute majority and plurality), have an average 60:40 split between the ethnically dominant and the minority populations. In this respect, it may appear to provide a certain "even-handedness." Each "canton" includes "core districts" with a greater than 50 percent majority of the dominant ethnic group (darkly shaded areas), and "marginal districts" in which the dominant group is outnumbered by the combined minority populations (lightly shaded areas on the map in *Figure 2)*. The ratio of "core" to "marginal" districts is most favorable in the "Serb Canton" (7.76), less favorable in the "Croat Canton" (3.34), and least favorable in the "Muslim Canton" (1.68). This heterogeneity and inherent instability is formalized in the next model.

The "Four-Canton Model" is composed of the three ethnic "core cantons" described above, which are comprised of districts with an absolute majority (dominance greater than 50 percent) of the respective three principal ethnic groups. An additional "Canton of Shared Dominance" is constructed from the remaining districts in which none of the three ethnic groups holds an absolute majority. The areas covered by these districts are mapped in *Figure 3* (dotted). The table accompanying the legend in *Figure 3* presents the ethnic distribution in percentages for the four cantons of this model. The relationship to absolute population numbers and areas of coverage is presented in the lower part of *Table 1*.

The four-canton model consolidates regional ethnic dominance by relying on those "core" districts that have absolute majority rather than plurality. However, the resulting "cantons" become less inclusive in the process. In the "core canton" of Muslim Slavs, for example *(Figure 3,* gray), Muslims would hold a 67.6 percent majority (as compared with 56.5 percent in the three-canton model). This means that 32.4 percent of the population in this "canton" would be non-Muslim minorities (as compared with 43.5 percent in the three-canton model). However, the "Muslim Canton" of the four-canton model would include only 49.7 percent of all Muslim Slavs of Bosnia-Hercegovina (as compared with the 64.3 percent in the three-canton model), leaving more than half of them (50.3 percent) outside that region. Similarly, the Serbs would hold a 65.2 percent majority vs. a 34.8 percent minority within their "core canton" *(Figure 3,* striped). This canton would include only 43.5 percent of the Serbs of Bosnia-Hercegovina, leaving 56.5 percent outside. In the Croat "core canton" *(Figure 3,* checkered), Croats would hold a 77.8 percent majority over 22.2 percent of non-Croat minorities. A region characterized by this dominance includes only 32.0 percent of all Croats living in Bosnia-Hercegovina, with 68.0 percent remaining outside that region. A corresponding reduction in surface coverage of the three ethnic cantons is shown in the lower right part of *Table 1*.

The fourth "canton of shared dominance" would cover 12,312 square kilometers, or 24 percent of the republic's total surface area. It would include 40 percent of the total population of Bosnia-Hercegovina, distributed in 24 out of 100 census districts. Most of the suburbs of the capital city of Sarajevo

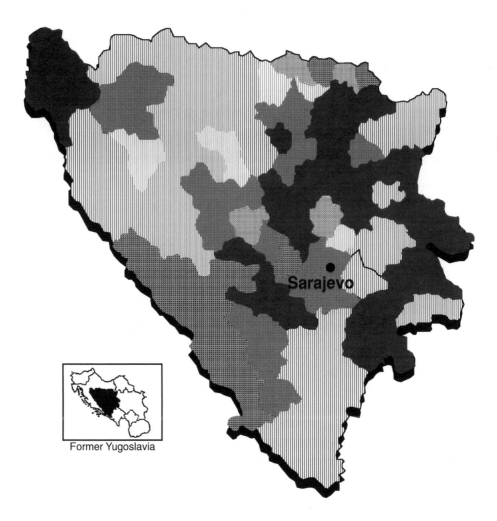

	Muslims	Serbs	Croats	Others
REPUBLIC B-H	43.6	31.3	17.3	7.8
Muslim Canton	56.5	23.1	12.1	8.3
Serbian Canton	21.5	61.5	9.5	7.5
Croatian Canton	18.2	10.9	65.7	5.2

Darker symbols–over 50%; lighter symbols–under 50%

Figure 2. Bosnia-Hercegovina Three-Canton Model—Percent Population

Table I
PREWAR (1991) POPULATION DISTRIBUTION OF BOSNIA-HERCEGOVINA IN AREAS CHARACTERIZED BY ETHNIC DOMINANCE

Cantons	Total No.	% Muslim	Serb	Croat	Other	Minor.	Surface Km²	% Area	Density No./Km²
Bosnia-Hercegovina	4,364,574	43.6	31.4	17.3	5.5	56.4	51,129	100	85
Three-Canton Model									
Muslims	2,806,856	56.5	23.1	12.1	8.3	43.5	22,083	43	127 (103)
Serbs	1,080,469	21.5	61.5	9.5	7.6	38.5	22,405	44	48
Croats	477,249	18.2	10.9	65.7	5.2	34.3	6,642	13	72
Four-Canton Model									
Muslims	1,397,127	67.6	19.4	7.6	5.3	32.4	13,856	27	101
Serbs	914,825	20.3	65.2	6.6	8.0	34.8	19,848	39	46
Croats	311,103	13.6	5.7	77.8	2.8	22.2	5,113	10	61
Shared	1,741,519	42.0	27.6	19.9	10.6	58.0	12,312	24	142 (99)

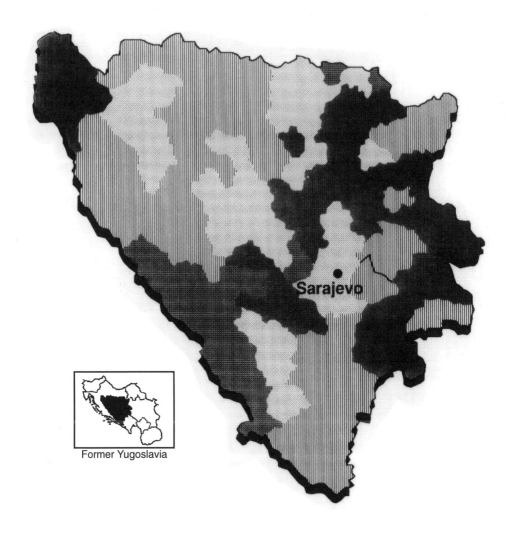

	Muslims	Serbs	Croats	Others
REPUBLIC B-H	43.6	31.3	17.3	7.8
Muslim Canton	67.6	19.4	7.6	5.4
Serbian Canton	20.3	65.2	6.6	7.9
Croatian Canton	13.6	5.7	77.8	2.9
Shared Canton	42.0	27.6	19.8	10.6

Figure 3. Bosnia-Hercegovina Four-Canton Model—Percent Population

would fall within this "canton" (the Serb-dominated suburb Pale has been included within the Serb cantons in both maps, *Figures 2* and *3)*. In the "canton of shared dominance," Muslim Slavs would dominate by plurality in 14 districts (5 with Serbs and 9 with Croats as co-dominant groups), Serbs in 4 districts (2 with Muslim Slavs and 2 with Croats as co-dominant groups) and Croats in 6 districts (4 with Muslim Slavs and 2 with Serbs as co-dominant groups). In 11 of these 24 districts, the difference between the dominant and co-dominant group would be less than 5 percent. In the entire region of shared dominance, Muslim Slavs would have a majority of 42.0 percent, followed by Serbs with 27.7 percent, and Croats with 19.6 percent, a proportion quite similar to that of Bosnia-Hercegovina as a whole (43.6 percent Muslim, 31.4 percent Serb, 17.3 percent Croat).

The analysis of the ethnic composition of Bosnia-Hercegovina based on the most recent population census, invoking two models that use ethnic dominance as the criterion for administrative subdivision, demonstrates that the areas of dominance of the three principal ethnic groups are neither homogeneous nor contiguous. Each of these areas is discontinuous, leaving "islands" within other ethnic areas. Each includes only a fraction of its total ethnic population, leaving between 35 percent and 68 percent of that ethnic group outside of the area of their dominance. Most importantly, ethnic dominance does not correlate with ethnic purity. Each area characterized by ethnic dominance includes a substantial percentage of minorities of ethnic identities other than the dominant group. The percentage of minorities can be as low as 22 percent, and as high as 43 percent. Therefore, neither the three-canton nor the four-canton models provide an acceptable blueprint for ethnic separation, although both are based on objective and internally consistent criteria of ethnic dominance. No third model can be objectively derived from these data.

IN JANUARY 1993 Owen and Vance, co-chairmen of ICFY, proposed a comprehensive peace plan for Bosnia-Hercegovina and presented it to the UN Security Council and to the parties at war. This plan has been accepted and, to date, signed by the representatives of the Bosnian Croats and (under considerable pressure from the West) by the multinational Bosnian government which also represents Bosnian Muslim interests. The Bosnian Serbs, however, have rejected the plan at every step. It has, nonetheless, become the focal point of peace negotiations concerning the war in Bosnia-Hercegovina.

The Owen-Vance Plan has put forward the "constitutional principles for Bosnia-Hercegovina," proposed a "constitutional structure" for the country, and provided a "map indicating the suggested delimitation of the provinces." The plan conceives the future Bosnia-Hercegovina as a decentralized state with a significant proportion of administrative functions carried out by 10 autonomous provinces.*

*ICFY/4/Rev. 1, January 4, 1993

The plan contains a short-term goal of a cessation of hostilities and separation of the warring parties into "designated provinces"—a de facto ethnic separation, and a long-term goal of demilitarization and ethnic integration of Bosnia-Hercegovina into a multi-ethnic democratic society. Taken as such, these goals are mutually contradictory.

The Owen-Vance map *(Figure 4)* uses ethnic dominance as the principal criterion for a division into provinces. The direct implication is that each of the three constituent ethnic groups would, at least initially, be in control of three provinces, with the capital city of Sarajevo remaining "neutral." Under this scenario, Bosnia-Hercegovina would be effectively divided between the three warring parties, each region under the control of its respective ethnically defined military leadership. This, by itself, would completely invalidate the stated long-term goals of ethnic integration, and the "progressive demilitarization" of Bosnia-Hercegovina.

By its own choice of wording, the Owen-Vance plan is supposed to "culminate" in the relocation of the military forces involved in the conflict to "designated provinces" within forty five days. The Owen-Vance map allocates these provinces to each of the three ethnic groups. A subsequent "progressive demilitarization" is required by the proposed constitutional design and is to be carried out under UN/EC supervision (apparently as a long-term objective). However, this objective is not supported by any specific procedural steps, and no obligatory timing or deadlines are given. Without such specifications and, particularly, without mechanisms to carry out a successful implementation of all the plan's objectives, the Owen-Vance plan, in its present version, is inadequate. Without appropriate backing, there is a danger that its execution may settle for only a partial completion of its objectives by confirming the military status quo while abandoning the more difficult goal of establishing an integrated civilian society with all the constitutional guarantees it offers in theory.

The Owen-Vance map, like the cantonal models, relies primarily on ethnic dominance in delimiting the provinces. Other criteria may have been taken in consideration but they do not alleviate the serious shortcomings of this map. Again, like the cantonal models, the Owen-Vance plan also fails to solve the problem of ethnic minorities within designated provinces, an issue which, according to our demographic analysis, and confirmed by the tragic events of the past year, is clearly the most vital. The Owen-Vance plan states that "many of the provinces will have a considerable majority of one of the three major groups" but "most will have a significant representation of minorities." In fact, all provinces designated by the Owen-Vance map would have between one-third and two-thirds minority populations (with percentages as low as 29.0 percent and as high as 58.4 percent, *Table 2).*

As a device for territorial division, the Owen-Vance map introduces glaring inequities. It apportions only 27 percent of the surface area of Bosnia-Hercegovina to the control of Muslim Slavs (who constitute 43.6 percent of population of Bosnia-Hercegovina), while 43 percent of the territory is placed under the control of Serbs (31.4 percent of the population), and 25 percent

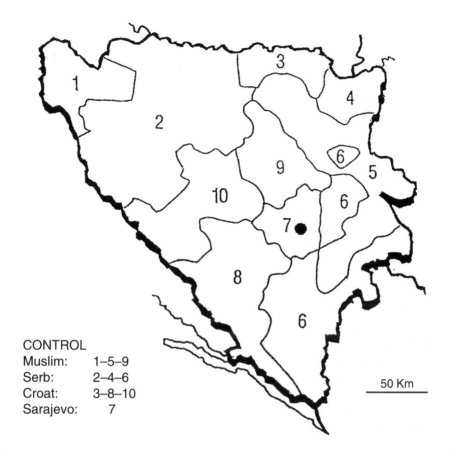

CONTROL
Muslim: 1–5–9
Serb: 2–4–6
Croat: 3–8–10
Sarajevo: 7

Figure 4. Owen-Vance Plan

under the control of Croats (17.3 percent of the population). "Inter-ethnic" Sarajevo would cover 4 percent of the territory. According to this plan, a 38 percent non-Muslim minority would remain under Muslim Slav control, a 42 percent non-Serb minority under Serb control, and a 51 percent non-Croat minority under Croat control. The Owen-Vance plan, however, does not specifically regulate or safeguard the relationships between the respective majorities and minorities.

The Owen-Vance map introduces compromise boundaries across territories with no distinct ethnic dominance. In order to consolidate certain ethnic territories, and connect ethnic islands marooned in the "wrong" province, narrow corridors have been cut across areas dominated by other ethnic groups. For example, corridors are cut across areas of Muslim ethnic dominance in the south-east part of Bosnia-Hercegovina to connect one Serb-dominated area to another. These broad-brush strokes on the map appear to sacrifice the principle of ethnic dominance for the sake of simplicity. Even so, the Owen-Vance map

Table 2
PREWAR (1991) POPULATION DISTRIBUTION OF BOSNIA-HERCEGOVINA IN PROVINCES DESIGNATED BY OWEN-VANCE PLAN

No.	Control	Total No.	Muslim	Serb	% Croat	Other	Minor.	Surface Km²	% Area	Density No./Km²
1	Muslim	352,501	70.1	22.1	3.0	4.8	29.9	2,991	6	118
9	Muslim	475,522	58.3	15.6	18.0	8.1	41.7	6,570	13	134
5	Muslim	882,681	60.7	26.4	5.9	7.1	39.3	4,254	8	112
	Sum	1,710,704	62.0	22.5	8.7	6.9	38.0	13,815	27	124
2	Serb	760,212	21.2	61.3	9.2	8.3	38.7	14,188	28	54
4	Serb	288,065	39.5	41.6	11.3	7.6	58.4	6,488	13	23
6	Serb	147,678	24.6	71.0	0.8	3.7	29.0	1,503	3	192
	Sum	1,195,955	26.0	57.7	8.6	7.6	42.3	22,180	43	54
3	Croat	181,977	11.9	32.1	48.6	7.5	51.4	1,984	4	92
10	Croat	383,422	37.3	12.8	44.4	5.5	55.6	5,808	12	61
8	Croat	353,896	28.9	11.0	54.2	5.8	45.8	5,220	10	73
	Sum	919,295	29.0	15.9	49.0	6.0	51.0	13,012	25	70
7	Sarajevo	538,620	49.3	26.8	9.6	14.2	50.7	2122	4	254

remains exceedingly complex, retaining islands and enclaves in the "wrong" ethnic territories. For example, Province 1 in the northwest, Province 3 in the
north, and the Sekovići district (northernmost Province 6) in the east would
remain separated from the other respective Muslim, Croat, and Serb areas.

Furthermore, the Owen-Vance map appears to contradict the general
spirit of the Owen-Vance plan. Provided that the plan does indeed proceed successfully beyond the provision that requires a relocation of (hostile) "forces to
designated provinces" (within forty-five days), and proceeds (at a yet-to-be-
specified schedule) toward the establishment of a desired integration of the
population into a democratic, multi-ethnic civil society—as the constitutional
provisions of the plan propose—the Owen-Vance map together with the principle of ethnic dominance on which it is based, loses its significance. If, however, the separation of military powers and continuation of their regional
control should be of any permanence, the Owen-Vance map is grossly inadequate regarding the protection of minorities. Leaving large numbers of minority civilians at the mercy of various warlords would be recklessly irresponsible,
particularly following unprecedented atrocities committed throughout Bosnia-
Hercegovina by military and paramilitary groups. Should the Owen-Vance
map be implemented, but "ethnic cleansing" continue toward achieving the
goal of ethnic separation and purity, over 1,600,000 people, or 37.2 percent of
the entire prewar population of Bosnia-Hercegovina would be affected.

In addition, given the fact that boundaries between provinces of the
Owen-Vance map run straight through major population centers, this provision would create scores of new "Berlins," "Beiruts," and "Belfasts," with walls
dividing streets, gardens, and families. Towns such as Bosanski Novi, Prijedor,
and Sanski Most would remain cut and divided between provinces, which
would create additional hardship for tens of thousands of people and become
administrative nightmares.

The laudable long-term aspirations of the Owen-Vance plan (constitutional provisions to enforce human, civil and political, and group rights,
achieve "group balance" in governmental bodies and civil services, and accomplish ethnic recognition and integration) could never be implemented if the
short-term plan, as presently prescribed, divides and distributes Bosnia-Hercegovina into the hands of local warlords while failing to disarm them.

NEITHER THE CANTONAL nor the Owen-Vance methods of subdivision, both
based on ethnic dominance, offer a viable solution to the current crisis. Ethnic separation cannot be accomplished without "ethnic cleansing," There is,
therefore, an obvious need for a more innovative, insightful, and prudent
approach to the problem.

First, one must acknowledge that the peoples of Bosnia-Hercegovina are
confined to live in the limited geography of the republic, and, regardless of
current animosities, will have to continue do so into the future. Second, an
objective basis for a solution should be sought in the properties and require-

ments of the land and the peoples who inhabit it, rather than the factions who now feud over it. The pursuit of a lasting peace must turn toward future social and economic needs, and not toward attempted rectification of injustices of the past, real or perceived. Therefore, the physiographic properties of the land and its resources, and the potential for peaceful co-existence among the peoples of Bosnia-Hercegovina, reflected in centuries of religious and ethnic tolerance and cultural diversity, is the basic foundation of our approach.

In proposing a "Natural Administrative Subdivision by Watersheds," we take the view that the drawing of provincial boundaries should be based first and foremost on the existing topography and hydrography, and only secondarily upon ethnic and cultural identities. A subdivision of Bosnia-Hercegovina is useful only if it facilitates the management of natural resources at the local level. A decentralized management performs more efficiently than a centralized one, and, in this case, would foster civic responsibility. To enable sustainable development, governmental entities at every level of organization (from local to national) must bear the responsibility for the long-term management of the resources on the territory under their respective jurisdiction. The rights to exploit those resources must come second.

Following these basic principles, the administrative subdivision of Bosnia-Hercegovina should be drawn along the natural boundaries of watersheds drained by the country's major rivers. Water is the most important natural resource for both population and industry alike. In addition, it is the main carrier of human and industrial wastes. As such, its proper management is of foremost importance for the present and future economic and environmental well-being of the inhabitants of the region.

Prudent use of water and water-transported resources in a given watershed can be optimized if coordinated under one management. Historically, watershed basins (surface catchment areas), fringed by mountain ranges, provided natural boundaries for human settlement and served as effective population separators.* Swiss mountain cantons developed in this manner, and have benefited from policies of uniform management and responsibility over entire alpine watershed basins under a singular cantonal jurisdiction.

Cutting and dividing watershed basins between different and potentially conflicting managements, as the Owen-Vance map does, is a poor management practice. Each watershed is particularly vulnerable to intentional and unintentional damage inflicted in its upstream areas, which would affect much larger areas downstream. For example, massive flooding, soil erosion, and land slides, due to excessive lumbering in the upper watershed areas, have often caused damage and clogging of reservoirs downstream. Irrigation programs in the upper areas of watersheds have been known to divert water and cause shortages downstream. In addition, pollution caused by industries

---

* The most common population separators in the lowlands are rivers, not mountains. They are, however, less suited as management boundaries because they require sharing and coordination of responsibilities between neighbors.

located upstream affect the water supply of communities downstream.

Incidents of intentional environmental damage and ecological black-mail have occurred during the current war on the territory of the former Yugoslavia. Threats to destroy dams on the river Drina (at Zvornik and Višegrad), and the actual mining and subsequent explosion at the Peruca dam on the river Cetina (in Dalmatia), held hostage thousands of inhabitants downstream along the valleys of these rivers. These, and similar events, have a potential for major ecological disasters.

Honoring the above principles, a map of Bosnia-Hercegovina can be designed with administrative subdivisions that roughly coincide with the watershed basins of the republic's major rivers (Figure 5). Bosnia-Hercegovina is naturally partitioned along the peninsular divide between waters draining northward as tributaries of the river Sava, emptying via the Danube into the Black Sea, and those draining southward, emptying into the Adriatic Sea. This natural divide forms the basis for the first order North-South subdivision of Bosnia-Hercegovina. The northern part is further subdivided into watershed basins of four major tributaries of the river Sava (from west to east): Una,

1 Upper Una
2 Una-Center
3 Lower Una
4 Vrbas
5 Bosna
6 Drina
7 Neretva
8 Viduša
9 Sarajevo

Figure 5. Mountain-Crest Divided Watersheds

Vrbas, Bosna, and Drina. The southern part includes the River Neretva, and a series of karstic fields with short and temporary rivers interconnected underground by numerous cave systems.

The rivers Una, Sava, and Drina mark, in parts of their flow, the external frontiers of Bosnia-Hercegovina. The river Una runs along the Republic's western and northwestern borders, forming a bow in between. Its basin can, therefore, be conveniently subdivided into three administrative units. The upper part of the river includes its tributary Unac and extends in the southeast-northwest direction (province "Upper Una" on the map). The central bow includes the westernmost district of the republic ("Una-Center"). Its lower course receives only its eastern tributaries from the territory of Bosnia-Hercegovina, with the river Sava draining the largest part of the watershed ("Lower Una"). The basin of the Vrbas lies east of the Una, generally draining in a South-North direction ("Vrbas"). The basin of the river Bosna lies to the East ("Bosna"). The southernmost part of this basin contains the district of the capital city of Sarajevo, which the Owen-Vance proposal treats as a separate province. The easternmost basin is that of the river Drina, which comprises, in part, the border between Bosnia-Hercegovina and Serbia ("Drina").

All tributaries which drain into the Adriatic sea lie within the karstic region of the republic. Only one major river, the Neretva, characterizes this region by its surface flow ("Neretva" province). In the absence of rivers with surface flow, other topographic features and ethnic considerations have been used in delimitation between the two southern provinces. The karstic fields west of the Neretva are included in the Neretva basin within a single administrative unit, while those east of the Neretva were separated, mainly by ethnic considerations ("Viduša").

The topography delimiting the watershed basins provides unambiguous, natural boundaries for an administrative subdivision of Bosnia-Hercegovina. Since mountain crests and rivers have been important determinants for human settlement from the earliest times, it should not come as a surprise that the distribution of ethnic groups coincides to some degree with these boundaries. Combining topographic and ethnic criteria, the Una watershed basin and the karstic region were further subdivided, defining the ethnic boundaries further while still complying with the criteria of resource management.

For the sake of comparison with other subdivisions based more or less on ethnic dominance, the proposed Watershed Subdivision of Bosnia-Hercegovina was also subjected to demographic analysis. The ethnic composition of the resulting 9 provinces is presented in *Table 3*. According to distribution of districts in relation to watershed-based provinces, Muslim Slavs would be the dominant population in the proposed provinces "Una-Center" and "Bosna," with significant concentrations of Croats in the southern and northern ends of the latter basin. Serbs would dominate in the provinces "Upper Una," "Vrbas," and "Viduša." Croats in the "Neretva" province, with an increased concentration of Muslim Slavs toward the east of the province, and Serbs in the upper parts of the Neretva river basin. The Provinces "Lower Una" and

Table 3
PREWAR (1991) POPULATION DISTRIBUTION OF BOSNIA-HERCEGOVINA IN PROVINCES BASED ON TOPOGRAPHY OF WATERSHED BASINS

No.	Province	Total No.	% Muslim	Serb	Croat	Other	Minor.	Surface Km²	% Area	Density No./Km²
1	Upper Una	63,018	10.1	80.9	6.4	2.6	19.1	3,886	7	16
2	Una-Center	245,435	81.9	11.7	2.2	4.2	18.1	2,214	4	111
3	Lower Una	282,940	41.0	49.0	3.7	6.3	51.0	4,586	9	62
4	Vrbas	668,785	21.6	51.9	17.8	8.6	48.1	7,971	15	84
5	Bosna	1,569,760	50.3	20.3	20.9	8.5	49.7	11,499	23	135
6	Drina	507,741	51.7	44.4	0.2	3.7	48.3	7,572	15	67
7	Neretva	45,8219	25.2	14.6	54.7	5.4	45.3	9,101	18	50
8	Vidusa	42,696	22.1	74.7	0.0	3.2	24.3	2,971	6	14
9	Sarajevo	525,980	49.3	29.9	6.6	14.2	50.7	1,329	3	396

"Drina" would be almost evenly shared by Serbs and Muslim Slavs. Comparison of *Table 3* with *Table 2* shows that in 3 out of 9 Watershed Provinces, the ratio between the ethnically dominant population and minorities is higher than in any of the provinces of the Owen-Vance map. Conversely, 3 out of the 10 provinces outlined in the Owen-Vance map (3, 4, and 10) have this ratio lower than the lowest ratio of the Watershed province design (Lower Una). Thus, even from a point of view of ethnic relations, the Watershed map turns out to be superior to that designed by Owen-Vance.

THE IMPLEMENTATION OF the Watershed Subdivision of Bosnia-Hercegovina, which accommodates the long-term needs for sensible resource management, is also consistent with the immediate needs for a restoration of normal civilian life. The first objective in implementing a successful peace plan is to eliminate protracted bickering over new boundaries. Because the boundaries of the Watershed Plan are inherently objective, and thus less controversial than other criteria for drawing political boundaries, this would remove the stumbling block which has, up to now, prevented any progress in peace negotiations for Bosnia-Hercegovina.

A second objective is to achieve and enforce a lasting cease-fire. In this respect, the Watershed Division has strategic advantages as well. By placing boundaries along the crests of mountain ranges, international peace-keeping forces could ensure that no one side could use mountain crests for military advantage over another. Misuse of the exclusive possession of topographic heights is exemplified by the shelling and destruction of Sarajevo from the hills surrounding the city. In peacetime, the mountain-crest boundaries become common property shared by neighbors, each side overlooking the territory of its respective responsibility and management.

A third objective, which has not been adequately addressed by the official brokers of peace negotiations, is the necessity of effectively reversing "ethnic cleansing" in order to provide for the safe return of millions of refugees. A plan for the repatriation of all refugees must take into consideration both where people originally lived, but also where they would now feel safe resettling. Many refugees would not want to return to their burned homes or to sites where family members had been killed. These people should be free to settle elsewhere. Children of mixed marriages may feel most comfortable in highly integrated and secularized regions of Bosnia-Hercegovina, while others should be able to settle among people of their own ethnic extraction. The Watershed Plan is compatible with the accommodation of the needs of both groups.

Within the Watershed Provinces, demographic analysis of the prewar ethnic distribution identified districts with the highest degree of ethnic integration as well as nuclei of maximum ethnic purity. Examples of districts with the most diverse and integrated population before the war were: Tuzla, Bosanski Brod, Brčko, and Maglaj. Districts within which at least two ethnic groups evenly shared dominance were: Travnik, Bosanski Samac, Zepće, Prijedor, Vitez, Sanski Most, Fojnica, Bugojno, and Ključ. On the other hand, examples of districts with ethnic concentrations of over 90 percent were: Cazin and Velika Kladuša for Muslim Slavs; Titov Drvar, Bosansko Grahovo, and Sekovići for Serbs; and Grude, Posušje, Lištica, Duvno, Citluk, and Ljubuški for Croats.

In the developing of policies for the return or re-settlement of refugees, it will be of the utmost importance that individuals be allowed to make decisions about their settlement strictly on a voluntary basis, free of any coercion or fear-generating propaganda, under international supervision and protection. To facilitate the reunification of families and friends, the return of properties to their rightful owners, and the resolution of property rights and exchanges, in the course of the resettlement, an information database should be created and implemented. (This would be a logical contribution for the United States and Japan to make.)

A fourth objective toward long-term peace and stability is to assist in the formation of a functioning government. Recent peace negotiations have forwarded proposals for a rotating presidency for Bosnia-Hercegovina, with a representational system of governors and provincial governments based on ethnic quotas. Ethnic quotas, however, are an investment in endless quibbling, and it was the rotating presidency that precipitated the undoing of Yugoslavia. A more acceptable arrangement for an electorate as disparate as that of Bosnia-Hercegovina would be a system of representation similar to that of the United States. A bicameral system, consisting of a House of Representatives which reflects the population numerically, by each of the administrative districts, and a Senate in which each of the four constituent groups (Muslim Slavs, Serbs, Croats, and Others) is represented equally, would function as both a workable and judicious system for the republic. A similar administrative structure, incorporating both majority and minority representation, should also be implemented within the Watershed Provinces. This would facilitate the security and confidence of minorities, perhaps the most critical factor in the long-term stability of Bosnia-Hercegovina.

The apprehension and prosecution of war criminals has been identified as an important objective, for which an International War Crimes Tribunal is being organized. In addition to laudable efforts to hunt down and bring to justice war criminals, this Tribunal could also serve the useful purpose of screening individuals for recruitment into civil, inter-ethnic police forces and international patrols. These patrols should be of international and mixed ethnic composition, similar to those introduced in occupied Vienna and Berlin following the Second World War. To ensure a nonpartisan execution of law and order, representatives of the local majority and minority (in addition to UN/EC representatives) should be required in each patrol.

Once the country returns to normalcy, it will be possible for the best features of the Watershed Plan to be realized in economic development, ecological recovery, and social harmony. Because all inhabitants of Bosnia-Hercegovina—Muslim Slavs, Orthodox Serbs, Catholic Croats, and Others—are first and foremost citizens of the republic, they are entitled to equal rights; they are, however, also equally responsible for the managing of the resources available to them within that region. It is the quality of this management which will determine the economic success of the region, its competitiveness on the world market, and the quality of life and acceptable living standard of its inhabitants. These factors are essential in securing the long-term stability of the region. No political or military solution to the current crisis that aspires to any permanence can afford to ignore this fact.

Presently, however, the nature of the war, the stated goals and aspirations of the parties at war and their split loyalties, as well as those diplomatic proposals which appease them and legitimize their gains, all promote divisive politics, and work in the opposite direction. This trend will only further exacerbate the conflict and prolong the suffering of the peoples of Bosnia-Hercegovina.

The premise that tribal animosities prevent these people from living together is a false one. The present disintegration of the social fabric of Bosnia-Hercegovina was caused primarily by divisive politics rather than age-old hatreds. The West's tacit acceptance of ethnic separation and the radical demands of warlords confer legitimacy to illegitimate elements of the current political scene; it also silences those voices of reason, who speak for the interests of the majority of the population.

Bosnia-Hercegovina was exemplary for its ethnic and religious tolerance which thrived for centuries, the disruption thereof during World War II notwithstanding. The demographic complexity of the republic bears this out. The formation of a mosaic of ethnic mixtures that was revealed in our demographic analysis would not be possible otherwise. Nor could numerous mosques, churches, and other cultural monuments survive side by side for centuries, only to be destroyed in the current conflict.

One year of violence, however brutal, is not sufficient to destroy the capacity of members of an entire population to relate reasonably and with tolerance toward one another. The joint suffering of Muslim Slavs, Serbs, and Croats in besieged Sarajevo is a vivid testament to the fact that such tolerance has not yet perished.

In Bosnia-Hercegovina, historic developments brought together people of different cultural backgrounds that developed split identities: some adopting the national "Bosnian" identity while others maintained their original cultural traditions. Industrialization and urbanization in Bosnia-Hercegovina, as in other developing nations, caused a migration of the majority of the republic's population from rural into urban settings, promoting integration, while remote villages remained faithful to their separate cultural traditions. The problems associated with balancing the tendencies of integration with those of cultural distinction in Bosnia-Hercegovina is, in principle, not different from those faced by the Jews and Gypsies in Europe, the Chinese in Indonesia, or for that matter, any immigrant group in the United States.

Exploitation of racial, ethnic, or cultural distinctions for political gains is also neither unique nor new. It is the least educated and economically most-deprived sectors of the population who are most susceptible to this type of manipulation. Dreams of the formation of a "greater Serbia" found fertile ground in the economically depressed "Krajina" regions of Croatia and Bosnia-Hercegovina. Memories of the suffering of the Serbian population at the hands the right-extremist Croatian Ustaše puppet regime during World War II and of Serb suffering under Ottoman rule centuries ago are now used to legitimize unprecedented criminal actions and atrocities against non-Serb civilians.

Accusing entire ethnically defined groups of civilians (including the elderly, women, and children) of historic wrong-doing, be they Croat, Muslim, or Serb, cannot be perceived as anything but absurd. Moreover, the passage of fifty years, and the complete replacement of one generation by another, born subsequent to the Yugoslav national reconciliation, makes the historical retribution argument a hollow one.

Driving people from their homes, raping and killing them, and destroying their possessions and livelihoods radicalizes the survivors, regardless of their ethnic, religious, or cultural identity. It is human nature to identify an enemy in response and to seek retribution. The world community's inaction has allowed the problem to fester and spread to the point that ethnic and religious polarization became the only practical means of recognizing friend from foe. Thus, it is important to realize that the ethnic/religious hatreds now characteristic of the war in Bosnia-Hercegovina are, for the general public of that region, not the primary cause but the consequence of the increasingly violent disintegration of the multi-ethnic Communist state.

Our demographic analysis of Bosnia-Hercegovina demonstrates that ethnic dominance is clearly not an acceptable criterion for any division or subdivision of the country. This conclusion renders cantonal models inadequate as a means of solving the country's ethnic problems. Similarly inappropriate are other proposed divisions that are based on ethnic dominance, such as those incorporated in the Owen-Vance Plan. We fear that their artificially derived set of provinces, whose sole justification appears to be military disengagement, will actually magnify the difficulty in realizing Owen and Vance's own stated long-term goals.

The primary deficiency of the current Owen-Vance peace proposal is the attempt to appease the radical perpetrators of the war. By dividing the country along ethnic lines, the proposal legitimizes their conquests, including the "ethnic cleansing" that has already occurred and offers no effective barrier to its continuation. The Owen-Vance Plan, in its present form, is a clear case of realpolitik that sacrifices the interests of the very people it purports to protect.

Instead, a natural physiographic administrative subdivision, as suggested in the present study, would promote future economic development and resource management, while achieving a comparable, if not superior, ethnic balance than the Owen-Vance Plan. Most importantly, the Watershed Plan is objective and promotes the ethnic integration and tolerance that sooner or later will have to return and prevail. A reasonable and workable solution needs to take into consideration the properties and needs of the land and its people

Table 4
1991 POPULATION CENSUS OF BOSNIA-HERCEGOVINA

		Total	Muslim	Serb	Croat	Other
1	Sarajevo	525,980	49.3	29.9	6.6	14.2
2	Banovići	26,507	72.4	16.8	0.0	10.8
3	Banja Luka	195,139	14.6	54.8	14.9	15.7
4	Bihać	70,896	66.6	17.8	7.7	7.9
5	Bijeljina	96,796	31.3	59.4	0.0	9.3
6	Bileća	13,269	14.7	80.3	0.0	5.0
7	Bos. Dubica	31,577	20.5	69.1	0.0	10.4
8	Bos. Gradiška	60,062	26.7	59.5	5.9	7.9
9	Bos. Krupa	58,212	74.5	23.6	0.0	1.9
10	Bos. Brod	33,962	12.2	33.8	41.0	13.0
11	Bos. Novi	41,541	33.9	60.4	0.0	5.7
12	Bos. Petrovac	15,552	21.1	75.2	0.0	3.7
13	Bos. Samac	32,835	6.8	41.5	44.7	7.0
14	Bos. Grahovo	8,303	0.0	95.5	2.6	1.9
15	Bratunac	33,575	64.2	34.2	0.0	1.6
16	Brčko	87,332	44.4	20.8	25.4	9.4
17	Breza	17,266	75.6	12.3	5.0	7.1
18	Bugojno	46,843	42.1	18.9	34.1	4.9
19	Busovača	18,883	44.9	0.0	48.1	7.0
20	Cazin	63,406	97.6	0.0	0.0	2.4
21	Cajniče	8,919	44.9	52.9	0.0	2.2
22	Capljina	27,852	27.7	13.5	53.9	4.9
23	Celinac	18,666	7.7	88.9	0.0	3.4
24	Citluk	14,709	0.0	0.0	98.9	1.1
25	Derventa	56,328	12.6	40.8	39.0	7.6
26	Doboj	102,546	40.2	39.0	13.0	7.8
27	Donji Vakuf	24,232	55.3	38.7	0.0	6.0
28	Duvno (TG)	29,261	0.0	0.0	99.2	0.0
29	Foča	40,513	51.6	45.3	0.0	3.1
30	Fojnica	16,227	49.4	0.0	40.9	9.7
31	Gacko	10,844	35.3	62.4	0.0	2.3
32	Glamoč	12,421	18.1	79.3	0.0	2.6
33	Goražde	37,505	70.2	26.2	0.0	3.6
34	Gornji Vakuf	25,130	56.1	0.0	42.6	1.3
35	Gračanica	59,050	72.2	23.0	0.0	4.8
36	Gradačac	56,378	60.2	19.8	15.1	4.9
37	Grude	15,976	0.0	0.0	99.8	0.2
38	Han Pijesak	6,346	40.1	58.3	0.0	1.6
39	Jablanica	12,664	72.1	4.0	17.8	6.1
40	Jajce	44,903	38.8	19.3	35.1	6.8
41	Kakanj	55,857	54.5	8.8	29.8	6.9
42	Kalesija	41,795	79.5	18.3	0.0	2.2
43	Kalinovik	4,657	37.1	60.6	0.0	2.3
44	Kiseljak	24,081	40.9	0.0	51.7	7.4
45	Kladanj	16,028	73.3	23.9	0.0	2.8
46	Ključ	37,233	47.6	49.5	0.0	2.9
47	Konjic	43,636	54.5	15.2	26.0	4.3
48	Kotor Varos	36,670	30.4	38.1	29.0	2.5
49	Kreševo	6,699	22.8	0.0	70.7	6.5
50	Kupres	9,663	8.4	50.7	39.6	1.3

		Total	Muslim	Serb	Croat	Other
51	Laktaši	29,910	0.0	81.7	8.7	9.6
52	Lištica (SB)	26,437	0.0	0.0	99.2	0.0
53	Livno	39,526	15.0	9.6	72.0	3.4
54	Lopare	32,400	37.7	55.5	3.9	2.9
55	Lukavac	56,830	66.7	21.6	3.8	7.9
56	Ljubinj	4,162	7.9	89.9	0.0	2.2
57	Ljubuški	27,182	5.8	0.0	92.6	1.6
58	Maglaj	43,294	45.4	30.7	19.3	4.6
59	Modrica	35,413	29.5	35.3	27.3	7.9
60	Mostar	126,067	34.8	19.0	33.8	12.4
61	Mrkonjić Grad	27,379	12.0	77.3	7.8	2.9
62	Neum	4,268	4.6	0.0	87.6	7.8
63	Nevesinje	14,421	23.0	74.5	0.0	2.5
64	Odžak	30,651	20.3	19.8	54.2	5.7
65	Olovo	16,901	75.0	18.0	3.9	3.1
66	Orašje	28,201	6.7	15.0	75.3	3.0
67	Posusje	16,659	0.0	0.0	99.5	0.5
68	Prijedor	112,470	44.0	42.5	5.6	7.9
69	Prnjavor	46,601	37.7	0.0	62.3	0.0
71	Pučarevo	30,624	38.0	13.3	39.6	9.1
72	Rogatica	21,812	60.4	39.6	0.0	0.0
73	Rudo	11,572	27.2	70.8	0.0	2.0
74	Sanski Most	60,119	47.0	42.2	7.1	3.7
75	Skender Vakuf	19,416	5.6	69.6	24.8	0.0
76	Sokolac	14,833	30.2	68.6	0.0	1.2
77	Srbac	21,660	4.3	89.1	0.0	6.6
78	Srebrenica	37,211	74.8	25.2	0.0	0.0
79	Srebrenik	40,769	75.0	13.1	6.8	5.1
80	Stolac	18,845	44.9	22.0	33.1	0.0
81	Sekovići	9,639	5.7	94.3	0.0	0.0
82	Sipovo	15,553	20.8	79.2	0.0	0.0
83	Teslić	592	21.5	55.1	16.0	7.4
84	Tesanj	48,390	72.2	6.4	18.5	2.9
85	Titov Drvar	17,079	0.0	97.3	0.0	2.7
86	Travnik	70,402	45.3	11.0	36.9	6.8
87	Trebinje	30,879	17.9	69.3	4.0	8.8
88	Tuzla	131,861	47.6	15.5	15.6	21.3
89	Ugljevik	25,641	40.6	56.2	0.0	3.2
90	Vares	22,114	30.4	16.4	40.6	12.6
91	Vel. Kladuša	52,921	91.8	4.3	0.0	3.9
92	Visoko	46,130	74.5	16.0	4.3	5.2
93	Višegrad	21,202	62.8	32.8	0.0	4.4
94	Vitez	27,728	41.4	5.4	45.7	7.5
95	Vlasenica	33,817	55.3	42.5	0.0	2.2
96	Zavidovići	57,153	60.1	20.4	13.2	6.3
97	Zenica	145,577	55.2	15.5	15.6	13.7
98	Zvornik	81,111	59.4	38.0	0.0	2.6
99	Zepće	22,840	47.2	10.0	39.8	3.0
100	Zivinice	54,653	80.6	6.4	7.3	5.7
	Bosnia-Hercegovina	4,364,574	43.6	31.4	17.3	5.5

rather than dwell on the conflicting interests and political ambitions of armed extremist groups. The foremost priority, therefore, should be directed toward an organized transfer of power from military to civilian authorities—a program demanding detailed consideration, a firm time-table, and a determined and forceful international backing.

Bosnia-Hercegovina is not alone in its tragedy. Numerous regional conflicts with similar problems, warlords, and demagogues, are emerging in the wake of the Cold War and the collapse of the reign of the superpowers. These conflicts will spread, multiply, and become increasingly unmanageable unless the western civilized democracies, the inheritors of a disordered new world, show the insight and courage to act in accordance with the principles upon which they are founded.

Caught in Another's Dream in Bosnia

Slavoj Žižek

PROPOS OF THE French Revolution, Kant wrote that its world-historical significance is not to be sought in what actually happened on the streets of Paris, but in the enthusiasm that this endeavor to realize freedom aroused in the eyes of its observers, the educated, enlightened public.

It may well be true that what actually took place in Paris was horrifying, that the most repulsive passions were let loose, yet the reverberations of these events within the enlightened public all around Europe bear witness not only to the possibility of freedom, but to the very actualization of freedom. The same step—the shift from the event's immediate reality to its inscription into the Other epitomized by passive observers—was to be repeated during the violent anti-immigrant outbursts in the summer of 1992 in Rostock and other cities in former East Germany. The true meaning of these events is to be sought in the fact that the neo-Nazi pogroms met with the approval or at least the "understanding" of the silent majority of observers; even some top Social Democratic politicians used them as an argument for reconsidering German liberal immigrant laws. This shift in the Zeitgeist is where real danger lurks: it prepares the ground for the possible hegemony of an ideology which perceives the presence of "aliens" as a threat to national identity, as the principal cause of antagonisms that divide the political body.

What we must be particularly attentive to is the difference between this "postmodern" racism which now rages around Europe and the traditional form of racism. The old racism was direct and raw—"they" (Jews, Blacks, Arabs, Eastern Europeans) are lazy, violent, plotting, eroding our national substance—whereas the new racism is "reflected," which is why it can well assume the form of its opposite, of the fight against racism. Etienne Balibar hit the mark by baptizing it "metaracism." That is to say, how does a "postmodern" racist react to the outbursts in Rostock? He or she begins by expressing horror and repulsion at the neo-Nazi violence, yet is quick to add that these events, deplorable as they are, must be seen in their context: they are actually a perverted, distorted expression and effect of a true problem, namely that in the contemporary Babylon the experience of belonging to a well-defined eth-

nic community, which gives meaning to the individual's life, is losing ground
. . . in short, the true culprits are cosmopolitan universalists who, in the name
of "multiculturalism," mix races and thereby set in motion natural self-defense
mechanisms. Apartheid is thus legitimized as the ultimate form of anti-racism,
as an endeavor to prevent racial tensions and conflicts. What we have here is a
palpable example of what Lacan has in mind when he insists that "there is no
metalanguage": the distance between metaracism and racism is void,
metaracism is racism pure and simple, all the more dangerous for posing as its
opposite and advocating racist measures as the very form of fighting racism.

At a different level, we encounter the same paradox in the way Western
media report on the recent war in Bosnia. The first thing that strikes the eye is
the contrast to the reporting on the 1991 Gulf War where we had the standard
ideological personification: instead of providing information on social, political, religious, and like trends and antagonisms in Iraq, the media ultimately
reduced the conflict to a quarrel with Saddam Hussein, Evil personified, the
outlaw who excluded himself from the civilized international community—
even more than military destruction, the true aim was presented as psychological, as the humiliation of Saddam who was to "lose face." In the case of the
Bosnian war, however, notwithstanding isolated cases of the demonization of
the Serbian president, Milošević, the predominant attitude is that of a quasi-
anthropological observer. The media outdo one another in giving us lessons
on the ethnic and religious background of the conflict: centuries-old traumas
are being replayed and acted out, so that, in order to understand the roots of
the conflict, one has to know not only the history of Yugoslavia, but the entire
history of the Balkans from the medieval times. In this conflict, it is therefore
not possible simply to take sides, one can only patiently try to grasp the background of this savage spectacle, alien to our civilized system of values.

Yet this opposite procedure involves an ideological mystification even more
cunning than the demonization of Saddam Hussein. The comfortable attitude of
a distant observer, the evocation of the allegedly intricate context of religious and
ethnic struggles in Balkan countries, is here to enable the West to shed its responsibility toward the Balkan countries, that is, to avoid the bitter truth that, far from
presenting the case of an eccentric ethnic conflict, the Bosnian war is a direct
result of the failure of the West to grasp the political dynamic of the disintegration of Yugoslavia. The logic is therefore ultimately the same as that of
metaracism: what we have is the actual bias, the support of "ethnic cleansing,"
under the guise of its opposite, the distance of an impartial observer.

RECENT EVENTS IN former Yugoslavia exemplify perfectly the properly dialecti-
cal reversal in which something that, within a given set of circumstances,
appeared as the most backward element, a remnant of the past, suddenly
emerges as the premonition of what lies ahead. The outbursts of Balkan nationalism were first dismissed as the convulsions of the dying Communist totalitarianism disguised in new nationalist clothes, as a ridiculous anachronism that

properly belongs to the nineteenth-century age of nation-states, not to our present era of multinationals and world-integration. But suddenly it became clear that the ethnic conflicts of former Yugoslavia are the first clear taste of the twenty-first century, the prototype of the post-Cold War armed conflicts.

Hegel said that the moment of victory of a political force is the very moment of its splitting. The recent deadlocks of the triumphant liberal-democratic "new world order" seem to endorse fully this view: today's world is more and more marked by the frontier separating its "inside" from its "outside"—the frontier between those who succeeded in remaining "within" (the "developed," those to whom the rules of human rights, social security, and so forth, apply), and the others, the excluded (apropos of whom the main concern of the "developed" is to contain their explosive potential, even if the price to be paid is the neglect of elementary democratic principles). This opposition, not the one between capitalism and socialism, is what defines the world today: the socialist bloc was the true "third way," a desperate attempt at modernization outside the constraints of capitalism. What is effectively at stake in the present crisis of post-socialist states is precisely the struggle for one's place, now that the illusion of the "third way" has evaporated: who will be admitted "inside," integrated into the developed capitalist order, and who will remain excluded from it?

This antagonistic splitting opens up the field for Khmer Rouge, Sendero Luminoso, and other similar movements which seem to personify "radical Evil" in today's politics: if—to use the Hegelian opposition of negative and infinite judgment—"fundamentalism" functions as a kind of "negative judgment" on liberal capitalism, as an inherent negation of the universalist claim of liberal capitalism, then movements like Sendero Luminoso enact an "infinite judgment" on it. In his Philosophy of Right, Hegel conceives the "rabble" *(Poebel)* as a necessary product of the modern society: a non-integrated segment within the legal order, prevented from participating in its benefits, and for this very reason delivered from responsibilities toward it—a necessary surplus excluded from the closed-circuit of the social edifice.

It seems as if it is only today, with the advent of late capitalism, that this notion of "rabble" has achieved its adequate realization in social reality, with the political forces which paradoxically unite the most radical indigenous anti-modernism (the refusal of everything that defined modernity: market, money, individualism) with the eminently modern project of effacing the entire symbolic tradition and of beginning from a zero-point (in the case of Khmer Rouge, the abolition of the entire system of education and the physical liquidation of intellectuals). In what, precisely, does the "shining path" of the Senderistas consist? In the idea to reinscribe socialism within the framework of a return to the ancient Inca empire (Khmer Rouge also conceived their regime as the return to the lost grandeur of the old Khmer kingdom). The result of this desperate endeavor to surmount the antagonism between tradition and modernity is a double negation. A radically anti-capitalist movement (the refusal of integration within the world market) is coupled with a systematic dissolution of all traditional hierarchical social links, beginning with the family. At the level of "micro-power," the regime of the Khmer Rouge functioned as the dictatorship of adolescents provoked into denouncing their parents, that is to say, as an "anti-oedipal" regime in its purest form. The truth articulated in an inverted form in the paradox of this double negation is that capitalism cannot reproduce itself without the support of precapitalist forms of social linkage.

In other words, far from presenting a case of exotic barbarism, the "radical Evil" of the Khmer Rouge and the Senderistas is conceivable only against the background of the constitutive antagonism of today's capitalism. There is more than a contingent idiosyncrasy in the fact that, in both cases, the leaders of the movements are intellectuals, well-skilled in the subtleties of Western culture (prior to becoming a revolutionary, Pol Pot was a professor at a French lycée in Phnom Penh, known for his subtle readings of Rimbaud and Mallarmé; Abimael Guzman, the "presidente Gonzalo," the leader of the Senderistas, is a philosophy professor whose preferred authors are Hegel and Heidegger and whose doctoral thesis was on Kant's theory of space). For that reason, it is too simple to conceive these movements as the last embodiment of the millenarian radicalism which structures the social space as the exclusive antagonism between "us" and "them," allowing for no possible forms of mediation. They rather present a desperate attempt to break out of the constitutive imbalance of capitalism, without seeking support in some previous tradition supposed to enable us to master this imbalance (the Islamic fundamentalism which remains within this logic is for that reason ultimately a perverted instrument of modernization). In other words, behind Sendero Luminoso's endeavor to erase the entire tradition and to begin from the zero-point in an act of creative sublimation, there is the correct insight into the complementary relationship of modernity and tradition: any true return to tradition is today a priori impossible, its role is simply to serve as a shock-absorber for the process of modernization. The Khmer Rouge and the Senderistas as the "infinite judgment" on late capitalism are therefore, in Hegel's terms, an integral part of its notion: if one wants to understand capitalism as a world-system, one must take into account its inherent negation, the "fundamentalism," as well as its absolute negation, the infinite judgment on it.

In Europe, former Yugoslavia is the exemplary case of this split inherent in capitalism as world-system: every actor in the blood-play of its disintegration endeavors to legitimize its place "inside" by presenting itself as the last bastion of European civilization (the current ideological designation for the capitalist "inside") in the face of oriental barbarism. For the right-wing nationalist Austrian, this imaginary frontier is Karavanke, the mountain chain between Austria and Slovenia: beyond it, the rule of the Slavic horde begins. For the nationalist Slovenes, this frontier is the river Kolpa, separating Slovenia from Croatia: we are Mitteleuropa, while the Croats are already Balkan, involved in the irrational ethnic feuds which really do not concern us—we are on their side, we sympathize with them, yet in the same way one sympathizes with a third-world victim of aggression. For the Croats, the crucial frontier, of course, is the one between them and the Serbs, that is, between the Western Catholic civilization and the Eastern Orthodox collective spirit which cannot grasp the values of Western individualism. The Serbs, finally, conceive themselves as the last line of defense of Christian Europe against the fundamentalist danger embodied in the Muslim Bosnians and Albanians.

It should be clear now who, within the space of former Yugoslavia, effectively behaves in the civilized "European" way: those at the very bottom of this ladder, excluded from all—Muslim Bosnians and Albanians. And today, they are paying the price for it. Slovenia and Croatia moved fast and aggressively against the will of the West: they proclaimed independence, and attained their goal, including being recognized by the West, whereas Alija Izetbegović, the Bosnian president, behaved as the model pupil of the West: he followed Western suggestions closely and proceeded with extreme caution, always ready to give another chance to any formula of a "new Yugoslavia," abstained from "provoking the Serbs" even when the Yugoslav Army was already fortifying artillery-sites on the mountains around Sarajevo—all in exchange for Western assurances that they would keep in check the Serbs and prevent the Yugoslav Army from attacking non-Serbs in Bosnia. He was paid for trusting the West and for playing its "civilized" game by the total destruction of his country: when Western promises proved void and the Army did attack, the West quickly threw up its hands and assumed the convenient posture of a distant observer, appalled at the outburst of primitive Balkan passions.

What is, then, the status of these notorious Balkan "archaic ethnic passions"? There is a well-known story about an anthropological expedition trying to contact a wild tribe in the New Zealand jungle who allegedly danced a terrible war dance in grotesque death-masks. When they reached the tribe in the evening, they asked them to dance for them, and the dance performed the next morning did in fact match the description. Satisfied, the expedition returned to civilization and wrote a much-praised report on the savage rites of the primitives. However, shortly after, when another expedition arrived at the place of this tribe and learned to speak their language properly, it was shown that this terrible dance did not exist in itself at all: in their discussions with the first group of explorers, the aborigines somehow guessed what the strangers wanted and quickly, in the night following their arrival, invented it especially for them, to satisfy their demand. In short, the explorers received back from the aborigines their own message in its inverted, true form.

Therein consists the lure to be dispelled if one is to understand what the Yugoslav crisis is about. There is nothing autochthonous in its "ethnic conflicts"; the gaze of the West was from the very beginning included—Lord Carrington and James Baker, Lord Owen and Cyrus Vance and Warren Christopher, among others, are today's version of the expedition to the New Zealand tribe: they act and react in exactly the same way, overlooking the entire spectacle; "old hatreds suddenly erupting in their primordial cruelty" is a dance staged for their eyes, a dance for which the West is thoroughly responsible.

SO WHY DOES the West accept this narrative of the "outburst of ethnic passions"? Recently, the world-famous Austrian writer Peter Handke expressed doubts about Slovene independence, claiming that the notion of an independent state is something imposed on Slovenes from the outside, not part of the inherent logic of their national development. Handke's mother was Slovene and, within his artistic universe, Slovenia functions as a mythical point of reference, a kind of maternal paradise, a country where words still directly refer to objects, somehow miraculously by-passing commodification, where people are still organically rooted in their landscape. What ultimately bothers him is, therefore, simply the fact that the actual Slovenia does not want to behave according to his private myth, and thus disturbs the balance of his artistic universe.

If an artist proceeds like this, the affair is still manageable—Handke himself entitled his recent booklet on Slovenia *Dreamer's Farewell to the Fairyland*. Problems begin when the same logic takes over in politics where, for a long time past, "Balkan" is one of the privileged sites of phantasmic investments. Gilles Deleuze said somewhere: *si vous êtes pris dans le rêve de l'autre, vous êtes foutu*— if you are caught in another's dream, you are lost. In former Yugoslavia, we are lost not because of our primitive dreams and myths preventing us from speaking the enlightened language of Europe, but because we pay in flesh the price for being the stuff the Other's dreams are made of. The fantasy which has organized the perception of former Yugoslavia is that of "Balkan" as the Other of the West: the place of savage ethnic conflicts long overcome by the civilized Europe, the place where nothing is forgotten and nothing learned, where old traumas are being replayed again and again, where symbolic links are simultaneously devalued (dozens of cease-fires broken) and over-valued (primitive warrior's notions of honor and pride). Against this background, a multitude of myths flourished. For the "democratic left," Tito's Yugoslavia was the mirage of the "third way" of self-management beyond capitalism and state-socialism; for the cultured literati it was the exotic land of refreshing folkloric diversity (the films of Makavejev and Kusturica); for Milan Kundera, the place where the idyll of Mitteleuropa meets oriental barbarism; for the Western Realpolitiker of the late eighties, the disintegration of Yugoslavia functioned as a metaphor for what might arrive in the Soviet Union; for France and Great Britain, it resuscitated the phantom of the German fourth Reich perturbing the delicate balance of European politics; behind all of it lurked the primordial trauma of Sarajevo, of the Balkans as the gunpowder threatening to blow up all of Europe. Far from being the Other of Europe, former Yugoslavia was rather Europe itself in its Otherness, the screen onto which Europe projected its own repressed reverse.

Regarding this gaze of Europe on the Balkans, we recall Hegel's dictum that Evil does not reside in the object perceived as bad, but in the innocent gaze which perceives Evil all around. The principal obstacle to peace in former Yugoslavia is not "archaic ethnic passions," but the innocent gaze of Europe fascinated by the spectacle of these passions. Against today's journalistic commonplace about the Balkans as the madhouse of thriving nationalisms where rational rules of behavior are suspended, one must point out again and again that the moves of every political agent in former Yugoslavia, reprehensible as they may be, are totally rational within the goals they want to attain—the only exception, the only truly irrational factor in it, is the gaze of the West, babbling about archaic ethnic passions.

Old ethnic hatreds, of course, are far from being simply imagined: they are a historical legacy. Nevertheless, the key question is why they exploded at precisely this moment, not earlier or later. There is one simple answer to it: the political crisis in Serbia. The determining factor of the Yugoslav tragedy is the survival of the old power structure (the Communist bureaucracy, the Federal Army) in Serbia and Montenegro: it succeeded in prolonging its domination by putting on nationalist clothes. The moment a truly democratic overture was to take place in Serbia, the flames of "centennial passions" would extinguish themselves in a couple of weeks.

It may seem that now the Serbian game is over, that the West "finally got it" and put the blame on the true culprit. The true desire of the West is nevertheless discernible in innumerable telltale details: the continuous compulsive search for stains also on the other side, with the aim to establish a kind of balance of guilt where "everybody is equally mad," where the equals sign is placed between the aggressor and its victim; the centering of attention on humanitarian problems (who will receive the flood of refugees?) which not only treats the conflict as if it were a kind of natural disaster, but also helps the Serbs in carrying out their program of "ethnic cleansing" in a more human way; the invention of ever new excuses against the military intervention (the Balkan countryside as the ideal ground for a prolonged guerrilla warfare); the ridiculous rejection of the desperate Bosnian plea to be allowed to buy arms and thus defend itself, characterized as "pouring oil on the flames." Suffice it to quote *Time*: "Western weaponry would probably not be useful to Bosnians without special training . . ."—the blatant racism of it strikes the eye. How come Serbs in Bosnia can handle sophisticated weaponry, including MIG fighter planes? How come the same problem did not prevent the United States from arming anti-Communist rebels in Afghanistan?

All the talk about the need for more severe measures to stop the Serbian "ethnic cleansing" continues to serve the purpose of precisely putting off the actual implementation of these measures. Consequently, there is no need for psychoanalytic theories of the "death drive" to understand the atrocities actually going on in Bosnia; the proper object for a psychoanalytic approach is rather the hysterical split that characterizes the attitude of the West, the uncanny antagonism between its "official" politics (preventing the Serbian "ethnic cleansing") and its "true desire" (to allow the Serbs to finish their work and then, after the fait accompli, to impose peace). In all probability, the West follows the geopolitical estimation according to which there will be no peace in the Balkans without a satisfied Serbia—the interests of all other parties can be sacrificed, only Serbia must be allowed to save face.

"Honorable exit for Serbia" is the secret obsession of the West today.

Meanwhile, all of Bosnia continues to linger on "between the two deaths": still alive, yet already written off, treated as a kind of political AIDS-patient, stigmatized as a mad place where people kill each other for the sheer pleasure of doing it. Are we to blame them if, in the end, they will become "Muslim fundamentalists" and resort to desperate "terrorist" measures?

The Blue River

Mak Dizdar

No one knows where it is
We know little but it is known

Behind the mountain behind the valley
Behind seven behind eight

And even further and even worse
Over the bitter over the torturous

Over the hawthorne over the corpse
Over the summer heat over the oppression

Beyond foreboding beyond doubt
Behind nine behind ten

And even deeper and even stronger
Through silence through darkness

Where the roosters do not sing
Where the sound of horn is not heard

And even worse and even madder
Beyond sense beyond God

There is one blue river
It is wide it is deep

A hundred years wide
A thousand years deep

About the length do not even think
Jetsam and flotsam unmending

There is one blue river

There is one blue river
We must cross the river

Translated by Vasa Mihailovich

PART IV

I was born in Goražde, on the Drina, in 1889. There I spent my childhood. I swam in the Drina and, during those years, collected within my eyes the glittering light of the sun that glowed from the skies and the round stones along Drina's banks. The house of my parents was first on the waterfront, but, after several floods, we moved it to higher ground, to the foot of a hill.

The river could be seen from the new location. I climbed to all the high hills, screamed with the other children, both Muslim and Christian. I grew with them. We fought, bloodied each other's heads, but it was as if we all belonged to the same mother and father. We ate cakes on Passover, round flour cakes on Bayram, and pretzels on Easter.

Cheerful, full of the sun, rosy-cheeked, I loved a little girl, though I was myself only a child. I took that last spring, which was bright, full of birds, flowers, blossoms; full of Drina, wooded groves, forests, songs; full of games, laughter, and the good eyes of my love, to Sarajevo where my soul was torn at once, since I could not find my bearings in the city. Since then, I am constantly rising to my feet and falling. But all of that sun, all those songs, all those smiles, are still flowing out of my eyes whenever I am happy . . .

—From an autobiographical text by Isak Samokovlija,
   a Jewish prosaist from Goražde, 1928

Here lies
The soldier Gorčin
In his land
Inherited by
A stranger

—MAK DIZDAR

The Destruction of
Bosnia-Hercegovina

Branka Magaš

T HE YEAR 1992, scheduled to be a milestone on the road to European unity, saw Sarajevo and other Bosnian cities bombarded slowly to pieces and their inhabitants starved before the TV eyes of the world. Since April 1992, two million Bosnian Muslims have been threatened with Europe's first genocide since World War II; most of them already driven deliberately from their homes by massacre, rape and terror, thrown into concentration camps or made refugees in their own country or outside it—all in the full knowledge of the outside world. It has been a year which has seen Bosnia's legal, multinational government holed up in Sarajevo, treated as a mere "warring party" and pressed to surrender by Western governments eager for peace at any price. Short-sighted and cynical, divided among themselves, determined to avoid intervention, seeking an eventual accommodation with the military strongman of the Balkans, these governments have settled for "humanitarian" palliatives that amount to little more than prolonging the agony of the victims. These same governments protested loudly about "ethnic cleansing" only when its reality was exposed by their domestic media, months after they had in fact known about it. Above all, they have maintained an embargo on the arms which alone would allow the Bosnian government to repel the aggression, reassert its authority over the whole territory of Bosnia-Hercegovina, and create conditions for the expelled population to return.

It has also been a year which has seen the Western Left largely silent before, or actively complicit with, these crimes: parroting the disinformation so artfully encouraged by their local chancelleries; too indolent or ignorant to distinguish between fact and propaganda; refusing to accept that the war did not just "break out," but was launched as a conscious act of policy by Belgrade; choosing instead to accept the easier, essentially racist, interpretation, facilitated by centuries of world domination, that Balkan—or all Eastern— peoples (frequently referred to as "tribes," almost never as real nations) are somehow genetically programmed for violence and thus all equally to blame for the cataclysm.

But no excuse this time that "We didn't know!" Everybody knows what is happening, so the search is on for reasons to do nothing about it. Nostalgia for the Yugoslavia created by the Partisans, finally buried in June 1991, when a so-called People's Army outside legitimate political control attacked one of the nation states making up the Partisan-created federation—Slovenia. A repugnance for nationalism that makes no distinction between mobilization behind an expansionary chauvinist project and mobilization in defense of national sovereignty under military attack. Resentment of Germany, ignobly fostered for their own petty purposes by now weaker postimperial powers like Britain and France, and yet more ignobly echoed on the social democratic and even Marxist left. Fetishization of supra-national states in the East by the very people who fear them like poison in the West. Above all, perhaps, cynical indifference to the democratic rights of other peoples, which can be airily traded away for this or that ephemeral tactical or pragmatic consideration borrowed from the instrumentarium of their own governments: "Why couldn't they have waited?" "It was all the fault of the Germans, pressing for recognition," "Bosnia-Hercegovina was never viable as an independent state," "Ethnic cleansing is dreadful, but they all do it, you know," "Once the lid came off . . . old ethnic passions . . . goes back to World War II . . . goes back centuries . . . warring factions . . . competing nationalisms . . ."—the siren dehumanizing litany is unending.

And yet, there is another voice with which the Left can respond to events such as those which have been unfolding in former Yugoslavia. It did not, after all, get things quite so wrong in the former Soviet Union, when for the most part—despite its hopes that Gorbachev would succeed in negotiating some new common arrangement—it responded to the August Coup (in which Belgrade had incidentally invested high hopes) with a basic recognition that unity enforced by brute military might was a far worse option than acceptance of break-up. Until the attack on Slovenia, it was permissible to hope against hope that the Yugoslav federation might somehow be saved. After June 27, 1991, however, a new and different commitment was necessary: to the future viability of the legitimate successor states of the former Yugoslavia—a future that offers the best, indeed only, hope of a democratic development for all the peoples of what was once a far-from-artificial state, born of a genuine revolution, which was not fated to disintegrate but has nevertheless been destroyed.

FOR YUGOSLAVIA, TITO'S death in 1980 marked a point of no return. Despite the fact that his death was to be the occasion for an authentic outpouring of Yugoslav patriotism, the country had already entered a period of dramatic and potentially disintegrative change. Yugoslavia now stood at a crossroad. One path led toward democratization, the other toward repression. Which path would be taken? The forces favoring the second soon showed their hand: in 1981 in Kosovo, where force was used against student-led demonstrations, and then in 1984 in Belgrade, where intellectuals were put on trial for taking part in unofficial debating societies. Subsequent events proved, however, that

the decentralization upon which the country had embarked in the more optimistic 1960s—embodied in the country's 1974 constitution—precluded the
federal Party and state organs from acting as effective instruments for conservative reaction, spearheaded as it then was by active or retired army and police
chiefs. Though that decentralization—a devolution of powers to the republics
and provinces—had not been accompanied by any significant loosening of the
ruling party's monopoly of political initiative, it did allow a greater public air-
ing of differences between the constituent states, hence also of alternative
views within those states. If Yugoslavia was to be united on a neo-conservative
platform, it would first have to be recentralized.

The neo-conservative project changed radically with the capture of
power in Serbia by Great Serb nationalists. In the mid 1980s, Belgrade was to
become the headquarters simultaneously of a new Yugoslav unitarism and of
a "Serb national renewal." The history of Yugoslavia appeared now to be running backwards: the more the Serb nationalists embraced the cause of
"Yugoslavia," the more anti-federal that Yugoslavia of theirs became—and,
inevitably, the greater the resistance to it in other parts of the country.
National co-existence would henceforth be threatened not only by power
struggles within the institutions of the federal state, but by the readiness of the
new Serbian regime headed by Slobodan Milošević to use extra-legal means—
mass mobilization on an ethnic basis—to bring down the 1974 constitution.

The aim was not just a return to the pre-1974 situation, but a complete
revision of the postwar settlement based on the principle of national equality.
What Belgrade sought was nothing less than the destruction of the federal
arrangement—in the name of a "strong federation"! By proclaiming its right
to speak in the name not only of Serbia but of all Serbs in Yugoslavia, by seeking to redefine internal borders as purely administrative, and by erasing the
autonomy of the provinces, the Belgrade regime negated the very foundations
of the second, federal Yugoslavia. Milošević thus emerged as the spokesman
not just for a conservative backlash, but for counter-revolution in the Yugoslav
lands. What is more, this counter-revolution was armed and ready, if defied,
to resort to war. Serbia's annexation of Kosovo and Vojvodina was the first case
in postwar Europe of alteration (obliteration) of recognized political borders
by force. By the end of the 1980s—before multiparty elections ever took
place—it had become clear that, unless Milošević was stopped, Yugoslavia was
doomed either to become a Greater Serbia or to fall apart.

The method used by Milošević to mobilize a Serb nationalist force capable
of destroying the federal order was relatively simple. Systematic recourse was made
to Stalin's old trick of creating enemies against whom mass anger could be turned.
Albanians, "bureaucrats," Vojvodina "autonomists," Slovenes, Croats, and "Muslim Fundamentalists" were denounced in succession as enemies of Serbia and
Yugoslavia. By the end of the process, the list had been broadened to include Germany (because of its support for Slovenia and Croatia), the European Community
(EC) (because of its decision to accept the dissolution of Yugoslavia), and the
Americans (because of their support for Bosnia-Hercegovina).

A brief resumé of events since 1987, the year in which Milošević won untrammeled power in Serbia, demonstrates a clear pattern of anti-federal campaigns. First, anti-Albanian sentiment was fanned by the Belgrade mass media, while Serbia's intellectual elite grouped in the Academy of Arts and Sciences and the Writers' Association—fresh from drafting a new national program for a "Greater Serbia" (the notorious 1986 Memorandum)—set about organizing a rebellion of the Serb minority in Kosovo against Albanian majority rule. The Kosovo issue was then used (at the climactic Eighth Session of the Serbian Party's Central Committee meeting in the autumn of 1987) to eliminate the more constitutionally-minded wing of the Party loyal to the republican president, Ivan Stambolić. A so-called "anti-bureaucratic revolution" was set in motion designed to extend Milošević's power across all Yugoslavia. After he felt strong enough to directly attack the Vojvodina Party and state leaders, accusing them of being "autonomists" (i.e. against Serbian state unity), they were brought down in October 1988 by a carefully organized "spontaneous" mass mobilization, after which the Vojvodina Party too was purged. Kosovo, Serbia's other province, proved a tougher nut to crack, since the Albanian population rose as one in November 1988 and February 1989, defending not so much their leaders as their hard-won national rights enshrined in the province's autonomy. Although the mass demonstrations were peaceful, the province was immediately placed under a state of emergency: the federal state voted for this measure for fear of Serbia's forces marching into the province on their own. Mass pressure was also brought to bear on the Montenegrin Party and state leadership, which was forced to resign from office in January 1989.

As a result of this march through the institutions, by 1989 Serbia had acquired control of four out of eight votes on the federal state presidency, five out of nine votes on the federal Party presidency. These bodies were thus completely paralyzed.

Why did Milošević's opponents remain passive in the face of his challenge? Their main problem was that from the onset he protected his flank by seeking support among Party hard-liners throughout the country—both in the federal establishment (the army, in particular) and in other republics—on a neo-conservative program: insistence on "democratic centralism," in their minds the *sine qua non* of Party and state unity; rejection of all forms of political pluralism or, of course, economic reform (the two republics most strongly associated with such "deviations" were Slovenia and Croatia). More generally, the federal and other republican leaders made a cardinal mistake in treating the purges in Serbia as an internal Serbian affair, since once accomplished they served to free Milošević from any all-Yugoslav political constraint.

The federal Party and state were already in deep crisis over a multitude of questions which the Thirteenth Congress (held in 1986) had done nothing to resolve. The disarray of the ruling party became evident at its 1988 all-Yugoslav Conference, which brought to public attention the existence of two main ideological fronts within it: one represented by Milošević, the other by the Slovene leader Milan Kučan. Kučan sought a reform of inner-party life guaranteeing minority rights. This Slovene demand, however, was denounced, in a manner reminiscent of Brezhnev's doctrine of limited sovereignty, as an attack on Party unity and a first step toward the disintegration of Yugoslavia, since it would have meant recognizing the right of each republic to follow its own "path to socialism." Kučan understood that the "anti-bureaucratic revolution" would not stop at Serbia's borders, but could also engulf Slovenia. Since Milošević (like Mao before him) used "spontaneous" mass rallies to hammer his opponents, the intraparty dispute acquired the dimensions of an inter-national struggle: the Serbian masses were now encouraged to denounce the Slovene leaders as enemies equally of Serbia, of all Serbs, and of Yugoslavia. The anti-Slovene campaign drew its strength also from the fact that 1988 saw the beginning of what became known as the "Slovene Spring": a growing democratization of political life, characterized in particular by the emergence of so-called "alternative movements." This democratic cancer was not going to be tolerated by Milošević and the army.

In October 1988, at the height of the purges in Vojvodina and after the first unsuccessful attempt to bring down the Montenegrin leadership, the seventeenth plenum of the Yugoslav Party's Central Committee took place. The split now simultaneously deepened and broadened. The representatives of Slovenia, Croatia, Bosnia-Hercegovina, Kosovo (in what turned out to be their swan song), and partly Macedonia tried to persuade the Serbian side that Yugoslav and Party unity could not be built by force. Belgrade, for its part, rejected all charges of "unitarism," "hegemonic aspirations," or wishing to create a "Greater Serbia." In a desperate attempt to preserve Party unity, the federal leaders sat on the fence. However, the fall of the Montenegrin leadership in January 1989 proved beyond all doubt that Milošević was indeed intent on exporting the "anti-bureaucratic revolution," and that the republics would accordingly have to protect themselves. Milošević's next planned provocation—a threat to hold a big rally of Serb nationalists in Ljubljana, Slovenia's capital city, in March 1989—was met by a stiffening of Slovene resistance. In February 1989, a large meeting took place in Ljubljana in solidarity with a strike of Albanian miners at the Stari Trg mine in Kosovo. At the meeting, Kučan declared that the miners were defending Yugoslavia as created in the revolutionary war of 1941–1945. When the Serb militants tried to enter Slovenia, the Slovene authorities banned the rally and sent a message that they would be stopped by force at the Slovene border. Serbia responded by imposing a boycott of Slovene goods. It was at this juncture, it seems, that Milošević opted for a war with Slovenia.

Once Kosovo had been crushed and Vojvodina and Montenegro swallowed up, the resistance to Milošević was inevitably led by Slovenia and Croatia, whence came a first strategic counter-offensive in the decision taken in the winter of 1989 to hold multiparty elections in the following April. The final parting of the ways between pro-Milošević and anti-Milošević forces took place in February-March 1990, at the Fourteenth Congress of the League of Communists of Yugoslavia—a congress which was also its last. The disintegration of the

LCY was followed by multiparty elections throughout the country, in which Communists (albeit under a new name) won only in Serbia and Montenegro.

Yugoslavia thus did not die a natural death: it was destroyed for the sake of a Greater Serbia. With the army on his side, Milošević felt confident of victory. What Serbia had failed to gain in two Balkan Wars and two World Wars suddenly seemed within reach. The nation was seemingly united behind the counter-revolutionary project—which had been formulated, indeed, by its most eminent intellectuals. It is difficult to underestimate the role this self-confidence played in Yugoslavia's disintegration. The armed counter-revolution rejected all compromise solutions that might have kept the country together. After the elections, Slovenia and Croatia, flanked by Macedonia and Bosnia-Hercegovina, offered Serbia a confederal compromise, that is, the transformation of Yugoslavia into an association of sovereign states. The offer was rejected out of hand. The Great Serb bloc stood firm, believing that the army would deliver whatever it wished. Slovenia was allowed to go, after a brief military incursion in June 1991, by mutual consent. But neither Croatia nor Bosnia-Hercegovina were allowed to leave and would be squeezed to relinquish as much of their territories as the army could hold. As the war that began in earnest in August 1991 progressed, the contours of the projected, racially homogeneous "Greater Serbia" became increasingly visible.

WHAT THE GREAT Serb bloc underestimated, however, was the readiness of Yugoslavia's constituent nations to defend themselves. In dismissing this factor of the people's war, the Serbian-dominated army made its biggest mistake. Neither in Slovenia nor in Croatia nor in Bosnia-Hercegovina was the aggression to be the anticipated walkover, despite the defenders' lack of arms. In Croatia, Serbia's great military advantage led to occupation of one third of the republic's territory, but failed nevertheless to achieve Belgrade's minimal strategic goals: the establishment of a physical link between the disparate parts of the so-called Serb Krajina; and the capture of a coastline commensurate with Serbia's ambition to become an Adriatic power. Each defeat suffered by the Serbian armies, however, served only to increase their destructive determination. The very fact that Croatia survived and received international recognition ensured that the onslaught on Bosnia-Hercegovina, when it came, would be that much more bloody and devastating.

Whereas in Croatia the war gradually built up from local Serb "uprisings" in the summer of 1990 to a full-scale war in the summer of 1991, Serbia's aggression against Bosnia-Hercegovina took the form of a blitzkrieg. In Croatia, "ethnic cleansing" was to produce some 300,000 refugees in the course of one and a half years; in the case of Bosnia-Hercegovina, the victims of the same policy on a larger scale numbered almost two million within six months. A U.S. Senate report estimated that during this period as many as thirty five thousand people were killed in Bosnia as a result of "ethnic cleansing" alone. In Croatia, Serbia fought the war ostensibly to defend a Serb minority threatened by a "fascist regime." No such pretext was possible in the case of Bosnia-Hercegovina, where Serbs were not a minority but one of three formally recognized constituent nations. The Bosnian elections of November 1990 produced an assembly in which Serbs were represented in numbers reflecting their weight in the population as a whole. A government was formed with appropriate Serb representation. Despite this, the war against Bosnia-Hercegovina was from the start waged with one aim only: complete destruction of the republic. It was here that the "Great Serbian" project was finally to reveal fully its true criminal nature.

The preparations for the assault on Bosnia-Hercegovina followed a pattern already set in Croatia. Once again a Serb Democratic Party (SDS) was set up which, prior to the elections of November 1990, immediately proceeded to declare itself sole representative of Bosnian Serbs, who were to be viewed as part of a seamless Serb nation. A Serb National Assembly and Serb National Council were set up in Banja Luka in October 1990, as sovereign legislative and executive bodies wholly independent from Sarajevo. From October 1990 to December 1991, the SDS was busy consolidating this structure (including its police and armed forces) and demarcating new internal borders in Bosnia-Hercegovina. Six so-called Serb Autonomous Regions (SAOs) had been established by the end of this process: Bosanska Krajina, Northern Bosnia, Northeastern Bosnia, Romanija, Hercegovina, and Old Hercegovina. These were then proclaimed parts of a "Serb Republic of Bosnia-Hercegovina," later renamed the "Serb Republic." Many non-Serb areas found themselves included in this self-proclaimed mono-ethnic state. The first aim of Serbian military operations in Bosnia-Hercegovina was subsequently to be the establishment of corridors between the different SAOs, cleared of all non-Serb population.

As the political arm of Serbia's impending aggression against Bosnia-Hercegovina, the SDS acted throughout the crucial 1991 escalation of war to prevent all moves the Bosnian government might make to save the republic. The elections had produced a coalition government and state presidency made up of representatives of the three main parties—the SDS, the Muslim-based Party of Democratic Action (SDA), and the Croatian Democratic Union (HDZ). These three parties between them controlled 86 percent of National Assembly seats (72, 86, and 44 respectively, out of a total of 240). Thanks to the obstructionist policy of the SDS, the new administration found itself unable to take any strategic decisions regarding the republic's future. The National Assembly came to be de facto divided between two blocs of uneven size. The majority bloc, composed of deputies belonging to the SDA, the HDZ, and most of the smaller parties, wished Bosnia-Hercegovina to become a sovereign state within Yugoslavia, or failing that, an independent state. The minority, made up of the SDS and its satellite parties, wanted the republic either to join Serbia en bloc (with some "federal" facade) or to be broken up. Again, no compromise was possible. Thus, in February 1991, the SDS turned down a proposal by the SDA (supported by the HDZ) to adopt a declaration giving the Bosnian legislature precedence over the "federal" one, now controlled by Serbia.

As in other republics, the departing Communist administration had introduced constitutional amendments designed to enhance the republic's integrity and sovereignty. In October 1991, the National Assembly adopted a draft Memorandum confirming these constitutional amendments. Though falling short of a declaration of independence, the Memorandum affirmed the inviolability of the republic's borders, while expressing support for a Yugoslavia made up of sovereign states. The SDS deputies walked out before the vote was taken. Their leader, Radovan Karadžić, warned not only that Bosnian sovereignty could not be achieved without Serb consent (which in any case would not be forthcoming), but also that insistence on sovereignty was leading the republic "into a hell in which the Muslims will perhaps perish."

For the Bosnian leaders, however, defining the republic's status was an urgent political matter, given that the EC-sponsored conference on Yugoslavia was about to begin. It was also a matter of trying to keep Bosnia-Hercegovina out of the war already raging in Croatia. Adoption of the Memorandum provided an occasion to declare Bosnian neutrality in this war—although, in reality, the army had from the start been using the territory under SDS control as a base for its war in Croatia. Strive as the National Assembly might to distance itself from the war, Bosnian integrity was more and more called into question.

The National Assembly's affirmation of sovereignty was immediately followed by the SDS's proclamation of a separate Serb state—the so-called Serb Republic of Bosnia-Hercegovina. Proclamation of the Serb Republic was followed by local HDZ leaders establishing two so-called Croat Communities, one in the north (Community of the Sava Valley) and one in the south (Herceg-Bosna). Although these Croat communities did not at first have the formal state structures characteristic of those set up by the SDS, the intention behind them was unmistakable: the Sarajevo government would be recognized only as long as it retained its independence from the former or any future Yugoslavia. At the same time, the Bosnian HDZ leadership (supported by most Bosnian Croats and nearly all Croatian parties) denounced these moves toward an effective division of Bosnia-Hercegovina.

Whereas Serbia never hid its territorial ambitions in regard to Bosnia-Hercegovina, Croatia's position was more ambiguous. While it did not initiate the war in the neighboring republic, it could hardly fail to disregard the fate of the latter's considerable Croat population, or Bosnia's geostrategic importance for its own destiny, in circumstances in which it was still the victim of Serbian aggression and Bosnia was about to become so too. In any case, Croatia's president, Franjo Tudjman, made clear quite early on that he believed neither in the likely survival of Bosnia-Hercegovina, nor in its historical legitimacy in the event of Yugoslavia's disintegration into national states. The logical solution, he claimed, was to partition the republic between Croatia and Serbia. This, however, infringed upon the very principle of the inviolability of Yugoslavia's internal borders upon which Croatia rested its own case for the return of its occupied territories! Unlike its Serbian counterpart, the Croatian regime was hampered, moreover, by the fact that the idea of dividing Bosnia-Hercegovina remained deeply unpopular in Croatia. In trying to square this particular circle, Croat officials followed the SDS in proposing "cantonization" of Bosnia-Hercegovina on an ethnic basis. The SDS had justified the creation of the six SAOs on the grounds that, in a centrally-run republic, Serbs would become an oppressed minority. Under Zagreb's influence, parts of the Bosnian HDZ now accepted the same logic. The EC too, to its eternal discredit, encouraged this "ethnically based" program—in whose name it has subsequently sought to qualify the Bosnian government's legitimacy.

The ethnic dispersion within Bosnia-Hercegovina, of course, makes the idea of cantonization on an ethnic basis dangerous nonsense. According to the 1981 census, out of 109 municipalities in Bosnia-Hercegovina, 35 had a Muslim absolute majority, 32 a Serb absolute majority, and 14 a Croat absolute majority (in several of these, moreover, the Serb or Muslim predominance was a matter of a few percentage points). A further 15 municipalities had a relative Muslim majority, 5 a relative Serb majority, and 7 a relative Croat majority. Since the combined population of these latter 27 municipalities in which no nationality could claim an absolute majority was about 1.7 million, it was clear that in order to create cantons with absolute national majorities an enormous proportion of Bosnia-Hercegovina's inhabitants would have to be uprooted and resettled. Cantonization, in other words, involved not just civil war, but destruction of the very identity of the Bosnian state created by the coexistence of the three nationalities. This is why the idea of cantonization was rejected by all Bosnian Muslims, by a majority of Bosnian Croats, probably by most Serbs in Bosnia's major cities, and by an unknown number of Serbs in areas under SDS control. Zagreb's acceptance of the principle of cantonization was divisive and would gravely imperil the defense of Bosnia-Hercegovina. Although Croatia repeatedly denied all territorial ambitions in regard to its neighbors, recognized Bosnia-Hercegovina within its borders, accepted half a million Bosnian refugees, helped generally with humanitarian relief, and provided the essential military supply route and rear base for Bosnia's armed resistance, the fact of its support for cantonization of the republic made it in this respect an objective accomplice of the regime in Belgrade.

Running against the clock, the Bosnian government was forced to give up appeasing Belgrade and the SDS. With EC recognition of Croatia and Slovenia in the air, on December 20, 1991, it, too, asked that it be recognized as an independent state. The SDS leaders proclaimed this decision to be null and void, warned again that one nation would "disappear" if the idea of Bosnian independence was not abandoned, and announced that, in the event of independence being granted, the "Serb Republic" would become "part of the federal state of Yugoslavia." Following the recognition of Croatia and Slovenia on January 15, 1992, the EC arbitration commission invited the Bosnian government to hold a referendum on the issue of independence, as a condition of recognition. On January 25 the SDA and HDZ deputies, supported by most of the smaller opposition parties, approved the holding of such a referendum under international supervision. The question submitted to the electorate on the weekend of March 1 was: "Are you in favor of a sovereign and independent Bosnia-Hercegovina, a state of equal citizens and nations of Muslims, Serbs, Croats, and others who live in it?" Almost two thirds of the population voted in favor. The Serbian army struck the day after Bosnia-Hercegovina was recognized as an independent state.

Was it right, in view of the attitude of the Serb Democratic Party—for which the majority of Bosnian Serbs had voted a year earlier, and which could thus claim to speak on their behalf—for the Bosnian government to seek independence? The fact is that the republic had no other choice. The alternative of joining a "Greater Serbia" was not simply unpalatable to the majority of its population—it entailed the disappearance of Bosnia as a state. What is more, the SDS certainly did not have any mandate for waging war against Bosnia in order to prevent its independence. Indeed, whatever legitimacy the SDS may have had at the beginning of this process, its participation in the terrible crimes committed against the people of Bosnia-Hercegovina has denied it all right to speak in the name of any part of it.

THE BOSNIAN STATE, however, was totally unprepared for war. The weapons of its Territorial Defense forces had been confiscated by the army prior to the elections. Its government had, in addition, been persuaded by the EC and the United States to allow in huge quantities of military personnel and armor leaving Slovenia and Croatia. (Although Zagreb had repeatedly asked of the EC mediators that heavy armor and tanks located in garrisons in Croatia be left there under international control, the West had insisted that they be allowed to depart for Bosnia-Hercegovina.) In moving toward independence, the Bosnian government clearly hoped for (and must indeed have been promised) international protection against aggression. Once war came, however, the EC countries and the United States accepted no responsibility for the country's defense. The same arms embargo which had given Belgrade's forces such an advantage in Croatia was maintained to still more catastrophic effect in Bosnia, directly contributing to the human and material devastation visited upon the republic by the amply equipped Serbian blitzkrieg. Bosnia-Hercegovina duly became a member of the United Nations, but its legitimate—and multinational—government was now increasingly treated as a mere "warring faction," or reduced to its Muslim component. Western rhetoric here accurately reflected Western policy, for although Bosnia-Hercegovina had fulfilled the conditions set by the EC for international recognition, the West subsequently bowed to Serbian pressure by conditioning that recognition upon Sarajevo's acceptance of cantonization. When, in the summer of 1992, the link between cantonization and "ethnic cleansing" became only too obvious, under pressure from Western public opinion, the idea was put on ice—but only temporarily. In the winter of 1992–1993, it was resuscitated with a vengeance in the guise of the Vance-Owen "peace" plan.

The schizophrenic split between high principle and shabby pragmatism characteristic of Western policy toward Croatia—leading to a settlement that seems intended to reward aggression and condemn the refugees to indefinite exile—was to acquire quite morbid proportions in relation to the far greater tragedy of Bosnia-Hercegovina. The West indeed condemned Serbia as the chief culprit of the war. It imposed economic sanctions on the self-proclaimed "Federal Republic of Yugoslavia" (made up of Serbia and Montenegro), yet did little to enforce their observance. It, indeed, denounced the Serbian policy of ethnic cleansing, the shelling of cities, the creation of concentration camps; yet the perpetrators of these crimes have regularly been welcomed in European capitals and treated as legitimate participants in the "peace process." The West has decried Serbia's and Croatia's annexationist ambitions, yet continues to press ahead with cantonization. Its appeasement of Belgrade's military power and de facto endorsement of its racialist logic have openly invited Zagreb to go down the same criminal—and suicidal—road: the Croat-Muslim hostilities that have threatened to spiral out of control since March 1993 in central Bosnia can be directly traced to the ethnic maps of Vance and Owen. The West pays lip-service to the integrity of the Bosnian state, yet by maintaining the arms embargo denies it the means to defend that integrity. By allowing Serbia to destroy much of Bosnia-Hercegovina, and by ignoring the difference between the victim and the assailant, the West became an active participant in Serbia's aggression.

What the West has always refused to do is acknowledge the singular character of Milošević's regime—a racially-based, proto-fascist formation that can survive only by creating new sources of war and conflict. The war it is waging in Bosnia-Hercegovina is a war not just for territories, but for territories devoid of population. The primary target of Serbia's blitzkrieg has not been objects of military significance, but the population itself. This is why the war has taken the form of mass terror. The aggression, moreover, is being conducted not just against the living people, but against their whole historic presence in the area, embodied in the architecture of cities and villages, in churches and graveyards, in archives and academic institutions, in museums and galleries. The scorched-earth policy practiced by Serbia in Bosnia-Hercegovina aims to create a tabula rasa, a new zero point in the history of this part of Europe. The genocide being conducted today against the Muslim population of Bosnia-Hercegovina, and the destruction of a unique society based on the centuries-long co-existence of different nations and religions, amount to a crime against humanity. How could this be allowed to happen in peacetime Europe?

Yet Bosnia lives. Despite the cataclysm that has engulfed it, Bosnia-Hercegovina has not surrendered. Its multinational government continues somehow to function. Sarajevo, under daily bombardment, continues to resist. The Bosnian defense forces still contain Muslims, Croats, and Serbs. Short of weapons and logistical support, in many places they have been resorting to forms of guerrilla struggle reminiscent of the Partisan war. Bosnia needs outside help, of that there can be no doubt; yet its strength lies in its own determination to survive. It does not even need to win the war outright.

Bosnia's mere survival means that the Great Serb project has no future, entailing inevitable repercussions in Serbia itself.

One can expect, however, that the Serbian regime, frustrated in Bosnia-Hercegovina but not thoroughly defeated there either, will be tempted to open up another theater of war, most obviously in Kosovo, and then Macedonia, which will then become the next victims of Serbian military aggression and "ethnic cleansing." The extension of war into Kosovo and Macedonia would inevitably draw in neighboring states. Thus, the more comprehensive the defeat for Serbian expansion in the present war, the better the chance of avoiding its successors.

IN THE EARLY 1980s, it was still possible to hope that the Yugoslav Federation, with its "system of socialist self-management," might be saved from disintegration through reform; that, under the pressure of an increasingly combative working class, an alliance of forces of progress could be forged, including reform-minded members of the League of Communists and democratic elements from among the intelligentsia and enterprise management. This would have been the "organic" way out, shedding the layers of Stalinist inheritance and corrupt bureaucratic rule in favor of political pluralism and economic reconstruction. It was clear from the outset that such an undertaking could succeed only as an all-Yugoslav effort, building on initiatives in each of the republics and provinces to produce a new vision of the country's future. There remained in the mind's eye the achievement of the Communist-led all-Yugoslav national and social revolution, still only one generation away. This was a scenario which *mutatis mutandis* the Left—whether conceiving it as social revolution, political revolution, or reformist evolution—at this time embraced not only for Yugoslavia, but also for the other countries of Eastern Europe. If it were to succeed anywhere, it would surely do so in Yugoslavia.

But, of course, Yugoslavia could not be isolated from events elsewhere. The political leadership necessary for the Yugoslav working class to assert itself as the primary subject of a positive social transformation could have been created only as part of a wider continental shift to the Left. This, after all, is what was happening in the late 1960s and early 1970s. By the 1980s, however, the continent was moving steadily to the right. The suppression and disintegration of the Solidarity movement in Poland—a movement initially supported by millions of workers—was to change the parameters of Yugoslav politics as well. Within the country, the working class ceased to be perceived as the force that might credibly deliver the final blow to an increasingly moribund system. The era of struggle for parliamentary democracy had arrived. Political vocabularies changed to suit local circumstances: in the Yugoslav west, "comrades" became "citizens"; in the east, *narodna volja* ["people's will"] replaced "working class interests."

Weakened by the dramatic fall in its living standards and by escalating unemployment; unprepared for the loss of self-confidence of the system that had produced it; confused by its growing realization that the party which still ruled the country in its name had abandoned it, the all-Yugoslav working class was only just taking its first steps toward political independence when crisis engulfed the country's entire superstructure. Belgrade-based counter-revolution now imposed a different agenda. Political struggle became inescapably focused on the defense of basic national and democratic rights. In Kosovo, miners spearheaded a general strike in defense of the province's autonomy, while in Serbia, workers were being mobilized behind chauvinist banners for a final assault on that same autonomy. A Yugoslav communist or democratic party unable to defend the miners, and a federal state unable to defend Kosovo, could not but break up.

In a multinational state like Yugoslavia, democracy—whatever its class basis—was inextricably bound up with a commitment to, and institutional safeguards for, equality between the constituent nations. An all-Yugoslav movement for democratic reform could have been built only within such parameters. Serbia, however, turned out to be the weak link; at the country's vital hour, it failed Yugoslavia and thus sealed its fate.

It can be argued that Yugoslavia, as a state, contained too many contradictions, especially in the field of economic development, to survive. The capitalist class emerging in the area at the beginning of the twentieth century favored Yugoslavia for economic reasons: the creation of a large and protected market. Yet the unequal economic development of the individual nations made a common economic policy always a matter of political contestation. Concentration of economic power at the Yugoslav center always led to concentration of political power as well, which in practice meant Serbian domination. Decentralization, on the other hand, not only provoked Serbian resistance but also fed centrifugal tendencies in the country as a whole. In this sense, therefore, one might argue that Yugoslavia came into existence too soon—well before the point at which its viability and stability could have become a natural concomitant of the area's economic growth. Yet the very fact that Yugoslavia did come into existence, not once but twice, suggests that there has always been a need for some sort of economic and political cooperation throughout the area. One thing is certain, however. If and when this need once again finds expression, it will not take the form of a common state. Yugoslavia's historical time has run out. But, unlike the war that has accompanied it, the break-up of Yugoslavia does not have to be seen as a tragedy. Once the Great Serb project has been defeated, allowing peace to return to the lands that once formed Yugoslavia, this need will seek and find its own channels and forms.

LETTER FROM SERBIA

"Greater Serbia" and Its Discontents

STOJAN CEROVIĆ

THE IDEA, "ALL Serbs in one state," is principally to blame for the war in Bosnia-Hercegovina, the brutality of which has horrified the world. It was this demand upon which Slobodan Milošević, the president of Serbia, obstinately insisted two years ago, during the course of crucial negotiations held to secure a peaceful resolution of the crisis. The leaders of the other republics of former Yugoslavia had proposed various solutions and compromises. The proposals outlined by Alija Izetbegović, president of Bosnia, and Kiro Gligorov, president of Macedonia, for the creation of a loose confederation of the South Slav republics were not only the most well-known but also the most realistic of all. But Slobodan Milošević sought all or nothing.

At this stage Yugoslavia—a state in which all Serbs lived—still existed, and Milošević formally posed as its defender. This stance by Milošević created great confusion both inside the country and among various foreign observers of the emerging crisis. But it was a stance which reflected a deeper political reality. Before the series of wars against the republics began, a convincing majority of the population favored the preservation of Yugoslavia; it was still an option, represented by the liberal reformist government of Ante Marković. While separatist tendencies were most intense in Slovenia and, in part, in Croatia, neither of these republics would have been in a position to break away, had Marković's government succeeded. At the very most the disaffected republics would have achieved a certain loosening of the federation; and, perhaps, before long, with the success of the reforms, both Slovenia and Croatia would have had little reason to seek further changes in the structure of Yugoslavia.

In 1990 and early 1991, of course, the populace still believed that liberal reforms—privatization, free markets, a multiparty system—would successfully, and with relative ease, replace communism in Eastern Europe. These expectations were at their highest during the days of Ante Marković. However, today as the euphoria aroused by the collapse of the Berlin Wall has subsided, it has become obvious that the collapse of communism has set in motion the destructive energy of old-fashioned nationalism. Therefore, in retrospect, many are now wont to conclude that neither Marković's reforms nor Yugoslavia had any real chance of survival.

Perhaps, there is some truth in such an argument. But in hindsight it is also possible to conclude that the disintegration of Yugoslavia would not have come to pass without a brutal war—of which, toward the end, a despairing Marković had given warning. The West, however, aside from promises, gave no significant support to Marković's reform program, expecting him, instead, to first resolve the internal, inter-republican, inter-ethnic conflicts. Of course, by that stage any resolution was impossible without external assistance. Marković's government was seeking to change a closed and monopolistic system, but wished to do so within the framework of a restructured Yugoslavia; while the republican governments in Serbia, Croatia, and Slovenia had precisely the opposite goal.

PERHAPS MORE THAN any other force it was Serbia which set out to destroy Marković's position and thus brought to an end the last Yugoslav government—proof enough that Milošević was a false champion of Yugoslavia. To many, it had long been obvious that Milošević aspired only to build a so-called "Greater Serbia." From the moment he came to power over five years ago, he began to raise the Serb national question in the context of Kosovo. Since then his political program has been defined only by methods designed to provoke confrontations between national groups. This stance met with swift responses; first in Croatia and Slovenia, and subsequently in Macedonia and among the Muslims in Bosnia.

By its very nature Milošević's political program could not have been considered pro-Yugoslav in any respect because it was not democratic. In a multinational country like Yugoslavia where—with the exception of homogeneous Slovenia—the people from different groups lived so intermingled with one another that minorities existed everywhere, tolerance for and acceptance of the other was an absolute necessity. Today, one might add, the very idea of Yugoslavia was more democratic than the Balkan national states that have come into being with its demise—the supposed objective of their independence being to resolve the national problem. It sounds absurd but Yugoslavia was destroyed precisely in the name of democracy and national liberation. Yet, in this instance a nation's right to self-determination meant the right not to live with other people who are different. The nationalisms emerging in former Yugoslavia are not only undemocratic and intolerant, but the states being formed around them cannot avoid the existence of minorities in their midst—unless ethnic cleansing of immense proportions is carried out.

Slobodan Milošević is considered by many to be the last Communist in Europe. However, he would not have successfully maintained himself in power had he not at the same time been one of the first post-Communist leaders as well. Communism for him was not so much an ideology as a certain type of government whose monopolistic essence he endeavored to retain as long as possible. Still, even Milošević recognized that, with the emergence of Mikhail Gorbachev, a crisis of legitimacy for such forms of state power was on the horizon. Therefore, he put his faith in growing Serbian nationalism and it brought him unprecedented popularity. In Serbia, where even today the wounds and divisions wrought by the civil war half-a-century ago are still sharply remembered, Milošević managed for over two years to act in such a manner that the most obdurate Communists were convinced that he was only using nationalism in order to stabilize communism, while the nationalists thought the opposite—that he was a Chetnik in Communist guise.

In any case, he was the first to declare that he wished to return dignity to the people. It became a familiar formula and was later heard from the lips of President Tudjman of Croatia. Like a common refrain it played across all of Eastern Europe. Yet the idea of a common state for all Serbs, ordinarily known as "Greater Serbia," was not a new concept nor one unique to Milošević. It was an ambition which originated in the nineteenth century, and became a constant, obsessive theme of Serbian politics, and, in some way, was built into the foundations of Yugoslavia as well. From the Croat and Slovene sides, other expectations were similarly embedded within the foundations of Yugoslavia and ultimately thwarted the consolidation of a common state. However, the "Great Serbian" project was undoubtedly always the most destructive of all the divergent elements.

Milošević came to power in Serbia at a stage when the Serbian national elite had expressed its disillusionment with Yugoslavia for the first time. This view was clearly formulated in the well-known, yet incomplete, "Memorandum" of the Serbian Academy of Sciences and Arts. This document, which came to light in 1986, vented Serbian grievances against the postwar structure of Yugoslavia. The memorandum became the basis for Milošević's program.

The essential reason for Serbian disillusionment with Yugoslavia was the realization that Yugoslavia was too big a country for Serbs to be able to dominate. Although the largest nationality, the Serbs only comprised about one-third of the population of Yugoslavia. The demand that all Serbs should live in one state thus had an unspoken addendum—namely, all Serbs should live in a *Serb* state.

Milošević's program was based on the resolve to retain as much Yugoslav territory as could be controlled from Belgrade without excessive difficulties. In its optimal form this would mean a Yugoslavia without Slovenes and Croats. The brief war in Slovenia made it quite obvious that Milošević was not interested in that republic; nor did the Yugoslav People's Army make more than a half-hearted effort to preserve Yugoslavia's borders. Evidently, Milošević, the Slovene leadership, and certain key generals had come to an agreement which would permit Slovenia's secession. Nevertheless, some sort of symbolic war had to be conducted for the benefit of all those uninformed people who actually believed in the value of preserving Yugoslavia. In this "mock" war, four Slovene "territorial" soldiers and approximately forty Yugoslav army recruits were killed.

However, in Croatia it was a completely different situation. Nearly 600,000 Serbs lived in Croatia and were, for the most part, intermixed with the Croatian population. The architects of "Greater Serbia" cared very little about the real circumstances of the local Serbs in Croatia: to them, it was really more a question of territory than of people. That is why the war in Croatia was launched into Slavonia and Baranja in eastern Croatia, as well as in the Krajina. In keeping with time-worn Serbian pretensions, the conquest of Dubrovnik was attempted even though there are practically no Serbs in the area. The battle fronts delineated the frontiers of "Greater Serbia" and it was fully understood that all territory to the southeast—Bosnia-Hercegovina, Montenegro, and Macedonia—belonged within the Serbian domain.

Croatia had to some extent prepared for war and local Serbs were numerically inferior. Despite its superiority in weaponry, the Yugoslav army did not prove to be particularly effective. For example, the siege of Vukovar lasted a full three months, during which time the city was completely destroyed by heavy artillery before its defenders were overwhelmed. Army recruits and reservists from Serbia deserted in droves. No amount of propaganda could convince them that they were defending their homes by fighting Croatia. When the question of territorial expansion and "Greater Serbia" was posed as part of a defense for endangered Serbs, it found a positive echo. But even so it is evident that it did not inspire mass enthusiasm for war. Anti-war protests began, reservists avoided mobilization *en masse,* thousands went into hiding and changed their addresses, and at least a hundred thousand young men left the country. In fact, this is one of the main reasons that the war came to a halt in Croatia. It was also the first time that the "Greater Serbia" project collided with reality.

Meanwhile, the process of attaining independence proceeded apace in Macedonia and Bosnia-Hercegovina. Milošević's Serbia became a monster from which everyone who was able to flee did so. Thus did Macedonia— which Serb nationalists consider southern Serbia—take its chance, the unfriendly encirclement and pretensions of its larger neighbors notwithstanding. For now Macedonia manages to exist as a "middle-ground" and buffer upon which an uncertain Balkan equilibrium rests. It is well understood that in case of a Serbian attack, Albania, Greece, and Bulgaria would be drawn into war over Macedonia. Milošević may also be pinning his hopes on the possibility that, in time, the Macedonians may seek a "natural ally" in Serbia.

AND SO, THE turn came for Bosnia-Hercegovina, where Serbs comprise just over a third of the population. Unlike Croatia, Bosnia already had received international recognition before the war broke out and this to some extent dictated Serbian strategy. International recognition of Bosnia-Hercegovina did not provoke the war as Serbian propaganda would have it: all preparations for war had already been made on the Serbian side. No agreement could be reached because the Serbs in Bosnia had already declared several of their own regions to be autonomous; the parceling up of Bosnia was already well under-way. However, it could not be fully accomplished without war and without the conquest of a large proportion of the territories in which the Serbs were a minority. The objective was to connect "Serb" territories within Bosnia, and to secure their bond to Serbia itself through virtual annexation. Thus, not only was war a necessity, but massive "ethnic cleansing" was a necessity as well.

This time, unlike in Croatia, the war could not be portrayed as defensive in character because it could not be demonstrated that Serbs in Bosnia were in genuine danger. Instead, therefore, the Serbs invoked their right to self-determination and their wish to live together with Serbia. They accused the Muslims and Croats of seeking domination within Bosnia by invoking a tyranny of the majority. There was some truth to these charges in the way in which Muslim and Croat deputies in the Parliament of Bosnia-Hercegovina passed legislation authorizing a referendum on the question of sovereignty: they had voted to go ahead in the face of a boycott by all the Serbian deputies. The Serb side used this event to vindicate their view that a tyranny of the majority would be established over their interests in Bosnia. On this basis they advanced the conclusion that Serbs could not live together with Croats and Muslims. This meant war.

However, it must be emphasized that there had been months of negotiations in Bosnia concerning the organization of a common state. During these discussions the Bosnian president and Muslim leader, Alija Izetbegović, displayed immense patience and goodwill. However, the Serb chieftain, Radovan Karadžić, was uncompromising. Izetbegović proposed repeatedly that Bosnia remain unified and that it retain some form of open borders with both Serbia and Croatia. Milošević rejected the proposal and, instead, offered Bosnia federation with Serbia.

At one point Izetbegović wavered, but anti-Serb sentiments were already so strong in Bosnia that it was impossible for him to accept such a federation. It happened on the eve of the war. A delegation of the moderate Muslim Bosnjak Organization, led by Adil Zulfikarpašić, visited Belgrade and reached an agreement with Milošević. It appears that Izetbegović gave his consent for such a dialogue. Perhaps he had only agreed as a means to gain time. Nevertheless, public reaction among Bosnian Muslims to Zulfikarpašić's mission was sharp, and the agreement collapsed. And the Serb side was not interested in trying to persuade the Muslims; they relied only on force, threats, and pressure.

The Serbian accusation that the European Community provoked the war by prematurely recognizing Bosnia-Hercegovina is, in fact, an indirect admission that the Serbs were the ones who first drew their weapons against the Community's action. Since the beginning of the war it has often been claimed that the European Community's recognition of Bosnia's independence denied the Serbs their right to self-determination, and that by supporting secession, Europe actually encouraged the dismemberment of Yugoslavia. On the contrary, Europe and the entire international community supported

Yugoslavia, but no one grasped the full complexity of the problem. Furthermore, the consequences of the collapse of Yugoslavia were not understood. All moves were made too late and many errors occurred. The international community vacillated and then acted in an extremely discordant manner. As a result, all the political actors in Yugoslavia, at one time or another, had the impression that they could count on the support of some powerful states.

The right to self-determination was denied to the Serbs outside Serbia while the same right was recognized as legitimate for the Slovenes, Croats, and—to some extent—for the Muslims. If Yugoslavia disintegrates along the borders of the republics, two and a half million Serbs will remain outside the borders of Serbia, which is why for years Serbia has sought to dispute the borders of the existing republics, insisting that they were unjust and drawn to the detriment of the Serbs by the Tito regime after the victory of communism. The truth, however, is that—with the exception of a small part of the frontier between Serbia and Croatia—all these borders are much older.

Furthermore, the key point to recognize is that any attempt to alter the existing borders in order to redress any injury done to perceived Serbian interests can only inflict a much greater injustice on another nation. The problem lies in the fact that the majority of Serbs in both Croatia and Bosnia live very far from Serbia. Their territories can only be reached by crossing Croat or Muslim areas. The Serb nationalists, in pursuit of "Greater Serbia," find their way around this dilemma by declaring that the Muslims are really converted Serbs and have no rights to an independent Bosnian nation. The Croatian nationalists have made similar claims. Thus, the nationalists in both Serbia and Croatia wish to deny the Bosnians their rights in order to lay claim to Bosnian territory.

The Bosnian Muslims have a very clear identity—one originally derived from their religious affiliation. Yet the very notion of religious fanaticism is alien to the vast majority the Muslims in Bosnia. While many have become almost completely indifferent toward religion, they have paradoxically lost nothing of their distinctive identity. Belief in the idea of Yugoslavia—which in principle transcended any quarrels among the various national groups—was very strong among the Bosnian Muslims. It offered them the possibility not only of existing between Serbia and Croatia but of being able to live together with Serbs and Croats in Bosnia.

As Yugoslavia disintegrated, Serbia assumed a much more aggressive stance toward the Bosnian Muslims than toward the Croatians, because it had become unequivocally clear that the Muslims would not voluntarily accede to being part of a new federation. Like other leaders in the republics, Izetbegović desired as much sovereignty and power as could possibly be achieved. By this stage following the war in Croatia, the Yugoslav People's Army had fallen under Milošević's control, and Milošević had begun to realize that the collapse of Yugoslavia had actually strengthened the existing internal boundaries based on republican borders. (The international community regarded these borders as recognized frontiers, because they assumed that they had to begin from some objective position. However, had a sincere Yugoslav policy been conducted from Serbia, and an expansionist variant of nationalism not prevailed, it is difficult to imagine that Bosnia or any republic—with the possible exception of Slovenia—would have managed to have broken away. In any case, the sympathies of the entire world would have been on the side of Belgrade.)

Milošević, having already demonstrated his capacity for brutality in Kosovo, now demanded for the Serbs outside of Serbia precisely that which he would not concede to the Albanians of Kosovo: the right to self-determination. Moreover, the Serb nationalists invoked their "historical rights" in the case of Kosovo, regardless of the fact that 90 percent of the inhabitants of the province are Albanian. At the same time the Serbian leadership sought to exercise the completely opposite principle with respect to the Serbs in Croatia and Bosnia, ignoring the historical fact that their territories had never been part of Serbia. Thus, in order to obscure this contradiction, Milošević was careful never to speak of the expansion of Serbia. He would talk about a Yugoslavia in which all Serbs wished to live. The subterfuge may have confused the uninformed foreigner, but everyone in Yugoslavia knew that he was building "Greater Serbia."

Following international recognition of Bosnia-Hercegovina, the Yugoslav People's Army could not be utilized as directly as it had been in Croatia, for under new circumstances, it might have created complications and provoked an international reaction. The open use of the Yugoslav army would have been seen as an act of external aggression even if the army was, for the moment, still located in Bosnia. Therefore, the Yugoslav People's Army had either to withdraw from Bosnia or place itself under the command of Alija Izetbegović. In fact, a section of the army did formally withdraw to Serbia and Montenegro, but hostilities had already broken out in Bosnia and the army placed an enormous proportion of its weapons and a large number of its officers at the disposal of Radovan Karadžić.

The Bosnian war began with the shooting in Sarajevo on April 5, 1992. Serb gunmen standing on top of the Holiday Inn fired upon anti-war demonstrators in the center of the city. One might also mark the outbreak of hostilities with the April 2nd raid by paramilitary units from Serbia on Bijeljina, a town near the Serbian border. Those who entered the city claimed that the Muslims in Bijeljina were planning a massacre of Serbs. The Serb units supposedly acted to prevent such an event. They took over the town and in the course of their operation they murdered at least several dozen Muslims. From that day until now, the war has unfolded according to a precise plan: non-Serb territories are encircled and Serbian majority areas are linked with one another. "Ethnic cleansing" has been an integral part of the entire plan. As Tadeusz Mazowiecki, Special Rapporteur of the UN Commission on Human Rights and former Prime Minister of Poland, put it: "ethnic cleansing" was the objective, and not a consequence, of the war.

The siege and devastation of Sarajevo—that most tragic, most terrible episode of the war which goes on—cannot be explained only by the existence of Serbia's territorial pretensions. From the beginning of the war the Serbian side has demanded that the city be physically divided between Serbs, Croats, and Muslims. The idea, of course, is absurd; all three communities have lived peacefully and successfully together in Sarajevo. It appears that the Serbian nationalists have destroyed the city precisely for this reason: to destroy it as a symbol of the very idea of co-existence which for centuries has been a way of life and survival in Bosnia-Hercegovina. Beneath the terror of Serbian artillery from the surrounding mountains, this unique spirit of urban community survived for months in Sarajevo. Many Serbs stayed in the city, refusing to join Karadžić's army—and in deference to them it was not said in Sarajevo that Serbs were bombarding the city, but that gangs of criminals were doing it. Today, a year after the beginning of the siege, the citizens of Sarajevo are still struggling to stay alive.

BOSNIA HAS, AND yet has not, been destroyed by this war. The degree of hatred between all three nationalities has undoubtedly intensified. The Muslim-Croat alliance in Bosnia is forced and insincere. The Croat units in Bosnia fought, in the first place, for their own territory; as a consequence fierce clashes have occasionally broken out within the alliance. In addition, Croatia has shown a clear desire to strike a deal with Serbia over the division of Bosnia at the expense of the Muslims. Yet it is not obvious how such a division could be effected. The problem remains the same as it was prior to the war. The population in Bosnia is deeply intermingled and no one will accept "ethnic cleansing" as an accomplished fact. But it is also difficult to imagine that a million and a half refugees will be able to return to their homes in the near future and live their lives as if nothing has happened.

It appears that the plan drawn up by Cyrus Vance and David Owen, which is concerned with bringing peace to Bosnia, is doomed to failure in advance because it is an attempt to discover a compromise that cannot be. The Serbs still desire their own state to join to a "Greater Serbia." However, the international community simply cannot permit them to do so, because doing so would mean rewarding and validating some of the most loathsome forms of violence. It would be a dangerous precedent which would call into question the entire international order. The Serbs have already conquered practically all the territories to which they have laid claim. They consider themselves the victors. The plan for the future organization of Bosnia, first proposed in Geneva, appears a capitulation to the Serbs. The Serbs are well aware that their actions expose them to the risk of international military intervention, and at times they endeavor to show goodwill to blunt the possibility. But they cannot and will not accept the essence of the Geneva plan, because to them it would mean they had fought in vain.

The Vance-Owen plan would create a decentralized Bosnian state with ten provinces that would accord roughly to ethnic divisions as they existed before the war. The problem for the Serbian side has been reduced to the issue of territorial corridors. They insist that their provinces be linked by corridors; in fact, they have already achieved this goal by means of war. They will not renounce these military gains. Yet no one should concede this territory to the Serbs, for only if the Serbs in Bosnia have no corridor or territorial link to Serbia will the Serbian regions be interested in the existence and survival of a unitary state in Bosnia. If the Serbian nationalists get the corridors, they will have gotten everything they wanted. They will then do everything in their power to detach these regions from Bosnia and secure their annexation to Serbia.

Given the prevailing realities in Bosnia, every political solution appears at this stage to be unrealistic. The most probable outcome will be the continuation of the war. The political projects and the territorial ambitions of the warring parties are simply irreconcilable. Moreover, the immense scale of the atrocities which have been committed are so extraordinary that they pose additional dilemmas. The most informed observers now recognize that the atrocities are part of a premeditated Serbian strategy which has been carried out so that the very idea of peaceful co-existence and a common future between all of Bosnia's national communities would be annihilated forever. National and confessional differences are not sufficient to explain a catastrophe whose proportions have already surpassed the suffering experienced in this region during the Second World War. A war as irrational and destructive as this one is a reflection on a form of nationalism which has freed itself of all moral considerations and civilized practices. It is not clear when or how this conflict will finally end.

TRANSLATED BY MARKO PRELEC AND DOROTHEA HANSON

The Roots of
Yugoslavia's Dissolution

MIHAILO CRNOBRNJA

IN APRIL 27, 1992, the Socialist Federative Republic of Yugoslavia, also sometimes referred to as the Second Yugoslavia, definitively ceased to exist. One by one the republics had left it. At that moment, Slovenia, having declared and secured its independence, was completely outside the problematic picture; Croatia had gained independence but was still waiting for a lasting political solution, with UN troops on its territory maintaining a shaky peace; Bosnia-Hercegovina was being torn apart by a violent war, though it, too, had gained international recognition as an independent state; Macedonia, though not at war, was unable to overcome the Greek objection to its use of the name "Macedonia" in its quest for international recognition; Albanians of Kosovo, under colonial oppression by the Serbs, had proclaimed their own republic which was as yet unrecognized even by Albania.

On that day Serbia and Montenegro proclaimed a new Federal Republic of Yugoslavia, hoping that the continued use of the name "Yugoslavia" would place them in the privileged position of natural successor to the old one—which did not happen.

But was that the day Yugoslavia came to an end, or did the end occur much earlier? When does a state stop functioning and cease to be?

In actual fact, Yugoslavia had been in a state of dissolution from that moment when aggressive nationalism came to supersede the country's Communist legacy. Even before this happened, economic and political cracks had begun to appear in the structure of the state which, unattended, slowly led to the break-up.

It could be argued that Yugoslavia was no longer a state at the time when the first republics passed constitutions that were not in conformity with the constitution of Yugoslavia. A further blow occurred when the republics started withholding revenues belonging to the federation and—worse—printing their own currencies. The federal state was hollow and helpless when the republics declared boycotts of goods originating from each other, or imposed additional taxes on the products, services, or property of citizens from other republics. All of this—and more—happened before de facto and de jure recognition was conferred on the states leaving this increasingly unhappy federation.

By a series of mutually reinforcing events, a negative spiral was set in motion, leading ultimately to the final termination of the state. There was no *one single cause* or one source of explanation for the disappearance of the Second Yugoslavia—or for the tragic war through which it disappeared. Some of the explanations include: the national and other complexities that lay in the foundation of Yugoslavia; the Serb domination of the country in the interwar period; the traumas of the conflicts during the Second World War; the considerable economic differences between the republics; Tito's particular, non-democratic formula for holding the federation together; the new wave of aggressive nationalism led by former Communists like Milošević, Kučan, and Tudjman; the rather confused state of collective security in Europe after the ending of the Cold War. As in a test with multiple choice answers the correct one is: *all of the above.* *

The weakening of the Yugoslav federation and its dissolution was a long process leading to a crisis which in turn speeded up the separation. It would be impossible to judge at such close historical quarter, as events are still unfolding, when the point of no return was reached. But the slowness and the length of the process suggest that the destruction was not inevitable: Yugoslavia did not blow up the moment that Tito, the force that allegedly held it together, was no longer around. Admittedly, this is not conclusive proof, but it does suggest that there was more "glue" than sheer political force which held the country together. Another strong, but again not definite, argument against the inevitability thesis lies in the contention that Yugoslavia was created twice. Both times the opposing forces were symbolic while the political forces in favor of Yugoslavia were overwhelming.

Under Tito, Yugoslavia created a unique system which was considered to be a viable alternative to the Soviet bloc of Socialist states. And for a long time, in fact, it was. Tito was a masterful politician. His quest for power was stronger then his loyalty or fear of the USSR and he was clever enough to let the West pay the price for Yugoslavia's independence from the Soviet Union. As a result, the Yugoslavs lived well and had a reputation and a political clout in world matters way beyond their real economic or demographic significance.

But there were a number of significant negative elements in Tito's political order. The system, though more open and liberal than the Soviet alternative, was far from democratic. This caused serious problems in the transition to the post-Tito era. Afraid the Communist hold on power was threatened, Tito personally intervened to stop economic reforms in the mid-sixties, and removed the Serb (and Slovene) liberals from the Party and the government in the early seventies. That was the first real, but lost, opportunity to change the future course of events—it was also a strong blow to the Serbs.

*For a more detailed account, see Mihailo Crnobrnja, *The Yugoslav Drama* (McGill-Queens University Press, 1993).

Tito then gave his blessing to the 1974 constitution which made Yugoslavia a confederal federation and conferred the status of statehood on both Yugoslavia and its republics. But which were the citizens to prefer: Yugoslavia or the republic states? This arrangement made the separation of the republics—once aggressive nationalism entered the stage—that much easier. At the same time, Serbia was reduced in political status to a second-rate republic in Yugoslavia, since two of its provinces were elevated into federal units. This was the second blow to the Serbs. It is little wonder then that the Serbs wanted to redress the (con)federal political arrangement. They were justified in their grievances, but their objective was set too high and the choice of method was the worst possible.

After Tito an inertia set in. The loss of positive political dynamics produced internal pressures and tensions. The first to surface openly were the economic tensions, caused by Yugoslavia's increasing foreign debt, superimposed on an economic system that was growing increasingly inefficient. A high-powered commission, formed by the Presidency of Yugoslavia—and led by a Slovene—toyed around with the idea of economic reform for almost two years. These reforms were never implemented.

The obstacle was a political system that could not accommodate the progressive economic reforms being suggested. Another high-powered commission was formed by the same Presidency—this time led by a Croat—to address the question of what political changes were necessary to revive the economy and establish a new political dynamic. The commission ended its work in total failure. The lines of division were ideological, rather than ethnic. The bureaucratic hold on power, rather then true concern about the well being of ethnicities, was the *spiritus movens;* economics was only the context in which the beginning of the debate occurred.

The economic system, dubbed the "contractual economy," since it was neither a command nor a market driven one, needed a major overhaul. All the republics were suffering from its inefficient performance. But, contrary to popular belief, the line of division lay not between the relatively more developed republics and those that, as the less developed ones, were receiving aid through transfers. The lines of division were more blurred in their ethnic dimension, but much clearer in the ideological. Odd as it might seem now, Milošević was then a young, upcoming liberal economic reformer.

The incompetent leadership that succeeded Tito did not read these pressures as a clear warning requiring a new round of progressive dynamic reforms, such as reviving the economic reforms that were abolished in the early seventies and moving toward a more democratic political structure that would better reflect the realities of Yugoslavia. At that juncture it would probably have been unrealistic to expect a sudden move toward a multi-party democracy. But a political dynamic in that direction would have gone a long way in providing an arrangement which would eventually address the main issues, still dormant in the wings: more decentralization for Slovenia and, potentially, Croatia—and the reinstatement of Serbia as a state at par with others. A second opportunity to move naturally and gradually toward a democratic and economically viable system was thus wasted.

And under the surface of these small and insignificant changes a dramatic change occurred in the overall balance of political intentions within the constituent republics. Instead of directing their efforts toward maintaining the viability of Yugoslavia, the republics shifted their emphasis toward securing better positions within Yugoslavia. This was extremely dangerous.

Yugoslavia, as complex as it was, could survive through the rough times of political turmoil only if deliberate political efforts were forthcoming to secure it against the centrifugal forces of the constituent parts. In other words, the real interests of a common country, though present, by themselves were insufficient to weather the storms without a positive political effort in that direction, and certainly were not strong enough to fight against active political encouragement of centrifugal forces.

In the absence of a positive and progressive alignment of political forces, and in the presence of a deteriorating economic situation, the politicians in the various republics perceived the situation as a zero-sum game—the gain of one being the loss of the other—and the logic of the situation became increasingly confrontational. In Tito's Yugoslavia not only were the differences between its constituent republics played down, but, in reality, they had also been greatly reduced. Now the favored political ploy of the nationalists was to make the differences stand out, and, if necessary, to exaggerate their magnitude through aggressive propaganda.

Before the outbreak of the crisis no political force in Yugoslavia—not even the Slovenes—considered the maintenance of Yugoslavia an impossibility: the objective was to change Yugoslavia's economic and political structures. This would seem to suggest that those forces favoring integration within Yugoslavia were at the time sufficiently strong. But they were weakened by the day, principally by irresponsible actions of the political leadership, both at the federal and the republican level.

Since no one at the stage reached during the mid-1980s actually challenged the legitimacy of Yugoslavia itself, the logical course of action was to proclaim one's own interpretation of it as the only correct one and to simultaneously accuse the other side for being anti-Yugoslav. This political confrontation occurred within the only real Yugoslav political forum—the League of Communists of Yugoslavia—breaking it up gradually into nationalist fractions. Very soon the Communists were representatives of nations, *first,* and Communists, *after.*

Tolerance—conceived as the ability to live with differences—was an early victim. Political actions gradually became manifestly contrary to the logic of life in a common state. Instead of identifying the commonality of interests, energy was increasingly used to point out, even to create, differences. The complex Yugoslav state could never be made operational by suppressing or ignoring the differences. But it gradually became totally dysfunctional because the differences were politically interpreted as plots and conspiracies of the "other" side. In the end they were deliberately tied to the national issue, even when there was no call for it.

The new crop of political leaders in most of the republics amplified the problems by their choice of political method: unable and unprepared to deal with these problems in a democratic manner, they resorted to nationalism. Their personal style—to which, unfortunately, too few objected and many applauded—was commanding and totally arrogant, incompatible with tolerance and negotiation. With such a style and attitude each and every problem became unsolvable. Disagreement turned to conflict, conflict to war.

The new leaders of the republics of Yugoslavia totally disregarded Hume's principle that a state will be more stable and closer to a natural equilibrium the more it relies on agreement and the less it uses force. The Yugoslav drama, among other things, demonstrates how easily common sense can break down. In the end, all it took was a few unscrupulous men to stir up hatreds.

SERB NATIONALISM BEARS the greatest responsibility (albeit not exclusively) for the tragic outcome. The irony is that Serbia needed Yugoslavia the most: it was an existing arrangement by which all Serbs lived in one country. Therefore, the Serbs are, paradoxically, the biggest losers from the destruction of Yugoslavia.

It can be argued quite convincingly that Serbia had no clear strategy in the course of events that took place. The objective was to improve the Serb position in the Yugoslav context. The feeling that one gets, after having lived through the Serb aggressive approach, is that the Serb question was in some ways above the question of Yugoslavia and not a part of it. Yugoslavia, though not necessarily undesirable, was dispensable if it stood in the way. The implied fall-back position at the beginning of the crisis was the making of a Greater Serbia on the ruins of Yugoslavia. If that failed—and few thought that it would—there was still the fall-back position of inheriting a rump Yugoslavia.

Yugoslavia was destroyed; "Greater Serbia" was not and will not be created and even Serbia proper is very insecure from without and from within. The second fall-back position—that of a rump Yugoslavia—is fighting a desperate up-hill battle with heavy odds against it.

The confusion about goals was followed by a confusion in the choice of means of achieving them. The simplistic logic that these three goals—a stronger Serbia in Yugoslavia, a "Greater Serbia," and a rump Yugoslavia— were, like the Russian dolls, contained one in the other, proved to be not only wrong but very costly. These goals were mutually exclusive and every one of them required a different tactic. Through this confusion Serbia found itself in a war, pulling others into it as well. Without loosing on the battlefield, Serbia lost practically everything it wanted to achieve, gaining, in the process, an extremely negative image.

So why did the Serbs act in this way? What brought about the resurgence of nationalism in Serbia? To be sure, in all republics there were some expressions of nationalism, even during the Tito years. These expressions presumably were only the front of a somewhat broader feeling of national discontent. But this feeling of national discontent was never in the center of the political stage.

The Serb political leadership before Milošević tried to solve the Serbian grievances without recourse to nationalism. They failed. That gave Milošević the idea to trump up the nationalist fever, to bring it onto the center of the political stage, and to use it as a powerful weapon in an otherwise purely political confrontation. Nationalist ideology frequently has a very narrow, if emotional base and is therefore unrealistic. The cardinal mistake that Serbs, led by Milošević, made was in assuming that a simple expansionist ideology, similar to that of the nineteenth century, would yield the same kind of results.

As far as Milošević himself is concerned, he put his immense popularity and charisma at the service of this nationalist drive, calculating that his popularity would bring him into a position of power and hold him there. Like communism previously, nationalism for him was not so much an ideological program as it was an instrument in a power play. An expansionist nationalist platform was combined with unyielding and uncompromising tactics. Like Pompey two thousand years before him, Milošević led the political battle from a platform according to which all those who were not with him were against him. That was why all the republics eventually left Yugoslavia: they feared that it would be dominated by the Serbs. At one point, even tiny Montenegro almost joined the ranks of those leaving. Caesar, in defeating Pompey, had fought from a platform which proclaimed that all those who were not against him were with him. A similar attitude from Milošević might have saved Yugoslavia. It would certainly have achieved better results for the Serbs.

The awakening of the Serb national spirit, transformed into an aggressive nationalist policy, awakened the dormant national spirits of others in Yugoslavia. This, of course, made a political settlement less likely.

Milošević and his strategists quite probably factored this into their deliberations. But what they considered to be a decisive element was the size of Serbia, the number of Serbs, and the fact that they were the first to start the process—thus catching others unprepared. Using the tactic of bullying and intimidation, they would scare small and frightened opponents into submission. If war was to break out, Serbs again felt confident of winning, since they had the striking power of the Yugoslav People's Army (JNA) pretty solidly on their side.

It has been said that Milošević was the first to discover that Tito was politically dead. It was a necessary but not a sufficient condition for the destruction that followed. The other precondition, without which things would not have gone the way they did, was the willingness of the Serbs to be nationalistically aggressive, tough, and unyielding. Serbia as a whole, thus, deliberately chose to behave in Yugoslavia like a bull in a china store.

The Serbs were quick to draw the gun at moments when other methods would have been far more appropriate for their cause. When the Slovenes and the Croats declared their independence, the principles governing statehood, as well as the position of the main outside factors, were still very much in favor of the unity of Yugoslavia. The Serbs should have organized a diplomatic rather then a military offensive. They should have pointed out that the declaration of independence by Slovenia and Croatia was against the principle established by the Conference on Security and Co-operation in Europe (CSCE) of non-unilateral changes of borders.

True, nations have a right to self-determination, but they cannot arbitrarily and unilaterally change borders—which is precisely what the Slovenes and Croats did. On top of that, there was ample evidence that the Serbs in Croatia were being persecuted—which, again, was in stark violation of CSCE principles on national minorities. Instead of seeking a diplomatic and political resolution, Serbia chose to take the law into its own hands and, heavy guns blazing, went to war.

It was the undeclared war Serbs waged against the Croats—and later against the Muslims in Bosnia-Hercegovina—in which they always denied Serbia's involvement, that ultimately tipped the scale against Serbia. Serbia was slow to recognize that the war was not only against Croats, Slovenes, and Muslims, but against the basic principle of modern-day security arrangements in Europe.

The declaration of independence by Slovenia and Croatia, in violation of CSCE principles, became a minor and, indeed, an easily forgotten offense in view of the Serb attempt to address the question by force. Post-war Europe was, and still is, extremely sensitive to the use of force to change or maintain borders, even if it is done by the JNA in "defense" of Yugoslav territorial integrity. By waging a war, the Serbs could not count on gaining friends in Europe; yet they were genuinely surprised by the solid block of condemnation they soon faced.

The Croat and, particularly, the Slovene position during the impending crisis was not one of attempting to contain aggressive Serb nationalism within the framework of a more democratic Yugoslavia. True, the Slovenes did attempt for a while to open a political dialogue within the Yugoslav framework. But their position was also characterized by extremist expectations and an unwillingness to seek a compromise. They scored a public relations point by consistently pretending to promote democratic initiatives but, at the same time, making sure that none of their nationalist aims were in any way compromised.

The best example was their constant blocking of free and democratic multiparty elections for Yugoslavia's federal parliament. Throughout the critical year 1990, repeated attempts were made by the federal government to establish a clean political slate by having a new, democratically elected Parliament. The Slovenes insisted on a change of constitution first—a change which would include a one-house federal parliament with national representatives appointed by national assemblies and not elected by the citizens.

The Slovene voters were not to be allowed to create a new multiparty democracy as citizens of Yugoslavia, but as a citizens of a national republic.

The moment that voters cast their votes only as citizens of republics, objectively and independently of their will and desire, they ceased to be citizens of Yugoslavia. This was the Slovene contribution *par excellence* to the destruction of Yugoslavia.

They, as well as the Croats, were willing to take a gamble even if it meant confronting the aggressive Serb position. Knowing the Serbs and their belligerent attitude, they actually provoked a confrontation once the crisis started to unravel fast. They anticipated—correctly—that this would tip the scale of world opinion in their favor.

It could be said that the Serbs loaded the gun but the Slovenes and the Croats fired the first shot in what became a war in Yugoslavia. And what is the war about? Borders! It is not a war of national hatreds, religious intolerance, or historical animosity. All of these, to the extent that they did exist, were converted into powerful instruments in a conflict which, in essence, is a conflict of self-interest designed to achieve political sovereignty.

The Slovenes wanted to redraw the borders of Yugoslavia, breaking away from it. The Croats wanted to secure the borders inherited from Tito's Yugoslavia, which included a sizable and vocal Serb minority. The Serbs wanted to change the borders, which they considered arbitrary and administrative. The Muslims attempted to maintain the unity of Bosnia-Hercegovina, in spite of what happened to Yugoslavia itself before Bosnia-Hercegovina was declared independent and sovereign.

Hatred was inspired, then used as an instrument to galvanize the population of respective nations to achieve concrete political objectives. Irrational means, such as nationalism, were abused to secure very definite and rational ends, no matter how objectionable these ends were. The results were to be attained even if this meant open confrontation. Finally, the nations of Yugoslavia went brutally at each other.

The consequences of almost two years of fighting are disastrous and tragic in many ways. There are many known and unknown victims, and many types of victims in this war, but the best-known victim is—Yugoslavia itself.

IF THERE WAS some doubt about, or hope for (depending on which way one looks at it), the possibility of coexistence of the Yugoslav republics before the war, that doubt or hope has perished—both inside and outside Yugoslavia. The violence and induced hatreds have effectively and rapidly brought an end to this country.

But bringing a country to an end has not brought peace to its peoples. The outlook for a stable and lasting peace is still very gloomy—and that is putting it mildly. Chances are better then ever that things will continue to be bad—and perhaps get even worse—before they start getting better. The negative spiral is still not over and the balance of political forces which is needed to stop the fighting has not yet been reached.

How long this will last is anyone's guess. A pessimistic and somewhat cynical view would have this type of instability in what was Yugoslavia go on for decades. However, the prevailing view among specialists is that a solution could be reached sooner. Once the fighting and the period of tectonic settlement is over, what would be the characteristics of a long-run and stable solution?

Since I have already discarded the most pessimistic scenario—perpetual conflict—in my view there are only three possibilities. These possibilities are presented here in their simplest, most essential form; it is relatively easy to build on the variations. The first one could be labeled the "land for peace" solution. It would involve negotiated and voluntary changes of borders, according to CSCE criteria. It would have the Croats yield territory to Serbs of Croatia who could then hook-up with Serbia. In their turn, Serbs would have to yield territory to Albanians in Kosovo. Bosnia-Hercegovina would definitely be partitioned, largely at the expense of the Muslim population. The dreams of "Greater Croatia" and "Greater Serbia" would be partially accomplished and at some territorial cost. The dream of "Greater Albania" would be accomplished fully, at least as far as Kosovo is concerned.

This solution seems extremely unlikely. Neither the Croats nor the Serbs are ready to yield one inch of their respective territories. The Muslims, who are squeezed between the two, have the world's sympathy on their side (and so far little else, but things could change). They would oppose this solution as long as possible.

The second solution could be called the "massive transfer" solution. Like the Greek-Turk and the India-Pakistan resettlement, it would lead to millions of people changing their geographic habitat in order to be "with their own" ethnic group. The unfortunate and unforgivable ethnic cleansing policies of Serbs—and, to a lesser extent, Croats—are the negative off-spring of this "solution." Rather then change borders, this solution would relocate people. But relocate them where? According to the Croats, Serbs would have to go all the way to Serbia, and according to the Serbs, the Albanians of Kosovo would have to go back to Albania.

This "solution" also seems highly unlikely. It is difficult to see close to five million people willingly accept moving their homes for the sake of a political solution. Again, the cynic might point out that over two million people have been removed forcibly from their homes already. True, but the majority of them hope and expect to go back to their homes eventually and will not accept an alternative.

If the first two "solutions" are unlikely, then the remaining one—which could be called "the coexistence" solution—is both the most likely and also the least costly solution. This solution would gradually reduce the significance of borders by making them open, transparent, and free to cross, and would eliminate the need for large population transfers since the rights of people could, and would, be protected even if they belonged to a country in which another ethnic group was dominant.

This solution is the one which accords with the CSCE principles and the long-term interests of the peoples of former Yugoslavia. Though it would be unrealistic to advocate a reconstruction or the creation of a Third Yugoslavia, this solution would nevertheless encourage the various ethnic groups and states to look toward each other in solving common problems, the biggest of which is the ethnic mix.

This solution will become much less of a utopia the moment rampant nationalism is moved off center stage in all the territories of former Yugoslavia. For this to happen a major change must occur in Serbia first. The Serbs must do away with their own nationalism if Serbs outside of Serbia are to have a prospect for decent living. This is easier said then done, but it is not impossible. Serbia does have a liberal tradition in its history as well: it was not always dominated by authoritarian, aggressive nationalists. Reviving this spirit is the key to resolving the Yugoslav drama.

The character of the conflict explained earlier would suggest the possibility of a political reconciliation. If the dissolution was impelled mainly by factors which were political rather than more fundamental in nature, then the possibility of reversing the process exists. Of course, healing the wounds and eliminating the fear will take a long time: because the roots of the conflict were long in the making, its resolution, too, will take time. Unfortunately, there is no quick-fix solution for the tragedy that is taking its toll on the peoples of former Yugoslavia.

Things Fall Apart

JELENA LOVRIĆ

TODAY, IN THE new countries on the territory of the former Yugoslavia, it has become fashionable to say that Yugoslavia was marked for disintegration at birth: it was constituted in such a way that it was impossible for it to function, and thus, could only be kept together by force. And yet, at the same time, the bitter war raging in these lands gives credence to the argument of those who claim that the peoples and the republics of what they once called Yugoslavia could not have separated peacefully; that the peoples are so intermixed and the new states so interdependent that separation was virtually impossible. Whatever the weight of the competing arguments, this much at any rate is certain: this is a highly complex region which defies any simple explanations or solutions.

The peoples who live in the space formerly constituting Yugoslavia, and the conditions under which they live, are exceedingly diverse. In the six republics of former Yugoslavia there were six nations, several national minorities (of which some national minorities—the Albanians, for example—were more numerous than the entire population of some nations); people spoke three or four languages (depending on whether one considers the language spoken by Croats and Serbs one language or two, which is most often a political question); there were three religions, and two civilizations which collided or flowed into one another. Furthermore, between the Yugoslav North and South there is a gap in development of global proportions. The river Drina has been, and is, the link—or border—between the Eastern and Western Empires, and, today, between Western and Eastern Europe. Therefore, the Croat and Serb peoples, who are perhaps the most kindred in spirit and who speak literally identical languages, belong in fact not only to two different religions but also, in some measure, to different civilizations. Composed of such heterogeneous elements, Yugoslavia was, indeed, a very complicated construct. The question is, could something so complex function at all.

If pluralism were wealth, then Yugoslavia had a chance. Even though in its blend of ethnic groups it was somewhat similar to America, its effort at melting its peoples together into some new Yugoslav nation did not succeed for many reasons. For one, this, after all, was not the New World. Had Yugoslavia emerged and evolved under more democratic circumstances, it might of course have been the forerunner of European integration, resembling what is today considered the European model: each community—national and political—retaining its own distinctiveness, and yet not obstructing or imperiling unification. However, a flaw was built into the Yugoslav state as it came to be constituted: confronted with the problem of its own diversity, it embarked on the leveling of differences. But as a unitary, centralized state it could not function, even though—and this may be a paradox—this was the only form in which it had ever existed. Slovenia and Kosovo, for example, could not live under the same laws: Slovenia was an industrialized republic on the edge of Central Europe, and Kosovo was a relatively pre-industrial society still based on clans. In order to encompass such differences and, accordingly, to create conditions for the progress of each republic, Yugoslavia needed to have a truly democratic and decentralized structure. Anything less would have transformed her into a Procrustean bed—intolerably uncomfortable for one or another republic.

FOR ALL THESE reasons, it is hard to determine the exact moment that marked the beginning of the end of Yugoslavia. I am inclined to argue that it began in the early 1970s when Tito refused to support the largely emancipatory movements in the two largest republics. This happened in 1971, when, (as we now know) under pressure from the Soviet Union, Tito crushed the "Croatian Spring" and, somewhat later, suppressed the so-called Serbian liberals in an equally brutal fashion. In this respect, Tito always tried to be even-handed. Although more is known about the Croat "mass movement," the elimination of the Serbian liberal circle may have been the more fateful step for Yugoslavia. The liberal current in Serbia had sought to turn the republic's attention inward, pulling it back from its perceived role as the supreme guardian of Yugoslavia. The Serbian leadership of the time, therefore, took the view that Yugoslavia was not synonymous with Serbia but was the collective concern of all its peoples; the Serbs were not, nor should they be, more responsible for it than the others. Serbia had its own house to set in order and would, in the long run, do more for the Yugoslav federation by focusing on its own development and modernization. The liberals were acutely aware of the backwardness of their republic, and took account of the fact that the remote Serbian hinterland bore little resemblance to "liberal" Belgrade. With the purge of the liberal circle, the movement to "separate" Serbia from Yugoslavia was permanently derailed; and the option of a democratic Serbia was closed. Another option, however, remained—an option which was to grow ever louder.

Two years later, in 1974, Tito promulgated a constitution which was to become the forerunner of the confederal organization of Yugoslavia. It conferred upon the republics that same measure of autonomy which the Croatian Spring had sought, but it came too late. The leaders who might have worked the new constitution successfully, those who represented the spirit of the future, had been purged and replaced; Tito could now only turn to the trusted, rigid cadres. Thus while the constitution offered many possibilities, these were never realized, for Tito was old, his statesmanship was in decline, his imperial tendencies were ascendant, and he was surrounded by cowards and yes-men. And so the time of a liberal constitution was transformed into the time of great purges, show trials, and the party and police state at the height of their power. The jails were full of Croats—a fact which traumatized both the Croats and the Serbs. For the Croats, this was incontrovertible proof of persecution and injustice; the consequences of "preserving" Yugoslavia by throwing Croats into prison thus surfaced with a vengeance. When Slobodan Milošević began to destroy Yugoslavia, the Croats wholeheartedly supported his efforts—not only was it impossible to live with his repressive policies, but the time also revealed that the Croats still bore the open wounds of the brutal suppression of their "Spring." For the Serbs, on the other hand, the fact that the jails were full of Croats was proof positive that the Croats could not be trusted, that Yugoslavia was in peril, and that they had to resume their role and mission as its guardians. Therefore the people of Serbia were again mobilized to watch over Yugoslavia, and to be even more vigorous because of the "immanent danger" to Yugoslavia's survival. Distrust between these two peoples had received a new impulse.

The constitution of 1974 could only work under democratic circumstances; that, indeed, was the premise on which it was based. Yugoslavia, however, had been emptied of all democracy. Given the reality on the ground, the process of the disintegration of Yugoslavia, built into the confederal structure of the constitution, commenced.

A view widely held today is that the new constitution, in fact, destroyed Yugoslavia because it was grist for the mill of the "secessionist republics." I think that, on the contrary, the destructive factor was built into the constitutional position of Serbia—a position which was thoroughly irrational. The autonomous provinces, Vojvodina and Kosovo, which were part of Serbia, were raised in their authority to the level of republics. This, apparently, was part of Tito's objective to weaken Serbia once he was gone and thus to stabilize a certain balance of power in Yugoslavia. At first, of course, Serbia itself was not opposed to the obvious implications of this move for its own standing within the federation. The elevation in the status of its two provinces had given each a vote: this, in effect, meant that Serbia, unlike all the other republics, had three votes in federal matters rather than one. However, this apparent advantage soon became its weakness instead of its strength, because the provinces soon emancipated themselves to the point at which they were regularly in disagreement with Serbia. Such a situation emphasized the absurdity of an arrangement that gave the provinces within a republic a direct link to the federation and the right to vote without the republic itself, while the republic, without the support of the provinces (the central part of Serbia), could not. Vojvodina and Kosovo began to function as de facto republics, or

rather as states-within-a-state, and their representatives to the federal Presidency, even after Tito's death, took their turn as presidents of Yugoslavia. (Of
course, the high degree of autonomy given to the provinces in Serbia had been
largely translated into the inflated privileges of the ruling elite. And, therefore,
as in other parts of Yugoslavia, none of this had necessarily materialized as
more democracy for the people.)

The entire situation vis à vis its status in the federation was intolerable
for Serbia, but the rest of Yugoslavia was slow to sense this. Everywhere rigid
dogmatists were in power, who dared not act; authority was mummified. As
Tito's health declined, the Yugoslav People's Army (JNA) gained influence,
through formal and informal channels. The JNA even had its own representative in the presidency of the League of Communists, as a "seventh republic."
Although little was known of this at the time, there were already indications
that the JNA was soon to play a crucial role—on the occasion of Milošević's
coup in Serbia.

AFTER TITO DIED, the cement holding the Yugoslav community together
became soft and unreliable. His successors underscored their inadequacy even
by their slogans, such as: "And after Tito, Tito." They flocked, frightened,
under the remains of his charisma, not daring to upset or change anything. It
was clear that these heirs of Tito possessed not even a scintilla of his skill with
which to address or defuse the growing crisis. The process of life having been
arrested, negative energy, the unfulfilled need for change, which had begun to
accumulate even before Tito's death, now began to seep from all the cracks
that had started to appear in the political system. Thus while Yugoslavia had
the appearance of a stagnant and lifeless pond—some will say that this was a
dead time in which nothing happened—the storm that would sweep all before
it was stirring beneath the surface.

The Serbs were the first to realize two facts, identical only at first glance:
one, Tito was gone, which meant that the time had come for realizing all
thwarted, repressed ambitions; and, two, Tito's place was vacant. From the
Serbian Academy of Sciences and Arts, under the strong, direct influence of
Dobrica Ćosić—considered at the time the father of the Serbian nation and
under the disfavor of official authorities—was launched the so-called "Memorandum." This was, in fact, the project of Greater Serbia, the policy which
has become known around the world and is encapsulated in the phrase, "all
Serbs in one state." The Memorandum's persuasiveness came from analysis
which was often quite accurate; but even official Serbian circles judged the
solutions it offered as "in memoriam Yugoslavia." However, those who saw
that the Memorandum was in fact burying Yugoslavia were soon replaced by
a classic party coup. A new leader arose in Serbia, who, significantly, had not
condemned the Memorandum, and who reached for power by inflaming the
issue of Kosovo.

The Albanian disturbances in Kosovo, which were rooted in the postwar

period when the Albanian population of the province had been subject to terror at the hands of Yugoslavia's chief policeman, heightened Serbia's frustration. This geographical and political region had long been tense; the Albanian
commotion at the time seemed emancipatory, but the Serbs considered it a
threat to the Serbian nation. In fact it was not easy for the people in Kosovo
or anywhere else in Yugoslavia. Kosovo, in fact, became the testing ground for
what would later occur in all of Yugoslavia—the clash of different nationalisms. The smoldering conflict in Kosovo was further fueled by the Serbian
side; those who know something of the role of the "myth of Kosovo" in the
collective Serbian consciousness will immediately realize how dangerously
easy it was to use that myth to inflame, mobilize, and set into motion both the
Serbs and Serbia.

When Slobodan Milošević carried out his coup in Serbia in 1987, there
was an initiative from the other parts of Yugoslavia to examine what was happening in Serbia. But nonetheless Milošević actions met with no serious challenge. There were several reasons why this was so. The autonomous provinces
did not want their votes in the presidency to get them involved in the struggle
within the Serbian leadership; rather they hoped that they would draw some
advantage from the Serbian quarrel, because whatever weakened Serbia could
strengthen them. Similarly the other republics, while loud in their objections
in the corridors, took no official action, because by intervening in Serbia they
risked being called to account in similar fashion. Clearly, even then there was
a tacit agreement not to meddle in each other's "internal affairs." Furthermore,
the federal leadership was at odds with itself, rendered powerless by its own
incompetence. Then, as now, Milošević allowed nothing to stand in his way;
he led the entire dance, using, as he himself acknowledged, any means possible: "institutional, noninstitutional; statutory, nonstatutory . . ." Thus at the
celebration of the six-hundredth anniversary of the Battle of Kosovo, in the
presence of almost the entire Yugoslav leadership, his warning was unambiguous when he declared, "even armed struggle is not excluded."

Claiming to restore dignity to the Serb people, Milošević destroyed the
leadership in the autonomous provinces with his own special brand of a populist movement—the so-called anti-bureaucratic revolution.* While the governments were indeed hopelessly bureaucratized, what Milošević sought and
achieved was the destruction of the autonomous status of the provinces. He
then moved against Yugoslavia as a whole, gradually transforming his nationalist movement into fascism.

When Milošević first captured power, there was still a struggle going on
in Serbia over whether the Serbian question, opened by the movements in
Kosovo, would become a question of democratic change and renewal, or
whether nationalism would become the political platform of the Serbian gov-

---

*The "anti-bureaucratic revolution" in Vojvodina was also known as the "Yoghurt Revolution,"
because of the containers of yoghurt hurled by the crowds. The phenomenon of mass demonstrations was, more generally, called *dogadjanje naroda* or the "happening of the nation."

ernment and the Serb nation. At this stage, Milošević was not yet the *Fuhrer,* he was only the *vožd.** While he was predisposed to the extremes of totalitarianism, he was no born nationalist but a Communist apparatchik, eternally hungry for power and ready to do anything to stay in power; furthermore he was not completely sane. A true-born nationalist was the father of the Memorandum, Dobrica Cosić. Neither a Chetnik, nor a fascist himself, Cosić perhaps truly believed that his ideas could be realized by pursuing a course other than the one that Milošević embarked upon. But to anyone slightly familiar with the situation in the Balkans it had to be obvious that the Great Serbian plans could only be carried out in the way they were: by fire and sword. In the beginning it was only nationalism, but in the five years of Milošević's campaign this brand of nationalism gave birth to fascism.

WITH MILOŠEVIĆ'S enthronement, the democratic option lost the battle; nationalism became the official Serbian political program. The aims of that program were realized through the methods of the so-called anti-bureaucratic revolution, which were a combination of populism and the most rigid Stalinist purges. Serbia rang with the sound of mass demonstrations; the nation was "happening" on the streets, which gave it a feeling of participation and political decisionmaking. It seemed as if the odious bureaucratized structures were indeed being destroyed by the people's will. This gave the people a sense of power. The collective frustration built up over the years rolled through the streets, the force of its energy frightening those who did not participate—especially those nations against whom it was directed. The Serb nation was animated—and deceived—by the feeling that instead of being an object it had suddenly become a subject. The people carried flags through the streets and wanted to plant them at the farthest points of "Serbian land." They declared that any land where there was even one Serbian grave was their territory; they wanted to impose their own truth in every region of Yugoslavia; and they tried to introduce their "demonstrations of truth" into Ljubljana and Zagreb.

It seemed as if chaos was "happening" in Yugoslavia. But even at the time there was a sense—as has become quite clear by now—that there was some method to the madness. Although manipulated by the rhetoric about restoring national dignity, in this choreographed national movement there was also some genuine enthusiasm. Crowded and deafened at demonstrations, the people could not see their own unsteady path. Driven crazy and hysterical, they could not see that with their "yogurt" and other revolutions, even as they were destroying a government they did not like, they were establishing and reinforcing another kind that would quickly do them in. Sweeping purges were carried out in all parts of society, always finding new internal enemies and accomplices. Immediately after the fall of the Vojvodina "autonomist" ruling circle, more than five thousand people were purged in that province. It

*"Leader," with popular, slightly archaic connotations.

was the same in all parts of Serbia. The "cleansing" encompassed all parts of society, from the political leadership, the media, and factory directors down to the grassroots. Whoever did not join in the game, whoever tried to preserve even a little human dignity and reason, was regarded as an insufficiently good Serb. Such people, as indeed all independent political thinkers, were dealt with drastically.

The changes in the editorial teams in television, newspapers, and radio were drastic and fundamental. Almost all the media were hitched to the same wagon. The national question was the only criterion, there was no room for doubt, with the largest newspapers becoming vehicles for witch-hunts, exposing and expelling supposed national traitors. The papers would give the starting signal for the political execution of individuals; with a verbal lynching they would mark the target, and everything that happened after that—expulsion from work and society, even physical extermination—was just the logical consequence. The media, and everything else, purged itself with daily discoveries of suspected fifth columnists, conducting and legitimizing Stalinist show trials in an instant, newspaper version. The nation was pumped full of hate every day in order to accept these war cries as a way of life. All Croats were called "Ustaše," Muslims were labeled Islamic fundamentalists. The Serbian media became a harbinger of crimes later committed by people—crimes the media inspired, encouraged, and legitimized. Stojan Cerović observes that Serbia was probably the first place in the world to establish television dictatorship as a new model of power. Although there are now opposition newspapers and journals, they are not important in a backward and impoverished country that reads less and less, lacking the money even for bread. The events of the last elections show that when the ground is well prepared, television alone is enough to make people choose whatever government is presented to them through the electronic media.

Three factors thus determined that a national movement would be perverted into fascism, and that the nation would choose that fascist option in generally free elections: first, a radical and exclusivist nationalism presented as a state plan and national program which did not allow national emancipation to become a question of democracy; second, populism and its inevitable corollary, autocratic government, which used all available means to eliminate and destroy all that it regarded as undesirable, and whose political purges were just the forerunners of what we today call "ethnic cleansing"; third, unbelievably furious and hysterical propaganda, with strict discipline of the media and particular abuse of television, combined with the nation's backwardness and illiteracy. The whole picture is of course much more complex: there were several other significant factors such as the political and economic misery of the people with attendant national and social frustrations, the deterioration of civilized standards, and a militant spirit fully able to express itself through the means provided by Serbia's huge military potential.

Latinka Perović, a respected Serbian intellectual who was forced to leave politics during the attack against Serbian liberalism, recently wrote about the existence of two long-conflicting Serbian national programs. She noted that, quite separate and opposed to the the policy of Greater Serbia, there does exist the alternative program of resolving the Serbian question within a union of Balkan and South Slavic nations: "Greater Serbia, created through conquest, would perforce become a military-police state which would have to invest all its forces into simply preserving itself from external enemies." She concluded that "in politics it is results not intentions that matter, and the results are, from the point of view of the Serbian national interest, so horrendous that it is difficult to find any comparable era in Serbian political history. Serbia is fighting everyone with whom it still shares any state territory; because of the Serbian diaspora it is not prepared to delimit its own boundaries. Within Serbia, unity was long ago established on the basis of opposition to everyone without. In such circumstances democracy becomes mere pretense." Everything that has happened in Yugoslavia, not only its dissolution but even the bloody scenario by which it was carried out, all the incomprehensible horror which will end who knows when—all this is the logical, although not the inevitable, consequence of the policy which once and for all destroyed the possibility of unity in the region. This is not to say that others did not work on the same plan. Milošević was the first and the most important actor, but he was not the only one. While he provoked other nationalisms, these in turn fed and supported him—not only out of gratitude for his having released their spirits from the bottle, but out of common interests. It could even be said that the Slovenian and Croatian side in some way used Milošević; their "secessionist" dreams could only be realized through him and the "impossible" Yugoslavia he wanted to impose on all. The Croatian president, Franjo Tudjman, found a common language with Milošević in this as in other matters: the division of Bosnia-Hercegovina was the subject of their deepest mutual understanding. That is why, even if one accepts that Yugoslavia began to fall apart long ago, it is completely uncertain when and how that process will finally end.

TRANSLATED BY DOROTHEA HANSON AND MARKO PRELEC

A PERSONAL REPORT

The Last Days of Yugoslavia

BOGDAN DENITCH

B Y THE SPRING OF 1991 Yugoslavia was nearing ter-
minal illness. With the withdrawal of the Slovenian and Croatian organizations the federal League
of Communists of Yugoslavia (LCY) had ceased to exist. While Prime Minister Ante Marković's economic program managed to maintain relatively high
wages and a stable currency, the political crisis was obvious to all. There was
an end-game, apocalyptic atmosphere in the circles of intellectuals I moved
among in Belgrade, Zagreb, and Ljubljana. A familiar, worn-out regime was
clearly on its last legs, but there was little joy and much fear about the
prospects for the future. We did not expect any velvet revolution or magical
fixes from the new mantra, "market and privatization," and yet none of us
could even imagine just how terrible the next two years would be.

Only in Sarajevo, of all places, were intellectuals and dissident activists
still relatively optimistic in early 1991. There were several reasons for this optimism. To begin with, both the local LCY leadership and the democratic intellectual dissidents, who had gathered first around the Zagreb-based journal
Praxis and later around the anti-nationalist Association for Democratic Alternatives in Yugoslavia (UJDI), were firmly committed to a multi-ethnic democratic state and united in their opposition to Serbian, Muslim, or Croatian
nationalism. The dissidents were mostly university teachers, journalists, writers, and actors who were still committed to the idea of Yugoslavia. They
wanted to move forward toward the democratization of the system within
some form of mixed economy combined with worker self-management freed
of the dominant role of the League nomenklatura. In short, they hoped for the
transformation of Yugoslavia into some form of a democratic civic state. In
pursuing this goal, they found they had more and more in common with the
increasingly dominant reform wing of the Bosnian League of Communists
and Marković's federal government. Non-nationalist democrats in Bosnia did
not feel isolated, as their opposite numbers in Belgrade and Zagreb increasingly did in 1990–1991. They communicated with those in power, and even
in the election in which nationalist parties achieved surprising success in
Bosnia, Marković's non-nationalist reformists (whom UJDI backed) and the

reformed League of Communists did quite well and formed the governing coalition in Tuzla.

My friends in Sarajevo were an ethnically mixed lot, some were children of intermarriage, or had spouses of a different ethnic origin. Intermarriage is now too often an overlooked category when discussing the ethnic makeup of Bosnia. Almost twenty-five percent of the marriages in Bosnia were inter-ethnic, but of course that number was much greater in the cities like Sarajevo, Tuzla, Zenica, Banja Luka, and Mostar. Intermarriage was especially common among cosmopolitan intellectuals, at home in Belgrade and Zagreb and often in Paris, London, and New York. For these people, who were overwhelmingly secular and mostly described themselves in the population census as "Yugoslav," the onslaught of nationalism was a horrible nightmare, a revival of primitive patriarchal parochialism.

Many of them stayed in Sarajevo. Zdravko Grebo, whom I last saw in December 1992, stayed to run a fine radio program; others like Gajo Sekulić were less visible. A Serb friend is the deputy commander of the Bosnian armed forces; another is an editor at *Oslobodjenje,* the last surviving daily paper still publishing in Sarajevo. All stayed while the city they had known and loved was slowly murdered during the endless months of siege while the European Community, the United States, and the United Nations dithered.

I had become deeply involved in the debates in the media throughout the country, having joined with some democratic socialists and radical democrats in organizing the UJDI, the first open non-Communist political group in Yugoslavia in 1989. The UJDI was organized in all the major cities including Zagreb, Belgrade, Sarajevo, Ljubljana, Skopje, Rijeka, and Split. Most of us had known each other through decades of meetings and activities. Thus UJDI included many of the student generation of 1968, some feminists, and peace activists. We had also gathered together most former members of the *Praxis* circle, with the notable absence of Mihailo Marković, a major academic from Belgrade. His absence signaled how many personal friends with whom we had collaborated for years would be lost to Serbian or Croatian nationalism. Marković—a well-known democratic socialist dissident until the late eighties and a leader of the Belgrade Eight—shocked us by becoming the vice president and spokesman of Milošević's ruling authoritarian Serbian Socialist Party, which was the old Serbian League of Communists with ever more aggressive nationalist politics: all that had remained of its "socialism" was the loyalty of the secret police and the old nomenklatura. Under Milošević, the party had become an essentially "peronist" organization, with vestiges of leftist social demagoguery, xenophobic paranoia toward the outside world, harsh nationalism, an alliance with openly fascist Chetnik thugs of Sešelj's Radical party and gangsters from Arkan's " Tigers," and, of course and above all, it has developed a cult of its leader. It has nothing in common with the earlier multinational, revolutionary, self-management tradition of Yugoslav communism.

My own situation was complicated. As a dual American-Yugoslav citizen, I would now have to opt for the citizenship in one of the new states.

When not in New York I have lived in Croatia on the Dalmatian coast since 1967. On the other hand, while active in academic and dissident circles in Zagreb, I am a Serb with many ties of family and friendship in Belgrade. Increasing national polarization put me in a difficult position, making me a target for both Serbian and Croatian nationalists, the first because of my politics—I had openly opposed Milošević and the Serbian nationalists—and the second because of my ethnicity. My position became even more uncomfortable after the right-wing nationalists won the first pluralist elections in Croatia. I was not only a Serb, but to make things worse, an active and very visible participant in left-wing Croatian politics. Armed paramilitary groups of the urban lumpen type were now increasingly visible on the streets of Zagreb and Belgrade. And by the autumn of 1991 it became a genuine issue whether or not to carry licensed arms. My friends recommended it while traveling or speaking in small industrial towns and rougher neighborhoods, and, after the autumn of 1991, while traveling through Bosnia, something unimaginable during the long Titoist twilight.

I remember my initial shock when I first saw Chetnik insignia on bearded young thugs in the center of Belgrade peddling chauvinist tape cassettes and blood-curdling pamphlets. They looked like caricatures of Chetniks from the Second World War. The only models the young had were from the war movies which glorified the Communist Partisans and treated the Chetniks as collaborators, rapists, looters, and killers. And that was precisely what had made them attractive to the new converts! The Chetniks had become the Serbian folk version of the skin-heads and young neo-Nazis in the West. Similar cultural blends were on show among the Croatian paramilitary groups who mixed Ustaša symbols with heavy-metal, skin-head, and Rambo images, sometimes topped off with Catholic prayer beads and a cross. These were the groups that would do some of the fighting and commit most of the atrocities in the wars which started that summer.

The Swedish Institute of the Workers' Movement had given me a modest grant to try to help democrats and social-democrats in Yugoslavia through a project optimistically called "Transitions to Democracy in a World Perspective."[1] The grant made possible minimal material aid to the democratic left, like fax machines and a newsletter (in English) to maintain a network of individuals and institutions in Yugoslavia and Eastern Europe. We also organized meetings with new unionists among the media, shipyard workers, and teachers in Croatia and Serbia.

As the war spread in the summer of 1991, the UJDI became an obvious anachronism. Our members turned to organizing social democratic parties in their respective republics. If Yugoslavia were to come apart we wanted to make sure that our new states were democratic at least, had reasonable social programs, and were open to cooperation across the new frontiers. Most of us believed that this could only be done by organizing new social-democratic parties and unions, since that would be the only way to organize broadly and to compete against populism and nationalism. Some of my friends in Macedonia and Slovenia stayed in the reformed former Communist parties which in those two states had evolved into genuine social-democratic organizations.[2] Some younger intellectuals preferred to work with social movements, which in practice meant ecological, women's, and peace groups. An important group in Belgrade around Vesna Pešić of the Democratic Reformist Party argued that it was premature to raise leftist political issues in Serbia, since the most urgent goal was to establish peace, minimal democratic norms, a law-abiding state, and human rights.[3] The advocates of these various views cooperated with remarkable non-sectarian amity and continue to do so to this day. I joined the Croatian social-democratic organization, the Social Democratic Union (SDU) led by Professor Branko Horvat, arguably the leading democratic socialist economist in Eastern Europe.

By midsummer 1991, an ever more brutal armed conflict in Croatia had grown from a local revolt by the Serbian minority into a war of aggression by the Yugoslav Army and the Serbian government. By autumn, communications between Croatia and Serbia were cut; travel and phone messages between Eastern and Western parts of former Yugoslavia now had to be routed through Hungary or Bosnia-Hercegovina.

Yet throughout that summer and autumn, as the war in Croatia escalated, the democratic opposition from the various republics still managed to organize round-table meetings of the federal government and opposition. These meetings took place mostly in Sarajevo—a city where we, as members of the democratic opposition, had considerable support. We were all known as democratic dissidents, a rubric defining dissent ranging from attacking the Soviet invasion of Czechoslovakia in 1968 to backing Solidarity in Poland and protesting its military repression, to demanding free speech and free pluralist elections in Yugoslavia. We saw ourselves as *democratic* socialists and throughout the eighties, after Tito's death, we found our views converging with an ever larger part of the reform wing of the LCY and many of the more open-minded journalists and intellectuals associated with the League who were moving to an explicitly democratic view of socialism. It was clear that the Yugoslav system desperately needed to be democratized if it were to survive.

By 1990 the majority of the Slovenian League supported pluralist elections and the complete abolition of censorship; strong sections of the Macedonian, Bosnian, and Croatian League had the same view. Alas, the Serbian League had been in the iron grip of the Milošević leadership since 1987; massive purges of thousands of members in Serbia, Kosovo, and Vojvodina had expelled the reformist wing from the League organization which had traditionally been the stronghold of reform forces. Those who were not expelled were effectively silenced. Increasingly the Milošević leadership rested on a tacit alliance of the old regime hacks and non-Communist radical nationalists who organized the "spontaneous" mass demonstrations in support of Milošević's assertive nationalism, first in Kosovo where the local League leadership was toppled, followed by Vojvodina and Montenegro where the local leaders were removed under the pressure of "peronist" crowds chanting a mix of nationalist and social slogans in the streets. All this was done under the benevolent eyes of both the regular and the political police of Serbia. The federal institutions were paralyzed gradually and completely. When Milošević's supporters proposed to send the traveling "spontaneous" demonstrations to Slovenia and Croatia in 1990, it was clear that the end was near. The leaders of the two western republics had a clear choice: to be toppled by "spontaneous" organized crowds of Serbian nationalists in the service of Milošević's regime, or to bar these meetings from their republics and prepare to secede.

The alternative—to use the federal institutions, the LCY, the Army, and the state to defend the decentralized Constitution of 1974 from Milošević—had been frittered away in the years between 1987 and 1990. The time to do so was when Milošević moved against Kosovo and later against Vojvodina. But the leaders of the other republics, with the exception of Slovenia, were too timid: their inaction and their acquiescence to Milošević's tactics made them accomplices of the Belgrade hardliners. They—the Croatian, Bosnian, and Macedonian representatives in the federal League and Government—believed, until much too late, that Milošević would be satisfied with the integration of Kosovo and Vojvodina into Serbia, and would go no further. No true democrats themselves, they reassured themselves by seeing Milošević—as he, indeed, liked to be seen at the time—as just a hardline Communist who wanted to centralize Serbia in order to defend Yugoslav communism from excessive pressures for democratic reform.

My own project on "Transitions to Democracy" organized a conference in Subotica near the Hungarian border in autumn 1991, with participants from the democratic opposition and some independent intellectuals, as well as democratic socialists from Western Europe, Russia, and Eastern Europe. International participants and solidarity helped the morale a little. We tried to make sense of what was happening and to work out some joint proposals. These were modest efforts to keep some kind of non-nationalist and democratic leftist community together. Old personal ties and friendships crumbled as many of the intellectuals I knew, as well as friends and family members, rallied to the defense of their own nation.

The pressure to do so was immense. Revived images in the media of the near-genocidal massacres of the Serbs in Croatia during the Second World War traumatized people who had seemed immune to nationalism. My Croatian friends were constantly bombarded with current pictures of burning cities—including Dubrovnik, a cultural icon—and the massive destruction of churches and monuments. Television on both sides repeatedly showed horrendous images of massacred and mutilated bodies in vivid color. This reached a point where child psychologists in Belgrade and Ljubljana protested that children were showing massive war neuroses and fears. By the spring of 1992 television in Belgrade and Zagreb had become unbearable while the relatively objective station run by the federal government from Sarajevo was inevitably an early casualty of the war in Bosnia.

The second multiparty election in Croatia took place in August 1992 while the new war in Bosnia had been raging for several months. Although Tudjman's ruling Croatian nationalists imposed an electoral law grossly tilted in their favor, we decided to participate anyway as did all opposition parties. We tried and failed to negotiate a general coalition with other democratic leftists and the regional parties from Istia and Dalmatia in time for the election. The best that we could do was to have a joint democratic socialist candidate for president who got a respectable 4.5 percent of the vote in a field of sixteen. We also helped elect five members from the regional parties in a parliament of 137.

What we did manage was to campaign in the teeth of wartime nationalist hysteria and get a respectable hearing and very high visibility. Branko Horvat, Nikola Visković (a popular gadfly member of the outgoing parliament), and I campaigned in the media, temporarily accessible during the elections, and before grim audiences of unemployed workers and veterans from the Slavonian front where we received a surprisingly respectful hearing. While there were innumerable threatening phone calls and depressingly voluminous hate mail, there were also letters from pensioners, school teachers and ordinary workers, and members of the traumatized Serbian minority who were grateful for the campaign.

Since the spring of 1992 the Croatian government had emphasized its support of an independent Bosnia against Serbian aggression. This was quite popular given the increasing evidence of massive atrocities by Serbian paramilitary groups in Bosnia during the summer of 1992. Evidence of mass rapes and concentration camps in the service of the unspeakable policy of "ethnic cleansing" was widely available and quite convincing. (I personally interviewed some children in Mostar, thirteen- and fourteen-year-old Muslim girls, who had been gang-raped in front of their families in August 1992.) There were almost half a million refugees from Bosnia in Croatia by the end of the summer. By that stage, however, the scandalous complicity of the Croat authorities in the partition of Bosnia through the setting up of a separate Croat state in Bosnia-Hercegovina, much as the Serbs had done, became obvious to all.

While the major aggressors in Bosnia are the Serb nationalists supported by the Yugoslav Army, Croat troops have also occupied large parts of Bosnia where Croats represent a minority of the population and are outnumbered by Muslims in cities like Stolac, Mostar, Prozor, Jablanica, and Travnik. The territory occupied by Croat troops is treated as part of the Croat state of Bosnia (Herceg-Bosna), with Croatian currency and authorities in place. Croat troops have been in combat with the mostly Muslim troops of the Bosnian government, despite the earlier uneasy alliance they sometimes maintained against the more powerful Serbian aggressors. As the war between the Croatian and Bosnian government forces escalates, cases of Serbian-Croatian collaboration, sometimes tacit, sometimes open, against the Bosnian forces are also increasing. This war against the Bosnian Muslims is being sustained, on both Serbian and Croatian sides, by national myths which emphasize the centuries of wars against the Ottoman Turks. Muslim Slavs, ethnically and linguistically identical to the Croats and Serbs—and in the urban centers, entirely secular and culturally indistinguishable from their neighbors—are somehow transformed into the legendary Turkish enemy and made to pay for the years of Turkish dominance.

Unlike most American intellectuals, most Europeans, especially East Europeans, do not accept a multicultural and multi-ethnic environment as normal. Internationalism was always very fragile in the socialist movement, and was turned into a caricature by Communists in Eastern Europe (especially when internationalism became another word for Soviet patriotism). Of course, E. P. Thompson and others had always stressed the intimate link between communitarian localism and class consciousness. And yet during the years I had lived and worked in Yugoslavia it had seemed that a new heterogeneous popular culture was emerging among the young and among the urban workers. And it was no surprise that it was multi-ethnic Sarajevo that emerged as the major source of popular music and culture in Yugoslavia. The current wave of nationalism in Bosnia therefore strikes me as the revenge of provincial language and history teachers and all those who insist that they must preserve that which is specific to their nation. For the war in Bosnia is obviously also an urbicide. Cities I have known and loved have been relentlessly bombed into shambles—the work of those who have always hated the cities. These cities were the places where massive intermarriage and de-nationalization took place, where various national groups mixed and made friends, where women entered the professions, where the young rejected religion and tradition. They were seats of political authority and the source of hated modernity.

Being a citizen of Yugoslavia had meant to me being a member of a very heterogeneous community, an interesting place which permitted a wide range of individual ways in which one could be a citizen. The new identities we are now forced to assume are narrower, more parochial, and less flexible. A bridge between the old and new civic identities is only created partially and deliberately by the community of the democratic socialist movement. I now feel poorer, as do many citizens of former Yugoslavia. But that Yugoslavia which I mourn is now clearly dead.

IN THE DESTRUCTION of Yugoslavia the Yugoslav National Army (JNA) has played a crucial role. Conversations with top officials of the last federal government make clear that the JNA had become an independent force at least a year before the breakup of Yugoslavia in June 1991.[4] While committed to preserving the federal state, the army leadership was even more concerned with preserving Communist political power. Therefore they opposed the only kind of Yugoslavia which could have been preserved: a decentralized, economically reformed, and pluralistic Yugoslavia. The Yugoslavia they sought to preserve could only be preserved by naked force. They believed that they had a reliable ally in the Milošević regime. They were wrong because Milošević banked on an alliance with Serbian nationalists, who were anti-Titoist and who required the destruction of any kind of Yugoslavia that could have been acceptable to the other national groups.

At least twice before June 1991 the army had been on the verge of a coup to overthrow the reforming Marković federal government. They believed that the Soviet Army, which faced similar foes in its own country, was a firm ally. Their last chance vanished with the failed coup against Gorbachev in August 1991. The Yugoslav Army leadership had tied its fate to anti-reformist military and political conservatives in the Soviet Union. The defeat of the coup in Moscow faced the Yugoslav Army with total international isolation. Within months the old Titoist generals were pensioned off and replaced by a younger and more nationalist lot who have been fitting allies of the Serb nationalists' war in Bosnia-Hercegovina.

In tandem with the army, the political elites of the states of former Yugoslavia have wrought a great disaster on their peoples. The shell of former Yugoslavia—now reduced to Serbia with its two restive provinces of Kosovo and Vojvodina and an ever more reluctant Montenegro—has waged two wars of aggression in two short years and is now an international pariah subject to an ever-tightening economic blockade. The summary sacking of the relatively moderate president, Dobrica Cosić, open clashes between the opposition and the hard-fisted Serbian nationalist regime of Milošević—which is backed by Sešelj's fascists—have pushed Serbia itself closer to civil war. As for Croatia, large parts of its territory are now ineffective protectorates of the United Nations where a Serbian police state rules; there are a million refugees in its cities; and its economy is in rapid decline. Bosnia's government is now reduced to a few enclaves and forced to fight an increasingly two-front war against Serbian and Croatian nationalist armies. Macedonia hovers on the edge of economic and political disaster as a result of the craven acceptance by the European Community and the United States of Greece's objections to its recognition. Slovenia's living standards have been pushed back two decades to those of 1972, which makes it the least unfortunate of the new states which have emerged from the wreckage of Yugoslavia. Before breaking up in 1990–1991 Yugoslavia had a better case for EEC membership than Hungary, Poland, or the former Czechoslovakia. That is now obviously an unattainable goal.

The elites of former Yugoslavia are not alone. In most of Eastern Europe and the former Soviet Union, destructive, over-ambitious demagogues, often uncritically supported by a West relieved to see the last of the Communists in power, were able to secure sufficient popular mandates to take power. The electorates, unschooled in democratic politics as were a large section of their intelligentsia, wanted to celebrate their own repressed exclusivist nationalist urges. In the theater of politics they engaged in, it seemed all right to indulge in a little "harmless" national assertiveness against their minorities and neighbors: "just a little harmless funky national self-assertiveness," after decades of prim, preachy insistence by the old Communist rulers that chauvinism was forbidden and nationalism suspect.

As the simultaneously playful and thuggish soccer riots and recent skin-head riots against immigrants in Western Europe have already demonstrated, that theater can also be deadly. In fact many soccer fan clubs became the core of the nationalist paramilitary bands in Serbia and Croatia which, while small in number, are responsible for a major share of atrocities in the wars in Croatia and Bosnia. The heirs of these bands can be recognized in the Croatian paramilitary organization, Croatian Armed Forces (HOS), of the neo-fascist Croatian Party of Rights in Bosnia with its predilection for black shirts, swastikas, and icons of the Croatian wartime fascist leader Ante Pavelić. They take no prisoners. Their Serbian equivalent, Arkan's "Tigers," are sloppier when it comes to uniforms and ideological pedigree but even deadlier and more prone to atrocities against civilians of the wrong ethnic group.

Thus in most post-Communist states today, democracy is a form of expressive politics. The weakness and isolation of the dissidents and the severity of Communist repression had bred irresponsibility. There was no chance for a subject people to learn responsible politics as active citizens; to learn, therefore, that their decisions and actions can sometimes matter a great deal and may well become matters of life and death, war and peace. The experience for almost half a century was to the contrary—politics had been a sham and had bred deep cynicism.

Titoism was a history of repeated attempts, all ultimately unsuccessful, at internal reform of a Communist regime. They were defeated by the contradiction between an increasingly attenuated authoritarian Leninism, on the one hand, and democratic empowerment through self-management, on the other. The LCY had experimented with various mixes of decentralization and Party control for almost four decades. It introduced semi-syndicalist models of workers' councils, decentralization down to the levels of county governments, and ever greater autonomy for the republics and provinces. The League also introduced market criteria in the economy; and it even withdrew from direct control of culture and the arts. The basic weakness was that all these experiments, the good and the bad, were introduced from the top down by the Party and therefore provided no genuine sense of empowerment and responsibility which victories gained in prolonged political and economic struggles bring to the mass of the people.

Instead, the League's systematic repression of a normal development of responsible opposition groups, journals, and parties had created an intellectual and moral desert. This man-made desert became a happy hunting ground for charlatans, adventurers, and demagogues who came to prominence overnight as the system collapsed. There had been no time to develop alternate views and politics to be tested in debate and mutual criticism; the "new" non-and anti-Communist politicians had to develop overnight. A substantial part was played by the emigres, especially in Croatia, who had preserved a nasty kind of traditional xenophobic nationalism during the long years in diaspora. Centrists and liberals did not arouse passionate commitment, the democratic left was weak, fragmented, and compromised by the similarity of their language with that of the Communist reformers. Organic right-wing nationalism was at least "authentic." It fit nicely with a crude and selfish Social Darwinism associated with fash-

ionable new economic dogmas of privatization and an uncontrolled market—
and the devil take the hindmost, especially if he is nationally different.

Much of the hostility to communism in Yugoslavia in the late eighties was
based on an "echo effect" arising from the general collapse of communism
throughout the East European bloc. It did not matter that the performance of
the Yugoslav Communist system was substantially different from that of the
communism of the East European states or the Soviet Union. Countries one
admired for being orderly, progressive, and having a high living standard, that is,
Western Europe and an America, mostly known through movies and consumer
products, were emphatically not Communist. Communism had to be gotten rid
off for many reasons, and love of democracy was one of the least important ones
for most people. Alas, it never held a candle to the love for consumer goods.

Nationalist politics in Serbia and Croatia include an amalgam of cleri-
calism, romantic historiography, pseudo-scientific nationalist ethnography,
and arcane plot theories involving the freemasons, Jesuits, and espionage
agencies. All of this was now made available to the new anti-Communist,
nationalist politicians. Plot theories and political paranoia had long been
widespread in former Yugoslavia and throughout Eastern Europe. This was
encouraged by the ceaseless efforts of the political police and the police's
favorite journalists in order to develop a "security consciousness"—a general
paranoia about all foreigners, potential spies, and all those who were different
and might threaten the political order. There was ample room for a symbiosis
of the political universes of the right-wing emigres and the Communist pub-
licists: both loved dark plots with undefined alien forces of great power and
malignity. Proto-fascist and Communist-inspired paranoias fit together neatly
and helped corrupt and infect an already insecure public opinion faced with
the collapse of known comfortable beliefs and social and political systems and
with no readily available alternatives.

These are politics for intellectually and morally lazy people: almost everything is explained by conspiracies against "our very own poor victimized
nation." For the Serbian nationalists, therefore, it is self-evident that the Albanians and Bosnian Muslims are in cahoots with the world conspiracy of Islamic
fundamentalism, and eternally lust after pure Serbian womanhood. The Croats
are obviously an extension of the permanent plot of the Vatican against Orthodox Christianity, or alternately the German march to dominate Eastern
Europe. For the Croat nationalists the Serbs represent the barbarian non-Euro-
pean hordes of treacherous "Byzantines" out to destroy Western civilization
and Christian (that is, Catholic) culture; they are also natural Bolsheviks and
even biologically inferior. This horrible mythology helps to increase the circu-
lation of a mass chauvinist yellow press and corrupts television and radio. It is
a politics of identity reduced to its crudest form, "we" versus "they."

A DECENT SOLUTION to the Yugoslav crisis now appears almost unimaginable.
Bosnia probably has been destroyed as a viable multi-ethnic polity through the

brutal war and massive "ethnic cleansing" by the Serbian nationalists. In Serbian designs to partition the Bosnian state, the Croatian nationalists have been fully complicit.

Not surprisingly, therefore, chances for democracy are endangered in both Serbia and Croatia because two bitter dirty wars have been waged for maximalist national aims since 1991, with horrendous losses of lives and property. No one has won. The wars are a moral and political catastrophe. The price for the Milošević's regime's survival in power may well be an extension of military aggression to Kosovo, the Muslim areas of Serbia in the Sandjak, and even Macedonia. The Serbs are today less secure in Kosovo, in good part because of their repression of the Albanians. Because the principle of collective guilt is widely accepted, all Serbs, innocent and guilty, nationalist and anti-nationalist, now have good reason to feel less secure in Croatia and Bosnia-Hercegovina than at any time since 1945. Serbian nationalist politics have frightened and antagonized every neighbor.

In Croatia, ugly nationalist triumphalism, after the first free election in 1990, drove the Serbian minority in ever greater numbers to support Serbia's war against the Croatian bid for independence. The 1991 war, fought entirely on Croat soil, was hugely destructive, pulverizing whole cities and creating some 600,000 refugees. In 1992 another 400,000 refugees from the Bosnian war poured in. The war has encouraged strong tendencies toward authoritarian presidential rule by decree. By 1993 the last of the independent press was under siege. The Croatian authorities have been complicit in the discrimination against the now isolated and frightened Serbian minority whose members have been faced with large-scale dismissals from employment, denials of citizenship papers, and the destruction of their homes. Citizenship has been denied not only to Serbs but also to Albanians and Muslims who have lived for decades in Croatia. This has occurred despite the incorporation of enlightened provisions in the Croatian constitution and legal system for the protection of the minorities. Included under pressure from the European Community as a condition for its recognition of Croatia's independence, these guarantees remain a dead letter.

Just as no democracy is possible in Belgrade so long as the Serbian government represses Albanians in Kosovo, no real democracy is possible in Croatia so long as its Serbian minority is treated as second-class citizens. So long as Serbs are mistreated in the areas under the control of the Croatian government there is no chance at all that the Krajina areas, now under UN protection, will ever be reintegrated into Croatia. And without the reintegration of these areas into Croatia there can never be a stable democratic government in Croatia since it will always be subject to irredentist pressures.

When the war moved from Croatia to Bosnia in the spring of 1992, inter-communal violence and open warfare reached near genocidal proportions. By far the largest number of the victims were Muslim civilians. In what had been an exemplary multi-ethnic society, Serb and Croat nationalist leaders in Bosnia now rejected a state based on all the citizens rather than ethnic or national groups. Both now war against the Bosnian government—partitioning of the country and annexation of its territory is their only goal. Alas that is also what the Vance-Owen plan, sanctioned by the United Nations and the European Community, proposed in essence and thus urged all sides to fight on for their own ethnically "pure" areas. For it was impossible to have an ethnically based partition without massive transfers of population. The Vance-Owen plan allocated large areas with predominantly Muslim population to Serbs and, above all, to Croats who would end up with as much territory as the Muslims. That is, with 16 percent of the population the Croats were to get three provinces, just as many as the Muslims with 44 percent. The plan had no provision to disarm the nationalist militias and therefore guaranteed continued "ethnic cleansing." Today the consequences of the Vance-Owen plan have led to the virtual carve-up of Bosnia.

Instead of the Vance-Owen plan, held up by the Western powers as the only solution to the war in Bosnia, it was essential to demonstrate unmistakably to the military and political leadership in Serbia that their murderous goals were not achievable except at unacceptable cost. This is why a real blockade was a necessary step but only a step to changing the Serbian policies. Complete and enforced interdiction of Serbian entry into Bosnian air space together with the lifting of the arms embargo on the Bosnian state, thus permitting the Bosnian government to arm itself, were absolute imperatives which were rejected out of hand by the West. For Bosnia-Hercegovina to survive as a unified country today, the only workable medium-range solution appears to be some kind of an effective UN protectorate over the country, enforced by UN military forces, providing international supervision for courts and police, since none other will be considered either impartial or legitimate.

What might be imagined as a decent, if not optimal, outcome emerging from the wreckage? What is essential is for the new frontiers between the new national states to be absolutely inviolable and at the same time not too terribly relevant in the lives of most people and for the functioning of most economic institutions and transportation networks.

The first step is peace and mutual recognition, within their present borders, of all states emerging from Yugoslavia. Any attempt to re-draw these frontiers would lead to interminable military conflict. Attempts to re-draw the frontiers along "ethnic" lines reinforce two deadly myths: first, that it is possible to draw frontiers in such a way as to create ethnically "pure" national entities, and, secondly, that this is desirable. Both myths are born out of a desire to create ethnically homogeneous national states. This is inimical to democracy in a real world where states are increasingly multi-ethnic. Instead, there should be a systematic de-linking of exclusive ethnic and national symbols from those of the state which should be a state of all of its subjects, who should all be equal citizens.

A second step should create a free-trade zone, if at all possible with a customs union. There are many obvious reasons for this, including the interdependence of much of the industry and services in former Yugoslavia. It would be a good idea to revive the old proposal that the whole area become a military-free zone. This would make both civil society and democracy considerably safer than they would be in the presence of national armies composed of dissatisfied heroes of wars of national independence.

I believe that once all of the states which have emerged from Yugoslavia recognize each other's independence and borders, the tendency will be toward increasing cooperation and contacts. There are more than two and a half million people in mixed marriages, there are economic, institutional, and personal ties. There is also a discreet but widespread nostalgia for the "good old Titoist days," days of job security, rising incomes, and law and order in what was the most open Communist-ruled country in Europe. Real incomes in Croatia, Serbia, and Bosnia have dropped dramatically; huge numbers of workers are faced with massive dismissals purely at the discretion of the management; all vestiges of workers' control and self-management have been abolished; pensions have been cut in half, and social services, already inadequate, are further sharply reduced. Women's social policy gains, the right to abortion and place in the work force, are all under harsh attack by the nationalist and clerical right. Every fourth person in Croatia, fifth person in Serbia, and third person in Bosnia is now a refugee. Weimar Germany in the twenties was a paradise of stability compared to the ruins of Yugoslavia.

My best-hope scenario is based on the notion that the broad, class-based left has more resonance in the memory and politics of Croatia, Bosnia, and Serbia than does the nationalist right. There are social democratic and leftist parties in all of the former Yugoslav states which maintain loose networks and share a common democratic politics. They are members of the governments of Macedonia and Slovenia and in the opposition in Croatia, Bosnia, and new "Yugoslavia." They have broad support from dissident intellectuals and from former Communist democratic reformers. They draw support from the anti-war young and from the increasingly militant and bitter workers.

It is not at all certain that these forces can win. Much will depend on the support they get from the social democratic left in the European community. However they do represent a hope, a possibility, a set of goals worth fighting for and taking risks. This is as much as anyone has ever really had in Eastern Europe and the former Soviet Union.

Notes

This chapter is based on a shorter article published in *Dissent,* Winter 1993.

1. The idea of a "world perspective" was initially provided by the Mexican and Egyptian institutes which wanted to see what they could learn from the problems of transition to democracy in Yugoslavia and Eastern Europe. This formulation also enabled West European social democrats to participate in some of our activities.

2. In both Slovenia and Macedonia these social democratic former reform Communist parties are now in coalition governments.

3. Pešić is now a major leader of the Citizens' Group which unites the leading opposition to Milošević's regime.

4. This information is based on my own lengthy interviews and conversations with former cabinet members and ambassadors of the federal government of Ante Marković. Through cross-checking I am convinced that it is true. Both the prime minister and the secretary for international affairs were among the first targets of the military "hards" during the first half of 1991.

Regional Polarization in Postwar Yugoslavia and the Impact of Regional Policies

Iraj Hashi

THE END OF THE First World War and the breakup of the Austro-Hungarian and Ottoman empires witnessed the birth of a number of new states in Europe. The Kingdom of Serbs, Croats, and Slovenes, as Yugoslavia was originally called, was one of these new states which came into existence in 1918. Sanctioned by the peace treaties of St. Germain, Neuilly, and Trianon, its western and southern constituent parts separated from the former territories of Austria, Hungary, Bulgaria, and the Ottoman Empire and joined the kingdoms of Serbia and Montenegro which had existed as independent states before the War.

Economically, socially, and culturally the new state was one of the most diverse and heterogeneous countries of Europe: its population was made up of eight major and about twenty minor ethnic groups (Serbs being the largest group, followed by the Croats), speaking four languages (Serbo-Croatian, Slovenian, Macedonian, and Albanian), practicing three religions (Catholic and Orthodox Christianity and Islam), writing in two scripts (Latin and Cyrillic), and displaying great social, cultural, and economic differences. These differences played a major part in subsequent events and contributed to the growth of rivalry and discord between different nations and regions.

In the interwar period, Yugoslavia was governed by Serb-dominated governments under the Karadjordjević dynasty. The rightful aspirations of other nations for some form of self-rule and autonomy were disregarded, and seeds of national discord were sown. The monarchist period, or the "first" Yugoslavia, was brought to an end in April 1941 by the occupation of most of the country by Nazi forces and their allies and the formation of the Nazi puppet "Independent State of Croatia" (the Ustaša regime) where appalling atrocities were perpetrated against Serbs, Jews, and other minorities.

Before long, the "second" Yugoslavia—this time socialist and federal—was being built on the ruins of the "first." With the rise of the Yugoslav Communist Party to political power, the "nationalities question" was brought to the forefront of the country's political and economic agenda. The nationalities question, in this period, was closely bound with the economic problem of bridging the regional development gap and enabling the poorer regions of the country to grow rapidly.

From 1950, Yugoslavia embarked on her own unique development strategy based on workers' self-management and the increasing use of the market mechanism. The "second" Yugoslavia was associated with rapid transformation of a poor and predominantly rural society to a modern industrial country. But despite all her achievements, she did not succeed in closing the regional development gap and resolving the nationalities problem. The 1980s witnessed worsening economic conditions, mounting dissatisfaction with the national and regional policies, and the outbreak of civil strife. The increased democratization of the Yugoslav society in the mid-eighties and the weakening of the League of Communists of Yugoslavia created the conditions for the revival of opposition political parties, including the extreme nationalist organizations, in all parts of the country. This was followed by the election of non-Communist governments in Croatia and Slovenia in Spring 1990, which had campaigned on nationalist platforms (particularly extremist in Croatia). The unilateral declaration of independence by Slovenia and Croatia in June 1991 sparked open armed conflict which, by the beginning of 1992, had brought the "second" Yugoslavia to an end.

A comprehensive analysis of the roots of this conflict must involve the unraveling of intertwined economic, political, historical, and ethnic factors which have developed over most of this century. The purpose here is to highlight the impact of uneven economic development and widening regional disparities on the evolving relations between Yugoslavia's constituent regions, in particular, the nature and instruments of the government's regional policy in the "socialist" phase and the effectiveness of these policies.[1] In this context, although the conflict between Serbs and Croats has been at the center of recent developments, it is important to address the wider issue of the relations between all nationalities and regions of the former Yugoslavia.

THE SERB-CROAT conflict which precipitated the disintegration of Yugoslavia in 1992 and led to the subsequent war in Bosnia-Hercegovina has its roots in the formation of Yugoslavia in 1918. Before that, the two peoples had been separate from each other for centuries and there is little evidence of serious strife or animosity between them. Slovenia and Croatia had been, respectively, part of Austria and Hungary for nearly a millennia. Slovenia was never an independent state, while Croatia, which had been a kingdom in the early middle ages, had gone into voluntary union with Hungary in 1102 and had been ruled from Hungary ever since.[2]

Serbia, on the other hand, had been a major empire in the medieval period, ruling over most of the present day Bosnia-Hercegovina, Montenegro, and Macedonia, and reaching its zenith during the reign of Emperor Stefan Dušan (1331–1335). But by 1463, she had been completely conquered by the Ottoman empire. With the weakening of the Ottoman Empire, Serbia and Montenegro gained their independence during the nineteenth century and formed their independent kingdoms in 1878 and 1919, respectively. Austria annexed Bosnia-Hercegovina in 1908, thwarting the Serbian desire of uniting all Serbs, including those under Turkish and Austro-Hungarian rule, in one state.[3]

The idea of a state unifying all South Slavs was initially put forward by the Croatian, Slovenian, and Serbian intellectuals of the "Illyrian movement" in the middle of the last century. The outbreak of the First World War gave the intellectuals and politicians from the territories ruled by the Austro-Hungarian empire a renewed hope of realizing their aspirations of a unified state. In April 1915, in Paris, the Yugoslav Committee (*Jugoslovenski odbar*) was set up to campaign for the unification of all South Slavs in a Yugoslav state. The Committee entered negotiations with the Serbian government-in-exile toward the end of the War and on July 20, 1917, the "Corfu Declaration" was signed. The Declaration proclaimed the determination of Serbs, Croats, and Slovenes to form an independent, constitutional, democratic, and parliamentary state headed by the Karadjordjevic dynasty. It also recognized, at least formally, the equality of the three "tribes," three religions, and two alphabets.[4]

The events surrounding the formation of the new state profoundly affected Serbo-Croat relations. Serbia, which had fought a long war, was now part of the victorious Allies; Croatia was associated with Hungary's vanquished camp. The nationalist elements in the Serbian government, headed by Prime Minister Pašić, wanted a reward for Serbia's part in the Great War. Italy's claim to parts of Istria and Dalmatia further increased the pressure on the Croat and Slovene leaders to work with the Serbian government and participate in the peace negotiations as one team. They therefore hurriedly joined Serbia and agreed on the formation of the new state on largely Serbian terms.[5] The union neither clearly expounded the relationship between the nationalities nor did it provide legal guarantees for their rights and duties. The Kingdom of Serbs, Croats, and Slovenes formally came into existence on December 1, 1918.[6] In October 1929, the new state formally adopted the informal name of Yugoslavia (*Jugoslavia,* meaning the land of South Slavs) as its official name.

It is important to note that economic factors did not play a major part in the formation of Yugoslavia. Of course, one could envisage the potential advantages of a wider market or the complementary nature of the industrialized and agricultural regions, but these advantages were not used as justifications, or even important reasons, by the proponents of the idea of Yugoslavia in either the Illyrian movement or the Yugoslav Committee. For the Serbian government, of course, the access to the Adriatic and the control over the industrially developed areas of Croatia and Slovenia must have constituted important considerations.

The elections for a Constituent Assembly were held in November 1920. With the exception of the Yugoslav Communist Party (YCP)[7], all other parties had a strong regional base and nationalist orientation. The YCP campaigned for economic, political, and social reforms in all of the South Slav lands and won the third-largest number of seats in the Assembly. But before the Constituent Assembly could meet, the government issued a special decree banning all Communist organizations. In June 1921, in an atmosphere of hysteria and an anti-Communist witch-hunt, the new pro-Serbian constitution was passed by a narrow margin in the Assembly.[8] This constitution concentrated power in the hands of a Serb-dominated central government and denied any autonomy to other nationalities and regions. The mistrust created in the process of the formation of the new kingdom was now reinforced, and suspicions among other nationalities of the ultimate Serbian desire for hegemony became stronger. This mistrust was further intensified by the population resettlement which followed the government's limited Land Reform program in 1918. Through this program, many Serbian veterans of the First World War, as well as volunteers, paramilitary groups, and poor peasants, were given land and settled in territories outside Serbia, particularly in Croatia, Bosnia-Hercegovina, and Macedonia where large tracts of land were expropriated from Hungarian, Turkish, and local feudal landlords. This internal migration was supported by the Serb-dominated Army, with the resettled population being perceived as the instrument of Serbian rule in non-Serb areas.

The economic situation deteriorated badly in the postwar period. The infrastructure and national capital, particularly in Serbia and Macedonia, had suffered enormous damage during the war. The value of fixed assets and national income did not reach prewar levels until 1923. Rapid inflation and the widening price scissors (indicating the relative prices of agricultural and manufacturing goods), together with the monopolistic concentration of industrial and financial capital in few hands, largely foreign, resulted in a sharp decline in real wages of workers and government employees. Standards of living of the bulk of the population declined, falling well below the subsistence level.[9]

There was strong opposition to the government's economic and nationality policies led by the YCP, the Croatian Peasant Party, trade unions, and various sections of the population. But the opposition was met by more restrictive legislation and more repressive measures which contributed further to the deepening of national discord. Then, in January 1929, King Aleksandar declared a personal dictatorship, abandoning any pretense to parliamentary democracy. The suppression of the opposition, particularly the YCP and trade unions, further intensified.

In October 1934, as he arrived in Marseilles on a state visit, King Aleksandar was assassinated by a member of IMRO (the International Macedonian Revolutionary Organization), hired by the Croatian ultra-nationalist organization Ustaša which was dedicated to the setting up of a "racially pure" Croat state. Anti-Croat, anti-Italian, and anti-Hungarian demonstrations broke out in Yugoslavia; another wedge was driven between the two main nationalities, pushing them further apart.

On the eve of the Second World War, with mounting international tension and domestic discontent, the Serbian government embarked on the formation of a coalition government with the political opposition. They signed the famous Agreement of August 1939 *(Sporazum)* with the Croatian Peasant Party headed by Maček, setting up a broad-based government with Maček as Deputy Prime Minister. Thus, for the first time, the Belgrade government yielded to the Croatian people's demand for some form of autonomy and agreed to a Croatian parliament in Zagreb.

The coalition government retained Yugoslavia's neutrality until March 25, 1941, when it decided to join the Axis powers. Mass demonstrations broke out in many cities (though not in Zagreb) and on March 27 a group of air force officers organized a coup d'´etat ousting Prince Regent Paul and the prime minister. A new government was set up and the seventeen-year-old King Peter assumed power as the sovereign. Hitler, furious at the air force coup, ordered the invasion of Yugoslavia and a particularly barbaric bombardment of Belgrade on April 6, 1941, causing massive destruction and loss of life. On the same day, the German armies, supported by Hungarian, Bulgarian, and Italian armies invaded Yugoslavia. Within ten days, the Yugoslav government and King Peter had fled and, on April 17, their representative signed the capitulation documents.

Thus the "first" Yugoslav state ended in defeat, occupation, and disintegration, with relations between its nationalities badly damaged.[10] Most of Slovenia was annexed by Germany which also occupied most of Serbia and put her under the administration of a puppet "Serb" government headed by General Milan Nedić; Hungary took over northern Serbia; Italy occupied the rest of Slovenia, the Dalmatian coast and Montenegro; and Bulgaria occupied Macedonia. But, in terms of relations between the different nationalities, the worst development took place in Croatia. Under German and Italian protection, an "Independent State of Croatia" was declared in Zagreb on April 10, covering Croatia and most of Bosnia-Hercegovina, with its eastern borders extending to Zemun on the outskirts of Belgrade. The Ustaša leader, Ante Pavelić, until now a fugitive in Italy, returned to Zagreb on April 15 and took charge of the new state under the new title of *Poglavnik* (the headman).

With the blessing of the Croatian Catholic church and its Archbishop Aloysius Stepinac, Pavelić immediately embarked on the establishment of a racially pure, Catholic state in Croatia. He began passing anti-Serb and anti-Jewish laws through the Croatian parliament from May 1941, barely three weeks after taking power. Serbs and Jews first lost the right to own radio sets (May 16) and were then dismissed from public offices and obliged to wear distinguishing insignia (May 22). The campaign of terror, mass arrest, detention, deportation, and extermination began in the summer of 1941. The targets of this campaign were primarily Serbs of Croatia and Bosnia but also included Jews, Gypsies, and political opponents of the regime. Toward Serbs, the Ustaša policy was to eliminate or expel as many as possible and convert the rest to Catholicism by force. In the Jasenovac concentration camp, established along the lines of Nazi extermination camps and manned by Ustaša guards, tens of thousands of Serbs and other detainees were murdered. Tens of thousands more were deported to other extermination camps in Germany and Poland.[11] These atrocities left their enduring mark on Serb-Croat relations. It would be true to say that Serbs never forgot, and never got over, their sufferings in this period. After the war, many of the Ustaša leaders (though not Pavelić himself) were arrested, brought to trial, and punished.[12]

Whereas in Croatia the German invasion paved the way for the puppet Ustaša regime, in other parts of Yugoslavia the Germans faced hostile opposition. The principal opposition was organized by the Communist Party, which had moved its center of activity from industrial areas to the mountains of Bosnia-Hercegovina and Montenegro from whence it embarked on Partisan warfare. The YCP was the only political organization in Yugoslavia committed to the principle of federal unity and the equality of all nationalities. The crimes committed by Germans in their occupied territories and by the Ustaša in Croatia and Bosnia led increasing numbers of people, mainly from the countryside, to join the ranks of the Partisans as the last hope of saving their lives and their dignity. The YCP, with Tito as its leader, turned Yugoslavia into a major theater of war in the Balkans and engaged ever larger numbers of German forces. It survived large-scale German offensives aimed at its annihilation, and, with the Allies' support, beat back German advances in the Balkans and fought the German armies in retreat.

In addition to YCP, other political organizations were also active in different parts of occupied Yugoslavia, among them the ultra-nationalist Serbian groups, known as Chetniks.[13] The Chetniks, who operated mainly in Southern Serbia, Montenegro, and parts of Bosnia, were committed to the idea of uniting all Serbs in one nation state and were prepared to resort to ethnic terror to achieve their aim. They committed brutal acts of violence against the Croat and Muslim population in Serbia and Bosnia-Hercegovina and played a major role in the intensification of national discord in Yugoslavia. Soon it became clear that they considered the Partisans as their main enemy and turned to collaboration with the Nedić government and the Germans. Britain, which had supported the Chetniks, withdrew her military personnel and ceased further supplies to the Chetniks in December 1943.

BY THE END OF 1944, Yugoslavia was almost completely liberated from the occupation forces. The Constituent Assembly, elected in November 1945, formally deposed King Peter and declared the formation of the Federal Peoples Republic of Yugoslavia. The YCP now faced not only the uphill struggle of rebuilding a war-torn economy but also the much heavier task of national reconciliation.[14] The victims of the Ustaša, in particular the Serbs, were now the victors and demanded retribution. But although many Ustaša (and Chetnik) leaders and activists were arrested, tried, and punished, these trials could not encompass every supporter, sympathizer, petty informer, or minor official of the "Independent State of Croatia." Nor could they include all those among the Croatian population who silently observed the Ustaša atrocities. Wishing to make a fresh start and hoping for national reconciliation and healing of the wounds, the government severely discouraged any manifestation of nationalism or seeking of revenge, particularly by Serbs.[15] The legal framework for the improvement of nationalities relations was laid by the Constitution of 1946. From the start, the equality of all nationalities and their right to use their own language, and develop their cultural heritage and identity on the basis of their own conditions, were guaranteed under Article 13 of the Constitution. The six constituent republics were given equal standing in the federation irrespective of their size, population, wealth, or level of development.[16]

As in the period following the First World War, there was a strong population migration comprising of Partisans (mainly poor peasants of Serb, Montenegrin, and Bosnian nationality) moving into the land confiscated from churches, foreign (mainly German) landlords, and collaborators. In 1945, the Serbian National Committee declared that the resettled Serbs should seek their political future with the people of the regions where they had settled. With the population migration following the two wars, the nationalities were dispersed widely but unevenly throughout the country. In most regions, in addition to the majority nation, there were significant minorities of other nationalities. The uneven distribution of population remained largely unchanged during the postwar period. *Table 1*, representing the ethnic origin of the population in different parts of Yugoslavia, shows the complex mixture of population in most parts of the country. (In particular, with the present hostilities on everyone's mind, the composition of population in Bosnia-Hercegovina, Croatia, Vojvodina, Kosovo, and Serbia should be especially noted.)

The initial enthusiasm of the YCP, boosted by the idealism of its victorious Partisan cadres, had created the hope that in the new Yugoslavia socialist relations would soon develop and would supersede and replace the relations and attachments based on nationality. The "nationalities" problem, however, was now closely intertwined with the "regional development" problem. The disparities in the level of social and economic development of different regions in 1947/1948 are illustrated in *Table 2*.

The Party believed that the nationalities question would persist in Yugoslavia as long as these wide disparities persisted. It was feared that these disparities would result in regional rivalries and give rise to nationalist tendencies. Interestingly, it was no longer Serbs and Croats, but the more and the less developed regions which were on different sides of the divide. Slovenia and Croatia, the area north of river Sava, became the economically more developed region (MDR) of the new state. Bosnia-Hercegovina, Macedonia, Montenegro, and Kosovo formed the less developed region (LDR) of the country. Serbia, and its constituent Autonomous Province of Vojvodina, with an average level of development, roughly constituted the middle ground.

It was clear from the beginning that, even with radical social and economic policies, the development of the less developed regions could not be achieved by reliance on local resources alone. Additional resources were needed, both in the short and long term, in order to improve the economic

Table 1
ETHNIC ORIGIN OF THE POPULATION OF DIFFERENT REGIONS BY PERCENTAGE[17]

	Year	Serb	Croat	Muslim	Slovene	Albanian	Macedonian	Montenegrin	Hungarian	Yugoslav
Yugoslavia	1953	42	23	*	9	4	5	3	3	6*
	1981	36	20	9	8	8	6	3	2	5
Bosnia-Hercegovina	1953	44	23	*	•	•	•	•	•	31*
	1981	32	18	40	•	•	•	•	•	8
Croatia	1953	15	80	•	1	•	•	•	1	•
	1981	12	75	1	1	•	•	•	1	8
Macedonia	1953	3	•	•	•	12	66	•	•	•
	1981	2	•	2	•	20	67	•	•	1
Montenegro	1953	3	2	*	2	5	•	87	•	1*
	1981	3	1	13	•	7	•	68	•	5
Slovenia	1953	1	1	•	97	•	•	•	1	1
	1981	2	3	1	90	•	•	•	1	1
Serbia (All)	1953	74	2	*	•	12	•	1	6	1*
	1981	66	2	2	•	14	•	2	4	5
Serbia Proper	1953	92	1	*	•	1	•	1	1	1*
	1981	85	1	3	•	1	•	1	1	5
Kosovo	1953	24	1	*	•	65	•	4	•	1*
	1981	13	1	4	•	77	•	2	•	1*
Vojvodina	1953	51	7	*	•	•	1	2	25	1*
	1981	54	5	•	•	•	1	2	19	8

• Less than 1%
*Muslims were not classified as a separate nation at this stage; they were included under Yugoslavs.

Table 2

SOME INDICATORS OF REGIONAL DISPARITY IN YUGOSLAVIA IN 1947/1948[18]

	Yugoslavia	Slovenia	Croatia	Serbia Proper*	Vojvodina	Bosnia-Hercegovina	Macedonia	Montenegro	Kosovo
Natl income per capita, % of national average	100	175	107	96	110	84	62	71	52
Share of population %	100	9	24	26	11	16	7	2	5
Share of social product %	100	25	26	11	14	5	2	2	
Share of fixed assets % (1952)	100	20	28	23	9	13	4	1	2
Share of industry in social products %	25	36	30	20	17	21	20	10	20
Share of agriculture in social products %	45	30	39	53	67	41	55	52	66
Share of population in agriculture %	57	44	62	72	68	72	71	72	81
Illiteracy %**	25	2	16	27	12	45	40	26	63
Dependents per 100 active population	97	76	87	79	97	126	127	150	179
Natural increase per 1000 population	14	9	9	13	9	22	21	22	26
Infant mortality per 1000 live births	102	81	112	91	130	126	136	41	133
Inhabitants per physician (1952) in 1000s	2.6	1.7	1.9	2.1	5.7	3.3	4.3	4.5	8.5
Inhabitants per hospital bed (1952)	277	188	202	300	300	448	339	241	606

*Republic of Serbia excluding the autonomous provinces of Kosovo and Vojvodina.

**Share of illiterate population in total population over the age of 10.

capabilities and public services in these areas. The federal government had to pursue an active regional development policy in order to make the rapid development of the less developed regions possible. Only then would the working and living conditions of people across the whole country begin to converge and pronouncements on the "equality of nationalities" would be meaningful. The rest of the community, therefore, agreed to assist these regions, and the principle was enshrined in the Constitution.[19]

FROM THE EARLY postwar period to the late eighties, the Yugoslav economy went through three major stages: the central planning phase (1947–1952), the market-based system of workers' self-management (1952–1974), and the period of the reassertion of collective control through the concepts of "associated labor" *(udruzeni rad)* and "social compacts" *(drustveni dogovori)* (1974–1988). In each stage, with the change in the Federal government's ability to mobilize and deploy resources, the method of intervention also changed.

The Central Planning Period, 1947–1952. From 1947 to 1952, the Yugoslav economy was organized and administered along the lines of the Soviet model with the strict subordination of economic units to the central planning authorities. Prices and quantities, wages, employment, investment, foreign trade, and the like, were all determined at the central level. Each enterprise was, effectively, another layer in the administrative hierarchy of a ministry. All enterprise profits and taxes went into the collective "kitty," the federal budget. In return, the federal budget acted as the main source of funds for social and public services as well as for investment in different enterprises, sectors, and regions.

In terms of regional policy, in this period, the federal government had full control over development funds and was in a position to channel these funds as it saw fit. The control of investment and other resources, particularly of those earmarked for the LDRs, had enabled the federal government to pursue an active "regional policy." But, of course, resources were limited and the demand for development funds outstripped their supply. The intense competition between different regions for these resources, backed up by political pressure and influence, resulted in a final distribution which was neither satisfactory to any of the LDRs, nor willingly accepted by the MDRs.[20]

By the early fifties, the Yugoslav leaders decided to abandon the central planning strategy and devise their own model of socialism based on workers' self-management. The main factors contributing to this decision were the disappointing performance of the economy under central planning; the emergence of a powerful bureaucracy; the apparent contradictions between Marxist theory and economic and political practice; the expulsion from the Cominform; the desire to receive American aid; and, last but not least, the adverse impact of a system of unified economic management on regional and national autonomy. The last point is of particular relevance to our present discussion. The imposition of centralized control on the six constituent members of the federation was thought to be in conflict with the long standing commitment to regional and national autonomy. The diversity of the six republics required different approaches to economic construction in different areas—something for which a unified system of economic administration was ill equipped.

The Period of Market-Based Workers' Self-Management, 1952–1974. The system of workers' self-management was instituted in Yugoslavia between approximately 1952 and 1974 by means of a number of major economic reforms (notably in 1952, 1960–61 and 1965). These consisted of a comprehensive program of transformation of both the mechanism of resource allocation and the locus of decision making power. The essential idea of the new system was to develop autonomous enterprises with independent decisionmaking powers which were managed by their workers (through elected workers' councils) and linked together through the market mechanism. The workers' councils were to decide on issues such as the management structure; the division of revenue between employees' incomes, reserves, and investment; wages and bonuses. The state was to guide the economy by means of a system of non-compulsory indicative planning and provide for social services and the infrastructure. Most prices were liberalized and allowed to find their free market levels. Investment decisions were gradually transferred to enterprises as was the burden of investment financing. The budget ceased to be the source of investment resources given to enterprises freely. Funds were allocated to enterprises as "credits" and on a competitive basis through the General Investment Fund (in the fifties) and the banking system (from 1963 onwards). The allocation of credit was to be based on the borrower's credit worthiness and other purely economic criteria. The coordination between different enterprises and different industries and the matching of production to consumption requirements of the population was to be achieved by the "market mechanism."

In this period, the federal government's ability to direct resources for regional development purposes was weakened. Investment resources, separated from the federal budget in the early fifties, were provided as loans by a newly established General Investment Fund. During the fifties and early sixties, annual and five-year social plans earmarked certain amount of resources (as guaranteed bulk appropriation) from the General Investment Fund for allocation to enterprises in the LDRs on preferential terms.

Following the abolition of the General Investment Fund in 1963 and the transfer of its resources to the banking system, the mechanism of allocation and the amount of resources for the specific use of the LDRs had to change too. Eventually in 1965, after much dispute and discussion, the Federal Assembly passed a law to create the Federal Fund for Crediting Economic Development of Less Developed Republics and Regions. This fund then became the main instrument of regional policy and the vehicle of interregional transfer of resources. It was managed by an independent board consisting of eight members, one from each region. Its resources were formed by an obligatory contribution imposed on all enterprises in the socialized sector of the economy in the form of a percentage of their total social product. The level of contribution (which was initially set at 1.85 percent) as well as the distribution of the fund's resources between the LDRs were to be decided every five years by the agreement of all republics and provinces.

In addition to the fund, which was mainly concerned with the provision of investment resources for the LDRs, the federal government had always been required by the Constitution to provide additional resources for the financing of social services in the LDRs. This requirement aimed at ensuring that all Yugoslav citizens, irrespective of their place of residence and work, enjoyed a reasonable minimum level of social services. This type of assistance took the form of a subsidy paid to the LDRs from the federal budget in order to supplement their own revenues and enable them to provide social services at par with the average Yugoslav level. The level of this contribution was also decided every five years by the agreement of all the eight republics and provinces.

The crucial feature of Yugoslavia's regional policy, particularly in the fifties and sixties, was the way the federal resources earmarked for the LDRs were utilized. The regional development policy in Yugoslavia was dominated by the concept of "rapid industrialization," generally associated with the Soviet model of socialist construction. Not only was a continually high proportion of the national product spent on investment, but also investment resources were channeled into building large power stations, coal mines, raw material and metal extraction and processing plants, iron and steel complexes, chemical works, etc. What is more, the emphasis was on the setting-up of a comprehensive, vertically integrated industrial base in every region. This latter aspect, of course, corresponded to the underlying desire for economic independence present in all republics and provinces. A glance at *Table 3*, showing the rate and growth of investment in different parts of the country, confirms this high investment strategy which dominated the policy makers' thinking for over forty years.

Table 3 shows that, firstly, a high rate of investment was sustained in all areas of the country throughout this period. Secondly, while in Croatia and

Table 3
RATE AND GROWTH OF INVESTMENT* IN DIFFERENT REGIONS[21]

	Share of Investment in Social Product (%)** 1952–65	Expenditure (%) 1966–75	Increase in Investment 1952–1975
Yugoslavia	36	30	513
Bosnia-Hercegovina	37	37	305
Croatia	30	27	563
Macedonia	64	38	480
Montenegro	75	49	321
Slovenia	29	25	601
Serbia proper***	40	31	378
Kosovo	53	58	1333
Vojvodina	26	25	1698

*Based on constant 1972 prices.

**Social sector only.

***Republic of Serbia excluding the autonomous provinces of Kosovo and Vojvodina.

Slovenia the rate was 25-30 percent (quite high by international standards), in the LDRs the rate was even higher. Thirdly, the actual volume of investment, in real terms, increased significantly over the period under consideration: by four to seven times in most places and by fourteen times in the least developed region of Kosovo.

The development strategy based on high investment, however, failed to satisfy the high expectations of policy makers and, also, disappointed all those who had argued for the "preferential treatment" of LDRs in terms of access to investment resources. Two factors account for this failure. Firstly, the regional desire for a comprehensive economic base overshadowed the reality of the small size of the Yugoslav market. Secondly, in the midst of rivalry over obtaining resources to finance large-scale projects, the availability of other relevant resources and complementary economic activities were disregarded. Scarce resources were wasted on prestige projects and "political factories" to satisfy regional considerations; the gestation period of investment projects was much longer than expected; the location of industrial plants in relation to raw material and markets were not always properly considered; and sufficiently skilled man-power to run these projects was in short supply. The maintenance of fixed low prices for raw material, energy, agriculture, and transport, prevalent before 1965, benefited enterprises in the MDRs and adversely affected the LDRs which concentrated on these activities.

The performance of the self-management system, on the whole, was some-what mixed and, in terms of the aspirations of the Yugoslav leaders, certainly far from satisfactory. It is true that the Yugoslav economy grew very rapidly in this period (for a while at one of the highest rates of growth in the world). A pre-dominantly agricultural country was transformed into an industrial nation with a wide and modern industrial base. Standards of living grew fast. Health, educa-tion, and other social services improved and reached levels which could match those of other medium developed European nations. But along with these achievements, some unplanned and undesired features and tendencies had also begun to emerge. By the late sixties, when the system of market-based workers' self-management was fully established, these undesirable tendencies had become serious trends in the system and soon began to dominate it.

First, as the size and technological complexity of production units increased, the decisionmaking power was increasingly concentrated in the hands of the technical-managerial elite of each enterprise, and the influence of ordinary blue-collar production workers weakened. This gave rise to increas-ing labor turnover, worker absenteeism, work stoppages, and strikes.

Second, given the small size of the Yugoslav market, liberalization resulted in the strengthening of oligopolistic tendencies with adverse implica-tions for employment and price levels. Inefficient oligopolies could hide their inefficiencies by charging higher prices and offering their workers higher per-sonal incomes. At the macroeconomic level, this tendency was one of the main causes of the rising inflation and unemployment.

Thirdly, given that the conditions of demand, resource endowment, technology, and access to markets varied widely, the performance of enterprises were bound to be widely different too. As "performance" became the main determinant of enterprises' ability to attract investment credits and pay higher incomes, inequalities amongst enterprises and employees (and regions) also expanded. In particular, being more efficient and technologically advanced, enterprises in more developed regions were able to attract better quality human resources and more investment credits, and perform even better. Thus was generated a centrifugal force which widened the gap between different regions.

These unexpected consequences of self-management and market socialism caused much concern, disillusionment, and protest across the country. The demand for curtailing the increasing income differential came not only from the striking workers and LDRs but also from protesting students (of the 1968 student movement), all of which had thrown into the open the question of the legitimacy of the Party, now known as the League of Communists of Yugoslavia (LCY).[22] The Yugoslav government and party leaders had to come to terms with these unwanted and unexpected developments. While the economic consequences of the "market socialism" were at the center of the protesters' actions, the party bureaucracy was primarily concerned with the preservation of LCY's political power. Their answer, after a period of discussion in the late sixties and early seventies, was the 1974 Constitution which formally restored the "social authority" and "guiding role" of the Party and reasserted the primacy of collective interests over those of individual economic units. It reinforced the position of LCY and its involvement in social and economic affairs, and increased the authority and control of local governments over enterprises in their area.

The Period of 'Associated Labor' and 'Social Compacts', 1974–1988. The 1974 constitutional changes ushered in the principles of "associated labor," "social compact," and "consensus." Most enterprises were divided into smaller sub-units, called the Basic Organization of Associated Labor (BOAL), the smallest unit which was technically and economically identifiable. BOALs, with their own organs of self-management, became the basic decisionmaking unit, empowered to decide on all of their affairs. In terms of our earlier discussion, this provision aimed at reducing the size of the unit and enabling the workers to realize their self-management rights.

The relationship between the BOALs of an enterprise, as well as between enterprises, was to be governed by negotiated binding contracts called the "self-management agreements." On all important issues, the constituent BOALs had to reach a "consensus," effectively giving the workers' council of each BOAL the right of veto over the decisions and wishes of other BOALs. Wages and bonuses were to be regulated by "social compacts"—agreements negotiated between enterprises, their associations, trade unions, and the relevant governmental unit. Market forces were relegated to a secondary position, superseded by surrogates such as "self-management agreements" and "social compacts." The coordination of economic activity was to take place, not "by the blind forces of the markets," but through these surrogates. The net effect of all this was the creation of a cumbersome and slow decisionmaking process with detrimental consequences for enterprise efficiency.

In the context of the present discussion, an important aspect of 1974 constitutional changes was that the republics and provinces obtained the greatest degree of independence in Yugoslavia's short history. The powers of the federal government were severely restricted. Major decisions relating to the federation (such as the conduct of fiscal and monetary policy, taxation, public expenditure, the social plan of the federation, and the level of contribution to the Federal Fund for the Development of LDRs) had to be reached through social compacts and agreements which required the consent of all eight republics and provinces.[23] The decision on development programs and the methods of utilization of development funds were transferred to LDRs themselves—a decision which proved controversial later. The principle of solidarity, of course, remained unquestioned, at least until the mid-eighties, and in addition to the two types of resources mentioned earlier (the regional development fund and subsidies from the federal budget) additional measures, aimed particularly at Kosovo, were also taken. These included the priority allocation of the bulk of credits from World Bank and IMF; exemption from customs on the import of production equipment; higher than average export subsidies; the refunding of part of the LDRs' contribution to the federal budget; assistance with the repayment of their loans as well as additional assistance from the budget.

The size of contributions to the Funds for the Accelerated Development of LDRs and the subsidies from the federal budget, as well as their distribution amongst the LDRs, were decided upon every five years through hard negotiations. It must be pointed out that these contributions remained at relatively modest levels. The contribution to the Fund varied between 1.56 percent and 1.97 percent of the social product of enterprises in the social sector. The subsidies from the Federal Budget, to support the provision of social services, varied between 0.53 percent and 0.85 percent of Yugoslavia's national income. Of course, despite being modest, the resources of the Funds for Accelerated Development of LDRs accounted for a major share of total investment (18-33 percent) in most of these areas and up to 95 percent in Kosovo.

By the mid-eighties, it had become apparent that the system of BOALs, and all that was associated with the 1974 constitutional changes, had created more problems than they had solved. The "associated labor" extension of self-management had not resolved the basic problems faced by all socialist economies: incentives for workers and enterprises, innovative activity and efficiency, and meeting the aspirations of the poorer regions. Macroeconomic policy had become much more problematic because of the enhanced possibility of political intervention in economic affairs. Inflation, unemployment, falling productivity, increasing poverty particularly in some LDRs,[24] and rising foreign debt were some of the manifestations of the economy's poor performance. The system was badly in need of reform and preparations began for a new phase in the development of the Yugoslav model of socialism. The outcome of discussions and consultations were the 1988 Constitutional Amendments. The ideas of "associated labor" and consensus were abandoned. Market forces were to replace the "compacts" and "agreements" and to become the main mechanism of economic coordination, reminding the seasoned observers of conditions prevailing in the post-1965 period. The legal and constitutional conditions for the gradual evolution of a social market economy, one based on mixed ownership, private initiative, and state regulation, were prepared by subsequent laws. But with the separation of Croatia and Slovenia and the ensuing civil war, these plans were completely disrupted.

YUGOSLAVIA'S ACTIVE REGIONAL policy had involved the transfer of a large volume of resources to LDRs in order to make up for the shortage of their own resources, stimulate their faster economic development, and ensure the provision of social services in these areas. But what were the effects of this active inter-regional transfer of resources? How did the economies of LDRs respond to the additional resources provided in aid or grant by the Federation? The answers to these questions are not unambiguous and straightforward and, depending on the criteria chosen, conflicting results may be obtained. It is beyond dispute that in the postwar period, the economic and social conditions of the LDRs improved significantly. All measures of social and economic progress (indicators of health, education, care of the young and elderly, participation of women, social security, economic growth, employment and others) grew significantly and testify to the great improvement in the living conditions of people in the LDRs.

But these achievements were overshadowed by the slow pace of change in the LDRs in *comparison* with the rest of the country, particularly with Croatia and Slovenia. It is equally beyond dispute that the gap between the MDRs and LDRs had widened and the relative position of the latter had increasingly deteriorated. More significantly, the gap between the extremes of the two groups, Slovenia and Kosovo, had particularly widened. *Table 4* shows the change in the relative per-capita social product of different parts of Yugoslavia during the postwar period.

It is clear that while the position of Slovenia and Croatia had improved significantly in relation to the Yugoslav average, that of the LDRs, especially Kosovo, had continually deteriorated. The position of Serbia (a major contributor to the regional assistance efforts but not a recipient) had remained roughly around the Yugoslav average. This is a particularly stark observation in the light of four decades of an active regional policy. The successive reforms of the economic system, while paving the way for the operation of market forces and the process of decentralization, failed to improve the ability of the LDRs to break out of the "vicious circle" of underdevelopment despite a significant investment effort by the federation. Many factors contributed to the persistence of this vicious circle, among which the high rate of population growth, low labor productivity, low efficiency of investment, and the impact of the market mechanism deserve specific mention.

Table 4
SOCIAL PRODUCT PER CAPITA
IN DIFFERENT REGIONS AS % OF YUGOSLAV AVERAGE*[25]

Region	1947	1953	1965	1975	1988
Yugoslavia	100	100	100	100	100
Slovenia	163	161	183	205	208
Croatia	104	116	120	124	128
Serbia proper**	101	97	96	97	101
Vojvodina	100	100	113	115	119
Bosnia-Hercegovina	86	86	71	66	68
Macedonia	70	68	67	68	64
Montenegro	94	75	76	69	74
Kosovo	49	46	36	34	27
Slovenia as a proportion of Kosovo	3.3	4.1	5.0	6.1	7.4

*Based on constant 1972 prices.
**Excluding autonomous provinces of Kosovo and Vojvodina.

Firstly, the rate of growth of population in the LDRs had been significantly higher than that of the MDRs throughout the period under consideration, thus reducing the impact of the growth of output. Between the 1981 and 1991 census, for example, the natural growth of population was 6.5 per thousand for Yugoslavia as whole, ranging from 3.4 for Slovenia, 2.9 for Serbia, 1.9 for Croatia, and 0.6 for Vojvodina to 9.9 in Bosnia-Hercegovina, 10.8 in Montenegro, 12.2 in Macedonia, and 24.3 in Kosovo. More importantly, while in the postwar period the rate of growth of population dropped significantly in all regions, it remained almost unchanged in Kosovo. As a result, Kosovo's share of total population increased from 4.6 percent in 1948 to 8.3 percent in 1991.

A high population growth resulted in a high level of dependency on the active population as well as a high rate of unemployment. The expenditure on health, education, and other services, partly supported by subsidies from the federal budget, was greatly stretched with adverse effects on the quality of human resources. Similarly, the investment resources from the regional development fund were partly redirected to areas such as housing, transport, and communication which were directly affected by the population size.[26] In short, the rapid growth of population had, to some extent, undermined the development efforts and contributed to the vicious circle.

The second factor explaining the widening gap was the low factor productivity in the LDRs: low efficiency of investment and low productivity of labor. Efficiency of investment is measured by the increase in social product resulting from 100 dinars of investment; labor productivity by output per worker in the industrial sector of the economy. These two indicators are shown in *Tables 5* and *6* respectively.

The efficiency of investment in all the LDRs was well below the Yugoslav average throughout the period under consideration (with the exception of Bosnia-Hercegovina's slightly above-average figure for 1976-83). The

Table 5
PRODUCTIVITY OF INVESTMENT*
IN DIFFERENT REGIONS AS OF YUGOSLAV AVERAGE[27]

Region	1952-65	1966-75	1976-83
Yugoslavia	100	100	100
Slovenia	119	135	109
Croatia	111	108	89
Serbia proper**	101	97	117
Vojvodina	143	109	105
Bosnia-Hercegovina	80	77	103
Macedonia	63	87	90
Montenegro	43	50	82
Kosovo	77	65	44

*Measured by change in the social product per 100 dinar investment (in social sector).
**Republic of Serbia excluding the autonomous provinces of Kosovo and Vojvodina.

Table 6
LABOR PRODUCTIVITY IN INDUSTRY*
IN DIFFERENT REGIONS AS % OF YUGOSLAV AVERAGE[28]

Region	1952	1965	1975	1988
Yugoslavia	100	100	100	100
Slovenia	105	117	125	126
Croatia	98	102	108	105
Serbia proper**	106	105	96	98
Vojvodina	87	89	101	111
Bosnia-Hercegovina	95	93	84	85
Macedonia	105	78	77	86
Montenegro	137	103	89	88
Kosovo	88	79	77	71

*Measured by social product in industry per worker (in social sector only), based on constant 1972 prices.
**Republic of Serbia excluding the autonomous provinces of Kosovo and Vojvodina.

difference was particularly large in Montenegro and Kosovo. Similarly, labor productivity in the LDRs was below the Yugoslav average, in most periods, and had also declined over time. The nature and quality of investment projects (referred to earlier), the availability of suitable inputs (especially management) and complementary activities account for the low levels of efficiency of investment. The work force's lower levels of skill and qualification and a shorter experience of an industrial culture in the LDRs account for labor productivity trailing behind the rest of the country. At the same time, the deployment of more modern production technologies, the availability of complementary economic activities, higher levels of education and skill attainment, better housing, health, and other social services in the MDRs also contributed to the growing factor productivity gap.

The low levels of factor productivity, in turn, resulted in low levels of industrial output, income, and demand, and given the higher rate of growth of labor force, produced higher levels of unemployment too. The vicious circle of underdevelopment was completed by the lower standards of living, lower public expenditure on social services, and lower labor productivity. *Table 7* shows the extent of unemployment, measured by the number of job seekers, per 1000 employed, in different regions of Yugoslavia since the early fifties.

It is clear that the LDRs, particularly in the latter half of the period under review, had been suffering from much higher as well as increasing rates of unemployment. Slovenia and Croatia, on the other hand, had always had a lower than average unemployment rate which had also been falling in proportion to the national average. Slovenian unemployment rate was about 70 percent of the national rate in 1952 and dropped to 20 percent of the national average by 1988.

Finally, the differential impact of the decentralization process and developing market relations on different regions should be noted. Regions such as Slovenia and Croatia were less damaged during the war. They started with a better endowment of resources, a more educated and skilled work force, and a more diversified economy. Enterprises in these regions were more efficient, and with developing market relations, became more profitable, and better able to raise internal funds for expansion and to attract even more from the banking system. They rapidly gained from their advantageous position in the federation and prospered. The less developed regions, on the other hand, started from what can only be described as backward economic conditions, suffered serious damage during the war, had poor endowment of resources, insufficient technical know-how, and lower levels of education. Their enterprises were less efficient and could not compete with those from the MDRs. Their profitability was lower, their internal resources and those raised from the banking system were limited, and they had to rely heavily on outside assistance. The support available from the federation, in the amounts provided, could not transform their position significantly.

As mentioned earlier, during the postwar period, the emphasis on the faster development of the LDRs had focused attention on the relations between richer and poorer regions and nationalities, thus eclipsing the Serb-Croat rela-

Table 7
UNEMPLOYMENT*[29]

Region	1952	1965	1975	1989
Yugoslavia	26	65	113	175
Slovenia	19	17	15	35
Croatia	29	59	58	86
Serbia proper**	25	79	143	183
Vojvodina	30	47	119	156
Bosnia-Hercegovina	15	50	128	260
Macedonia	67	156	267	283
Montenegro	33	54	168	294
Kosovo	26	179	297	583

*Measured by the number of registered job seekers per 1000 employed.
**Excluding autonomous provinces of Kosovo and Vojvodina.

tion. The richer regions made their contributions to the LDRs under much pressure and, in the latter years, under great duress. It is certainly true, as *Table 8* shows, that the bulk of transferred resources came from the contributions made by enterprises outside the LDRs. But it is also important to note that Serbia (excluding Vojvodina and Kosovo), whose position throughout this period remained at about the Yugoslav average, made a major contribution, often higher than Slovenia and Croatia, to the transferred resources. And the Serbian enterprises made these contributions without the kind of complaint that was continually heard from the Croat and Slovene political leaders.

In sum, both sides of the regional divide became increasingly unhappy with the evolution of the regional policy. On the one hand, a substantial amount of resources had been allocated to, and spent on, the development of the LDRs. Some results had been obtained but they were far from sufficient and satisfactory, leaving the LDRs frustrated and suspicious. They resented the expanding regional gap and the insufficient help from their better-off neighbors. The more developed regions, on the other hand, felt that the LDRs were not using their increasing autonomy to direct the Federal assistance effectively. In their eyes, scarce investment resources were being transferred from their more efficient enterprises with higher productivity to enterprises in the LDRs with lower productivity, thus retarding the development of the MDRs. They wanted better application of economic and profitability criteria. They also wanted to have a say in how the transferred resources were being utilized and wished to encourage inter-regional joint ventures, in the hope of influencing the utilization of these resources.

The leaders of the more developed Croatia and Slovenia continually complained of the slow pace of economic reform. They saw their future in further decentralization, the extension of market-based economic reforms, and the limitation of the role of central authorities. They believed that further extension of the market mechanism and depoliticization of resource allocation would force enterprises in the LDRs to become more efficient and to base their decisions on profitability and other economic criteria.

Table 8
CONTRIBUTIONS OF DIFFERENT REGIONS
TO THE FUND FOR ACCELERATED DEVELOPMENT OF LDRS (% OF TOTAL)[30]

Region	1982	1983	1984	1985	1986	1987	1988	1989
MDRs	75	78	74	76	79	73	77	77
Slovenia	13	19	16	15	18	18	20	24
Croatia	23	26	27	25	23	24	24	26
Serbia*	27	24	21	27	21	18	26	19

*Serbia without the autonomous provinces.

The LDRs, however, felt that their enterprises were not at the same technological and efficiency levels as those of the MDRs and could not easily compete with them. The growing autonomy of regions under self-management was seen to be condemning them to a perpetual "poorer partner" position with slower rate of growth. The LDRs, with a preference for an active interventionist policy, became associated with opposition to reforms. The notion of the "progressive northwest" versus the "conservative southeast" found increasing currency.[31]

Regions resorted to restrictive practices and autarkic measures—remnant of the sixties—which effectively barred many enterprises from operating outside their own regions. Self-management agreements and social compacts were used as means of closing the market to "non-domestic" producers and workers. Each region, therefore, had to resort to hard bargaining in order to establish workable (if not ideal) economic relations with other regions. The field of economic policy was the most fertile ground for political and economic horse-trading, an ultimately unsatisfactory state of affairs. Economic disputes gradually were expressed in regional and national terms and took nationalistic tones, thus contributing to the rise of nationalism and the degeneration of nationality relations.

The argument between the two groups was essentially based on regional self-interest. The richer regions had been campaigning, since the sixties, to move rapidly toward a market economy. They did not wish to be held back by the slower moving regions. Nor did they believe in continuing the inter-regional transfer of resources to these regions. By 1991, with the disintegration of the LCY, the only mechanism for imposing some form of socialist solidarity had disappeared, creating conditions for Croatia and Slovenia to speed up their campaign for either a loose confederation or separate states.

Two points need to be emphasized before concluding this discussion. First, for nearly forty years, the MDRs operated in an environment where product markets were largely liberalized but input markets, particularly raw materials, energy, and minerals were subject to controls. The MDRs had a protected and ready market for their manufactured products in the LDRs where they faced little competition from local producers or from abroad. Their enterprises, specializing in manufactured goods, could fix (and raise) their prices according to market conditions but bought their inputs from the LDRs at controlled prices (which were always below the market level). These benefits never appeared on the loss-gain balance sheet of the relations between regions.

Second, the market-based self-management model of economic development chosen by the LCY was at the core of deteriorating regional economic and social disparities in Yugoslavia. With successive market-based reforms and the decentralization process, particularly in the post-1974 Constitution period, it was inevitable that the relative positions of the different regions would diverge. The 1974 Constitution effectively created eight separate and autonomous units, only loosely linked together by the federal state and party institutions. By the mid-eighties, the resources under federal government's control were severely curtailed, and thus its power of intervention in favor of poorer regions had been greatly reduced. The magnitude of transferred resources through the Fund for the Accelerated Development of the LDRs and the subsidies from the federal budget were simply insufficient to deal with the increasing regional disparities. These resources remained in the modest range of two to three percent of the social product of each region—and declined in the last decade. In the absence of more active intervention, backed by financial and technical resources, the operation of market forces could only create centrifugal forces amongst the regions. The regional government and party leaders lacked the political will to find more effective forms of regional policy which would augment the quality and quantity of transferred resources.

THE YUGOSLAV COMMUNIST Party was always aware of the existence of national and regional prejudices which had developed in the interwar period and intensified during the Pavelić regime. But the Party's own war-time experience had strengthened its deep belief in the possibility of peaceful development of relations between nationalities. The re-publication of Kardelj's prewar essay, *The Development of the Slovenian National Question* in 1958, drew public attention to the nationalities question again.[32] For a time, particularly in the fifties, the Party believed that with the development of self-management, the conditions would be created for the emergence of a "Yugoslav" identity, which would supersede the narrower national or regional identities. The idea of "Yugoslavianism" (*Jugoslovenstvo*) was promoted, and attempts were made to identify and spread a "Yugoslav" culture, and develop a new consensus about the relations between nationalities. However, the federal structure and the importance of regions in national affairs meant that the notion of nationality would survive all this. The idea of "Yugoslavianism" was eventually dropped at the Eighth Party Congress in 1964. From then on, the Party focused on the idea of "parity of representation," trying to ensure that regions and nationalities were represented in the national decisionmaking process.

With the liberalization of the Yugoslav society, however, public manifestations of nationalism (and even chauvinism) became possible. In the fifties and sixties, Serb and Croat writers and historians were in dispute over their cultural heritage, the status of Croatian as a language separate from Serbian, and the position of the Croatian Communist Party over the 1939 *Sporazum*. More serious was the struggle in the early sixties with an anti-reform group, headed by Aleksandar Ranković, the de facto leader of the Serbian Party and the most powerful member of the leadership after Tito. Although the struggle revolved around the direction and pace of reforms, and Ranković was aligned with many representatives from the LDRs, Serbian nationalism became the focus of criticism which culminated in the removal of Ranković in 1966.

In the late sixties and early seventies, when most of Yugoslavia was concerned with the consequences of market-based socialism (discussed earlier), the Croatian and Slovenian parties were pressing for greater autonomy and faster reforms, drawing an angry response from other parts of the country. The Serbian cultural organization *Matica Srpska,* the Serbian Orthodox Church, the Serbs in Croatia and their organization *Prosvjeta,* as well as the Croatian cultural organization *Matica Hrvatska,* and organizations of economists, writers, and students, all took active part in these exchanges. It was in this period that ideas such as a Croatian Republic, a separate Croatian Army, and a Serbian autonomous region in Croatia were publicly floated. This time, Croatian nationalism was the focus of criticism and resulted in large-scale resignations, purges, and arrests. The criticism was also used to strengthen the LCY's political power and pave the way for the 1974 constitutional amendments.

Despite these occasional outbursts of nationalism, relations between nationalities improved significantly during the "socialist" phase of Yugoslavia's history, albeit with the exception of Kosovo. The nationalities policy was, on the whole, successful and received public support. Incidents of public and open hostilities toward any nation were extremely rare. The evidence from the research work of several scholars in the fifties, sixties, and seventies, in Yugoslavia and abroad, indicated strongly that the "ethnic distance" had narrowed, the political incorporation of different regions into Yugoslavia had been accepted, and their political cohesion had been enhanced. This improvement in the relations between nationalities should be seen in the context of the rising economic prosperity and prestige enjoyed by Yugoslavia in the international community. It was not pure coincidence that by the late eighties, when the economy was in serious crisis, relations between the Yugoslav nationalities also deteriorated, reaching the point of fratricidal war in Bosnia-Hercegovina.

The only significant instance of violent confrontation between nationalities, prior to the recent events, occurred in Kosovo in 1981 and then in 1988–1989. Relations between Kosovo's Albanian nationality and the Serbian and federal governments deteriorated sharply during the eighties resulting in large-scale mass demonstrations which were violently suppressed by federal troops. The problem of Kosovo, where Albanians gradually became the largest and most dominant nationality in an area which had been inhabited by Serbs for centuries, remains one of Yugoslavia's most complex problems. This problem, however, has been more about the demands of the Albanian nationality for greater autonomy (including the status of a republic) and much less about relations between Albanians and Serbs. Although since 1988 the Serbian government, led by Milošević, has a lot to answer for concerning the escalation of tension in the Province, all members of the federation must share the blame for the decision to declare a "state of emergency" and deploy federal troops on the streets of Priština and other towns, and the disastrous consequences that followed.

The events of 1990 and 1991, leading to the breakup of the "second" Yugoslavia, have to be studied separately and in much greater detail.[33] Suffice it to say that the situation became very grim in Croatia in 1991, and even more so in Bosnia-Hercegovina, with serious loss of life, violation of basic human rights, and a massive onslaught against the civilian population by regular and irregular armies. While Serbia has deservedly received widespread international condemnation for its actions in Croatia and Bosnia, the role of Croatia in the conflict has largely escaped critical scrutiny. The deplorable practice of "ethnic cleansing" began early on when Croatian Serbs became victims of atrocities and were expelled from their villages in Western Slavonia, to all of which Zagreb turned a blind eye. Later, the Croat population in Eastern Slavonia was targeted by armed bands (calling themselves Chetniks again) supported by the JNA and the Serbian government. What was particularly serious in Croatia, however, was the systematic violation of the rights of minorities which was (and still is) tolerated by the state. The new Croatian Constitution declared that Croatia was the land of Croats; the use of Cyrillic alphabet for official communication was banned (even in areas where Serbs are in majority). The insignia and flags resembling the Ustaša began reappearing. The hidden agenda seemed to be to change the history of 1941–1945. Against international protest by the victims of the holocaust, the "Victims of Fascism Square" in Zagreb was renamed the "Croatian Heroes Square." The site of the former extermination camp at Jasenovac became a national park. The Croatian parliament rehabilitated Archbishop Stepinac. Arbitrary arrests, disappearance of Serbs, and unlawful killings began to happen again. Reports by the Amnesty International and other human rights organizations have been appearing regularly, indicating a deteriorating situation.[34] The EC recognition of Croatia, despite an unfavorable report on the rights of minorities by Judge Robert Badinter, the president of the French Constitutional Court, may prove to have been a mistake (particularly as it failed to stop further escalation of violence).

From March 1992, Bosnia-Hercegovina has been embroiled in ethnic conflict on an unprecedented scale, reminding us of the situation that prevailed there in the 1941–1945 period. Bands of new Chetniks, now vying for international respectability, have resorted to the most appalling methods to drive the mainly Muslim population from its homes in order to create a Serbian mini-state in Northern and Eastern Bosnia, linking Serbia proper with Serb-inhabited areas of Croatia. In this they have been supported by the Milošević government and the JNA. The Croat paramilitary organizations in Bosnia have also pursued a similar aim—the creation of a Croat mini-state in western Bosnia, and have resorted to similar methods, albeit on a smaller scale, to achieve their objective. The governments of Serbia and Croatia, by giving overt and covert support to their political followers in Bosnia, bear the main responsibility for the carve-up of this republic.

In the Second World War, it was the Partisan movement in Bosnia-Hercegovina which united different ethnic groups in their common struggle against fascist occupiers and their domestic allies. The agony of Bosnia will continue until the emergence of a new political force which is able to build on the positive lessons of history, unlike the present politicians who continually emphasize the negative aspects of the past in order to fan the flames of national hatred and ethnic discord.

One particular aspect of national question which deserves some clarification is the issue of Serbian overrepresentation in the party and state institutions. This is an issue which has received much attention in the context of the present hostilities. It is certainly true that under the pro-Serb governments of the "first" Yugoslavia, state institutions were dominated by Serbs, giving rise to strong feeling of subjugation by other nations, particularly Croats and Slovenes. In the immediate postwar period, too, Serbs and Montenegrins were heavily overrepresented in the army and state administration. But the reason for this was entirely different from that of the interwar period. The postwar political elite in Yugoslavia has its roots in the Partisan and the relatively small Communist movements. Serbs (and mainly Croatian Serbs) and Montenegrins were the most numerous ethnic components of the Partisan movement. All historians of the movement have pointed out that the Serb-populated areas of Croatia were the first areas to engage in armed uprising against the Pavelić regime and the Germans.[35]

The crucial point, however, is that, starting from the heavy overrepresentation of Serbs (and also Montenegrins), the party and the government made conscious attempts to change the status quo during the period of the "second" Yugoslavia. The notion of "national parity" was the vehicle by which these attempts were promoted.[36] At the higher levels of decisionmaking, the ethnic balance was certainly changed and some form of parity obtained. Republics and Provinces were well represented at the leading level of almost all federal institutions. But at lower echelons of federal institutions, the cadres and technical staff, the change was much slower, with Serbs and Montenegrins retaining their more-than-proportionate presence.

The change in the ethnic composition of two particularly important institutions deserve a brief mention. These are the LCY and the army. The membership of LCY had undergone much change in the postwar period. The total party membership increased steadily from a mere 161,000 in 1945 to over two million in 1983 when it started to decline slowly. The increase in membership, of course, was not homogeneous in different parts of the country. *Table 9* represents the ethnic composition of the LCY since the mid-fifties.

The table clearly shows that, between 1957 and 1988, the extent of overrepresentation of the Serb and Montenegrin nationalities gradually declined, though it was not eradicated. At the same time, the representation of Muslims, Macedonians, Albanians, Hungarians, and particularly "Yugoslavs" gradually increased. The Croat and Slovene underrepresentation, however, had somewhat increased, mainly because of a general drift away from the LCY in these two republics during the eighties.

The ethnic composition of the Yugoslav National Army (JNA) also went through a similar process in the postwar period. From a predominantly Serb and Montenegrin army, it was transformed into an army in which other nationalities were also represented, though the Serbian over-representation has persisted. This is illustrated in *Table 10*, showing the ethnic composition of the JNA leadership.

From a very high level in its early days, the overrepresentation of Serbs in the JNA reached 70 percent of the officers' corps in 1971, and then was

Table 9
NATIONAL ORIGIN OF MEMBERS
OF THE LEAGUE OF COMMUNISTS OF YUGOSLAVIA1957-1988 BY PERCENTAGE[37]

Members	1957 LCY	1957 Population	1971 LCY	1971 Population	1988 LCY	1988 Population*
Serb	54.5	41.7	49.4	41.7	44.2	38.4
Croat	19.0	23.5	17.4	22.9	12.6	20.5
Slovene	7.7	8.7	6.4	8.6	4.8	8.0
Macedonian	6.4	5.2	6.2	5.6	7.5	5.9
Montenegrin	6.7	2.1	6.4	2.4	5.5	2.5
Muslim	n/a	n/a	4.6	6.9	7.6	7.8
Albanian	2.4	4.5	3.4	4.7	4.7	5.6
Hungarian	1.1	3.0	1.1	2.7	1.2	2.2
Yugoslav	n/a	5.9	3.8	1.4	10.6	5.6
Others	2.2	5.4	4.3	3.1	1.3	3.5

*Population according to the 1981 Census.

Table 10
ETHNIC ORIGIN OF THE OFFICERS CORPS
OF THE YUGOSLAV NATIONAL ARMY (JNA) BY PERCENTAGE, (1991)[38]

Nationality	Share in Army	Share in Population*
Serb	60	36
Croat	13	20
Slovene	3	8
Montenegrin	6	3
Macedonian	6	6
Muslims	2	9
Albanian	1	8
Hungarian	1	2
Yugoslav	7	5
Others	2	3

*According to the 1981 Census.

slowly reduced to some 60 percent, as shown above. But the representation of other nationalities never reached the proportions warranted by their share in the total population. Again, as in the case of LCY itself, there was a process of change toward greater representation of other nationalities but the process was too slow. Of course, as long as the LCY was in control of the army, it was reasonable to expect that the army would be essentially concerned with its primary task: the defense of the territorial integrity of the federation. But with the rapid disintegration of the LCY in 1990–1991, the army gradually turned to an autonomous organization fighting for its own interests. The size of the JNA, as well as its human and material resources, could be justified only in the context of a twenty-three-million-strong nation. With the separation of four republics from the federation, the JNA would have to shrink to a much smaller size—not a welcome prospect for the JNA leaders.

IN CONCLUSION, THE causes of the deterioration of relations between Yugoslavia's nationalities were complex, but the role of regional development policies was central to the conflict which finally surfaced in the late eighties. Once this conflict erupted, history became a powerful weapon for competing nationalist causes. The pro-Serbian policies of the interwar government had resulted in disappointment among those intellectuals and politicians who had campaigned for the unification of South Slavs, and in disharmony and rancor between Serbs and other nationalities (particularly Croats). The Second World War created the conditions in which Croatian nationalists could realize their aspirations for an "independent" state, even though through a state delivered by Nazi invaders.

The "socialist" phase in Yugoslavia's history witnessed significant improvements in the relations between nationalities. Although the policies of the new state did not bring about full equality of representation and political power among its constituent nationalities and regions, it went a long way in that direction. Given the largely Serb and Montenegrin make-up of the Partisan movement and the Party, the subsequent gradual change in the ethnic balance of the Party, the army, and state institutions were the result of a conscious effort by the leaders of the "second" Yugoslavia. During this phase, the nationality question was linked to the uneven economic development of different regions. It was thought that only with economic convergence of different regions would national rivalries and disputes diminish and, eventually, disappear. The achievement of rapid economic growth in the LDRs, therefore, became the key to the nationalities question and the cornerstone of government policies. Throughout this period, the government pursued an active regional policy involving the redistribution of investment and budgetary resources in favor of the LDRs. As a result of these policies, there was significant economic progress in the LDRs.

But regional policy and policy instruments were themselves directly influenced by Yugoslavia's overall development strategy: the establishment of a system of market-based workers' self-management. This system, by its emphasis on market allocation of resources, decentralization and granting of unprecedented autonomy to the regions, weakened the federal government's ability to mobilize resources for inter-regional transfer. Decentralization and the market mechanism gave regions and republics increasing autonomy over their affairs, thus retaining and even expanding their differences. They also generated centrifugal forces which could not be weakened by the regional policy instruments utilized by the state.

The "high investment" strategy employed for the rapid development of the LDRs was, on the whole, unsuccessful. This was partly because of the concentration of investment in capital-intensive heavy industries and partly because of low labor productivity and low efficiency of investment in LDRs. The subsidies from the federal budget, aimed at improving the provision of social services, were insufficient to counteract the effects of high population growth rates. Over time, despite the continued involvement of the federation and the acceptance of the need for active regional policy by all concerned, the gap between the less developed and the more developed regions widened. The inter-regional transfer of resources satisfied neither the LDRs nor the MDRs. The LDRs believed that the resources provided by the federation were not sufficient to improve their relative position. The MDRs, however, maintained that any improvement should come from better utilization of these resources and not from their expansion. Serbia's position over this on-going debate was of particular relevance. While itself not one of the MDRs, Serbia supported the redistributive efforts of the federation and played a major part in providing supplementary resources for the LDRs. It is difficult to see if, in return, Serbia derived any special economic advantage during the life of the "second" Yugoslavia.

The generalized crisis of the Yugoslav economy during the 1980s, manifested by high rates of inflation, unemployment, inefficiency, rising foreign debt, poverty, etc., resulted, among other things, in the reduction of resources allocated to the development of poorer regions, precisely at a time when more resources were needed. The richer regions, notably Slovenia and Croatia, were unhappy with the contributions they were making to the less developed regions. The less developed regions, on the other hand, felt left out, unassisted, and exploited. Either a new solution to the problem of regional polarization and dispute had to be found or, the rapid deterioration of the situation was to be expected.

It may seem that the recent conflict in Yugoslavia has been more about the assertion of the right to statehood and the dismantling of the "socialist" state than about regional disparities and growing polarization. Economic factors, nevertheless, played an important role: in the end, Slovenia and Croatia did not wish to continue to "subsidize" the less developed parts of Yugoslavia and be slowed down by their pace of growth. Had regional policies been more successful and the gap between different regions narrower, the economic justification for separation would have been considerably weaker.

NOTES

This article was originally written in January–February 1992 and first appeared in *Capital and Class,* 48, October 1992. It has been edited for the present volume. The author is grateful to many friends and colleagues, particulary to Miša Crnobrnja, Gabi Herbert, and George Poltts, for their comments on an earlier version of the article.

1. Other aspects of the "nationalities problem," which have contributed to the unfolding of the present tragedy, have been left out because they are beyond the scope of this article.

2. Hungary's rule in Croatia had been particularly oppressive and brutal, giving rise to Croatian nationalism long before Serbs were a major factor on the scene.

3. For details see Ivo Banac, *The National Question in Yugoslavia: Origins, History, Politics* (Ithaca, 1984), and P. D. Ostović, *The Truth About Yugoslavia* (New York, 1952).

4. The question of the "nationhood" of Montenegrins, Macedonians, and Bosnian Muslims was shelved at this stage.

5. As it turned out, France and Britain had already (secretly) promised the disputed areas including the major ports of Trieste, Fiume (Rijeka), and Zadar to Italy by the London Treaty of 1915. Under pressure from the Allies and other neighbors, the Yugoslav delegation finally signed the Peace Treaty conceding the Italian claims. Most of these areas (though not Trieste) were recovered after the Second World War. Macedonia and Southern Serbia (including Kosovo) were returned to the new state at this stage—despite Bulgarian protests.

6. While some 700,000 of its potential citizens were left outside its borders (more than half of them in Italy), the new State was also "assigned" more than a million minority citizens of Magyar, Romanian, and German origin through various peace treaties. The national composition of the 12-million-strong population at this stage was: 39 percent Serb, 24 percent Croat, 9 percent Slovene, 6 percent Bosnian Muslim, 5 percent Macedonian, 4 percent Albanian, and 17 percent other nationalities including Germans, Hungarians, Austrians, Romanians, Turks, Jews, Italians, and other Slavs. For details see Ivo J. Lederer, *Yugoslavia at the Paris Peace Conference: A Study in Frontiermaking* (New Haven, 1963).

7. The Socialist Workers Party of Yugoslavia was formed in 1919 by the progressive elements of the Serbian, Croatian, and Slovenian social democratic parties, other leftist groups, and the returnees from the Russian front who had come in contact with the Bolshevik Revolution during the War. It was renamed the Yugoslav Communist Party (YCP) in 1920 and the League of Communists of Yugoslavia (LCY) in 1952.

8. Given the extent of opposition, it is useful to point out that had the YCP not been banned, the 1921 Constitution would not have been passed by the Assembly.

9. For details, see Rudolf Bićanić, *Economic Policy in Socialist Yugoslavia* (Cambridge, 1973), ch.1.

10. In her article "Lessons of History: War Returns to Yugoslavia," *Capital and Class,* 47 (1992), pp. 25-32, Branka Magaš has blamed Serbian nationalism, and not the the Nazi occupation and Ustaše collaboration, for the disintegration of the "first" Yugoslavia. In these "lessons of history," there is not a single reference to the Ustaša regime and its role in shaping the nationality relations in Yugoslavia.

11. The estimates of the number of victims of the Ustaša regime vary greatly (from tens of thousands to hundreds of thousands). The Croat nationalist historians have tried to minimize the extent of atrocities and blame it on the Serbs' behavior in the previous period. See, for example, Franjo Tudjman, *Nationalism in Contemporary Europe* (New York, 1981). The Serb nationalists, for similar reasons, have attempted to magnify the number of victims. But, in addition, there are the accounts of many foreign observers, particularly British army and intelligence personnel air dropped behind the enemy lines in Yugoslavia, who have also testified to these atrocities. Of course, no downward revision of the number of victims can or should reduce the severity and enormity of Ustaša crimes or their impact on the Serb-Croat relations. For some accounts see Zdenko Lownthal (ed.), *The Crimes of the Fascist Occupants and Their Collaborators Against the Jews in Yugoslavia* (Federation of Jewish Communities of The FPRJ, Belgrade, 1957), and Lenard Cohen and Paul Warwick, *Political Cohesion in a Fragile Mosaic: The Yugoslav Experience* (Boulder, 1983).

12. Archbishop Stepinac was brought to justice and, after a much publicized trial, was sentenced to sixteen years imprisonment. Pavelić and many of his henchmen, though, fled from Yugoslavia and with the help of the Catholic Church, the Vatican, and even the Allies, reached Argentina. There he reorganized the Ustaša movement, even publishing the the journal *Hrvatska Revija* (Croatian Review). The Ustaše, in exile, continued to organize terrorist activities against Yugoslav government officials. They have been responsible for scores of bombings at Yugoslav embassies and the murder of a number of Yugoslav diplomats around the world.

13. The Chetnik leader Draflza Mihailović, a colonel in the Serbian army during the First World War, was appointed the Minister of War by the exiled "Royal" Yugoslav government in London, and his Chetniks began receiving military support from Britain. Mihailović was arrested in March 1946, tried and condemned to death in July.

14. While the Party's basic line remained one of national reconciliation, the opposition (often with religious overtones) from some reactionary sections of some nationalities was severely put down. There were violent confrontations with the Albanian minority in Kosovo reaching the point of an armed uprising in 1944 with scores of deaths. Relations with the Catholic Church in Croatia and with the Islamic Religious Community in Bosnia became very tense. For a detailed discussion of the Party's relations with minorities in this period, see Paul Shoup, *Communism and the Yugoslav National Question* (New York, 1968).

15. By a law passed soon after the War, any incitement to hatred on the basis of nationality, religion, or race was made a criminal offence.

16. The decision to make Bosnia-Hercegovina a separate republic and the sixth unit of the Federation was taken, after much debate, at the second session of the Anti-Fascist National Liberation Council of Yugoslavia [AVNOJ] in November 1943. The status of Bosnian Muslims as a separate nationality, however, was not settled at this stage but had to wait until the early sixties. From then on "Muslim" has denoted a nationality rather than followers of a religion. For more details on this see Paul Shoup, *Communism and the Yugoslav National Question* (New York, 1968).

17. Sources: "Savezni zavod za statistiku," *Statistički Godišnjak Jugoslavije* [SGJ], 1960, 1970, 1973, 1987; and "Savezni zavod za stastistiku," *Jugoslavija 1945–1964* (Belgrade, 1965). The last proper census of population took place in 1981. There was indeed a 1991 census but the results (for areas other than Serbia and Montenegro) are partial and largely based on estimates. Some of the results have been published in *Yugoslav Survey*, 1 (1992). With minor exceptions, the general picture had remained largely unchanged. One of the notable exceptions was the continued decline (from 13 percent to 10 percent) in the share of Serbian nationality in Kosovo.

18. Sources: *Jugoslavija 1945–1964,* and *Yugoslavia 1945–1985* (Belgrade, 1986).

19. The Constitution of the Socialist Federative Republic of Yugoslavia [SFRY], 1974, Basic Principle III, p. 15. Similar pronouncements were made in earlier constitutions.

20. The scarcity of resources for regional development and the competing claims of different regions for these resources was, furthermore, compounded by Yugoslavia's expulsion from the Cominform in 1948. This resulted in serious disruption of external trade and diversion of resources from civilian to military industries. The associated dislocation meant that the scarce investment funds had to be allocated to those regions and projects with higher productivity of investment. This, in general, meant the more developed regions and their industrial projects.

21. Sources: SGJ, 1960; *Yugoslavia 1945–1985.*

22. The most well-known protests took place at Belgrade University, where students demanded the sharing of the burden of the reforms by all sections of the society and the curtailing of the power of the "red bourgeoisie."

23. The principle of "equality of all nations," therefore, gave Montenegro with half a million people exactly the same powers on the top decisionmaking body as Serbia with over seven million, and an effective veto power.

24. According to the research conducted at the Institut ekonomski nauka, between 1978 and 1989, the proportion of the population below the poverty line increased from 17.2 percent to 23.6 percent. The variation across the regions was even more startling: 2.9 percent in Slovenia and 81.9 percent in Kosovo. For detaisl see Aleksandra Pošarac, "Poverty in Yugoslavia," *Sudosteuropa,* Heft 2 (1991).

25. Sources: *SGJ,* 1980, 1989. *Yugoslavia, 1945–1985.*

26. In fact, if the population size is taken into account, the "high investment" regions of Table 3 will mostly change to "'low investment per capita" regions.

27. Source: *Yugoslavia 1945–1985.*

28. Sources: *SGJ,* 1990; *Yugoslavia 1945–1985.*

29. Sources: *SGJ,* 1990; *Yugoslavia 1945–1985.*

30. Sources: *SGJ,* 1988, 1990.

31. The most important example of this unity is the alliance supporting Aleksandar Ranković in the early sixties which actually succeeded in forcing the postponement of major economic reforms until 1965. In the late eighties, a similar alliance was formed around Milošević in order to thwart the dash of Slovenia and Croatia for a loose confederal state. For some of the documents of the Federal Presidency, see *Yugoslav Survey,* 4 (1990) and 1 (1991).

32. In this essay Kardelj argued that "nations" would continue to play an important role until the realization of socialism.

33. For an excellent analysis of the events of 1990–1992, see Mihailo Crnobrnja, *Le Drame Yugoslav* (Rennes, 1992).

34. The Amnesty International Report, EUR 48/26/91, November 1991; Helsinki Watch Report, *Guardian,* February 15, 1992; and *Index on Censorship,* 5 (1992).

35. For details see Lenard Cohen and Paul Warwick, *Political Cohesion in a Fragile Mosaic: The Yugoslav Experience.* A study of the ethnic origins of the surviving veterans of the partisan movement in 1977 reinforces this point further. See *Statistički Bilten,* 1174, April 1980.

36. The notion of "parity of representation," of course, is one that aroused much emotion in Yugoslavia and contributed to the rise of nationalism everywhere. Serbia was the largest republic, and Serbs constituted some 40 percent of the population. But they did not have the same proportion of the leading posts in Federal institutions. Montenegrins, who constituted less than 3 percent of the population, occupied a much greater proportion of leading positions. "Parity," for Serbs, has meant that in many areas of social and political life, they carried less weight than their numerical strength in the Federation warranted. This became a particularly thorny issue in the recent period and was heavily relied on by the nationalist forces and groups among the Serbs.

37. Sources: *Jugoslovenski Pregled,* July–August 1964; Boris Vušković, 'Temeljna demografska i socijalna oblijeza članstva Saveza Komunista Jugoslavije' in Marksistički Centar Konferencije SKJ Z O Split, *Struktura i dinamika članstva Saveza Komunista* (Split, 1985); and Izdavački centar komunist Beograd, "šta polazuju istaživanija SKJ," *Vanredni Kongres SKJ,* January 20–22, 1989 (Belgrade, 1989).

38. Source: *Vreme,* July 15, 1991.

The Albanians of Kosovo: Self-Determination Through Nonviolence

Shkelzen Maliqi

THE DISTANCE BETWEEN the Albanians and the Serbs of Kosovo has become almost unbridgeable, relations having deteriorated to the point where the two communities now live in completely separate worlds. The Serbs, a privileged minority, rule over Kosovo with the aid of the police and army. The Albanians, an overwhelming majority by a ratio of nine to one, are subjected to severe repression and have been completely marginalized in the province's political, social, and economic life.

A system has been created in Kosovo which displays all the characteristic features of national apartheid and segregation. The Serbian leadership under Milošević has not merely suspended the province's constitutionally established autonomous status, but has assumed all power in administrative, economic, and cultural institutions. The Albanians have been excluded from all public and civil institutions: hotels and restaurants; sports centers and football grounds; secondary schools, university buildings, student halls, libraries, and reading rooms; cultural centers, public halls, and swimming pools have all become "Serb." The existing relationship between Serbs and Albanians can be described as one of open enmity that has not yet developed into a state of open war. Yet the level of militarization is so great that nearly every day armed incidents occur. Typically the victims are of Albanian nationality. This state of neither war nor peace is accompanied by a fatalistic sense of the impossibility of overcoming the gulf and the inevitability of a final ethnic showdown.

The present Serbian regime is responsible for the militarization of the Kosovo question. It has made no secret that its aim is not merely the annexation of the province, but the fundamental alteration of the ethnic structure and composition of Kosovo. In Serbia the idea is propagated that Kosovo is a "Serb land" and that Serbs have the right to use all possible means to establish a Serb majority. The means and methods include the mass settlement of Serbs, the expulsion of "disloyal Albanians," a coerced reduction in the Albanian birthrate, and the active encouragement of emigration by economic measures. Such methods require a state of permanent military rule in order to prevent a revolt. But if these measures do not bear fruit then provoking a Serb-Albanian war will become a real option. As in Croatia and Bosnia this would lead to mass expulsions and massacres with the result that Kosovo would be "cleansed" of all Albanians. Unfortunately, when it comes to the question of Kosovo, this genocidal and warlike policy is even supported by much of the Serbian opposition in Belgrade.

During the first phase of Yugoslavia's disintegration in the spring of 1990, the Serbian authorities planned to provoke a military confrontation in Kosovo. The intent was to create a pretext throughout Yugoslavia for a broad militarization of the so-called "Serb Question." If an open rebellion could have been provoked in Kosovo, then a rationale for wars in Croatia and Bosnia could have been established. This was at a time when rationales were still sought. Several unprovoked massacres and armed incidents occurred in Albanian villages in Kosovo. In our view, each of these terrible incidents was a deliberate attempt to provoke a mass Albanian revolt. Such a revolt would have been used as a *casus belli* for a brutal campaign of bombardment against Albanian villages which would have been followed by mass repression and an inevitable exodus of the Albanian population.

> But the Albanians unexpectedly opted for a strategy of non-violent resistance. Superficially it may appear that this decision not to engage in armed resistance would make the formal annexation of Kosovo easier. Yet, in this instance, the strategy of non-violence blunted the aggressive ambitions of the Serbian war strategists. Albanian "Gandhianism" came as a surprise not only to the militarists in Serbia, but also to the Albanians themselves. They had never before imagined themselves in such a role. In the dominant stereotype of their traditions, the Albanians never gave particular prominence to values such as non-violence, patience, turning the other cheek, or sacrificing national pride for the sake of preserving national survival. On the contrary, their self-perception and self-characterization emphasized the highlander's moral code of unsullied honor. This view assumed the capacity for violent heroism and a readiness to sacrifice oneself for liberty and national ideals, as expressed in the typical declaration: "We are all prepared to die for freedom and justice." The gallery of preferred national models in textbooks, historical novels, films, and posters which occupy a place of honor in Albanian homes are invariably made up of warrior heroes from earlier eras of resistance and wars of national liberation.

Until the very end of 1989 when Serbia moved to consolidate its annexation of Kosovo, the dominant mood among Albanians was one of desperate vengefulness. The population was simply waiting for the moment of maximum mobilization in order to begin the armed uprising. Some political agitators, who would later play key roles in the formation of political parties, considered an uprising inevitable. They were indifferent to the potential scale of casualties. Typically one would hear: "We shall lose fifty or a hundred thousand people, but we shall be free." When asked what if the number of casualties turned out to be vastly greater, they would give no answer. Instead, they considered such questions a provocation and an insult to national dignity.

But in the winter and spring of 1990 a sudden, radical change took place. Overnight, warriors became unfashionable. It is interesting that there were no great theoretical debates or organized propaganda campaigns about non-violence. Nor did a figure emerge seeking to take the role of an Albanian Gandhi. It was only later, when the concept had already been adopted spontaneously, that Ibrahim Rugova, the most influential leader in Kosovo came to the fore. The strategy of non-violence somehow imposed itself as the best, most pragmatic, and most effective response to Serbia's aggressive plans.

In part, it was the tide of democratic change which swept away Communist rule in Eastern Europe that became the inspiration for a dramatically different alternative to the more typical warlike and vengeful response expected from the Albanian people. The developments in Europe had awakened the hope that the resolution to Kosovo's key problem, the "Albanian Question," might lie in democracy. As elsewhere, the formula was presented simply: pluralism, the market, free elections, a multiparty parliament, and democratic institutions. These initial demands articulated in the early post-Communist period opened a space for the Albanians to express themselves for the first time. They believed that perhaps it was not necessary to go to war to establish in Kosovo a democratic majority government. Indeed, by democratic methods it might be possible to realize the ideal of an independent Kosovo.

However, the secret of the sudden turn toward non-violence can perhaps be more accurately identified as part of a process through which an identity was being constructed against the "Other." In this instance, the Albanians had to draw a clear line of distinction between themselves and their rival and enemy. For years they had been vilified as counter-revolutionaries, separatists, irredentists, and demonized as thugs and as monsters who poison the wells of their Serb neighbors. As a repressed, humiliated, and silenced population, the Albanians had developed a tendency, on the one hand, to search constantly for a collective alibi, and, on the other, to distance themselves from their abusers: "God forbid that we should have anything in common with people who lie and abuse us so much!" In other words, the Albanians were reaffirming themselves by emphasizing the difference and the distance between themselves and the Serbs: they were *not* who the Serbs said they were.

The political articulation of this self-recognition was first demonstrated by the Trepca miners in November 1988, when they embarked on their fifty-mile protest march from their mine to Priština and back. In addition to their political demands the miners gave an answer, through their dignified conduct, to the mass rallies that had already been organized throughout Serbia by the bellicose Milošević. At these gatherings Albanians were portrayed as the main enemy of Serbs: as chauvinist beasts, murderers, arsonists, poisoners, defilers of Serb women, desecrators of Serb graves and holy places, a primitive and violent people who deliberately used a high birth rate to Albanize and take holy Serb lands away. At these turbulent meetings, Milošević began the ethnic war which would envelop all Yugoslavia by stirring Serb chauvinism into a frenzied pitch of murderous bigotry.

By contrast the Trepca miners brought hundreds of thousands of people out to fill all the roads of Kosovo, marching in columns in quiet protest. They marched night and day in the cold and snow. In every aspect of their behavior they tried to demonstrate that Albanians were not as the Serbs described them. During this protracted demonstration in which four hundred thousand people took part there was not a single incident of vandalism or destruction. Not even a single window was broken. Great self-discipline was required to prevent hatred and fury from erupting. The message conveyed by this self-control was: "We are not what you say we are. We do not rape and kill. We express our political will in a dignified way which is different from yours."

The miners in fact made a conscious effort to avoid any gesture or slogan that might offend the Serb people. At the principal gathering of the Priština demonstrators one particular slogan stood out: "Long live the brave Serb nation!" The intention was to draw a line between the regime in Belgrade and the Serb people and to say, "We do not hate other nations. We do not call for the expulsion or extermination of other nations." In contrast, at Milošević's rallies in Serbia the shouts that were heard were those of "Death to Albanians" and "Albanians Out."

There was an ironic symbolism in the fact that the Albanian demonstrations in Priština in November 1988 were the last pro-Yugoslav and pro-Titoist demonstrations. Albanian flags were tied together with Yugoslav ones. Albanians carried Tito's pictures and hailed the 1974 Constitution. The cynics behind Serbian propaganda spoke of Albanian hypocrisy and declared that those who marched in Kosovo were only using Tito as a cover for their anti-Serbism. Yet the demonstrators were certainly expressing loyalty to a state and a project in which for the first time in their history they had been treated as an equal subject. However, in the course of the following months Titoism in Kosovo was extinguished by tanks. Since Kosovo had a place at the federal summit and possessed the right of veto in the Yugoslav federation, not only was the concept of Tito's Yugoslavia destroyed but so was Yugoslavia itself.

By the spring of 1990 the Albanians with their strategy of non-violence had completed the circle of their self-understanding. They identified themselves as a peaceful and democratic nation in conflict with a warlike and undemocratic regime. What Serbian propaganda had ascribed to Albanians now revealed itself to be a projection of the Serbs' own hegemonistic intentions. The victim and the thug, as originally conceived by the Serb chauvinist, in reality were to exchange places. Serbian prejudices against Albanians were to serve as rationales and justifications for the most terrible of crimes.

Kosovo thus became a remarkable example of a crossroad between two confrontational forms of national awareness and self-assertion. If the Albanians chose democracy, the Serbs saw democracy in Kosovo as tantamount to the loss of Serb lands; if the former were liberating themselves from tradition-alism, folklorism, and inherited prejudice, the latter were sinking into myths, obsessed with the revival of Serb military glory and the need for revenge for the defeat six centuries ago in the battle of Kosovo.

SERBIAN CHAUVINISM, first nurtured in Kosovo, soon became rampant in Croatia and Bosnia. Through acts of collective vengeance it began to replicate the ethnic slaughterhouse of World War II. With indescribable brutality a Balkan war began with millions of people of the "wrong" nationality expelled from their homes. Territories were "ethnically cleansed" by means of massacres and concentration camps. It was Serbian aggression, supported by the former federal army with its enormous armaments which has brought Serbia to a complete rupture with the civilized world.

The ultimate imposition of international sanctions against Serbia repre-sented a great moral victory for the Albanians of Kosovo who had been the first to face Milošević's aggression with dignity. They had shown themselves and others that they were more civilized than their tormentors. Recognition for the stance taken in Kosovo has come from wise and peaceful Serbs. The distinguished Serbian poet and novelist, Mirko Kovač, has written in *Borba* of Belgrade of March 13, 1992, that "Albanians are politically the most mature nation in Yugoslavia. I accept the thesis of the Slovene philosopher and writer Slavoj Žižek that Kosovo's Albanians are a European people that is endowed with patience, that in the political sense uses Gandhian methods, and that insists on negotiations and rejects violence."

This, however, is not the end of the story. Although Albanians have held a referendum on independence and proclaimed Kosovo a republic, indepen-dence has not yet been established. European states, fearful of setting "bad" precedents for their own national minorities which seek self-determination, do not wish to open the question of revising frontiers. Thus they attempt to situate the problem of Kosovo strictly within the domain of safeguarding human rights and securing Kosovo's autonomy within the borders of Serbia. The Albanians are, therefore, urged to conceive of Kosovo's future as defined by a new democratic order which will establish democratic institutions enabling the Serbs and the Albanians to live together in tolerance. But this optimistic argument ignores the fact that the problem of Kosovo is acute pre-cisely because, under the existing circumstances of absolute suspicion, hostil-ity, and a complete unwillingness to co-exist, conditions for the creation of a new democratic order simply do not exist. Without prior declarations of loy-alty by the Albanians of Kosovo, the Serbian regime is not willing to lift the state of emergency and the drastic restrictions it has imposed on the civil lib-erties and human rights of the Albanian community. For their part the Alba-nians are not prepared to discuss the question of coexistence with the Serbs without the formal restoration of Kosovo's assembly and its government— including the restoration of the powers vested in these self-governing bodies prior to their forced dissolution. Moreover, they insist that decisions taken by these organs—which continued to meet underground or in exile—must be recognized as legitimate. A serious Albanian-Serb dialogue is possible only on the question of self-determination for Kosovo and the modalities of Kosovo's acquisition of independence. At a subsequent stage, negotiations concerning economic and political ties between Kosovo and Serbia would be appropriate.

Can there be a compromise solution of the Kosovo question? Opposition circles in Serbia have, on occasion, raised the possibility of what is described as a *historic compromise* between the Serbs and the Albanians. During the summer of 1991, before war had engulfed Bosnia-Hercegovina, the Muslim Bosnian Organization sought to promote such a compromise between Serbs and Bosnian Muslims. But the possibility of such a compromise collapsed because the vast majority of Bosnian Muslims did not trust Milošević's Serbia. Among the many reasons for this distrust was the memory of how Milošević had "solved" the Kosovo question. It is for this reason that the absolute precondition for reaching any compromise in Kosovo must be the abrogation of all measures imposed in Kosovo by Milošević's regime and the establishment of democracy.

Were this stage ever to be reached a new question would immediately arise: what would be the institutional framework for democracy in Kosovo? The Serbian side wants the framework to be the Serbian parliament, while the Albanian side insists on a separate parliament for Kosovo. The Serbian parliament suspended Kosovo's parliament precisely because it feared that free elections in Kosovo would legitimize Albanian majority rule and would become a prelude to secession.

Thus, the issue of a historic compromise between Albanians and Serbs is essentially bound up with this impossible-to-resolve dispute over the framework of democracy in Kosovo. In certain Serbian circles it is said that any agreement between the two sides would be based on the definition of Serbia as a state of its *citizens* that would guarantee the collective rights of all national minorities which at the moment constitute one-third of Serbia's population. Thus, Serbia would not be a Serb national state but a state of all its citizens.

However, the present realities of Serbian political life simply fail to offer a convincing basis for the realization of a secular and democratic state of equal citizens. All key institutions in Serbia today are preoccupied with resolving the so-called "Serb question" in quite a different manner. The disintegration of Yugoslavia itself is linked in many ways to the Serb desire to solve this question through the creation of a Serb "national state" in which the greatest possible number of Serbs would live. The protagonists of what has emerged as the dominant option have declared that it is irrelevant whether the new state is called Serbia or Yugoslavia. They are unambiguous in their objective: to gather in as many Serbs and Serb territories as possible. At the moment the state is composed of Serbia and Montenegro; the idea, however, is to extend its territory by attaching to it the Serb Krajinas in Croatia and the so-called Serb Republic of Bosnia-Hercegovina.

The offer of a historic compromise within the framework of a "Greater Serbia" which would allegedly be a state of its citizens is therefore not at all a persuasive one for the Albanian side. Under the present circumstances it is illusory to think that the option of a citizens' state will prevail anywhere in the Balkans. The creation of national states in the sick East of Europe has become an unstoppable epidemic. A "state of citizens" without corresponding economic relations and civil institutions is only a phrase. In fact, the present constitution of Serbia also declares that Serbia is a state of its citizens. Yet the instruments of the state are not used to guarantee the rights of its citizens. In Kosovo total domination by the Serbian regime has led to the imposition of various forms of national segregation between its citizens. This has taken the extreme form of imposing from Belgrade a virtual regime of apartheid that now separates Serbs and Albanians in Kosovo.

Thus, the solution of the Serb national question is sought by implementing the idea of ethnic demarcation by the establishment of ethnic territories. This has happened in Vojvodina and in Croatia. It is now taking place in conditions of great violence in Bosnia-Hercegovina. Everywhere that Serbs live in any numbers the policy is being pursued single-mindedly. In the context of the Serbian regime's policy of ethnic demarcation, the Albanian-Serb conflict in Kosovo would be one of the easiest to resolve when compared to the other confrontation in the Balkans. This is so because the separation of Serbs from Albanians could be more easily achieved than separation of Serbs from Croats or Bosnian Muslims. In Kosovo and southern Serbia the Albanians form a compact and overwhelming majority in all municipalities except for a few bordering on Serbia, Sandjak, and Montenegro. In Kosovo, the Serb population represents only 1.5 percent of all Serbs in the Balkans. The Albanians in Kosovo represent 38 percent of the Albanian population in the Balkans. (If one includes Albanians living in Macedonia, then the total rises to half of all Albanians in the Balkans.) If Serbia's existing claim is sustained and Kosovo is treated as an exclusive domain of Serbia, then an intolerable anomaly will be created whereby 1.5 percent of all Serbs in the region will hold under colonial occupation 38 percent of all Albanians. The Albanians in Kosovo form a compact majority of at least two-thirds of the population in 95 percent of the districts they inhabit. In other words, everywhere in Kosovo they are a majority, not a minority. Set in its right framework, the question of Kosovo is one of decolonization. If democracy is based on self-government and the right of a nation to self-determination, then with any establishment of a democratic system the Albanians, constituting the majority of Kosovo's population, will seek independence. They will do so because their rights have been violently suppressed and also because—historically since 1912 and the formation of the first Yugoslavia, but especially since 1981—they have had no positive experience of fruitful civic cohabitation with the Serbs. The Albanians are prepared to enter into negotiations but only as an independent subject. They are willing to be represented and to take part in decisions on the basis of equality but not as a minority whose destiny will be decided by others.

Bosnia Tune

JOSEPH BRODSKY

As you sip your brand of scotch,
crush a roach, or scratch your crotch,
as your hand adjusts your tie,
people die.

In the towns with funny names,
hit by bullets, caught in flames,
by and large not knowing why,
people die.

In small places you don't know
of yet big for having no
chance to scream or say good-bye,
people die.

People die as you elect
brand new dudes who preach neglect,
self-restraint, etc.—whereby
people die.

Too far off to practice love
for thy neighbor/brother Slav,
where your cherubs dread to fly,
people die.

While the statues disagree,
Cain's version, history
for its fuel tends to buy
those who die.

As you watch the athletes score,
check your latest statement, or
sing your child a lullaby,
people die.

Time, whose sharp blood-thirsty quill
parts the killed from those who kill,
will pronounce the latter band
as your brand.

A Chronology

c. 925	Croat kingdom begins under Tomislav.
1102	After the extinction of the Croat dynasty in 1091, Croatia's dynastic union with Hungary is finally sealed. It lasts until 1918.
1314–53	Emergence of the Bosnian kindom. Reign of Stefan II Kotromanić. Subjoining of Hum (Hercegovina) to Bosnia.
1353–91	Reign of Stefan Tvrtko I in Bosnia, high point of medieval Bosnian kingdom which, after 1377, includes much of Serbia.
1389	Battle of the Field of Kosovo; decisive Ottoman victory; Prince Lazar of Serbia beheaded by the Turks after the battle.
1463	Ottomans conquer Bosnia (and, in 1483, Hercegovina).
1526	Ottoman conquest of most of Hungary and Croatia, whose estates elect Ferdinand the Habsburg to the thrones of the two countries.
1878	Treaties of San Stefan and Berlin recognize Serbia as an independent kingdom. Habsburg Monarchy occupies Bosnia-Hercegovina.
1908	Habsburg Monarchy annexes Bosnia-Hercegovina.
1912–13	Balkan wars. Serbia roughly doubles in size with the conquest of Kosovo and Vardar Macedonia. Atrocities committed against Albanian and Macedonian population and clergy.
1918	Dissolution of the Habsburg and Ottoman empires at the end of the First World War. Formation of first Yugoslav state under Serbian Karadjordjević dynasty.
1929	Aleksandar abolishes the Constitution and declares royal dictatorship over Yugoslavia.

1941 Germany, Italy, Hungary, and Bulgaria invade Yugoslavia. Proclamation of Independent State of Croatia under Axis auspices in Zagreb. Ustaša massacres of Serbs and Jews in puppet Croatian state. Serbian Chetniks massacre Muslims and Croats.

1941–45 Successful multinational anti-fascist Partisan resistance organised by the Communist Party of Yugoslavia led by Josip Broz Tito.

1945 Defeat of the Axis powers. Establishment of the second Yugoslavia led by Tito.

1968 Student demonstrations in Belgrade and Zagreb.

1971 "Croatian Spring" movement suppressed. Croatian party leadership purged.

1972 Liberal Serbian party leadership purged.

1974 Last Yugoslav constitution promulgated, giving republics effective sovereignty including the right to secession.

1980 Death of Tito; succeeded by a collective presidency drawn from the six republics and two provinces.

1981 Albanian demonstrations in Kosovo suppressed by Serbian and Yugoslav security forces.

1987 Slobodan Milošević assumes leadership of Serbian party; purges party leaderships of Vojvodina, Kosovo, and Montenegro.

1989 Milošević abolishes the autonomous status of Vojvodina and Kosovo.

1990

Jan. At Fourteenth Extraordinary Congress of the League of Communists of Yugoslavia, conflict between Slovenian and Serbian delegations provokes a split in the LCY and leads to the end of one-party rule.

Mar.–Apr. Free, multiparty elections in Slovenia (won by democratic nationalist coalition) and Croatia (won by the center-right nationalist Croatian Democratic Union, the HDZ, led by Franjo Tudjman).

Sept. Serbia adopts a new constitution eliminating the autonomy of its two provinces, Vojvodina and Kosovo.

Nov.–Dec. Multiparty elections in Bosnia-Hercegovina bring three national parties to power. Alija Izetbegović, leader of the Party for Democratic Action (SDA), becomes president of the the collective Presidency.

Dec.　　Elections in Serbia and Montenegro bring victory to Milošević and his allies.

　　　　Slovenian referendum mandates independence within six months if the restructuring of Yugoslavia cannot be negotiated.

1991

Jan.　　Yugoslav Federal Presidency orders dissolution of all Republic armed forces and surrender of weapons to the federal army. Orders ignored in Slovenia and Croatia.

Jan.–Apr.　　Expanded meetings of the Yugoslav Presidency, including presidents of the republics and leaders of the Yugoslav People's Army (JNA), aimed at resolving the Yugoslav crisis.

　　　　Alija Izetbegović of Bosnia-Hercegovina and Kiro Gligorov of Macedonia attempt to secure the agreement of Slovenia, Croatia, and Serbia to a compromise plan on a restructured Yugoslavia which would prevent Slovenian and Croatian secession from the Federation. Mediation unsuccessful.

Mar.　　Demonstrations against Milošević in Belgrade, suppressed by the intervention of the JNA.

　　　　Meeting between Franjo Tudjman and Slobodan Milošević at Karadjordjevo where the two agree on the partition of Bosnia-Hercegovina between Croatia and Serbia.

　　　　First clashes between Croatian police and Serbian paramilitary groups in Croatia.

May　　Croatian referendum mandates independence from Yugoslavia.

Jun.　　Slovenia and Croatia declare independence from Yugoslavia. JNA invades Slovenia.

Jul.　　European Community convinces Slovenia and Croatia to suspend the implementation of the declarations of independence for three months. In return, JNA agrees to suspend military operations against the republics.

　　　　The JNA withdraws from Slovenia into Croatia and Bosnia-Hercegovina.

Aug.　　Serbia and the JNA launch their war against Croatia.

Sept.   The United Nations Security Council imposes an arms
               embargo on Yugoslavia.

Oct.   Both Slovenia and Croatia reaffirm their decision to leave
               Yugoslavia.

               Parliament of Bosnia-Hercegovina approves documents
               providing the legal basis for the republic's independence.
               Members of the Serbian Democratic Party (SDS) led by
               Radovan Karadžić walk out before voting takes place.

Nov.   The SDS announces the formation of six "Serb Autonomous
               Regions" on two-thirds of Bosnian territory and, after holding
               a "plebicite," announces the establishment of a "Serbian
               Republic" within Bosnia-Hercegovina.

Dec.   Following destruction and occupation of the city of Vukovar,
               Germany announces its intention to recognize Slovenia and
               Croatia as independent states.

               The parliament of Bosnia-Hercegovina passes a Declaration
               of Sovereignty and President Izetbegović applies to the EC for
               recognition of his country as an independent state.

1992

Jan.   EC countries join Germany in recognizing Slovenia and
               Croatia.

               UN Special Envoy Cyrus Vance negotiates a Serbo-Croat
               ceasefire.

Feb.   Stjepan Kljuić, leader of the HDZ, the Croat party of Bosnia-
               Hercegovina, is ousted for his opposition to the division of
               the country. He is replaced by representative of the minority
               faction, Mate Boban, with the backing of President Tudjman
               of Croatia.

               Referendum in Bosnia-Hercegovina mandates independence;
               Serb voters largely abstain from voting.

               EC peace conference on Bosnia in Lisbon proposes partitioning
               the state into three ethnic cantons. After initially accepting,
               Izetbegovi´c rejects the proposal because of strong domestic
               opposition; advocates preserving Bosnia as a single state.

Mar.   War in Bosnia begins with the erection of Serbian barricades
               in the capital city of Sarajevo.

Apr.   EC and US recognize independence of Bosnia-Hercegovina.
               At this time US also recognizes Slovenia and Croatia.

JNA and Serbian paramilitary groups from Serbia invade Bosnia-Hercegovina. Siege and bombardment of Sarajevo begins.

May Bosnian Serb leader Radovan Karadžić and Bosnian Croat leader Mate Boban meet in Gratz, Austria, to work out an agreement on the division of Bosnia-Hercegovina between Serbs and Croats.

UN and EC impose sanctions against Serbia and Montenegro.

Serb forces begin "ethnic cleansing" operations in Bosnia.

Jul. Mate Boban's HDZ forms the "Croatian Union of Herceg-Bosna" within Bosnia-Hercegovina.

Aug. The London Conference, convened by the UN and EC, affirms the territorial integrity of the state of Bosnia-Hercegovina.

In the months that follow, war in Bosnia-Hercegovina continues. More and more towns and villages "cleansed" by Serbian forces or under siege; reports of systematic rape of women; discovery of Serb-run concentration camps; destruction of the Muslim-Ottoman heritage of Bosnia.

Dec. UN General Assembly votes in favor of lifting the arms embargo to allow the Bosnian forces to defend themselves against Serbian aggression. Security Council ignores General Assembly's call.

1993

Jan. Cyrus Vance and EC mediator David Owen present a plan to carve Bosnia into ten ethnic provinces with a weak central government. Only the Bosnian Croats accept the plan in full.

Bosnian Deputy Prime Minister Hakija Turajlić, traveling under the protection of UNPROFOR officers, killed at pointblank range at a Serbian roadblock by a Serb soldier.

Feb. US President Clinton, reversing earlier position on Bosnia, supports the Vance-Owen peace talks. Begins air-drops of food and medicine to besieged Bosnian towns.

Mar. Under pressure from the US, the Bosnian government accepts all parts of the Vance-Owen plan. The Serbs do not.

The UN Security Council, under pressure from the US and increased Serbian advances in Bosnia, considers US proposal

to arm the Bosnian forces and launch air strikes against
Serbian forces.

At a conference in Athens, Radovan Karadžić agrees to sign
the Vance-Owen plan.

War breaks out between Croat and Bosnian forces as the
Croat forces loyal to the HDZ begin military campaign to
secure territory for a future Croat state.

Apr.   Plans for Western military intervention collapse amidst
continuing Anglo-French resistance.

Bosnian Serb "parliament" rejects the Vance-Owen plan.

Siege of Sarajevo enters second year. The war continues.

May   US Secretary of State Warren Christopher once again fails to
secure the agreement of France and Britain to strike Serbian
artillery positions and to lift the arms embargo on the
Bosnian forces.

The Washington Agreement among the US and European
states on the creation of "safe havens" in Bosnia; no
subsequent agreement to defend the "safe havens."

Jun.   Security Council again votes against lifting the arms embargo.

Following Serb rejection, Vance-Owen plan is shelved.
Geneva Negotiations on the Milošević-Tudjman proposal for
the partitioning of Bosnia, conducted by David Owen and
Thorvald Stoltenberg, result in Owen's endorsement of the
partition, reversing principles of the 1992 London
Conference.

Aug.   Serbian forces tighten their siege of Sarajevo, cutting off
Sarajevo's last lines of supply with Bosnian held territory.

Owen and Stoltenberg announce the Geneva plan for the
partition of Bosnia into three ethnic states. Plan's assignment
of territory to the three states endorses Serb and Croat
conquests.

Karadžić says if the "Muslims" do not accept the plan, they
will get nothing; Serbs and Croats will take all.

Bosnian government under pressure from the EC and the US
to accept the partition plan.

The HDZ withdraws its members from the Bosnian
parliament. Croat "parliament" announces the establishment
of the "State of Herceg-Bosna."

Bosnian parliament rejects plan and seeks further negotiations on the territory assigned to the "Muslim" state and on the international status of Bosnia-Hercegovina.

Fifth US State Department official resigns in protest over US policy in Bosnia-Hercegovina.

Diego Arria, Permanent Representative of Venezuela on the Security Council, denounces Owen-Stoltenberg partition plan as a betrayal of the UN Charter.

The war continues.

Prepared with the assistance of Marko Prelec.

Contributors

T. D. ALLMAN is foreign correspondent for *Vanity Fair,* New York. He is the author of *Unmanifest Destiny* (Atlantic Monthly Press, 1987) and *Miami: City of The Future* (Dial Press, 1984).

ATTILA BALÁZS is a journalist and writer from Novi Sad, Vojvodina. In late 1991 he fled to Hungary in order to avoid being drafted by the Yugoslav army to fight in Croatia. He is now working for the Budapest newspaper, *Pesti Hírlap.*

SMAIL BALIĆ received his Ph.D. in Philosophy from the University of Vienna. He is affiliated with the Institute for the History of Arabic and Islamic Sciences at the University of Frankfurt and is a lecturer in Oriental Languages at the University for Economic Sciences in Vienna. He is the author of *Das unbekannte Bosnien: Europas Brücke zur islamischen Welt [The Unknown Bosnia]* (Böhlau, 1993).

IVO BANAC received his Ph.D. from Stanford University. He is Professor of History and Master of Pierson College at Yale University. His book, *The National Question in Yugoslavia: Origins, History, Politics* (Cornell, 1988), ranks as a classic in the literature of Southeast Europe.

JOSEPH BRODSKY was born in 1940 in Leningrad. In 1964 he was brought to trial in the Soviet Union on charges of "social parasitism" and sentenced to five years of hard labor. After serving the sentence for twenty months, he was released. In 1972 he left the Soviet Union and has since lived as an exile in the West. In 1987 he won the Nobel Prize for literature. His collections of poems and essays include *Elegy for John Donne and Other Poems, A Part of Speech, Less than One, To Urania, Marbles,* and *Watermark.*

ORHAN BOSNEVIĆ is a pseudonym for the author who is a Bosnian national and a former inmate of the Manjača concentration camp in Serb-held Bosnia-Hercegovina.

SUSAN CAMPBELL is a Research Associate in the Department of Biology at Boston University. She was an AAAS Science, Engineering, and Diplomacy Fellow at the US Agency for International Development in 1984-1985.

STOJAN CEROVIĆ, born in 1949 in Titograd, Montenegro, is co-founder and editor of the independent weekly *Vreme* in Belgrade, Serbia.

MIHAILO CRNOBRNJA has taught at the University of Belgrade. He was Chief Economist of Beogradska Banka; Minister of Economic Planning in the government of Serbia; and the last ambassador of Yugoslavia to the European Community. He now lives in Canada and is Professor in the Department of Management at McGill University. He is the author of *The Yugoslav Drama* (McGill-Queens University Press, 1993).

BOGDAN DENITCH is Professor of Sociology at the Center for Social Research, The Graduate School, City University of New York. He is the author of *End of the Cold War* (University of Minnesota Press, 1990) and *The Tragic Death of Yugoslavia* (University of Minnesota Press, forthcoming).

MAK (MEHMEDALIJA) DIZDAR, 1917-1971, is ranked amongst the greatest contemporary Bosnian poets. A post office worker who joined the Partisan resistance during the Second World War, he subsequently made his name as a poet, journalist, writer, and literary editor. He was a life-long student of ancient and medieval literature of Bosnia-Hercegovina. While he published several collections of his poetry, *Kameni spavač* or "Stone Sleeper" (1966) is considered his best, most dazzling work.

SLAVENKA DRACULIĆ is a writer and journalist. She is a contributing editor to *The Nation,* New York and the author of *Balkan Express* (Norton, 1993). She lives in Zagreb, Croatia.

STJEPKO GOLUBIĆ, from Croatia, is Professor of Biology at Boston University.

THOMAS GOLUBIĆ is a student in the College of Communications at Boston University.

THOMAS HARRISON is Executive Director of the Campaign for Peace and Democracy, New York.

IRAJ HASHI is Senior Lecturer in Economics at the Center for European Research in Economics and Business, Staffordshire University, United Kingdom.

CHRISTOPHER HITCHENS, writer and journalist, is a columnist at *The Nation,* New York. He is the author of *For the Sake of Argument: Essays and Minority Reports* (Verso, 1993).

FRANCIS R. JONES studied modern languages at the University of Cambridge. He has translated European literature in several languages (including Russian, French, German, Modern Greek, Hungarian) into English. In Serbo-Croat he has published two collections of the verse of Ivan V. Lalić— *The Works of Love* and *The Passionate Measure* (Anvil Press, 1981 and 1989). *The Passionate Measure* was awarded Britain's 1991 European Poetry Translation Prize. He is a lecturer in English as a Foreign Language at the University of Newcastle upon Tyne, United Kingdom.

IBRAHIM KAJAN, writer and poet, was born in 1944 in Mostar, Bosnia-Hercegovina. Most recently he published *Muslimanski danak u krvi*, a collection of documents and testimony on the war crimes against the Muslim population of Bosnia-Hercegovina, and *Zavodjenje*, a collection of essays. He is the president of *Preporod*, the cultural society of the Muslims of Croatia.

ENES KARIĆ was born in 1957 in Travnik, Bosnia-Hercegovina. He received his Ph.D. from Belgrade University. He is Assistant Professor of Islamic Theology, University of Sarajevo. He lives in Sarajevo.

DANILO KIŠ, 1935-1989, was born in Subotica, Vojvodina, to a Hungarian Jewish father and a Montenegrin mother. His father and almost all his family were murdered in Auschwitz. By the time of his own death in Paris, he was the best-known Yugoslav writer. His major works of fiction, which include *Garden, Ashes, A Tomb for Boris Davidović, Hourglass, The Encyclopaedia of the Dead*, have been translated into many languages.

MIRKO KOVAČ, born in 1938 in Petrovići, Montenegro, is a writer, poet, and playwright. His books have been translated into several European languages, including French, German, Swedish, and Hungarian. Until Serbia's war with Croatia, he lived in Belgrade. As a result of his participation in the peace movement, he was forced by the Milošević regime to leave Belgrade and now lives in exile in Rovinj, Croatia.

KEMAL KURSPAHIĆ is the editor-in-chief of the daily *Oslobodjenje*, Sarajevo, Bosnia-Hercegovina.

DŽEMALUDIN LATIĆ, born 1957 in Gornji Vakuf, Bosnia-Hercegovina, has published two collections of poems, *Mejtas i Vodica* (1980) and *Dome Davidov* (1990). He is currently the chief executive editor of *Ljiljana*, a paper for "a free Bosnia-Hercegovina." Published until recently from Zagreb, the paper has been forced by the Tudjman regime to move its operations from Croatia to Ljubljana, Slovenia.

JELENA LOVRIĆ, born 1948 in Tuzla, Bosnia-Hercegovina, has worked as a journalist since 1971. She lives in Zagreb, Croatia, and was a columnist for the *Slobodna Dalmacija,* a paper forced, in early 1993, to accept government-engineered changes in ownership initiated to curb the paper's independence. She is currently an editor at *Feral Tribune,* published from Split.

BRANKA MAGAŠ, is the author of *The Destruction of Yugoslavia* (Verso, 1993). She was a member of the Editorial Committee of the *New Left Review.* She lives in London.

SHKELZEN MALIQI, born in 1947, is founder of the Social Democratic Party of Kosovo and the editor-in-chief of *Thema,* a journal of philosophy and sociology published in Priština in the Albanian language.

MARKO PRELEC is a doctoral candidate in History at Yale University. He is specializing in the history of the Balkans.

DAVID RIEFF is a writer and contributing editor of *Harper's Magazine.* He is the author of *Going to Miami* (1987), *Los Angeles: Capital of the Third World* (1991), and *The Exile: Cuba in the Heart of Miami* (1993). He is writing a book on the Bosnian War.

MARK THOMPSON is a writer and journalist. He has translated fiction from French and Italian into English. *(Inferences from a Sabre,* by Claudio Magris, was shortlisted for the European Translation Prize.) He has been editor of the *European Nuclear Disarmament Journal.* From 1989 until 1992 he was London correspondent for *Mladina,* Slovenia. He is the author of *A Paper House, The Ending of Yugoslavia* (Pantheon, 1992). He lives in Zagreb, Croatia.

KASIM TRNKA, formerly Chief Justice of the Constitutional Court of Bosnia-Hercegovina, served as a legal expert to the Bosnian government's delegation during the Vance-Owen negotiations in Geneva and New York.

SLAVOJ ŽIŽEK teaches at the Institute of Social Sciences in Ljubljana, Slovenia. He ran as a pro-reform candidate for the presidency of the republic of Slovenia, then part of Yugoslavia, in 1990. He is the author of the tripartite series *Looking Awry: An Introduction to Jaques Lacan through Popular Culture, Enjoy Your Symptom,* and *Everything You Always Wanted to Know About Lacan But Were Afraid to Ask Hitchcock* (Routledge, 1992).

EDITORS

RABIA ALI received her Ph.D. from the University of Cambridge. She is working on a study of populist politics and authoritarian structures in modern Pakistan.

LAWRENCE LIFSCHULTZ has been South Asia Correspondent of the *Far Eastern Economic Review.* He has also written extensively on South and Southwest Asia for *The Guardian, Le Monde Diplomatique,* the *BBC,* and *The Nation.*